MINDFULNESS-INTEGRATED CBT

MINDFULNESS-INTEGRATED CBT

Principles and Practice

Bruno A. Cayoun, DPsych

WILEY-BLACKWELL

A John Wiley & Sons, Ltd., Publication

Registered Office
John Wiley & Sons Ltd, The Atrium, Southern Gate, Chichester, West Sussex, PO19 8SQ, United Kingdom

Editorial Offices
350 Main Street, Malden, MA 02148-5020, USA
9600 Garsington Road, Oxford, OX4 2DQ, UK
The Atrium, Southern Gate, Chichester, West Sussex, PO19 8SQ, UK

For details of our global editorial offices, for customer services, and for information about how to apply for permission to reuse the copyright material in this book please see our website at www.wiley.com/wiley-blackwell.

Library of Congress Cataloging-in-Publication Data

Mindfulness-integrated CBT : principles and practice / Bruno A. Cayoun.
    p. cm.
Includes bibliographical references and index.
ISBN 978-0-470-97496-4 (cloth) – ISBN 978-0-470-97495-7 (pbk.)
 1. Mindfulness-based cognitive therapy. 2. Meditation–Therapeutic use. I. Title.
RC489.M55C39 2011
616.89′1425–dc22

                                                          2010047203

A catalogue record for this book is available from the British Library.
This book is published in the following electronic formats: ePDFs 9781119993179; Wiley Online Library 9781119993162

Set in 10.5 on 13pt Minion by Toppan Best-set Premedia Limited
Printed in Malaysia by Ho Printing (M) Sdn Bhd

1   2011

Contents

About the Author

Bruno Cayoun is Director of the MiCBT Institute, which trains, accredits, and supports MiCBT practitioners. He is also a Clinical Psychologist in private practice and Research Associate at the School of Psychology, University of Tasmania.

Dr Cayoun's past research has involved the dysfunction of attentional systems and the human capacity for attentional and inhibitory control (two essential mechanisms in mindfulness training) in children with ADHD. Current research includes the efficacy of MiCBT in clients with complex co-morbidity, the effects of MiCBT on the experience of addiction and trauma, and the measurement of mindfulness mechanisms in clinical populations.

For the past 22 years, he has practiced Mindfulness meditation and participated in many intensive training courses in Vipassana centers in various countries (France, Nepal, India, and Australia). He is the principal developer of the MiCBT model, which integrates mindfulness skills training with well-established principles of traditional Cognitive Behavior Therapy.

Dr Cayoun provides continual training in MiCBT to various services and professional associations in Australia, New Zealand, and South East Asia. His mindfulness training CDs are used worldwide and he is the principal developer of two questionnaires, the Short Progress Assessment and the Mindfulness-based-Self Efficacy Scale, now translated in Portuguese and Dutch.

Acknowledgments

This book would not have seen the light of day without the invaluable teaching I received from my beloved teacher of mindfulness meditation, Satya Narayan Goenka, a celebrated teacher in the Burmese *Vipassana* tradition. His pragmatic teaching of mindfulness has paved the way to this integrated approach. In the early stage of writing, I greatly benefited from the precious encouragement and comments from my colleagues Vicki Sauvage, Dr Frances Martin, Dr George V. Wilson, Dr Christopher Williams, and Dr Christopher Walsh. I thank George Burns, Patrea O'Donoghue, and Tenzin Chönyi (Dr Diana Taylor) deeply for their comments and precious advice at a later stage of the manuscript. I also thank Professor J. Mark G. Williams for his encouragement and useful advice on the renaming of this therapy model a few years ago.

The advice and contribution of Dr Kathryn Elbourne was central in the production of MiCBT information sheets for clients (Appendix C), and I express my gratitude to Gabrielle Cayoun, Georgina Cooke, Linda Elliott, and Glenn Bilsborrow for their precious assistance with the design of client and therapist forms (Appendix C). My gratitude also goes to my dear and compassionate wife, Karen, whose support, patience, and suggestions have been invaluable. I express wholeheartedly my gratitude to the inspiring people who were once my clients for their willingness to include their moving and inspiring letters in this book.

Like other practitioners writing about the way of mindfulness, I stand on the shoulders of giants. I am especially indebted to one of the wisest men in history, Siddhartha Gautama, known as the Buddha, whose legacy continues to inspire humankind for peace and science, and whose teachings have enthused those involved in this domain of therapy and research.

Preface

This book has its origins in my first 10-day residential mindfulness meditation course in the Burmese Vipassana tradition, in March 1989. There, I began to informally conceptualize a model of information processing that integrates the Buddhist psychological system. It took another 12 years of daily personal practice, numerous intensive courses and study of cognitive and behavioral principles to formulate a model that integrates traditional mindfulness training with cognitive and behavioral principles for the purpose of addressing psychological distress. In the early days, this integration was called "Equanimity Training".

In 2001, I proposed and began to introduce a four-stage model of "Mindfulness-based Cognitive Behavior Therapy" (MCBT) for crisis intervention to various mental health services in Tasmania (Australia). About a year later, the book *Mindfulness-based Cognitive Therapy: A new approach for preventing relapse in depression* by Dr Zindel Segal, Dr John Teasdale, and Prof Mark Williams (2002) was published and has been a major influence in the proliferation of the use of mindfulness-integrated models in modern Western therapy. The acronym for this approach is MBCT. In the four years which followed, the similarity of acronyms between MBCT and the MCBT model I and others were using created some confusion. Although there are inevitable overlaps between the two approaches, there are also important differences. Repeatedly, therapists and researchers had often used these acronyms interchangeably.

Following a conversation with Mark Williams, it became clear that the name of MCBT had to be changed. However, since many clinicians and researchers attended training in MCBT and used it professionally or in their research, it was important that they had a say and that the switch of label was made together, as a group. I invited 211 colleagues and members of the Mindfulness-based Therapy and Research Interest Group worldwide to help in this process, which took several months of brainstorming and deliberating. The democratic process was inspiring for all of us. Fifty-three propositions were obtained and then distilled down to just a few options. From these, the new name "Mindfulness-integrated Cognitive Behavior Therapy"

(MiCBT) was coined to effectively represent the essence of the approach described in this book.

We were pleased with the new name. It kept the two essential approaches (Mindfulness and CBT) and their integration at all stages of the model. For example, we would use the so-called Socratic dialogue even at the very start with people who believe they cannot make time for practicing twice daily.

We were also satisfied with MiCBT because the notion of "theoretical integration" (rather than "technical eclecticism") has been our guiding principle from the start. MiCBT integrates numerous principles from both approaches. For example, in Stage 1, as will be described later, it uses the principles of operant learning, especially interoceptive conditioning and extinction to explain a number of experiences during body-scanning. It also uses neural network theory to explain thought intrusion (distractions) and deactivation during mindfulness of breath. It attempts to measure increased awareness of body sensations and explains it in terms of neuroplasticity. In Stage 4, it relates an aspect of Grounded Empathy practice ("Loving Kindness" towards all beings) to counter-conditioning principles.

Over the last seven years, writing this book has been a dynamic experience. My initial intention was simply to provide a comprehensive manual for postgraduate students and mental health professionals undertaking training in MiCBT. Smaller versions of this book, the "MCBT manual", and later the "MiCBT manual", have been used for several years by multidisciplinary clinicians in the field of mental health. Clinicians, researchers, and writers have referred to it on many occasions and expressed strong interest in its publication (e.g., Ivanovski and Malhi, 2007; Lindsay, 2007; Whitfield, 2006). I now feel that the "manual" has become a sufficiently comprehensive and reader-friendly guide for clinicians to integrate confidently mindfulness training with cognitive and behavioral skills and principles in a generic manner to address a wide range of conditions. I hope the reader will find it useful for this purpose.

Abbreviations

ACT:	Acceptance and Commitment Therapy.
ADHD:	Attention Deficit Hyperactivity Disorder.
CBT:	Cognitive Behavior Therapy.
CNS:	Central Nervous System.
DSM-V:	Diagnostic and Statistical Manual of Mental Disorder (5th edition).
EEG:	Electroencephalograph (measurement of brain waves).
FFMQ:	Five Facets of Mindfulness Questionnaire.
FMI:	Freiburg Mindfulness Inventory.
fMRI:	Functional Magnetic Resonance Imaging (photographing of the brain's blood flow during mental tasks).
GP:	General Practitioner. In Australia, a GP is a Medical Doctor.
ICD-10:	International Classification of Diseases (10th edition).
ICS:	Interacting Cognitive Sub-Systems.
KIMS:	Kentucky Inventory of Mindfulness Skills
MBCT:	Mindfulness Based Cognitive Therapy.
MBSR:	Mindfulness Based Stress Reduction.
MRI:	Magnetic Resonance Imaging (structural photographing of the brain)
MSES:	Mindfulness-based Self-Efficacy Scale.
OCD:	Obsessive Compulsive Disorder.
PMR:	Progressive Muscle Relaxation, also called Jacobsonian relaxation.
PTSD:	Post-Traumatic Stress Disorder.
SMA:	Supplementary Motor Area. the frontal lobe part of the motor system which enables the programming of movement sequences.
SPA:	Short Progress Assessment.
SUDS:	Subjective Units of Distress.

Introduction

Much learning does not teach understanding.
Heraclitus

Training ourselves to improve our capacity to remain calm and collected while facing the vicissitudes of life has a long history, dating back at least twenty-five centuries. It was, and remains in some Eastern traditions, a central feature of the yogic training taught by Buddhism. Its systematic approach embodies both a cosmological and a psychological system for the understanding of mental processes and remediation of psychological pains, which clearly departs from traditional ritualistic and religious practices (Goleman, 1977). It was in the most unusual way that I first experienced some of these principles.

Although it was over 29 years ago, I still remember sitting on the edge of a hotel bed in southern Israel, with an excruciating toothache. I had left France, my country of origin, several months earlier to visit the Middle East. There, I suddenly found myself with next to no money in my pocket after having lost my wallet and all my identification papers. It was about 2pm on a hot Saturday and the few dentists in the area were not available. I could not afford painkillers and didn't know anyone who could help. The pain was so paralyzing that I could not even walk to a hospital, several kilometers away.

I had minimal understanding of what was the problem and decided to think it through: "the nerve will not hurt me forever … it is just a matter of time before the infection kills the nerve and the pain will go away, so I just have to wait," I thought. This is just what I did, sitting on the side of the bed, waiting for the pain to pass. I pondered what would be the way to calm my inner agitation in the meantime. I am not sure why, but I thought that focusing on the pain to monitor the change and "go with the flow" could potentially accelerate the process. I was expecting to spend the rest of the day and at least part of the night with intense suffering, but there was not much else I could do. How long a tooth infection would take to kill the

Mindfulness-integrated CBT: Principles and Practice, First Edition. Bruno A. Cayoun.
© 2011 John Wiley & Sons, Ltd. Published 2011 by John Wiley & Sons, Ltd.

nerve in the root canal was central to my concerns. As I paid attention to the centre of the pain, I felt it more intensely for a short period and then, to my great surprise, it very rapidly diminished. After about ten minutes, the pain had largely disappeared. It was clear to me that the relief I experienced was due to the way in which I paid attention to the pain sensations rather than the desensitization of the tooth by the infection.

Being untrained in meditation techniques and unaware of their potential, this experience was incredible to me. My interest in the resources of the mind grew stronger from then on. I later understood that I had inadvertently used a technique well known in ancient Buddhist meditation practice, the practice of equanimity, a central component in what is known as Mindfulness Meditation. I also realized that I underestimated the constructive powers of human suffering. After all, it was pain and the necessity to accept it that taught me one of the greatest lessons in life; things change, even the most painful experience.

Buddhist teaching suggests that we create suffering because of our expectations. While wanted things don't often happen, unwanted things often do. When we do get wanted things, they soon change. Even if some wanted things don't seem to change, we do! We become habituated to what we have and eventually not so interested, and soon dissatisfied, once again. Becoming mindful of this simple but far-reaching universal reality in a way that alleviates suffering is an important aspect of the way of mindfulness. The establishment of mindfulness at all levels of experience (originally called *Satipatthana*) constitutes the essence of the practical aspect of Buddhist teaching. The meaning of the term "mindfulness" (*sati*, in Pali language spoken in ancient India) is traditionally expressed by meditation teachers as a mental factor which serves to keep our minds on the chosen object of concentration (Taylor, 2010) and this with a deeper understanding of the object of concentration. As will be described in detail in Chapter 1, we can recognize elements of sustained attention.

In the West, mindfulness has been defined as "paying attention in a particular way: on purpose, in the present moment, and non-judgmentally" (Kabat-Zinn, 1994, p.4). Well over a decade ago, Salmon, Santorelli and Kabat-Zinn (1998) already noted the fast growing interest for the mindfulness approach since its early integration with Western psychotherapy in 1979, with over 240 mindfulness-based programs implemented in North America and Europe. Researchers have proposed the formal integration of mindfulness-based approaches with existing cognitive, behavioral and other models of psychotherapy (e.g., Bennett-Goleman, 2001; Cayoun, 2003; Hayes, 2003; Hayes, Follette, and Linehan, 2004; Kutz, Borysenko, and Benson, 1985; Lau and McMain, 2005; Roemer and Orsillo, 2002; Shapiro and Carlson, 2009; Whitfield, 2006).

Proponents of this integration have proposed various operationalizations and rationales for the implementation of mindfulness-based therapy systems in accord with the theory of specific psychopathologies, guidelines for clinical interventions, and a description of the quality standards of the therapeutic approach (e.g., Kabat-Zinn, 1990; Kabat-Zinn, Lipworth, and Burney, 1985 [chronic pain and stress];

Carlson *et al.,* 2001 [depression and stress]; Linehan, 1993 [Borderline Personality Disorder]; Orsillo, Roemer and Barlow, 2003 [Generalised Anxiety Disorder]; Kabat-Zinn *et al.,* 1992 [Panic and other anxiety disorders]; Segal, Williams, and Teasdale, 2002 [depression]; Witkiewitz and Marlatt, 2006; Follette, Palm, and Pearson, 2006 [Post-Traumatic Stress Disorder]), and specific information processing issues (Breslin, Zack, and McMain, 2002; Teasdale, 1999; Teasdale and Barnard, 1993; Wells and Matthews, 1994).

Numerous authors, whose expertise varies from social categorization to cancer research, have demonstrated that the human capacity for mindfulness can be developed and put to good use in the process of health recovery (Grossman *et al.,* 2004; Lindsay, 2007; Speca *et al.,* 2000). There is evidence that including the principles of mindfulness in Western psychotherapy programs can be of benefit to a wide variety of conditions (e.g., Baer, 2003). In keeping with this trend, I have proposed a non-dualistic, integrative approach to cognitive and behavior modification founded on the combination of a traditional account of mindfulness, the well-established Western principles of operant conditioning and on the principles of "embodied cognition" and neural networks in information processing (Cayoun, 2005a).

The integration of mindfulness and cognitive-behavioral principles is actually not new at all. Numerous Buddhist parables recount twenty-five century-old stories that illustrate ways of using what we consider to be cognitive and behavioral skills to address people's suffering, as well as for teaching purposes.

In one such parable, a woman who could not have children for seven years finally gave birth to a boy. Unfortunately, the boy died of an illness at the age of two, leaving the mother distraught to the extent of carrying her child in the city streets as if nothing had happened, pretending that her child was fine, that he was only asleep and just needed help to wake-up. Of course, nobody from the dozens of neighbors she asked for help could wake the child. Touched by her disarray, an old man suggested she goes and speak with "Master Gautama at his ashram." Desperate for a miracle, she followed this advice and approached Master Siddhartha Gautama, better known as the Buddha, holding the boy's corpse in her arms: "My son is asleep and nobody can wake him up. Someone in town said you could help. Please sir, I will do anything …"

The Buddha saw that her emotional agony would not permit an understanding of the true cause of her suffering and she was not ready to be taught in the way of mindfulness. So he proposed what we would perceive as a "behavioral experiment" to initiate cognitive reappraisal using the following instructions: "Go to every household of the city and ask for five sesame seeds from each family and bring them to me, but you must accept the seeds only from families in which there has been no death." So she went, relentlessly knocking door after door, asking for the magical seeds that would save her son from eternal sleep. The unfeasibility of her task became clearer after each failure to find a deathless household. Everywhere, someone had died. By the time she returned to the Buddha, she had come back to her senses and before he even spoke, she said: "I understand sir, everybody dies; this is not just my son, this is how it is everywhere." The Buddha was pleased and thought she was ready for mindfulness training. As the story goes, she became a well-known and prominent teacher of mindfulness meditation, freed from what could have been deep-seated grief for much of her life.

Assuming this parable has historical correctness, it demonstrates one of the remarkably spontaneous and accurate ways with which the Buddha implemented behavior modification techniques within his mindfulness doctrine. In other parables, he integrates a questioning style that we would easily associate with what is known as the Socratic dialogue, bringing forward the inconsistency of certain thoughts and their underlying assumptions (see Axiom, 2002, for a collection of parables).

Sharing similar principles, the four-stage model of Mindfulness-integrated Cognitive Behavior Therapy (MiCBT) presented in this book is a sophisticated integration of mindfulness core principles and traditional Cognitive Behavior Therapy (CBT). It incorporates a set of evidence-based techniques to develop self-knowledge, a healthy sense of self-control and self-efficacy in multiple domains of living. These attributes are partly dependent upon the type of knowledge about ourselves from which we operate to solve problems.

Three Bases of Learning

According to Theravada teachings, which is believed by many to be the oldest Buddhist school of thought, there are three bases for self-knowledge: listening to and believing others (devotional, philosophical, religious, etc), rationalizing (one's own intellectual problem-solving abilities), and experiencing (one's own actual experience). This applies to how we learn about ourselves during therapy. We can think of these learning methods in terms of personal involvement dimensions, each offering information about ourselves from a narrow (passive listening) to a greater (experiencing) frame of reference.

Devotional learning

During psychotherapy, the client may learn about himself or herself based on what we say as therapists, colored by our own view of the world and operational paradigm. Our client acquires self-knowledge based on someone else's view, the therapist's: "the client's thought is irrational because it leads to emotional pain." If this is the only level of involvement (faith in the clinician), symptoms may be alleviated for some time but the client's sense of self-control and self-efficacy tends to remain poor and bound to the context and topic of the intervention. A potential danger is dependence on the clinician for approval or reassurance, leading to unnecessary long-term treatment.

Rational learning

The next level of involvement for self-knowledge is problem-solving by making sense of the information. This requires further personal involvement in the processing of information. It requires semantic processing with which the meaning of information is actively and critically evaluated and compared against already learned information stored in memory. For example, making sense of how our belief systems or "core schemas" (basic assumptions about the self and the world) create our reality, pleasant or unpleasant, has proven to be a useful skill in the course of Cognitive Therapy. Verification of this understanding via behavioral experiment (testing the validity of an assumption) has also been shown to help change our view and often the corresponding emotional distress. However, understanding our schemas does not always suffice to change our behavior. Despite the skilful attempts of the therapist to enhance a client's awareness of his/her unhelpful beliefs, the client may feel incapable of changing a view or habitual response. Below is a good example of the difference between rational realization and experiential realization, which is the next level of involvement.

In 1952, Donald Glaser, an expert in physics who was awarded the Nobel Prize, invented a machine called the "bubble chamber" to measure the rapidity with which subatomic particles composing the universe "arise and pass away" (Goenka, 1987). In liquid hydrogen maintained near its boiling point, ions produced by incoming energetic radioactive particles leave bubble tracks that can be photographed. He counted ion traces and calculated that the number of arising and passing ions equated 10^{22} Hz (cycles per second). In other words, Glaser discovered that subatomic particles arise and vanish 10^{22} times per second. This great discovery, demonstrating the dynamics of the transient nature of the physical universe, relied on a machine, an external means of measurement with which we can rationalize physical human nature.

Experiential learning

It is astonishing that twenty-five centuries earlier, a man with only his introspective capacity to apply awareness and equanimity from moment-to-moment made a similar discovery at an experiential level. Siddhartha Gautama (Buddha) discovered that "the entire material structure is composed of minute (subatomic) particles which are continuously arising and vanishing. In the snapping of a finger or the blinking of an eye, he said, each one of these particles arises and passes away many trillions of times" (Goenka, 1985, cited in Hart, 1987, p.32). Since there was no previous description or name for these vibrating particles, Gautama created the word *kalapa* – smallest indivisible unit of matter. Hence, these men's discovery was similar but the process and results of that same discovery were indescribably different. One man became free from worldly woes while the other grew old bound by the emotional afflictions of physical and mental decay.

MiCBT encompasses these three aspects of learning about ourselves, with an emphasis on experiential characteristics and their underlying neurobehavioral underpinnings. An increasing number of researchers and clinicians are considering the advantages of experiential paradigms and have already embraced the inclusion of mindfulness components in the cognitive-behavioral framework (Follette *et al.*, 2006; Hayes, Stroshal, and Wilson, 1999; Salzman and Goldin (2010); Teasdale, 1999; Teasdale, Segal, and Williams, 1995; Wells and Matthews, 1994; Williams *et al.*, 2000). This book is yet another reflection of the current thinking in psychotherapy, which considers that experiencing per se has significant therapeutic value.

About this Book

Rationale

Despite the growing number of research publications and excellent books on the use of mindfulness in therapy, most tend to orient their contents toward problem- or disorder-specific contexts (e.g., Baer, 2006; Williams *et al.*, 2007). There is no current practical set of general principles and guidelines for the applied integration of mindfulness meditation and the well-documented, evidence-based, techniques from traditional CBT to address multiple difficulties. Not only would such general principles help the efficacy of program delivery in heterogeneous groups, they would also help address the problem of co-morbidity, as informally illustrated by the various letters from ex-clients collated in Chapter 11. The need for such general principles and standardized guidelines has prompted the undertaking of this book. Much like that of Stephen Hayes and his colleagues with regard to their integrative model (Acceptance and Commitment Therapy, 1999), this book presents a rationale and general guidelines for the implementation of mindfulness meditation (not just attitude) tightly integrated with well-researched evidence-based CBT methods for a broad range of psychological dysfunctions.

Structure

This book places each chapter in order of implementation of the MiCBT four-stage program, although some features can be flexibly interchanged with individual delivery according to the client's condition and progress. This structure is based on nine years of piloting, implementation and standardization in various mental health services. Years of opportunities for modifications based on client feedback, supervision of students and experienced clinicians, and empirical data have led to the current structure and content of the program.

Chapters 1 and 2 present an operationalization of mindfulness and a robust theoretical framework for including mindfulness in psychological therapy. It offers a neurobehavioral account of the mechanisms of action through a detailed description of the co-emergence model of reinforcement, showing a clear interface between mindfulness training and CBT. There is also a summary of main points at the end of Chapter 2, which will help the reader recall the most important aspects of the concepts and skills. It will also help the reader to communicate the content of the program simply to clients and colleagues.

Chapters 3 to 6 explain the details of Stage 1 of MiCBT, which describes mindfulness-training skills to internalize attention in order to regulate attention and emotion. These chapters describe techniques to engage the client in the treatment plan using a combination of mindfulness and CBT skills (interoceptive exposure and Socratic questioning). The chapters describe some of the clinical relevance and implications of this particular integration of mindfulness and CBT, and provide a comprehensive description of the common difficulties and resolutions.

Chapters 7 to 9 describe how MiCBT externalizes newly acquired skills in Stage 1 (attention and emotion regulation) to equip clients with long-term cognitive and behavioral tools to address common stressors, avoidance mechanisms and interpersonal difficulties. This is achieved through strategies learned in Stages 2, 3 and 4. The rationale for the use of Loving-Kindness Meditation, in Chapter 9, will make much sense to cognitive behavioral therapists and scientists.

Chapters 10 and 11 discuss the benefits of MiCBT and the relevance of MiCBT to DSM-V Axis 1 and Axis 2 disorders. The view that problems due to a personality disorder cannot be changed is challenged. The notion of internal locus of reinforcement and the advantages of addressing maladaptive cognition and behavior at the experiential level are illustrated by case examples. The inspiring commentaries of ten of my ex-clients treated with MiCBT are included. The reader is also informed about useful measures of change produced by mindfulness approaches, emphasizing the notion of self-efficacy. An evaluation of mindfulness training based on Aaron T. Beck's (1976) standards is included.

Chapter 12 provides a useful summary of the weekly implementation protocol for adult clients. Note that reference to the use of compact discs (CDs) is frequently made, should the clinician choose to use the CDs typically used with MiCBT to assist both clients and clinicians in their daily training (available online from the MiCBT Institute: www.mindfulness.com.au. The experience of most MiCBT practitioners is that both practice CDs (Stage 1 and Advanced Training) would complement the practical use of this book, and are advantageous when delivering the program.

Chapter 13 addresses the importance of professional training. It includes a short review of the research on therapists trained in Mindfulness skills and the structure of the Vocational Graduate Diploma in MiCBT offered by the MiCBT Institute, a course that is now nationally accredited in Australia.

Chapter 14 is a compilation of questions by clients, clinicians and researchers, addressed to me over the past nine years, which I answered to the best of my ability. Since the exchanges with clients and colleagues were in simple conversational language, this chapter preserves the same conversational style to provide questions and replies grounded in the complex reality of clinical work.

The appendices contain three scripts that can be used by clinicians who want to instruct clients personally, rather than using CDs, during group sessions or one-on-one consultations. There are also several forms which clinicians will find very helpful for the delivery of the program.

Style

Unfortunately, academic references to Eastern teachers and writers who devotedly provided the bases for mindfulness training are often ignored. In this book, references are made to traditional conceptualizations and implementation of mindfulness training, and to its originator, the historical Buddha. Of course, this does not make it a "Buddhist" book, but it seems important that the reader has an opportunity to relate current concepts in behavioral science to ancient, well-established Eastern wisdom.

Finally, while the writing style of this book is mostly conversational, some technical language remains necessary, especially since most researchers, mental health professionals and interns would be familiar with many of the non-elaborated concepts. The reader is encouraged to refer to the glossary of terms at the end of the book when necessary.

Part I
Theoretical Foundation

Chapter 1

Operationalization of Mindfulness

Therapeutic progress depends upon awareness;
in fact the attempt to become more conscious is the therapy.
                                                    Edward Whitmont

Definition of MiCBT

As a mental state, mindfulness is experienced as a heightened sensory awareness of the present moment, free from judgment, reactivity and identification to the experience. As a training, mindfulness requires deliberate sustained attentional focus on sensory processes with unconditional acceptance of the sensory experience. Mindfulness-integrated Cognitive Behavior Therapy (MiCBT) is a systemic therapy approach that integrates mindfulness meditation with core elements of cognitive and behavioral methods for the purpose of teaching clients to internalize attention in order to regulate emotion and attention, and externalize these skills to the contexts in which their impairment is triggered or maintained.

The 4-stage model of delivery

This integration can be applied flexibly within a 4-stage model.

Personal stage
In stage 1, Mindfulness meditation training is taught to internalize attention in a way that promotes deep levels of experiential awareness and acceptance. The

Mindfulness-integrated CBT: Principles and Practice, First Edition. Bruno A. Cayoun.

emphasis is on the internal context of experience to equip clients with an increased sense of self-control and self-efficacy in handling thoughts and emotions before addressing daily stressors. We learn to regulate attention and emotions.

Exposure stage
Stage 2 is the first externalizing stage. It introduces various exposure procedures, first in imagery and then *in vivo*, to decrease avoidance and increase self-confidence. We learn to decrease reactivity to external situations.

Interpersonal stage
Stage 3 requires externalizing attention further towards others by decentering attention from self to others. It includes mindfulness-based interpersonal skills to understand experientially others' ways of communicating, combined with assertiveness and other social skills training to address the interpersonal context of psychological difficulties and help prevent relapse. We learn to prevent our reaction to others' reactivity.

Empathic stage
Stage 4 teaches empathic skills grounded in the bodily experience of the present moment. It includes developing ethical awareness and action, self-compassion and compassion towards others in a way that acts as a counter-conditioning method and helps prevent relapse. We learn to feel connected to ourselves and to others.

Case Illustration with Generalized Anxiety Disorder

Before diving into the science and theoretical aspects of MiCBT, looking at clients' impression might be of interest. The example below is a good reflection of how most clients perceive the program. There are ten other cases discussed in Chapter 10, where people (ex-clients of the author) express their views and transformations.

"Jo," a physically active middle-aged lady, was severely anxious about receiving the confirmation of her physical condition. Assessments from several specialists pointed to a diagnosis of Multiple Sclerosis, but they needed to perform further tests. It seemed to her that they were waiting to see some aggravations before being able to ascertain the diagnosis. She had been a worrier for most of her life and had been experiencing clinical levels of generalized anxiety for over twenty five years. Her mood had been mildly depressed for several years, and became clinically low since the tentative diagnosis was made, about nine months prior to our first meeting. In addition to the unappealing prospect of such a severe illness, living in future uncertainty had become excruciating. Catastrophic thoughts about the future had taken over most of her waking hours. Her GP referred her for symptoms of anxiety and depression. Fortunately, her partner was very warm and supportive. The MiCBT intervention included nine sessions, after which we both felt confident that she would be able to withstand the uncertainty and the final diagnosis, and ultimately, prevent relapse.

Following an intake assessment, we discussed a "therapy contract" (see Chapter 12) and the four main delivery steps of the MiCBT program (also in Chapter 12). She benefited from practicing Progressive Muscle Relaxation in the first week, which helped reschedule her day to include a thirty-minute practice of mindfulness meditation twice daily in the forthcoming weeks (see Chapters 3 to 6). Stage 2 (see Chapter 7) started on the fourth week, Stage 3 (see Chapter 8) on the sixth week, and Stage 4 (see Chapter 9) started on the seventh week. The ninth week was a follow-up session. Below is a letter which she wrote to express her experience.

Seeking help from a psychologist wasn't something I'd ever considered. After all, I didn't really need to – did I? A few years ago I knew that, for apparently no particular reason, I was feeling a bit down. My relationship was solid, my home life was good, I knew that the conditions of my life were, comparatively, excellent. Of course, there were always ups and downs with work, as with the rest of life. Generally, however, I couldn't complain.

Nearly 12 months ago I began having a health related issue which potentially may develop into a debilitating condition. I love being active – bike riding, surfing and bushwalking. I own a farm and breed horses. Not being able to do all these things, the things I love doing, was not part of my future life plan! I found it really hard to move my mind away from thoughts about the future – thoughts that were almost invariably negative. My moods were becoming increasingly dark as these thoughts occupied my mind, more and more. I know my partner was worried about my mental state. She had suggested seeing someone to try and work out some strategies to help a number of times. However, I've never been comfortable with the idea of 'airing the laundry' to a complete stranger, preferring instead to try and work things out myself.

Consequently it was some time before I agreed to see someone – a psychologist recommended by a personal friend. I was seeking some ideas, some things I could 'do' to be able to help myself break free of the dark cloud. After the third session of talk, a couple of relaxation CDs and a month of a 'snap out of it' rubber band strategy, nothing was really changing. I can, however, thank this person for referring me on to Dr Cayoun, suggesting that his MiCBT program could provide some answers for me.

I have worked with Dr Cayoun for nearly 3 months. So what has changed? Quite a lot really – everything from my daily routine to the way I perceive each minute of each day. Twice daily I spend at least half an hour learning about my mind, my body, sensations, emotions, feelings and the inter-relationships between each of these. As I began training with basic relaxation and breath mediation exercises I realized my mind was totally in control of my sensations. I was constantly fighting to keep random (usually negative) streams of thought from dominating my mindspace and I was living in the future and not for the present. Further into body scanning methods, I have been learning more and more about the connection between thoughts and body sensations, but importantly, living more in the present moment.

So, what does this mean for me? Even though the concerns about my health remain, my emotions do not dominate my life as they did previously. I can enjoy what I have now as I am more observant and aware of all my experiences, all my body sensations. I am able to see situations with increased clarity – like the dusting settling after the road train has passed! I have learnt to recognize destructive thought patterns early – early enough to control my reactions to body sensations that accompany them and halt the emotional dip that usually follows. This increased level of equanimity has benefitted all areas of my life. At work I can focus more easily and am more patient with people who I previously found it difficult to work with. At home my ever supportive partner says that I'm more positive and easier to get along with. I have upped my exercise regime as I live in the moment and enjoy my life as it is at present, even making plans for the future – something I haven't been able to do for some time.

Whatever happens in the future, I know that Dr Cayoun's program will continue to be an important part of my life.

Western Understanding of Eastern Conceptualization

The formal establishment of mindfulness (*Satipatthana*) has been traditionally initiated through a meditation technique called *Vipassana*, meaning "seeing objectively" or "Insight," which is said to facilitate the shift of personality (Doshi, 1989; Fleischman, 1989). Elements of vipassana meditation, re-branded as "mindfulness," have entered the field of cognitive-behavioral psychology in various ways (Solomon, 2006). In part, this is because both traditions present important overlapping features and are complementary in several ways.

Relationship between mindfulness and modern Learning Theory

In many ways, mindfulness is a state of heightened awareness of natural laws. As such, developing mindfulness has been traditionally conceptualized as the highest standard of studying ecology. For instance, when we are able to sit still and merely witness internal passing events (thoughts and body sensations) we witness the law of impermanence within.

In effect, we have been using the law of impermanence for almost a century in conditioning research, and later in behavior therapy. The change over time that we observe when, for example, a learned behavior is decreased, is called an "extinction" phenomenon. The practice of CBT relies heavily on reinforcement and extinction principles, from the behavioral analysis stage to the planning and implementation of treatment. We will briefly discuss some of these principles later, although the scope of this book does not permit an elaborate discussion of the traditional views of the ways in which human behavior is modified (see Corsini and Wedding, 2005, for a useful summary).

The traditional teaching of mindfulness includes an awareness of the power of reinforcement that comes from grasping at attachments and abhorrence with aversions. Learned behaviors, thoughts and emotions are thought to lose their strength when they are not reacted to (Goenka, 1987); a principle known as 'extinction' in Western behavioral science. Whereas Western Psychology has termed and investigated reinforcement and extinction principles for about a century, Eastern conceptualizations of behavior have included a sequence of mental events called the Law of Causation for well over twenty-five centuries. In these conceptualizations, interoception (i.e., the ability to feel body sensations) has prime importance in either strengthening or eradicating behavior (Solé-Leris, 1992; see also Woodward, 1939, for an accurate translation).

Hence, the notions of reinforcement and extinction were not only well understood twenty-five centuries ago, they were also used as a means of self-acceptance and psychological change to decrease human suffering.

Mindfulness of human suffering

Mindfulness, as originally conceptualized in Theravada Buddhism, must serve to realize three central human conditions, one of which (Selflessness) will be discussed in more detail later. These are (a) the changing nature of all things, (b) the consequent substancelessness of the self ("Egolessness" or "Selflessness"), and (c) the suffering that springs from a lack of awareness of the impermanent nature of all phenomena, including the self and its aggregate components (Genther and Kawamura, 1975). From this perspective, being mindful facilitates this realization in all encountered internal and external events, knowing (not just thinking or hoping) that "this will also change." Thus, as mentioned in the introduction of this book, the traditional conceptualization of mindfulness involves an increased ability to remain aware of a natural law, impermanence (i.e., the omnipresence of continuous and uncontrollable change), and its consequences in daily living (see Marlatt, 2002; Marlatt, Witkiewitz, Dillworth *et al.*, 2004; for applications to treatment of addictive behavior). What is meant by "mindfulness" throughout this volume is precisely what this long-established tradition encompasses.

Paul Fleischman, a Psychiatrist and experienced mindfulness teacher in Northern America, pointed out that "Vipassana is a training in psychological culture" (Fleischman, 1999, p. 63). In terms of Kelly's (1955) constructivist view of personality, undergoing traditional mindfulness-based training involves testing the hypothesis that all thoughts and physical sensations have the same characteristics of arising and passing away. By experiencing this law of perpetual change within ourselves, we learn to alter the self-construct by being a more objective, scientific observer producing more accurate analyses of ongoing events and making predictions that are more sensible and realistic, thus enhancing the sense of control over our life.

Attention regulation training

Yi-Yuan Tang, Michael Posner, and other experts of attention research have argued that mindfulness practice requires the recruitment of numerous brain networks that enable important functions of our attention systems. When we pay attention to our breath, for example, we teach ourselves three crucial attentional skills that are very familiar to attention researchers and clinicians working with attentional disorders (e.g., Cayoun, 2010; Tang *et al.*, 2007). These are known as *sustained attention*, *response inhibition* and *attention shifting*. Observation and measurement of these three functions of attention are well established in the research literature, as reflected by the numerous tests of the so-called *executive functions*, which will be briefly discussed later, as they relate to mindfulness meditation skills.

Sustained attention

First we train ourselves to sustain attention to a target, our natural, non-controlled breath (a script is provided in Appendix A). While we do our best to remain vigilant of our breath, we also learn to detect thoughts and other unwanted stimuli intruding into our conscious awareness. This task helps improve our vigilance and focus in daily activities. It also helps improve our objectivity and detachment. It is only when we can perceive a thought or body sensation arising in its own right that we can learn not to get lost in it, not to identify with it. We learn to differentiate our internal experiences from the sense of self.

Response inhibition

As soon as we realize that a thought or body sensation has emerged in conscious awareness, we endeavor not to react to it in any way, whether mentally by producing a value judgment or otherwise. We "inhibit" our otherwise automatic reaction. This task leads to a progressive sense of being an agent of self-control and helps us learn to accept or tolerate the presence of unpleasant experiences and the absence of pleasant ones.

Response re-engagement

We learn not to grasp and "cling" to thoughts, which allows us to switch and reallocate attention to the intended target, in this case our breath. This is one of the most difficult attentional skills because it relies on both sustained attention and response inhibition. Research into the aetiology and maintenance of Attention Deficit Hyperactivity Disorder shows that people who are accurately diagnosed with this condition have some response inhibition deficits in some contexts and are most impaired in response re-engagement (e.g., Cayoun, 2010). Our ability to switch attention back to the experience of breathing or to other body sensations when a thought has emerged results in greater cognitive flexibility, which helps us "let go" of all sorts of unhelpful thoughts and emotions.

A few years ago, a team of North American and Canadian researchers met in an effort to produce an operational definition of mindfulness so that the mindfulness construct can be scientifically and efficiently measured (Bishop *et al.*, 2004). Their conceptualization integrates (and is not limited to) these three functions of attention in a manner very similar to that mentioned above, with minor differences. Scott Bishop and his colleagues have termed this aspect of mindfulness training "attention regulation," which effectively reflects the consequence of improving our ability to use these three skills simultaneously. Attention regulation, added to a non-judgmental and accepting attitude towards our *whole* experience, allows us to adopt a specific attitude called "equanimity." As briefly discussed below and more in detail in the next chapter, equanimity is considered a core mechanism in the process of extinguishment of both implicit and explicit learned responses.

Equanimity: a core mechanism

The term "equanimity" loosely means balance, equipoise, composure, calmness, level-headedness, equilibrium and self-control. In the *Abhidhamma* (texts regrouping the Buddhist psychological system), it is referred to as "a mind which abides in the state of non-attachment, non-hatred, and non-deludedness coupled with assiduousness ... Its function is not to provide occasions for emotional instability" (Pradhan, 1950, p. 6). It is the refusal to be caught in aversion or attachment (Taylor, 2010) and a "state of mind free from craving, aversion, ignorance" (Goenka, 1987, p.162). In the therapeutic context, equanimity may be defined as: *the conscious and deliberate act of being non-reactive towards an event experienced within the framework of one's body and thoughts as a result of non-judgmental observation.* This implies that unless we are aware of an actual (internal) experience, we cannot be equanimous towards it. Thus defined, equanimity is a state of experiential acceptance that relies on awareness of thoughts and somatic sensations.

Interestingly, about fifty years ago, Russian behavior scientists reported on the importance of what was termed "interoceptive conditioning" (e.g., Bykov, 1957; Razran, 1960, 1961; Voronin, 1962). These studies, according to Yates (1970, p. 416), "are of critical significance for behavior therapists." As will be discussed later in this and other chapters, interoceptive awareness and acceptance are central mechanisms in both mindfulness meditation traditionally taught in the Burmese tradition and in MiCBT, in which it is integrated.

In many ways, equanimity requires more objectivity about the event we are experiencing. The more able we are to be aware of thoughts and body sensations just as they are unfolding, the more equanimous we become. In that sense, we become more scientific about our own experiences. Our mind and body can be a little like our private laboratory, where our observations are significantly closer to scientific assessments than our usual judgmental evaluations. Hence, some researchers and teachers of mindfulness have argued that mindfulness meditation is a science.

Neuroanatomically, it is proposed that equanimity relies on inhibitory neural networks in the temporal regions (inhibition of verbal responses in auditory cortex), right-prefrontal and limbic regions (inhibition of behavioral responses in emotional pathways, especially amygdala), and excitatory networks in the parietal regions (facilitation of neuroplasticity in somatosensory networks). Equanimity also seems to be associated with secretion of endorphins, whereas reactivity is related to secretion of adrenaline and cortisol. Equanimity is tied to activation of the parasympathetic nervous system and increased immune response (Davidson, Kabat-Zinn, Schumacher *et al.*, 2003; Tang *et al.*, 2007; Fan *et al.*, 2010).

Overview of basic practice components

During formal training (i.e., sitting meditation), we learn to see a thought for what it is, just a thought, no matter what its content may be. Though content is acknowledged, we learn not to cling to it, give it importance, identify with it, or react to it. We learn to perceive an emerging thought more objectively as an arising and passing mental event. As such, the thought cannot truly affect us, the observer. The benefits gained through this process are obvious for depressed and anxious individuals, whose capacity to prevent ruminations are almost immediate (e.g., Ramel *et al.*, 2004).

We learn to identify when and for how long the mind has wandered in thoughts. In doing so, we progressively develop an awareness of our ongoing thoughts as they manifest themselves in consciousness. This skill has been termed "metacognitive insight," which is another important skill that helps address depression and anxiety symptoms (Teasdale, 1999).

We also learn to perceive a body sensation merely as a body sensation, regardless of its hedonic qualities (pleasant, unpleasant, or neutral). We train to remain as objective as possible and observe the transient characteristics of body sensations, how quickly or slowly they change, whether they are intense or feeble, acceptable or unacceptable. Often with stupefaction, we discover that, much like thoughts, body sensations arise and pass away and they are essentially impersonal phenomena.

Developing this kind of detachment has several advantages. For instance, consider hyperarousal-based disorders (e.g., panic, post-traumatic stress disorder [PTSD], impulse control disorder, etc), or even chronic pain. What would happen to your client with these kinds of symptoms if he or she could train to experience their intrusive thoughts and accompanying body states with more objectivity and acceptance, and "let them go"?

Changes in Western Clinical Psychology

In the last decade and a half, there has been a significant shift in our conceptualization of human cognitive and emotional processing. For example, John Teasdale and his colleagues led the way by claiming that emotions are produced by patterns of sensorily-derived information and are maintained by self-perpetuating mechanisms via feedback loops (Teasdale *et al.*, 1995). Teasdale and Barnard's (1993) Interacting Cognitive Subsystems (ICS) model of information processing integrates the various ways of human cognition and emotion with an ecological notion of self-organized systems. The ICS approach also emphasizes experiential aspects of cognition which have been insufficiently taken into account to explain how reinforcement is actually experienced.

Others have also widened the net of possible reinforcing factors in their view of learning principles. For instance, modern learning theory acknowledges that cognitive and other internal experiences can be involved in learning. Bouton, Mineka, and Barlow's (2001) comprehensive review of basic conditioning research in relation to panic underscores these involvements. The authors propose that Panic Disorder develops because exposure to panic attacks causes the conditioning of anxiety to cues outside the person as well as cues experienced in the body. In line with the model presented here, Bouton *et al.*, (2001) conceive that this process fundamentally involves emotional learning that is best explained by conditioning principles.

Moreover, Stephen Hayes and his colleagues proposed a "post Skinnerian" account of learning, through their Relational Frame Theory (RFT). This approach proposes that human language and the use of it to communicate or make sense of the world requires deriving relations among events, highlighting the important role of human language and cognition in human learning, see Hayes, Barnes-Holmes, and Roche (2001) for detailed account.

Current status in Western psychotherapy

It has been proposed that mindfulness is a common factor across various therapeutic orientations (Martin, 1997). The basis for this view is that the development of mindfulness promotes access to new perspectives and the disengagement from habitual response sets, including automatic thoughts and behaviors (Langer, 1989, 1992; Roemer, and Orsillo, 2002; Teasdale *et al.*, 1995; Wells, 2002).

By itself, mindfulness training can provide us with opportunities to review our beliefs since we train daily not to buy into our thoughts. It allows us to challenge our own established views about ourselves, others, our values, our future, as well as the external world (Kabat-Zinn, 1982, 1990), without necessarily reviewing the deep-routed belief systems that we began to establish in childhood (our "schemas") or involving exposure to specific triggers as implemented in traditional cognitive-behavioral approaches (e.g., Beck, 1976; Mahoney, 1974; Meichenbaum; 1977). Accordingly, it is understandable that some authors have expressed reservations regarding what exactly are the active ingredients in mindfulness training (e.g., McLaren, 2006; Pridmore, 2006).

Some authors indicated the lack of adequate control in several studies of mindfulness training, as taught in MBSR, for depression and anxiety disorders (Toneatto and Nguyen, 2007) and questioned the construct of mindfulness, the effectiveness of such programs, the mechanisms of action, and the methodology used for treatment outcome studies (Bishop, 2002). The recent proliferation of publications has clarified some of these questions (e.g., Allen, Chambers, Knight, and Melbourne Academic Mindfulness Interest Group, 2006), but the active mechanisms of mindfulness seem to remain unclear (Kostanski and Hassed, 2008).

During her research at the University of Canterbury, examining the effects of MiCBT on the health behavior of diabetes sufferers, Melanie Lindsay (2007) noted the following:

Within the context of Western psychology, mindfulness research for physical and psychological health is a fledgling field. The variety of ways in which mindfulness has been conceptualized reflects the lack of theoretical consensus (Bishop *et al.*, 2004) and much of the research on mindfulness highlights the problematic process of capturing a definition of mindfulness (Baer, 2003; Brown and Ryan, 2003). There is potential for confusion in the use of the word mindfulness (Hayes and Wilson, 2003) because mindfulness may be described as a group of behaviours and represent an outcome (Baer, Smith, and Allen, 2004; Feldman, Hayes, Kumar, and Greeson, 2004), a practice (Thera, 1969), a therapeutic process (Germer, 2005), a technology (Hayes and Shenk, 2004; Linehan, 1993), a state and a trait (Bishop *et al.*, 2004; Siegel, 2009a).

The following chapter attempts to address some of these questions using a model of reinforcement that does not rely on Cartesian dualism, by which the endorsement of a dichotomy of mind and matter has dominated Western Psychology for over a century. Rather, it proposes that mind and body cannot be separated during an experience. It is an integrative approach to behavior maintenance and change that rests on a neuro-behavioral model reinforcement.

Summary of Main Points

- Mindfulness practice requires the development of cognitive and behavioral skills, including sustained sensory awareness, and unconditional experiential acceptance and response prevention; traditionally summarized by the term "equanimity."
- MiCBT is a four-stage therapy model that integrates mindfulness meditation with core elements of cognitive and behavioral methods into a systemic approach to teach clients to regulate emotion and attention, and to externalize these skills to the contexts in which their impairment is triggered or maintained.
- There is a strong overlap between mindfulness principles and modern Learning Theory, both of which recognize the importance of reinforcement for the maintenance, enhancement and extinguishment of habitual reactions to stressors.
- In agreement with the traditional principles for the establishment of mindfulness in the East (*Satipattana*), the MiCBT therapy system proposes that equanimity is the principal mechanism of action for the transformative effect of mindfulness meditation. Other mechanisms of action include sustained attention, response inhibition to intrusive thoughts, response re-engagement (attention shifting), and non-identification with the experience.
- In the last fifteen years, there have been significant changes in the Western understanding of human cognitive and emotional processing. The notion of Cartesian Dualism has given way to the concept of embodied cognition, where mind and body cannot be separated during an experience. Numerous health clinicians have successfully used mindfulness training to address the experiential aspect of their patients' conditions.

Chapter 2

The Co-emergence Model of Reinforcement: A Rationale for Mindfulness Integration

There are many cakes but only few ingredients.
(Ex-client, 26 October 2009)

In the area of cognitive neuroscience, in accord with the model presented below, some empirical researchers have predicted a major paradigm shift in our appraisal of information processing. Amongst those who share the view that cognitive science is shifting towards neurophenomenology, Varela's (1999) position was as follows:

> One of the major key realizations over the last few years in science has been to understand that you cannot have anything close to a mind or a mental capacity without it being completely embodied, enfolded with the world. It arises through an immediate coping, inextricably bound in a body that is active, moving and coping with the world. This might sound obvious but it is not so within the world of research where other ideas have been predominant especially the computational idea. ... Cognition is not only enactively embodied but is enactively emergent, in that technical sense that I just tried to sketch. Some people might call that by various names: self-organization, complexity, or non-linear dynamics. The core principle is the same: the passage from the local to the global. (Varela, 1999, pp. 72–76)

The model described below extends our understanding of learning principles through the neurophenomenology of reinforcement, the actual experience of reinforcement mechanisms. It is an integrated conceptualization of how mind and matter "co-emerge" to produce an experience. The model is anchored in modern Learning Theory and the phenomenology of mindfulness meditation and principles (see Narada, 1968, for traditional conceptualization). The operationalization of the model is entrenched in a cognitive-behavioral framework. It is presented in a simple

Mindfulness-integrated CBT: Principles and Practice, First Edition. Bruno A. Cayoun.
© 2011 John Wiley & Sons, Ltd. Published 2011 by John Wiley & Sons, Ltd.

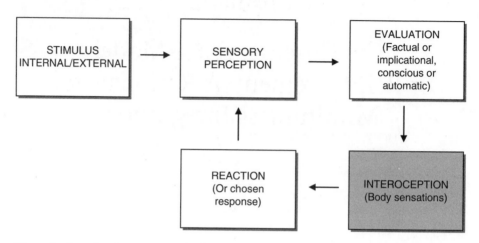

Figure 1. Functional components in the co-emergence model of reinforcement.

form by means of generic functional components, rather than a complex conceptual architecture.

Integrating Essential Components of Behavior Change

The non-pathological functioning of the overall information system necessary for the reinforcement of what we learn is presented in Figure 1. In brief, the stimulus is perceived (consciously or subconsciously) through the senses, evaluated according to previously formed categories and beliefs that spring from past experiences, personality, expectations, needs and values, leading to the emergence of body sensations, to which we are likely to react with a learned response when these reach a sufficient level of intensity – even though they may remain below awareness level. These four generic components function in equilibrium when mental health is optimum and in disequilibrium when normal functioning is challenged, as we will see later in this chapter.

Despite the apparent hierarchy of the model, input into the perceptual component (Sensory Perception) may also be generated by the person's thoughts, body sensations, or reactions. In this case, they constitute an internal stimulus. In addition, well-learned patterns of reacting bypass our awareness of the Evaluation component (so called "automatic thought"); the stimulus appears to move from Sensory Perception directly to stimulating Body Sensation. Because of the great rapidity with which each component continuously manifests itself, we experience a sense of continuity and wholeness, comparable to a Gestalt principle in perception (such as the apparent motion of flashing lights animating casinos at night).

Another particularity of this cognitive flow is its reliance on continuous input. The last stage, Reaction, becomes the input (Stimulus) perceived for the next cycle to begin, so that the flow never ceases, even during sleep. As soon as a reaction takes place, it "fuels" the next perception and the cycle continues through self-reinforcement. As is elaborated later via a "neural-networks" explanation of intrusive thoughts, one reason for the incessant flow of information-processing is that recently or frequently activated memory pathways in the brain remain with a degree of activation that becomes (or remains) conscious when we relax or sleep. Thus, the end of a cycle leads to the beginning of the next, allowing mental continuity, response reinforcement and our identification with this continual process. From an experiential point of view, the process of thinking "organizes itself" in sets of stable idiosyncratic patterns with which we fully identify. We usually feel that we *are* our thoughts. It is of no surprise that the idea of "stopping to think" through "meditation" can sometimes worry some people because the idea of stopping to think seems like "stopping to be" or losing control.

However, the flow of cognitive activity can be altered by conscious will and its typical patterns transformed by adequate training. This is reflected during the experience of mindfulness training, especially when experiencing an increased sense of control over our own continually emerging thoughts.

In his discussion of the therapeutic effect of acceptance, Greenberg (1994) proposed the existence of a continuous internal experiencing process. As proposed in the present model, Greenberg argues that this experiencing process is automatic, not subject to conscious, deliberate control, yet is affected by conscious symbolization of it.

Role and Phenomenology of the Four Functional Components

Sensory perception

Of the four functional components of the model, the first allows contact between sense organs and an inner stimulus (thought or body sensation) or an outer stimulus (any stimulus from the environment). It is the reception of perceptual stimuli that enables us to sense the world. This function translates neural impulses into smell, taste, sound, touch and visual image. Some argue that this processing occurs mostly below awareness levels and that what is reaching conscious awareness is a representation of it. Others, especially proponents of Ecological Psychology, propose a more direct route whereby the stimulus is directly perceived and evaluated by the organism, so that no representation is necessary.

Although experts in sensory perception have described these principles at length (e.g., Bower, 1977; Sekuler and Blake, 1994), they have been generally limited to the five common senses: sight, smell, taste, hearing, and touch. The present model highlights two more important perceptual abilities that develop, to great extents during mindfulness meditation, a sixth and a seventh sense. One is known as "meta-cognitive insight" (Teasdale, 1999), which allows us to know when a thought manifests itself; just as olfaction lets us know that an odor has stimulated our sense of smell. The development of awareness of spontaneous thoughts is central to mindfulness training. Equally important is the other perceptual ability, known as "interoception" (perception of internal states), which allows us to feel sensations in the body. Of course, interoception can be a conscious or subconscious experience. Before being translated into categories of experience, basic manifestations such as hunger, coldness or painfulness, are initially processed via sensorimotor feedback in the form of four basic constituents that are in continual interaction: mass, temperature, motion, and cohesiveness, as discussed below in the section on Interoception.

Evaluation

This constitutes a vast area of research within the field of cognitive sciences and presenting a complex architecture of the cognitive system and subsystems according to various conceptualizations is beyond the scope of this book. For the purpose of presenting the model described here, it may be useful to simply mention two very broad types of processing observed during mindfulness practice: one has a descriptive role, the other serves an evaluative or judgmental function.

Following the sensory perception of a stimulus, the first broad processing is a rapid sequence of stimulus recognition and categorization, for example, "there is a pencil on the desk." Unless we are trained to attend purposefully to this early mental event, as is the case in mindfulness training (metacognitive awareness), it generally takes place below our awareness threshold. This initial, neutral, stimulus identification is based on consensus, norms, and factual knowledge, and enables us to make sense of the world.

If the stimulus has a degree of personal importance at the time of recognition, it is immediately followed by a second broad processing category, an evaluation of what has just been recognized, a judgment of it. Teasdale and Barnard's (1993) Interacting Cognitive Subsystems' (ICS) "central engine," is also made-up of a "propositional" coding system (factual, descriptive thinking) and an "implicational" coding system (evaluative, judgmental thinking). These coding systems roughly correspond to the notion of "cold" and "hot" cognitions.

Following sufficient repetition, the evaluation is learned and becomes automatic, enabling rapid judgment based on past experiences, values, personality, present emotional state, expectations and needs. Since the appraisal of the world relies primarily on past references (Langer, 1992), the evaluative component contaminates some or all aspects of the stimulus. Consequently, the "implicational" evaluation of a present life event is largely dependent upon rules and beliefs established in the past, our so-called schemas. In the co-emergence model, as in traditional cognitive models, evaluative processing does not only mean conscious thinking. Beck (1976) and others have long argued that much of our behavior is directly dependent upon automatic thoughts. This component of cognitive processing is highly subjective, idiosyncratic, and often associated with emotional states, although it is not exclusively manifested with emotional content. In line with Buddhist conceptualization of mind and the co-emergence principles described below, the ICS approach also proposes that implicational coding leads directly to sensorimotor processing.

Interoception

Stimulation of the judgmental (implicational) aspect of information processing causes the emergence of a qualitatively different phenomenon; one or more sensations occur somewhere in the body. This component involves all body sensations from the subtlest to the grossest, whether they are felt consciously or subconsciously. The extent to which a thought has personal implications, to that extent it will produce salient body sensations. In other words, the intensity of our thought-related body sensations is a function of the personal implication contained in the meaning of the thought, even if the thought is not consciously accessible at the time.

Evaluative thinking leads to interoception because it projects the information from the cerebral cortex deep into the center of the brain to stimulate emotional pathways. It has been shown that regions in the right prefrontal cortex are systematically activated when negative thoughts take place (e.g., Davidson *et al.*, 2003). These regions of the brain have excitatory pathways projecting to the amygdala, which has a central role in the production of stress responses. The stimulation of these pathways is a function of the intensity with which the stimulus is evaluated, whether consciously or automatically.

However, interoceptive processing does not present only in a descending hierarchical order. It also emerges because of environmental conditions (e.g., pollution, air temperature, etc) or physical activity and conditions (e.g., body movements, digestion, heartbeat, fever, blood flow, muscle tension, etc). In this case, it constitutes the internal stimulus in the chain of events, causing a thought or thought-stream to co-emerge. Presumably, this happens as a result of previous associations between the present interoceptive experience and its typical appraisal. Thus, the emerging body sensation causes a network to auto-activate, either below or above the threshold of awareness.

An important assertion in the model is that body sensations exist at all times throughout the body, except where neurons are absent (e.g., hair and the external part of fingernails and toenails) or where neural connection are insufficiently strengthened to allow conscious interoception. Many are mostly too subtle to be detected by individuals untrained in mindfulness meditation. Body sensations are detectable when they intensify sufficiently to reach our threshold of awareness. This is greatly affected by emotional load and stress levels, as will be discussed later. Arousal is the process that takes place when body sensations are grossly intensified following contact with a pleasant or unpleasant stimulus.

Learning "to survive," whether in the jungle, in the classroom or at work, is primarily an automatic process. The extent to which our recognition of a context has personal implications, will determine the intensity of co-emerging body sensations. The more implicational is the thought, the more intense is the body sensation,

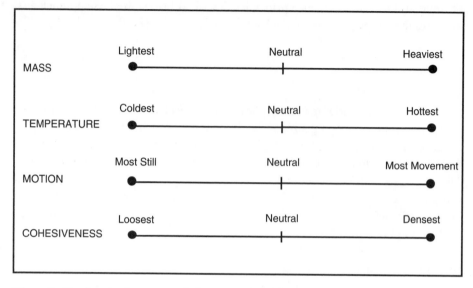

Figure 2. The four basic perceptual characteristics of interoception.

which then becomes the main determinant of our response, as will be described later. Without this relative reliance on body sensations to recall the significance of events, we may not be able to remember which context is potentially harmful. Thus, co-emerging body sensations play a very important role in the maintenance and availability of emotional memories. Whereas factual thoughts (propositional coding) serve to inform us about factual aspects of a phenomenon, "implicational" thoughts help us survive. With the latter, body sensations that are coupled with the thought immediately prepare the nervous system for rapid reaction. When we encounter ambiguous situations, in particular, it is what we feel in the body that mostly tells us about the context we're in and whether it is safe, not our rational thinking. This is one reason for which it is so difficult for PTSD clients to remain rational and factual about their intrusive traumatic memories. We can access more readily and rapidly the body sensations encoded during the event and the formation of its memory.

Body sensations are experienced on a hedonic continuum in three principal ways: pleasant, neutral or unpleasant. Neutral sensations often lead to unpleasant ones in sensation-seeking contexts (adolescence, pre-manic stage in Bipolar Affective Disorder, etc). The traditional approach to mindfulness also identifies four basic characteristics of body sensations, the intensity of which varies along a continuum, as shown in Figure 2.

They are "perceptual" characteristics because they can be appraised as such only "perceptually" (Sensory Perception), not "judgmentally" (Evaluation). The ability to perceive body sensations in their perceptual dimensions is a function of the acquired equanimity. These four characteristics continuously interact during the individual's experience, providing an infinite possibility of interoceptive combinations. This can be compared to other perceptual modalities, such as sight, where the four basic constituents of colors (red, yellow, blue, and grey scale from white to black) provide infinite color combinations. Similarly, for the sense of taste, the four basic elements (sweet, sour, salty, and bitter) allow infinite taste combinations.

Mass	With mass, there are sensations of weight, from feeling extreme lightness to extreme heaviness.
Temperature	The continuum of temperature involves sensations of temperature, from feeling extremely cold to extremely hot.
Motion	With motion, there are sensations of movement, from the subtlest vibration to the grossest shaking experiences.
Cohesiveness	The cohesiveness continuum provides sensations of solidity or density, from the loosest to the most compounded sensation, typically letting us feel the shape of the sensation.

Some practical considerations can help avoid confusion in clients. The characteristic of cohesiveness tends to be more ambiguous at the start of training. It is usually not difficult to feel the shape of our limb or face. The experience of solidity or density, which leads to the impression of form, can be easily experienced, for example, when the chest is constricted or there is tightness of throat during anxiety symptoms, though it can sometimes be confused with the sensation of mass. With advanced scanning methods, as will be described later, trainees can feel very subtle tingling sensations vibrating *en masse* throughout the body, as if there is no solidity — a very pleasant experience. This makes the cohesiveness continuum clearly discernable, but it may have to be explained a little more to clients in the early stage of training, perhaps asking them to try feeling the shape of their hand or other body parts.

The context in which body sensations are experienced is important. A subtle sensation for one person may appear intense for another; depending on the person's ability for somatic awareness. In addition, a relatively neutral body sensation at a particular point in time may appear pleasant or unpleasant at another, depending largely on the person's current awareness threshold. This is because regular and skilled practice allows us to be increasingly sensitive to very subtle body sensations. What seemed to be a faint experience at the early stage of training may appear relatively intense as skill improves. This is best explained in terms of increased interoceptive awareness.

After some practice of mindfulness meditation, pleasant and unpleasant sensations are relatively "easy" to deal with. In contrast, neutral sensations require more skill, partly because their lack of apparent salience requires more sustained attention. The typical reaction to neutral body sensations is the experience of boredom, and a subsequent tendency to be distracted due to the lack of sensory stimulation and/or feeling drowsy. Ultimately, feeling bored leads to frustration and possibly an aversive response. This is typically emphasized in sensation-seeking behavior.

Interoception occupies one of the most important roles in mindfulness training. As emphasized in MiCBT, clients practice body-scanning techniques for lengthy periods in a continued effort to develop interoception and improve their perception of early cues of distress. It has recently been shown that mindfulness training produces plasticity in brain pathways needed to operate interoceptive awareness (Lazar *et al.*, 2005), and it may be argued that neural plasticity similarly develops in frontal pathways that promote metacognitive awareness (Kabat-Zinn, 2005). Neuroplasticity is the capacity of neurons to adapt to a changed environment (FitzGerald and Folan-Curran, 2002). According to Hebbian learning, pre-synaptic terminals change in numbers according to usage and each learning experience strengthens existing neuronal connections (Hebb, 1949).

Reaction

Most body sensations lead to immediate responses, most of which are generated by the Central Nervous System (CNS). The awareness of both body sensations and reactions varies according to their intensity and the individual's awareness threshold. It follows that stress, with its associated gross sensations, prevents the detection of subtle sensations. Especially with over-learned ("automatic") responses, the CNS constantly initiates or alters behavior without having to rely on our conscious knowledge. Automatically scratching oneself following an itching sensation is a typical example. Another good example is during sleep, when our grasp of sensory events is far remote from awareness (Goenka, 1987; also in Hart, 1987). The buzzing of a mosquito about our head can lead our hand to wave towards the sound to distance the insect, although we are sound asleep. Since the CNS is not wired to respond specifically to mosquito buzz at birth — newborns do not show aversion to it — the CNS has learned to react according to our initially conscious aversion to the body sensation following one or more mosquito bites. As the night gets chilly, although conscious awareness is still absent, the body "feels" the cold and our hands take the blanket to cover neck and shoulders. Who gave the order? Thus, based on learned patterns of reactions, reactive behavior can be subconscious, whether in sleeping or waking states. Put simply, we react to what the evaluation "feels like."

Reactions are either overt or covert and suppressed or expressed through mental, verbal or physical responses. Mental events (such as self-talk) that may or may not be acted upon verbally or physically also need to be taken into account. In the treatment of addiction, for example, "The critical juncture of potential drop-out is the client's reactions to his or her first lapse" (Marlatt, 1994, p. 186). The process by which a mental reaction is carried out is part of cognitive automaticity. For any person, the cyclic nature of the entire process relies on interactions between the functional components described in Figure 1. This is clearly emphasized in panic sufferers. As the physical sensations associated with the condition (e.g., tingling in hands and arms, tightness and pressure in the chests, etc) reach the person's awareness threshold, the reactive (often catastrophic) thoughts also become increasingly apparent. The reader will benefit from reading Bouton's comprehensive review of the panic literature and undoubtedly relate modern Learning Theory to a number of propositions advanced in the present model (see Bouton *et al.*, 2001).

Consistent with Clark's (1986) model of panic, reactions feed back into the system to act as the new input. However, the present model conceives this self-perpetuating reinforcement process as applicable to *all* learned responses and not restricted to panic attacks. Even the most legitimate fear is experienced as thought (e.g., a child is very late coming home from school) co-emerging with body sensations (e.g., pressure and movement in abdominal areas and temperature change in various areas).

A reaction may take the form of a reflex-like physical movement, a thought or thought pattern, or an emotion (combination of thought, intense body sensation and a relieving behavior). There are two direct relationships between Interoception and Reaction. First, the severity of the reaction depends on the intensity of the body sensation. The extent to which a body sensation is intense, to that extent a reaction is likely to take place. Second, the type of reaction depends on the type of body sensation and previous associations. The extent to which a body sensation is experienced as pleasant, to that extent the reaction will be an attempt to prolong its duration and increase its frequency. The extent to which a body sensation is experienced as unpleasant, to that extent the reaction will be an attempt to reduce both duration and frequency of occurrence (e.g., avoidance). As this pattern of behavior is learned, we crave for pleasant sensations and experience aversion for unpleasant sensations, whether present or imagined. Whether learned or inherent in the CNS, craving and aversion are linked to both pleasant or unpleasant body sensations and mental unrest (see Hart, 1987, for a comprehensive description). This phenomenological account not only fits well with the basic principles of learning theories, especially those of operant conditioning, it also highlights the "missing link" in the unfolding of conditioning principles: reinforcement relies on interoception.

Widening the Scope of Learning Theory

The craving behavior is (positively) reinforced each time a pleasant body sensation is successfully maintained or increased. The aversive behavior is (negatively) reinforced each time an unpleasant body sensation is successfully decreased, typically through avoidant behavior. As explained in the traditional work of B.F. Skinner (1953), operant learning takes place when the behavior "operates" on the environment to generate consequences. His demonstrations of operant conditioning relied on the pleasant and unpleasant consequences of a stimulus on the organism. Attempting to increase pleasant body sensations and decrease unpleasant ones also constitute operant behaviors, except that they manifest at the experiential level of behavior, often at a sub-threshold level of awareness (i.e., automatically). The incessant "flow" of operant behavior is precisely the target of mindfulness meditation and is accordingly emphasized in MiCBT.

From the above description, a strong implication arises: *all* learned behaviors undergo operant behavior, however subtle and covert the level of processing may be. It is suggested that all forms of conditioning include operant learning and depend on it. They are layers of superimposed conditions that can produce learning *only* if operant learning is activated at the source. Beneath the apparent coupling of a stimulus and a response, there are body sensations we must experience and to which we must respond. Technically speaking, interoception "operates" on the response. From this point of view, body sensations are the sole real operants, universally manifesting themselves at the source of all learning.

To illustrate this phenomenon, let us take the example of how classical conditioning depends on operant processes. For example, imagine that you are travelling in a developing country and order a green salad over the counter of a small restaurant. You trekked for several weeks and you are bored with eating tinned food. The owner says hello with a welcoming smile. You say hello and smile back. As you read the menu, you see all the healthy fresh local produce and ingredients included in the dish and you feel hungry and excited. This is because in the past, you have associated these ingredients with health and well-being, a concept which, for you, was also associated with reassurance or perhaps even happiness. In other words, your positive response is "classically conditioned." Printed words of the ingredients are conditioned stimuli and your positive response is a conditioned response. So far so good. As you wait for your dish to arrive, you decide to read more about the region in your tour guide and you come across a paragraph on the farming habits of the locals. You read: "Because lettuces are difficult to grow in this area of the country and farmers cannot afford common fertilizers, they are sometimes grown using diluted human excrements as fertilizers." Since you have associated human excrement with dirt and possibly disease in the past, you begin to feel worried. As the dish is served, you look at the little piece of lettuce among other ingredients and spontaneously feel disgusted. This time, you don't smile back to the owner who serves you smilingly and you decide to return the whole dish. You pay for it, leave the restaurant and buy tinned vegetables at the corner store. You read that the produce was grown somewhere else and feel reassured and calmer. Here, your response is also "classically conditioned." In the first situation, the positive assumption that eating greens was going to be beneficial to you (implicational coding of agreeability) co-emerged with pleasant body sensations. Your response, a desire to eat and read more about food, was directly related to the pleasant body sensations. Had you been unable to feel body sensations, your response would have been different. In the second situation, your negative assumption that consuming lettuce contaminated by human excrement was going to be a threat to your health (implicational coding of disagreeability) co-emerged with unpleasant body sensations. Your response (returning the whole dish, leaving the premises, etc) was directly related to your unpleasant body sensations. Every time you are hungry while remaining in this area of the country, you feel unpleasant body sensations, which are alleviated by eating non-local tinned food while travelling in this country. Note that tinned food is now producing pleasant body sensations, not boredom anymore.

This negative response to tinned food has been "counter-conditioned" and is now extinguished because you are associating tinned food with hygiene and safety. Nonetheless, if the emergence of unpleasant body sensations generalizes to all foods of this country, you are likely to shorten your visit.

In the above example, only lettuce is the unconditioned stimulus, but soon all fresh produce (conditioned stimuli) are avoided (conditioned response) *because* of disagreeable thoughts of threat of illness co-emerging with unpleasant body sensations, which in turn give rise to an aversive reaction of disgust and avoidance. The underlying principle is operant conditioning. The aversive experience of unpleasant body sensations first eliminates the experience of hunger, and later the disinterest in tinned food. To be "conditioned," a response requires an experience.

A Dynamic Systems Explanation of Intrusive Thoughts

As mentioned earlier, practicing mindfulness meditation involves the development of a high ability for meta-cognitive awareness, sustained attention and inhibitory control over reactive habits. In general, models of attention have been developed and understood within the information-processing framework which necessarily involves a hierarchy of control. However, it has been pointed out that these models of attention "suffer from an inability to provide a satisfactory explanation of what orients attention" (Summers and Ford 1995, p. 79).

Alternatively, neural networks models of attention reject the hypotheses of hierarchical and serial processing (Cohen, Dunbar, and McClelland, 1990; Phaf, Heijden, and Hudson, 1990). They suggest that behavioral control is continuous with the biological structure of the brain, rather than modeling "the mind" on a digital computer. Similarly, Teasdale and Barnard's (1993) ICS approach integrates some aspects of neural network models, but it emphasizes the experiential aspects of cognitions. Their systems approach to the processing of information is more in line with human experience than is the traditional cognitive theory. Based on my personal 22 years of experience with regular mindfulness meditation, the multitude of other practitioners' subjective reports, and phenomenological data reported by research participants (Herring, 2005; Kornfield, 1979; Mason and Hargreave, 2001), descriptions of thoughts and simultaneous co-emerging body sensations during mindfulness training fit surprisingly well into a neural network model, and more so the ICS approach, in which cognition is said to be "embodied."

Simply described, neural network models of information processing (also called "connectionist models") have a common structure that consists of three layers of numerous interconnected neuron-like processing units, each having a current state of positive, neutral, or negative "activation," and each having an excitatory or inhibitory effect on other units. The "input layer" receives input from the environment and is activated by it; the "output layer" receives output from the system and is activated "internally;" and finally there is a third layer of "hidden units" which have neither direct input from, nor output to, the environment (McClelland, Rumelhart, and the PDP Research Group, 1986). These models propose that knowledge is distributed across sets of units in the form of patterns of activation, rather than being stored within a specific location and manipulated by a "central executive." Some networks ought to be more activated because of the person's expertise, frequency and recency of use, emotions linked to certain networks, etc.

Patterns of thoughts emerging dynamically in consciousness during mindfulness meditation can be explained in terms of intra- and inter-network activity. The client's usual mental reactions to pleasant or unpleasant body sensations and co-emerging thoughts automatically feed back into the system in the form of further activation, thus strengthening (reinforcing) the network for the maintenance of the information it produces, as described below.

Three internal causes of intrusive thoughts

Experienced mindfulness practitioners notice two main contexts in which uninvited thoughts intrude on consciousness. One is "external," the other is "internal." The external locus of distraction consists of all the stimuli perceived in the external environment. The smell of the neighbor's barbeque triggering a pleasant memory (with its co-emerging pleasant body sensations) of your best party some years ago, the sound of the passing motorbike in the street triggering the unpleasant memory (and its co-emerging unpleasant body sensations) of your own motorbike accident, etc. Since the sitting practice of mindfulness meditation requires minimizing such sensory stimulation by practicing in silence, immobile, and with closed eyes, the external cause of intrusive thoughts is usually only a challenge early in the course of training. Note that practicing indoors is, accordingly, the most conducive context.

The internal context, on the other hand, can remain difficult to address in some clients. It is a continual and self-organized source of intrusive thoughts that do not require external stimulation or the thinker to expect them. Rather than being stimulated by external events with which they are associated, intrusive thoughts emerge as a consequence of their associated neural activation strength. As we relax while attending to our natural (uncontrolled) breath or body sensations, neural networks with the greatest activation strength emerge first in consciousness; and we perceive a thought.

The activation strength of neural networks that enable a thought is determined by at least three internal factors: the *recency* and *frequency* with which thought networks are activated and the *emotional load* (associated body sensations) they carry. The more recently or frequently a pattern of activation has been stimulated, the stronger is the activation strength in the neurons that produced the thought. In other words, the more recently or frequently a thought or idea has taken place, the more it remains fired up in the brain cells that produced it and the more likely it is to reach consciousness easily as we relax. For example, this morning's inspiring discussion with a colleague, the image of a recent car accident or the ongoing fear of failing the upcoming exam, are highly likely to hijack our consciousness as we sit calmly after a hard day's work.

An extreme example of this principle is the experience of Obsessive-Compulsive Disorder (OCD). The maintenance of obsessive thoughts in OCD can be explained in terms of the maintenance of very frequently and very recently activated neural networks. The continuous rehearsal of obsessive thoughts keeps their corresponding neural networks highly activated and reinforces neural connections. Consequently, the so-called "obsessive thoughts" compete successfully with normal daily thinking and interfere with it.

During mindfulness meditation, as we attempt to minimize the tendency of producing new thoughts (the "input"), thoughts produced by these highly (recently and frequently) activated networks intrude in consciousness because new mental inputs are intentionally prevented. In turn, these networks are not being reacted to (reinforced) since the focus of attention is systematically shifted back to the breath or body sensations. Consequently, the activation strength of these networks decreases and the corresponding thoughts are progressively weakened. In behavioral science, this is typically considered to be an "extinction" procedure.

Thus, when input is decreased sufficiently below the usual level of processing activity via non-evaluative observation of breath or body sensations, inputs previously "stored" in memory networks are called for processing. Provided no new thought is generated as a response to experiencing the current one (i.e., provided reinforcement of those networks does not occur), thoughts that are less frequent and less recent emerge in conscious awareness. This is illustrated by the common re-experiencing of older memories during mindfulness meditation.

Among the important clinical implications of this procedure is that memories emerging spontaneously can be reprocessed in a more neutral way and without the need to challenge our thoughts. To borrow Teasdale and Barnard's (1993) terminology, memories are reprocessed through greater amount of "propositional coding" and lesser amount of "implicational coding." Daniel Siegel's recent work also mentions the necessity for "decoupling" the cognitive from the emotional aspects of painful memories and how mindfulness meditation can help in doing so (e.g., Siegel, 2009b). This does not mean that the memories are less accurate or cannot be recalled later. On the contrary, recalling seems to be facilitated when our attention is not crowded by continual automatic thinking and avoidance of emotions.

In addition to the recency and frequency of activation as explanations for intrusive thoughts, the *intensity* of activation is also a factor. As discussed earlier, the Evaluation component of the co-emergence model causes spontaneous stimulation in the Interoception component. At any given moment, the intensity of body sensations is a function of the degree and amount of judgmental thinking. This is because some thoughts (including old memories) have been encoded, and now co-emerge, with more salient body sensations. It follows that memories associated with more intense body sensations have stronger connections to emotional pathways and seem more resistant to extinction. From an evolutionary point of view, this is a clear advantage for survival; we recall more easily memories that remind us of potential threats and we tend not to forget them easily.

In the case of PTSD, flashbacks can be explained in terms of frequency of activation of both thought networks and associated body sensations. Remaining non-reactive (equanimous) decreases the intensity and duration of newly arising thoughts. Since these networks are not being reinforced either, even subtler associations (often corresponding to older memories) are being extinguished.

One explanation for the change in attitude following mindfulness training is related to an increase in awareness and acceptance of subtler experiences, which is likely to allow the reprocessing of schema-based associations. Taking a co-emergence standpoint (Figure 1), encoding cognitive events that evoke even the slightest emotion also encodes their concomitant body sensations. The decoding of the body sensation can then give access to the decoding of the cognitive dimension of the memory. In other words, if I read or hear that I failed my exam, the memory of this event will be encoded with some corresponding (co-emerging) body sensations somewhere in my body. If, years later, when practicing body-scanning techniques during mindfulness training, I come across the type of sensation which resembles closely that which I felt at the time of encoding the unpleasant event, I am likely to experience the intrusion of the memory of the old event (failing the exam). These are undoubtedly significant implications for what is known as mood-dependent memory; a phenomenon by which memory recall is enhanced by the emotional cue with which it was initially encoded. Perhaps, the notion of co-emergence can provide an "internal context" to explain mood-dependent memory. More importantly, it may help normalize our experience of intrusive thoughts during mindfulness meditation. When explained simply, clients feel reassured that their intrusive thoughts are part of the process, rather than due to their lack of ability.

The failure of long-term thought suppression

Based on the phenomena described above, thought suppression is not useful with intrusions when associated body sensations are not dealt with equanimously (i.e., when they are reacted to). They are more likely to be reinforced if we experience aversion towards the bodily experience (as yet subconscious) that led to suppression in the first place. The paradoxical effects of suppressing anxious thoughts during imminent threat were clearly observed by Koster et al., (2003). The authors demonstrated that while the duration of anxiety may decrease during suppression, the severity and frequency of anxiety symptoms are likely to increase when thought suppression stops. Hayes (1994, p. 17) stressed that forbidding oneself to think a negative thought requires the contact of a verbal rule that is normally designed to help avoid the thought but actually causes it to occur, since "it is not possible to follow the rule do not think of X without also thinking of X." The autonomic intrusion of what is usually termed "automatic thoughts" following a stressful event has been demonstrated (Horowitz, 1975), but it has not been explicitly associated with the physiological experience produced by body sensations.

New theoretical and clinically applied cognitive models that take into account the significance of mindfulness have emerged in the literature, whether for the treatment of anxiety disorders (e.g., Orsillo et al., 2003; Roemer and Orsillo, 2002;

Wells and Matthews, 1994), mood disorders (e.g., Segal *et al.*, 2002; Teasdale and Barnard, 1993), or addiction (Marlatt *et al.*, 2004, 2006; Witkiewitz and Marlatt, 2006). Wells' (1997) work shows a cognitive perspective that captures the notion of acceptance contained in the mindfulness approach, even though no reference is made to the simultaneous sensorimotor dimension (co-emerging body sensations); that is, the notion of impermanence is implicit:

> A specific processing strategy suggested by Wells and Matthews (1994) is detached mindfulness in which clients are instructed to disengage ruminative appraisal or active worry from intrusive thoughts. This is a selective "letting-go" of intrusions, in which awareness of the initial intrusion may remain but the client is instructed not to engage with the intrusion on a mental or behavioral level. The process may be assisted through self-instruction such as: "This is only a thought it isn't reality; I don't need to give my time to this thought." The intrusion should be allowed to decay in its own right … In addition, detached mindfulness can be employed as a behavioral experiment to determine what happens to intrusions and the distress they cause if they are "left to their own devices." This is the antithesis to thought suppression attempts, and can be used to challenge beliefs about intrusions and the distress associated to them. (Wells, 1997, p. 272)

Indeed, this perspective is relevant to the treatment of anxiety disorders where intrusions are central to the problem. However, the intrusive nature of common day-to-day cognitions (e.g., a melody that is initially contingent upon pleasant body sensations) often leads to the involuntary repetition of spontaneous reaction (e.g., singing or whistling of the melody), even though we may not wish to do so at that particular time. It follows that taking into account the embodied nature of cognitive processing, extends the notion of intrusion to a number of psychopathologies.

Maintaining Mental Illness

Although the Reaction component of the co-emergence model is an innate phenomenon linked to the CNS, its excessive and sustained activation leads to disequilibrium in the processing of information. The present model emphasizes that psychopathologies cannot coexist with a well-balanced information-processing mechanism.

Psychopathologies are facilitated and maintained when the disequilibrium is established as the predominant (stable) state of the system. It follows that equilibrium between the four functions may predict the likelihood of mental health and, to some extent, physical health (see Langer, 1989, 1992, for the relationship between mindfulness and longevity).

Figure 3 displays the system in the most common state of disequilibrium. A relative amount of attention is shifted from sensory perception (which becomes depleted) to the evaluative/judgmental component of the system (which becomes predominant). Much of the remaining resources are polarized by reactive processes, largely

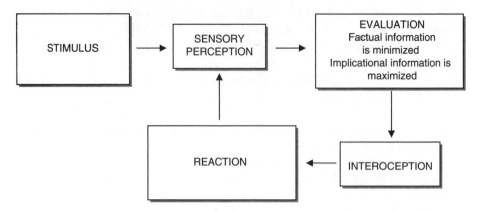

Figure 3. Schematic representation of reinforcement when disequilibrium in information processing occurs.

bypassing interoceptive capacity (body sensations), unless these are very intense as in panic attacks. The over-processing of evaluative and reactive functions reflects automaticity. We produce automatic thoughts and reactions and, as described by others (e.g., Segal *et al.,* 2002), we function on "automatic pilot."

Hence, reliance on perceptual (neutral) features of stimuli and awareness of body sensations are minimized, whereas reliance on evaluative and reactive habit patterns is maximized. This is consistently observed during the early stage of mindfulness meditation practice. The more a person is affected by stress or experiences such as depressive or anxious states, the less he or she is able to feel common body sensations, such as the weight and touch of hands on the armchair's sides or pressure under the feet. On the other hand, more relaxed individuals, although untrained, seem to be able to access common body sensations with little difficulty. Of course, we can easily feel more intense sensations, especially those which we tend to like or dislike. However, someone with a panic disorder will tend to be vigilant to gross sensations associated with panic, but is not likely to feel more subtle, commonly occurring, sensations at the same time.

Although common, and sometimes necessary, stress responses also lead to such disequilibrium, their consequence when over-emphasized and sustained is maladaptive functioning because disequilibrium becomes the stable state of the information processing system. Indeed, our clients typically report feeling that they have become over-judgmental and over-reactive in common situations. This configuration is especially, but not only, emphasized during arousal periods.

Using an evolutionary rationale, it is possible to explain this pattern in terms of differences in the allocation of attention during perception of threat — note that the application of the model is not limited to fear and other forms of arousal. For example, say it is 50 000 year ago, a furry object (Stimulus) is moving behind a large bush. It could equally be a rabbit or a large threatening animal, like a grizzly bear. The wind blows from behind you, towards the bush, and you know that you will be smelt within the next few seconds. The object is ambiguous and therefore perceived as a potential threat. Do you linger there like an objective scientist trying to guess whether this fur belongs to a dangerous or placid animal? Do you come closer to gather counter-evidence for your possible irrational fear? Probably not. Your brain would not allow it unless it was specifically trained to do so. Unless trained otherwise, you are likely to perceive the shape and other aspects of the animal hastily (depleted Sensory Perception) and rely predominantly on past categorization and "implicational" assumptions of a potential threat (increased Evaluation leading to automatic catastrophic thoughts). You may start assuming that there is a bear and that it is moving to chase you. This would be especially the case if you have memories of this happening to you or to others. Since you cannot make predictions based on "objective" sensory perception, the brain falls back on the next available source of information to resolve the problem, your memory, whether explicit or implicit. The question "what is?" is replaced by "what is it like?" and within less than a second, you make out that if it looks like a bear, then it might as well be a bear.

In a similar vein, trainees in the police force are formally taught to assume that an individual with a hand in the pocket or behind their back is hiding a weapon, and that they must therefore be on guard. Basically, the brain tends to perceive an ambiguity as a potential threat and the way to preserve the survival of the species is to assume the worst and prepare for it.

From an information-processing standpoint, one of the reasons for the depleting of attention from the Sensory Perception and its reallocation to the Evaluation component is that Sensory Perception would require an unnecessarily long processing-time in the face of potential danger and being an objective scientist in this kind of situations would put oneself in jeopardy. Because implicational thoughts co-emerge with somatosensory processing, once a fear schema is engaged, our fight-or-flight physiology is produced simultaneously and we begin to feel intense body sensations. Since being aware of increased interoception (perception of body sensations) also requires unnecessary processing-time and does not serve a life-saving purpose, the brain depletes attention from the Interoception component and reallocates it to the Reaction component. We freeze or run to safety, bare feet yet unaware of the pain caused by thorns, broken branches and sharp stones; it is out of the question to feel a mosquito bite that occurred during the flight. When we find a safe place and retrieve our calm, we begin to feel the aftermath of the chase and wonder how we injured our foot, and a little later, when more relaxed, we begin to feel the itch of the mosquito bite and the need to scratch. Thus, in such ambiguous situations, reacting occurs automatically because of the consequence (interoception) of our overemphasized evaluations, whether the furry object is the body part of a dangerous or placid animal. Nowadays, living in cities, threats such as dangerous animals have been replaced by status anxiety, mental or physical disease, unemployment, financial crises, lack of life purpose, loneliness, lack of love and other interpersonal concerns, but our brain functions very much in the same way.

In summary, since the processing of the perceptual aspects of stimuli and body sensations are time consuming and not crucial in the presence of a potential threat, the organism gains processing speed by altering the deployment of attention resources. A decrease in mental effort to process Sensory Perception and

Interoception, and an increase in mental energy to process Evaluation (schematic models/established memory networks) and Reaction (rapid automatic decision), can make the difference between life and death. Note that so-called catastrophic thoughts are not "distorted" cognitions in this case. On the contrary, they are integral part of a healthy survival response, without which we wouldn't feel the unpleasant body sensations that we attempt to decrease by reacting (running, in this case).

However valid this biological view may be in such circumscribed potentially threatening situations, the differential distribution of attention across the components is also proposed to be a result of avoidance strategies, since what is being avoided is also perceived as a potential threat (e.g., peer rejection). A parsimonious[1] explanation is the long-term habit of remaining distracted from processing body sensations because the state of mind (e.g., stressful, reactive) produces unpleasant experiences. In other words, disequilibrium can also be learned as an avoidance mechanism. The lack of objectivity resulting from such functional disequilibrium (as shown in Figure 3) keeps us in a cycle of maladaptive reinforcement. This arrangement fits with the concept of "experiential avoidance" (Hayes *et al.*, 1996). It also has important implications for the processes underlying operant learning, and in particular interoceptive conditioning, although such a discussion is beyond the scope of this book.

Whether we rationalize the attention switch to a disequilibrium state in terms of "hard-wired" biological reflexes toward survival or as a learned avoidance response to emotional cues, our brain keeps on processing stressful information in subcortical areas, increasing the likelihood of emotional reactivity and decreasing the likelihood of rational thinking. To become less reactive, the nervous system needs to learn to process stressful information in cortical areas, especially using inhibitory pathways in prefrontal parts of cortex, to inhibit the response and reengage in the desired behavior *while the emotion is taking place.*

Note also that the same pattern of functional disequilibrium occurs in depressed states and is not limited to represented states of arousal. Although our depressed clients often present with an apparent lack of arousal, their attention is also focused on negative evaluation of the situation and they tend to react with ruminative and other unhelpful thoughts that may or may not be expressed overtly. The main difference rests on the type of experience but the pattern in disequilibrium is much the same.

Recreating Balance in the System

Regaining equilibrium in the information-processing system necessitates the resetting of new parameters. Mindfulness training does just that. By learning to attend more objectively (perceptually and with factual categorization) to all body sensa-

---

[1] Parsimony is the scientific idea that the simplest explanation of a phenomenon is the best one. It is more logical to accept a hypothesis that depends on a small number of independent processes rather than based on a large number of processes.

tions and co-emerging thoughts while minimizing evaluating and reacting, more attention is available for Sensory Perception and Interoception and less is allocated to Evaluation and Reaction, bringing back greater balance between components (as in Figure 1). The functional equilibrium resulting from training oneself to continuously reallocate attention where it has been depleted allows us to see things from different angles and apply more choice before action. We become more "objective," more "realistic."

Note that during mindfulness practice, even though we endeavor to not produce new judgments (Evaluation) towards an emerging thought or body sensation (internal stimulus), the stimulus is more often than not already associated with past meanings and values (automatic thoughts). Consequently, their stimulation is likely to produce co-emerging body sensations. Even though our attitude is "non-judgmental" during training and we may not be directly aware of these automatic thoughts, we still feel the consequence (body sensations) of these well-learned judgments. The core task is to not react to these body sensations, with an understanding that they are stimulated by old associations. The effort not to reinforce the usual response (Reaction) is precisely what is meant by "equanimity."

Hence, reallocating attention to Sensory Perception and Interoception allows us to become aware of old associations of thoughts and body sensations that emerge spontaneously during practice and train the brain not to reinforce its usual reaction to them. We become more observant and aware that even though we do not judge a negative intrusive thought in a negative way, we still feel its concomitant unpleasant body sensations. Without sufficient reallocation of attention to the Interoception component, we continue to assume that the cause of our dissatisfaction and reactions is the stimulus. We misattribute the cause of our experience and blame the stimulus or try to change it.

The reallocation of attention proposed by the co-emergence model is well illustrated by the rapid increase in sensory perception in clients with PTSD and conditions that include dissociation. Soon after training begins, clients often report all sorts of strong sensory experiences, including feeling new pleasures with taste, smell, or sex (see case example 3 in Chapter 10). Kabat-Zinn (1990, 2005) also describes people's enhanced taste awareness during "the raisin exercise," during which group participants are asked to eat a raisin mindfully.

If the functional-equilibrium explanation is included in the rationale for the delivery of mindfulness training, therapy seems more understandable and appealing for the numerous clients who would not otherwise engage in a treatment with meditative features. The next chapter addresses specifically the delivery of the rationale for MiCBT.

Summary of Main Points

- During mindfulness meditation, the dynamic interaction (or "co-emergence") between body sensations and thoughts is evident. Because our conscious attention is usually unable to detect the few hundred milliseconds delay between the emergence of a thought and its concomitant body sensation, unless trained otherwise, we perceive their emergence to be simultaneous. This is the reason for which this phenomenon is called "co-emergence."

- According to the co-emergence model of reinforcement, every "implicational" thought co-emerges with its concomitant body sensation(s), whether one is aroused or not. This implies that every important memory is encoded and stored with a coupled bodily experience.

- There is a twofold interactive relationship between mind and body; intensity and quality: first, the intensity of the co-emerging body sensation is proportional to the extent that a thought has personal implication. Second, the quality of the co-emerging body sensation is also proportional to the extent that a thought is agreeable. An agreeable thought will co-emerge with a pleasant body sensation. This also works in the opposite direction. When we scan the body, certain kinds of sensations lead to thoughts that were associated with these sensations at the time of encoding and will co-emerge spontaneously.

- In many ways, when we scan the body, we also scan our mental state and memories. Accordingly, many (if not most) of our spontaneous cognitive and emotional experiences are based on our memories, our past, which we "project" into the present. This is the fundamental principle for the perpetuation of schemas. Well-established schemas can be very persistent when the therapy approach used to address them does not take somatosensory concomitants into account. This is principally why mindfulness training is a central part of MiCBT.

- When we react, we react to the consequences of our thoughts in the body (body sensations) in order to reduce them if they are unpleasant or increase them if they are pleasant. We do not react to thoughts themselves or to stimuli.

- Whereas sustained disequilibrium among the four components of the information-processing system increases the probability of psychopathology, creating and maintaining a functional equilibrium between the components (1) decreases the probability of psychopathology, and (2) increases the probability of recovery from crisis and prevention of relapse.

- There are three identifiable internal causal factors for intrusive thoughts: (1) frequency and (2) recency of neural activation, and (3) their co-emerging body sensations. Generally, the more frequently and/or the more recently we think a thought, the more likely it is to arise first during meditation. Some older memories also resurface when we experience a body sensation sufficiently similar to the one with which it was initially encoded.

- Body sensations that co-emerge with thoughts are fundamental memory cues that help us recognize if what we perceive is important. It is proposed that this somatosensory memory system is important for effective survival purposes.

- With each negative reaction to body sensations (memory cues), we reinforce our perception of threat and thereby the emotionality of memories. With each neutral response (equanimity) to these memory cues (body sensations), we extinguish our perception of threat and decouple the emotion from the memory, thus dismantling the fabric of schemas.

- Mindfulness meditation produces neuroplasticity in cortical areas associated with self-awareness and self-regulation of emotion. This promotes the transfer of equanimity to daily situations and allows us to feel more subtle body sensations, and detect early cues of distress. This usually results in increased general resilience and better coping skills in the face of with common stressors.
- It is proposed that all forms of conditioning principles include operant learning and depend on it. Beneath the apparent coupling of a stimulus and a response, there are body sensations that act as *fundamental operants*, which we must experience and to which we must respond. Through body scanning, remaining equanimous neutralizes these fundamental operants and produces rapid breaking down of conditioned responses. This is the reason (though formulated differently) for which equanimity is viewed as the main active mechanism of change in mindfulness meditation, as traditionally taught in the original Burmese practice.

Part II
Internalizing Skills

Chapter 3

Suitability and Rationale for MiCBT: Practical Guidelines for Therapists

A cat said: rabbits are not worth teaching!
Here I am, offering cheap lessons in catching mice and not a single rabbit taker!
Old Sufi Tale

A Transdiagnostic Assessment

A particularity of MiCBT is its "trans-diagnosis" approach which deals with fundamental patterns of information-processing imbalance (micro-level of reinforcement) rather than specific types of symptoms (macro-level of manifestation). The fundamental problem of our depressed, anxious, psychotic, angry or dissociating clients is their reactivity, whether mental, verbal or physical, overt or covert, conscious or subconscious. Since mindfulness meditation increases equanimity, thereby decreasing general reactivity in the nervous system, there is a good case for its use across a range of conditions, especially if it is integrated with other therapeutic tools shown to be effective across these conditions. However, for any psychotherapy system, client variables are fundamental in determining treatment efficacy and adherence to treatment. Taking into account the positive and negative indicators below, the success or failure with MiCBT treatment is not bound by typical DSM or ICD diagnostic categorization.

Positive indicators
- Sufficient distress (especially chronic conditions)
- Desire to change

Mindfulness-integrated CBT: Principles and Practice, First Edition. Bruno A. Cayoun.
© 2011 John Wiley & Sons, Ltd. Published 2011 by John Wiley & Sons, Ltd.

- Ability to form adequate therapeutic relationship with therapist
- Positive attitude toward treatment
- Capacity to use and understand MiCBT
- Availability of professional support, audio player, time, and adequate context.

The positive indicators should be weighed against the following negative indicators:

Negative indicators
- Intoxication or sedation
- Severely disorganized thought processes
- Pronounced intellectual disability
- Severe neurocognitive dysfunction (e.g., following brain injury)
- Severe attention deficits
- Characterological unsuitability.

These negative indicators should not be confused with "false enemies."

False enemies
- Low motivation (this feature *is* an integral part of depression, which we treat)
- Grief
- Over-reactivity (including impulse control problems and relaxation-induced anxiety)
- Severe physical pain.

Contraindications

The MiCBT program is usually safe and non-intrusive, delivered by professionals with training in compassion for others. Despite the empathic stance usually observed in therapists using a mindfulness-based therapy approach, some clients may react negatively. Some cases of negative responses to mindfulness-based programs have been reported in research papers and by service providers.

However, there is a more serious and, to some extent, predictable context in which the implementation of mindfulness meditation needs to be carefully dosed and guided. This is the context of potential psychosis and delusional states. With closed eyes, a psychotic client may begin to imagine all sorts of things, visualize all sorts of images and eventually hallucinate. This also applies to auditory hallucinations.

Paul Chadwick and his colleagues from the University of Southampton and the Royal South Hants Hospital in Southampton, UK, found that with caution, mindfulness meditation is still possible in this difficult client group (Chadwick, Newman, Taylor and Abba, 2005). They assessed the impact on clinical functioning of a six-session group-based mindfulness training along with standard psychiatric care for

11 people with current, subjectively distressing psychosis. People were taught mindfulness of breath and encouraged to let unpleasant experiences come into awareness, to observe and note them, and let them go without judgment, clinging or struggle. One of the particularities of the implementation protocol was that participants limited their practice to short periods and could practice with open eyes. As we found in our own pilot trials (none published as yet), there was a significant decrease in symptoms and improvement in mindfulness skills. The authors found the results to be encouraging and encouraged further controlled outcome and process research. Unfortunately, not much has been done since in this particular client group.

Generally speaking, it is not advisable for clients in extremely distressed states to practice mindfulness meditation on their own. People with lack of insight or poor understanding of the techniques who cannot handle distressing thoughts can sometimes feel worse when practicing. At this early stage of research in this area, it is not recommended to practice standard mindfulness meditation while experiencing psychotic states (e.g., delusions, hallucinations, paranoia), manic states (e.g., extreme anxiety or anger, uncontrollable agitation or impulse), or suicidal states in which the person may be at risk.

Keep in mind that the diagnosis is not necessarily the issue. These cautions are more based on the understanding that mindfulness meditation relies on the ability to access some degree of metacognitive insight, which in turn allows trainees to reappraise intrusive unhelpful thoughts for what they truly are during practice. If access to metacognitive awareness is compromised by cognitive distortions that are serious enough to impair perception, then the chances for reappraisal are low and distressing thoughts may be reinforced instead. Although most meditation-naive clients do include some degree of such reinforcement at the start of their practice, they usually extinguish more responses than they reinforce, making the practice challenging but beneficial.

Assessing Motivation to Change: A Proposed Script

When we propose the therapy of choice to our clients, occasionally they hesitate to commit, often on the basis of self-doubts. Depressed and anxious clients often experience a fear of failure which makes any new task appear difficult to achieve. Therapy-based expectations can become a new source of anxiety and a reason for dropping out. The communicative approach in the following dialogue can facilitate your client's motivation and commitment.

1. "If you were given the skills to change your condition, would you use it to change your situation?"
2. "How much would you be prepared to change out of a hundred?" (if less than 100%, clarify their reasons: possible self-doubts, fear of failure, low motivation, etc and challenge the view with standard cognitive therapy skills).

3. "It may sound a bit strange, but could you tell me why you would like to change?" – the following list shows examples of varying degrees of motivation. The last two points are likely to indicate higher probability of commitment and success.
    *   External pressures (e.g., legal/forensic reasons, insurance, accommodation, etc)
    *   To save a relationship or for the sake of the family
    *   To please someone else
    *   Physical health
    *   Emotional/mental difficulties
    *   Self-growth, change life-style.
4. "What could happen if you don't change?" (Some arousal may emerge at this point).
    **** The therapist stops here and provides a rationale for MiCBT (see next section), with the aim to both inform and demonstrate how quickly we can feel relieved from suffering when using effective skills, before proceeding with item 5 below.
5. Emphasize the "cost" (homework), mentioning it is sometimes difficult to keep up with the practice.
6. Emphasize the need for commitment. "When would you be prepared to spend 30 minutes morning and 30 minutes evening on your therapy?"
7. "Where could you practice?"

With a warm and supportive attitude, assertiveness about homework and commitment is essential to gain trust and commitment from the client. Integrity about outcome is also important (i.e., results depend on homework, which is acquired and clarified during therapy sessions).

Developing and Delivering an Appropriate Rationale

Why a rationale?

Presenting a rationale before starting any sort of psychological intervention is a form of acknowledgement of the client's intelligence, choice to go on with a therapy style and format, and right of information about treatment. Moreover, research shows that presenting a good rationale for the use of a therapy model enhances collaboration, decreases dropout rates and increases therapeutic gains. Experienced clinicians and researchers in CBT have emphasized the need for educating clients about CBT via appropriate rationale (e.g., Barlow, 2002; Beck, 1976; Beck, Emery, and Greenberg, 1985; Williams, 1984).

Part of a cognitive-behavioral program is to provide psycho-education that brings the client's attention to both internal and external variables which may not be easily linked to the problem. The client is asked about contextual, emotional, physiological, cognitive, and interpersonal factors, his or her own behavior, and how each of these variables may relate to the problem. The theoretical framework on which the therapy system is based is explained simply to the client and related to the presented problem.

When delivering the rationale for MiCBT, an experiential approach is the most direct and engaging way of demonstrating the central role of the *process* or *mechanism* of information processing in the maintenance of unnecessary suffering. Showing, not just discussing, how to disengage from the content of information and attend to its process with an experiential exposure exercise can, in the very first treatment session, alter the way in which a client perceives the situation. This helps to strengthen motivation and commitment to therapy.

Delivering the rationale for mindfulness training is primarily a means of demonstrating some experiential evidence for the predictability of change. The aim is for the client to realize that even the worst experience passes away more rapidly when it is understood and accepted as a transient and impersonal event rather than when it is reacted to (reinforced). This can be achieved in various ways:

1. One is to introduce mindfulness training at the level of thoughts. An experiential rationale for the mindfulness-with-breathing technique is described in some detail in the next section of this chapter. This reasoning helps demonstrate how thoughts continue to intrude into consciousness and affect behavior. Starting with breath-awareness, the exercises allow the client to discover the nature and effects of his or her own thoughts with a good understanding of the purpose and difficulties of the exercise. This exercise is best delivered as soon as possible, perhaps in the first or second week after your intake assessment, following which the initial body-scan technique is introduced via the rationale described below.

2. The delivery of a rationale for mindfulness training that focuses on body scanning is particular to MiCBT, which addresses crises rather than developing relapse prevention strategies as its main objective. When a client is deeply distressed, "exposure and response prevention" to the interoceptive cues (acceptance of body sensations) associated with emotions demonstrates to the client that mindfulness can work simply through an extinction procedure, as illustrated in the dialogue below.

3. The experiential understanding of how body sensations co-emerged with cognition in the client's latest difficult situation is very beneficial when it is acquired within the first or second session. This constitutes "the rationale" part of MiCBT, encouraging the client's trust, commitment and motivation for therapy. In addition, acquiring experiential evidence that a simple skill can help painful emotions change rapidly, gives clients an immediate impression that they will

feel more in control with the treatment. This also promotes a sense of direction in therapy, which helps clients commit to treatment despite the initial difficulties usually encountered. Thus, the immediate therapeutic effect of delivering the rationale for body scanning is a powerful means of engaging distressed clients in the program.

Whether to start the MiCBT program by presenting the rationale for mindfulness of breath or the rationale for body scanning will often depend on the client's emotional state; the more distressed, the more engaging and convincing the latter is likely to be. With mildly to moderately distressed clients, as well as with groups, it is recommended to begin with the rationale for mindfulness of breath only. Explaining and demonstrating how body-sensations pass away more easily and rapidly when consciously appraised and accepted for what they are can take place the following week, when thought intrusions are better understood and managed.

Example of rationale delivery
The following is an example of the rationale for the body-scan technique delivered in terms of a general rationale for mindfulness training in MiCBT. It is an actual dialogue between a male client with Schizo-affective Disorder, and the therapist (the author), taking place in the first therapy session, during the early stage of the rationale and just following the client's description of his main complaint. Note that the rationale for body scanning is the exercise of choice because the client presents with high arousal (anger).

THERAPIST: What do you feel when you think about this?
CLIENT: Bad, very angry.
THERAPIST: How do you know you feel angry?
CLIENT: Well I feel it!
THERAPIST: And how does anger feel?
CLIENT: Terrible!
THERAPIST: Could you tell how do you know it feels terrible?
CLIENT: (*after a short hesitation*) … Well, I know because I feel it now.
THERAPIST: Where do you feel it now?
CLIENT: Here in my chest (softly hitting the lower chest area with a clenched fist), it takes the whole space here.
THERAPIST: Are you saying that you experience anger in your chest as a strong body sensation?
CLIENT: Yes, very strong.
THERAPIST: Can you be more specific about this body sensation? How much space it occupies in your chest? … Keeping your eyes closed, could you show me how large it is with your hands?
CLIENT: Like this … about three inches.
THERAPIST: Tell me more about it, is it cold, hot? Does it move, is it still? Is it heavy or light? Look at it very carefully and very objectively, like a scientist in a laboratory.

CLIENT: It's hot, burning! And it's like a heavy pressure.

THERAPIST: Do you feel any other sensation in your body?

CLIENT: Yes, now I feel this tension in my shoulders and in my face.

THERAPIST: Do you feel this is part of the anger you were feeling before?

CLIENT: Yes, I think so.

THERAPIST: Now go back to the sensation in the chest area. Is it the same as before?

CLIENT: Actually, it's not so bad now.

THERAPIST: Are you saying that the emotion you felt in your chest is already changing?

CLIENT: Well apparently yes, it doesn't feel as painful anymore.

THERAPIST: How do you usually react to make yourself feel better when you feel these sensations in your body?

CLIENT: I slam doors or break something, I feel like being violent and sometimes I am.

THERAPIST: How long does it usually take you to calm down?

CLIENT: Normally a short time if I let it out, or it can take a long time if I don't.

THERAPIST: And how do you feel now?

CLIENT: Not too bad actually.

THERAPIST: Are you saying that your anger is gone?

CLIENT: Almost yeah.

THERAPIST: That's good. And how can you explain that it has almost gone in a few minutes without letting it out?

CLIENT: I'm not sure.

(In this case the belief that venting anger is necessary to feel relieved was successfully challenged at the experiential level).

THERAPIST: When you are ready, you can open your eyes. ...

The next stage links this initial experience with the therapy model.

THERAPIST: As most people do when I ask them to describe their emotions, you systematically pointed to your body. And as soon as you looked at your body sensations objectively, examining it with your full mind, without reacting to it, you felt better almost immediately. Would you agree with that?

CLIENT: Yeah, that was a surprise.

THERAPIST: We call this approach "mindfulness." Mindfulness-integrated Cognitive Behaviour Therapy, or MiCBT, is a therapy that uses evidence-based methods. By taking our mind and body into account, it helps create more balance in the nervous system so we become less reactive
             ...

Following the explanation in the above paragraph, some additional (but brief) information traditionally given about specific disorders can be included according to the client's diagnosis. For example, information about the physiology of fear or anger responses, or the cognitive triad in depression, can help focus the rationale and enhance rapport.

Now or in a later consultation, you can use the Diary of Reactive Habits (in Appendix C) and demonstrate a typical event; e.g., the latest anger episode.

Example

THERAPIST: From the MiCBT perspective, these are the stages in which we process information (*pointing to the model's components on the Diary of Reactive Habits*). Earlier, you described being very angry each time you speak with someone from your insurance company, right?

CLIENT: Yes, I don't like them … They don't care about people at all.

THERAPIST: Do you remember the last time it happened?

CLIENT: Four days ago, last Wednesday I think.

THERAPIST: Was it a man, a woman?

CLIENT: It was a woman.

THERAPIST: What did she actually say that led you to feel angry? Try to be specific.

CLIENT: She said she didn't think the insurance would pay for my car because I didn't tell them that I had the accident under the influence of alcohol, but I was just at the legal limit … When I explained that to her, she started asking me hundreds of questions about how much I drank that night, but that's not her business!

THERAPIST: Ok, her comment was the situation, an external situation (*showing the first component, Situation or Stimulus*). So we can write "phone conversation with the insurer who asked many questions" in the first box.

Then the second stage is the Perception stage; it is about the senses you use to perceive the information. This stage allows us to perceive what's happening inside or outside ourselves. In this case, it was a phone call so we can write "hearing" in this box.

Then (*pointing to the Evaluation component*), we have to make sense of the world, of what we perceive. We make a judgment so we know what to do. When you heard the woman speaking on the phone, you interpreted her talk according to your memories, values, your personality, your mood at the time and your expectations. This is the third component, the Evaluation component. So how did you interpret what the insurer was saying?

CLIENT: I thought she didn't believe me. It was a waste of time.

THERAPIST: Ok, so we can write it down here in the Evaluation box.

Once the client recalls the self-talk or how he or she interpreted the stimulus, it is useful to use elements of the so-called "downward arrow" technique from Cognitive Therapy. Simply put, this consists of asking the deeper meaning of a judgment until the client reaches deeper layers of his or her core belief. This is used in MiCBT to emulate the schema-based arousal involved in the client's current description, so that we can show how to diffuse it rapidly with interoceptive exposure. One way of doing so is as follows:

THERAPIST: What did it mean to you that she might not have believed you?

CLIENT: It was like she accused me of wanting to rip them off.

THERAPIST: If it were true that she accused you of that, what would it mean to you?

CLIENT: It means that I can't trust anyone to do their job … Now it is they who want to rip me off, not me, so really I should have lied in the first place … What's the point of being honest anyway?

THERAPIST: And what would be the consequence or the meaning that you can't trust anyone?

CLIENT: It means the world is pretty rotten and people will use their power to take advantage of you.

THERAPIST: So what does it mean to you?

CLIENT: It's just bloody unfair!

As arousal becomes noticeable, we switch to show how Interoception is a consequence of such (schematic) evaluative thoughts. We do so without obviously leading the client so that the experience remains a part of his/her own discovery.

Note that in contrast with traditional Cognitive Therapy, we do not attempt to challenge the "injustice" schema the client is experiencing and his "irrational expectations." We simply use the assumption and link it to the unpleasant experience with which it co-emerges in the body, perhaps as follows:

THERAPIST: So, how did it make you feel when you had the thought that "people are unfair"?

Note that the above question is constructed in order to subtly educate the client about his responsibility for feeling the way he did. This is done by placing the thought as the cause of feeling, rather than letting him believe that the stimulus (the insurer) caused him to feel the way he did.

CLIENT: I felt very angry.

THERAPIST: Ok, and how did you know it was anger and not joy or another emotion?

CLIENT: Well I could feel it in my body and I needed to breathe more …

THERAPIST: Do you mean that your emotion was in your body?

The above question is important in that it will help the client co-formulate a good rationale for using body scanning as a form of emotional regulation method.

CLIENT: Yeah, you bet it is!

THERAPIST: Good … so what type of sensation was it?

CLIENT: I felt hot everywhere and I could feel my heart pumping.

THERAPIST: Ok, so we can write it in the fourth box, which represents the Interoception stage. Let's write "temperature" for the heat and "motion" for your heart pumping. Does it make sense?

Then we react to make ourselves feel better. So how did you try to make yourself feel better in this situation?

CLIENT: I hung up on her.

THERAPIST: So you tried to stop feeling the way you did in the body by stopping the conversation. Did it work?

CLIENT: A little bit, but I was still thinking about it for the rest of the day.

THERAPIST: That's right, so we can write this in the last box, the Reaction stage. And of course, if it worked even a little bit, what do you think you'll do next time it happens?

CLIENT: Just the same I suppose ... that's what I do when it's too much.

THERAPIST: Exactly, we call this "reinforcement." If a reaction helps you decrease some discomfort or increase pleasures, we keep on using it and it becomes a habit of reacting, a learned response. Would you like to learn to change your habit?

CLIENT: Yeah! I've had enough of it ...

THERAPIST: Ok, so let's see what we need to do.

Note: The Situation (stimulus) may be an internal one such as intense body sensations, as is the case with "out-of-the-blue" panic attacks. In this case, write "interoception" (which is the ability to feel body sensations) in the Perception box, any catastrophic or other unhelpful thoughts about the symptoms in the Evaluation box, the increase in intensity of body sensations in the Body Sensation box, and whatever response is associated with increased intensity in the Reaction box. Now briefly explain the entire cycle using his/her story, emphasizing the reinforcement principle in each recurring event.

Example

THERAPIST: Let's have a look at how it works for you. First, a phone conversation happens. We cannot do anything about that. These things happen all the time, this is life.

Second, your senses perceived the voice, the intonations, etc. Here too, we can't do much at this stage. Then the information has been evaluated. Based on your past experiences and your way of thinking, you interpreted the questions of the insurer in a way that was unpleasant, negative, and simultaneously you experienced some very unpleasant sensations in certain areas of your body. Is that right? ...

Can you see how your interpretation created your experience? ... And when you felt so bad, then you reacted by hanging up the phone and you boiled in anger for ten minutes, then called back and abused her.

Can you see how your reaction was toward the unpleasant body sensations? ... This is important to understand: you didn't react to the situation because it is not yet an experience; you didn't react to your interpretation because it is not an experience either. You reacted to the unpleasant experience in your body, and these were created by your thoughts about the event. Do you understand how information was processed? ...

Ensure s/he understands; question if necessary. With arousal-based conditions, it is appropriate at this stage to explain briefly the fight-or-flight response in order to normalize the symptoms. Now briefly mention automaticity.

Example
Well, when our nervous system is used to reacting in a certain way to pleasant and unpleasant body sensations, we react subconsciously even if we try not to; reactions become just a habit and we are almost on automatic pilot. Have you felt that too? ... These parts become very big and these parts become very small.

On the form, (Diary of reactive habits) draw a large circle over Evaluation and another over Reaction, and a small circle within Perception and another small circle within Interoception.

The way we process information is unbalanced and the pattern has been established. With Mindfulness training, the main thing we are trying to do is to re-establish a balance in the way we process information. We try to become mindful at all levels, to be more objective, accurate and relaxed. So our task is to increase our objectivity and our ability to feel sensations (*showing Perception and Interoception*) and to decrease our negative thoughts and reactions (*showing Evaluation and Reaction*). Does this make sense? This is the first stage of therapy. This will require you to train every day because your habit is established for so long that it takes time and effort to change ... In the second stage, we will look at dealing with more specific situations in detail. Now, we start by learning the skill of mindfulness to decrease your reactivity.

Now proceed with items 5, 6, and 7 in the previous section ("Assessing Motivation to Change").

An Experiential Rationale for Mindfulness with Breathing

With clients who do not present with severe or unmanageable symptoms, it is useful to present a rationale and exercises to develop awareness and acceptance of thoughts through mindfulness of breathing, as explained in the next chapter. The following is an experiential task using the "finger task" to deliver a rationale for the client's weekly homework. It can also be used as an ad-hoc explanation for thought intrusion during practice if the information it contains has not been discussed prior to implementing mindfulness-with-breathing homework.

THERAPIST:

Pre-implementation opening: I will show you how and why your thoughts can be very intrusive in the coming week ...

Post-implementation opening: I will show you how and why your thoughts have been so intrusive this week ...

... First, try to sit with your back and your neck straight and, just for this exercise, rest the palm of your hands on your knees. Good, now confidently close your eyes and focus all your attention at the entrance of your nostrils and breathe naturally, normally and consciously ... Try not to control your breath. Just feel it as it is. Pay attention to details ... is the breath warm or cold when it enters and exits the nostrils? ... Does it go more through one nostril than the other? ... Try also to feel the touch of the breath on the inner walls and the outer rings of the nostrils and stay there patiently and attentively for the next few minutes, until I give you more instructions ...

Wait silently for about thirty seconds allowing the client to experience some intrusive thoughts.

You're doing a great job! Keeping your eyes closed and from now on, become very aware of thoughts that arise in your mind, whatever they are about ... maybe the conversation we just had, the chores you need to do when you go back home, or even these very instructions. To give me a sign that a thought has just arisen, slowly raise the index finger of your dominant hand, leaving your wrist at rest on your knee. Then keep your finger raised until you are able to bring your attention back to your nostrils and then gently let it rest again on your knee.

Do this with each thought that arises in your mind while you simply monitor your breath. You may have to do this many times in the next few minutes. This is not a problem and it is not a reflection of a lack of skill. What really matters is that you catch each thought as it arises, that you calmly and patiently let it go, and that you redirect your attention to the breath as soon as possible. Is that ok? ... (Briefly clarify potential questions).

Alright, do your best for the next few minutes, remembering to use your finger to help me understand what your thoughts are doing ... Note also that a sound is not a thought. The sounds of birds outside are not thoughts unless you start to think about them; like how beautiful they sound, etc. So raise your finger only if you actually think about the sounds you hear in the next few minutes.

Observe the client's attitude, body language and frequency of thought intrusion for about two minutes. In some cases, a client may show little or no intrusions. Some believe they have to perform and perhaps impress the therapist, especially if they have meditated before. This is mostly a case of clarifying what you are looking for. You may need to reframe your interest in terms of looking at their "ability to catch upcoming thoughts." This should do the trick! If not, the client might be so caught-up in his or her thoughts that even the difference between involuntary thinking and purposeful attention is blurred.

It is sometimes helpful with children or people with poor insight to redo the exercise after illustrating the task visually on a white board. Draw a crude, cartoon-like, little person with a bubble on one side of the head in which you write a thought that has just manifested, and another bubble on the other side of the head in which you write "this is just a thought." Then explain:

> We will redo the exercise and as soon as the first bubble pops up in your head, raise the index finger of your dominant hand and keep it up (*show your fingers rising*) until the second bubble pops up. As soon as you are aware that this thought has come up (*pointing to the 1ˢᵗ bubble*), focus all your attention back to the breath coming in and out of your nostrils (*point to the nostrils*) and bring your finger back down to your thigh (*show how you lower your finger on your thigh*). Is that ok? Let's have another go at it and see if it is the same or different now.

It is now very likely that the client recognizes and allows the intrusive process. After about a minute of silently observing the client, resume with the following statement.

> Have you noticed how agitated the mind is? We try to rest our mind peacefully and quietly on the breath and it doesn't let us (*here you normalize the difficulty by using "us" in your explanations*). There is no rest there, only busyness and agitation. Have you notice how this is similar when you try to relax at home? Unless we have a drink, watch TV, read a book or use other distractions it is difficult to unwind and free our mind from thoughts, especially negative ones … is that right? … Let me give you some explanations for this by looking at what happens in the brain when we process information …

> *Briefly and simply, explain the effects of frequency and recency of activation in neural networks as main reasons for intrusive thoughts, as discussed in Chapter 2. If you are certain that the client's level of insight will not permit good understanding, then using "the fasting metaphor" in Chapter 6 may be useful, then resume.*

So, let's summarize all this. With the mindfulness of the breathing exercise, we train to sustain attention to our breath, as it comes in and as it goes out of the nostrils. Of course, many thoughts we didn't choose to have will emerge in consciousness. The first skill to develop is the ability to detect thoughts and perceive them objectively, just as thoughts, no matter what they are about. This helps us not to identify with our thoughts, which means that *we* are the observer, not the thought. This is a very important skill because it gives us the option to respond in a way we choose. The second important skill is to prevent the usual reaction to the thought, which is to think it. We learn to say "thanks but no thanks," to accept that there is a thought but not engage with it. We call this "response inhibition." As soon as we have detected a thought and decided not to engage with it, the third important skill is the ability to refocus spontaneously on what we intended to focus on, the target, which is the breath at the entrance of the nostrils. For this, we need to reallocate attention to the breath, and we do this gently, without forcing, without frustration, with patience and tolerance

– though this remains hard work! Through this continual effort to shift attention, we develop an important skill called "cognitive flexibility." These are the three main skills that enable us to become quickly aware when we ruminate, to stop doing it, and to easily refocus on what we were doing, and sometime this means sleeping better and longer instead of tossing and turning in bed, wasting a lot of time thinking.

(*Prompt:*) Is that interesting? … Would you like to be the master of your own mind rather than a slave of it? … That's right, so this week you can use a CD to help you train your mind to do what *you* want it to do.

Then resume with explaining commitment to the practice, as well as a very brief explanation of the normality of agitation, drowsiness and other challenges usually encountered when one starts the training. These can be explained in more details, as discussed in Chapter 6, in the client's next session.

Modeling Acceptance and Equanimity in the 1st Interview

As in all psychotherapeutic systems, the clinician's attitude plays a role in the therapy. Since people tend to categorize each other within the first thirty seconds, being behaviorally consistent with the rationale of MiCBT is important from the very first moment of the initial consultation or group session. It is central to building rapport with the client and increases motivation to undertake some hard work. Implicit self-talk in the client may include: "she's nice, she doesn't get annoyed even though I'm being a pain," or "I wouldn't mind being as calm and peaceful … ," "She knows what she is talking about," or even "If I can become a bit more in control like him/her, it might be worth the effort."

McMillan *et al.,* (2002) pointed out the lack of skilled personnel for the delivery of mindfulness training. Admittedly, the most expert and efficient in implementing mindfulness training are those who, themselves, have trained in the technique and improved their own ability for equanimity. This assertion is congruent with the notion that mindfulness is an experiential approach, not one that is knowledge-based (see Dimidjian and Linehan, 2003, for comments).

However expert in his or her initial approach, a clinician who keeps scratching at the first itch, sneezing at the first dust particle, or reacting at the first frustration, is not going to be as efficient in modeling equanimity as one who remains calm and centered despite external and internal aversive events. Thus, an obvious benefit of being an equanimous therapist is the ability to be behaviorally consistent with the rationale offered to clients.

Summary of Main Points

- Since mindfulness meditation is meant to target the fundamental "operants" of unhelpful behavior, its efficacy is not limited to specific diagnoses. Accordingly, MiCBT suits a wide range of clinical and sub-clinical populations.

- There are a few contraindications for mindfulness meditation. These include severe states of mania, psychosis, paranoia, and uncontrollable anxiety symptoms.
- Providing a rationale for every stage and sub-stage is important. Delivering a rationale experientially is a significant advantage for engaging the client in the treatment plan. Using the Socratic Dialogue enhances client understanding and commitment.
- Modeling acceptance and equanimity from the start of therapy is essential.

Chapter 4

Stage 1 of MiCBT – Part I: How to Generalize Metacognitive and Interoceptive Exposure

I will now close my eyes, I will stop my ears, I will turn away my senses from their objects …; and thus, holding converse only with myself, and closely examining my nature, I will endeavor to obtain by degrees a more intimate and familiar knowledge of myself.

René Descartes

Set Up

Place as a cueing mechanism

When starting the training, it is best to choose a particular place and keep it only for the practice. This will decrease memory recall of associations of the place with other events. It will also work as a cue for the practice. It is also recommended to practice at the same times. This will promote a routine and minimize motivational effort.

When we begin to practice mindfulness meditation, we are sometimes under the impression that the whole world should stop. At home, we know it is not realistic but we still think that the phone should not ring, children should be silent, the floorboards should not creak and cars should not be so noisy at this time of day. In a group situation, we might think that other participants should not cough so loudly or move so much. We react and can become more tense. This is because the inhibitory neurons in our frontal lobe are not yet very good at inhibiting irrelevant stimuli entering our auditory cortex, so we get frustrated. Our expectation to practice well is co-responsible for our reactions. With practice and increased equanimity, the frontal lobe becomes more skilled at dismissing intrusive sounds and sustaining

Mindfulness-integrated CBT: Principles and Practice, First Edition. Bruno A. Cayoun.
© 2011 John Wiley & Sons, Ltd. Published 2011 by John Wiley & Sons, Ltd.

attention to the body (breath or body parts). We need to explain to clients that these noises are part of life and are useful in our training to increase our levels of equanimity and overall tolerance.

In contrast, some clients cannot say "no" to their pet. Some report meditating with the cat or dog on their lap. This is of course not recommended because it is such a pleasant source of distraction. If pets are unable to stay away from the client, they are best kept out of the room. Pets will get used to it and the client's guilt can be addressed using the Socratic dialogue to evaluate the validity of their beliefs (e.g., I don't want to be selfish, my dog will feel rejected, or my cat will end up leaving me).

Clothing

Suitable clothing is also important. Uncomfortable clothes can produce pressures that add to the flow of sensory input. This is an unnecessary discomfort or distraction the client needs to deal with. Very loose and sufficiently warm clothes are ideal. Sometimes, a shawl or small blanket over the knees can help avoid feeling cold as we become more relaxed.

Since the practice is done with closed eyes, it is not necessary to wear spectacles. Remind the client that the weight and pressure due to spectacles also add body sensations to the overall pool of interoceptive stimuli and can mask more subtle sensations around the nose area. Undoing tight belts and shoelaces is also a good idea.

Posture

Avoid strenuous yogic postures. Mindfulness is not about physical exercises or athletic discipline. Rather, the client chooses a comfortable sitting position on a chair or cross-legged and attempts to keep it. In any case, the back and neck must be kept "naturally" straight, which will help withstand fatigue and drowsiness. If drowsiness is found to be a pattern, it is recommended to ask the client to sit on a pillow (preferably high and firm) cross or semi-cross-legged. Moreover, when a client who initially chooses to sit in a chair develops a degree of equanimity, shifting to a cross-legged position may also improve posture stability and concentration.

A comfortable and helpful posture for most people who sit cross-legged on the floor is with the buttocks positioned higher than the knees, which gently rest on the floor. The feet also rest on the floor without crossing. A way of facilitating this posture is to place a thick book under one or two cushions to elevate the hips sufficiently. This will help keep the back straight without much effort.

Since all attempts to minimize sensory input must be made in order to avoid distractibility, clients are told to make the least possible movement. Initially, they can change position at will when discomfort builds up just a little beyond the usual limit of acceptability. However, as practice improves and clients report some ease in the practice, it is important to suggest practicing with immobility for a predetermined period within the sitting session – perhaps starting with 15 minutes, and later on (often the following week) extending to the entire session. This will rapidly improve equanimity.

Relaxation as a Preparatory Measure

It is essential that the procedure starts with a relaxed mind. For the majority of clients, the ability to feel ordinary body sensations is hindered by emotional distress, causing bodily discomfort and racing thoughts. Since interoception is enhanced by calm and stability, practicing a congruent form of relaxation is therefore an advantage.

The relaxation technique that is most compatible with body scanning is progressive muscle relaxation (PMR). PMR also deals with body sensations, even though it tends to operate at a very gross level of experience. The connection with the body, which is often decreased due to avoidance mechanisms and the redeployment of attention towards ruminative thoughts, is easily re-established and clients' small gains promote some confidence to go further. Clients are told that, along with relaxing, PMR helps "to be more in our body rather than staying in our head." It prepares them for a regular daily practice of mindfulness. If a client cannot even commit to 15 or 20 minutes of PMR twice daily, it is unlikely that he or she will commit to the 30-minutes mindfulness practice in the morning and evening. It is good to address commitment at this early stage, as there is evidence that practice frequency improves results (e.g., Rosenzweig *et al.*, 2010).

With PMR, clients start learning to observe and accept gross muscular tension in an easily practicable fashion and feel immediately benefited. Since feeling body sensations can be perceived negatively by some clients (e.g., chronic pain, PTSD, etc), the problem of avoidance tends to emerge at this early stage. Clients who dissociate may also find PMR challenging but more easily achieved than mindfulness exercises, which are considerably subtler. Hence, starting with PMR has numerous advantages.

Another good reason for choosing PMR is the empirical evidence for its effectiveness as a separate technique (e.g., Borkovec and Costello, 1993; Carlson and Hoyle, 1993). Using two evidence-based techniques is likely to be productive.

The main goal of mindfulness meditation is not relaxation but experiential-awareness and experiential-acceptance. As the training develops and the capacity for interoception increases, PMR is replaced by focusing on simple natural breath which allows focus on a more subtle level of experience. This is usually sufficient to bring calm and centeredness. If necessary, this "mindfulness-with-breathing" technique can be prolonged for as long as required until agitation subsides. In fact, though it is an integral feature of interoceptive exposure, it is also a technique of mindfulness meditation of its own in numerous treatment programs.

Additional to its use for relaxation and concentration prior to the interoceptive exposure procedure, breath awareness should be used during interoceptive exposure whenever and as much as necessary (i.e., until racing thoughts subside, drowsiness disappears, or agitation gives way to calm and attentional control).

Practice Overview: Description and Operationalization

The essence of mindfulness meditation is twofold: a continuous awareness of the full range of experiences in the present moment, and an unconditional acceptance of these experiences as they manifest themselves within the framework of the body and mind (Goenka, 1987; Hart, 1987; Marlatt and Kristeller, 1999). From a learning theory perspective, these two essential components may be operationalized as "generalized interoceptive and metacognitive exposure," or more simply put, "experiential exposure and acceptance" (Hayes and Wilson, 2003). Exposure to spontaneously emerging body sensations and concomitant thoughts is "generalized" because it is not targeting a particular behavior or experience. Rather, we simply prevent reactions to *any* experience, wherever it is manifested at the physiological or mental level.

The sustained lack of usual reaction to an emerging experience results in the progressive extinction of the conditioned response to that kind of experience. In its most simplistic formulation, it is a form of desensitization to private events (Hayes, 1994, 2002). The state of calm, tranquility and equilibrium that results from this desensitization is called "equanimity."

Mindfulness with breathing

For the first part of the session, as mentioned earlier, clients learn to "observe" (feel) natural breath in order to develop some control over racing thoughts (see Mindfulness with Breathing Script, Stage 1, in Appendix A). This consists of attentional training that uses an already existing function (the breath) that is integral to the client's actual ongoing experience. Clients focus their attention on breath patterns, which vary dynamically according to conscious or subconscious cognitive and somatic activity.

The first realization is that the mind from one moment to the next is anything but still, wandering either in the past or in the future but hardly ever remaining in the present reality. Monitoring these inherent mental patterns progressively silences and stabilizes the mind. Similarly, studies using the Dynamic Systems approach in an attempt to index attentional cost incurred by motor tasks have shown that attention plays an important role in the stabilization of spontaneous dynamic patterns (e.g., Cayoun, Tayler, and Summers, 2001; Temprado *et al.*, 1999; Wuyts *et al.*, 1996).

Three decades of research have provided evidence that attention is not a unitary entity or mechanism. Posner and Raichle (1997) have proposed a model of attention based on neuro-imaging studies, in which attention processes may be attributed to three major functions: orienting to sensory stimuli, establishing and maintaining alertness, and executing control of goal-directed behavior (including intention and inhibition of automatic responses). Within this framework, the first stage of mindfulness meditation (sustained monitoring of the breath) may involve improvement in both the executive control network and the vigilance/alertness network, neuroanatomically related to the midline frontal cortex (cingulated and SMA), basal ganglia (especially caudate), anterior prefrontal cortex, and anterior right parietal cortex (Swanson *et al.*, 1998).

Within the Information-Processing framework, executive processes are known to be involved in the management of the constant stream of sensory information competing for access to the processes controlling action, and in decisions about the appropriateness and timing of action (Denckla, 1996). This is consistent with this aspect of the mindfulness program, in which the client learns to decrease the duration of distractibility from both spontaneously emerging thoughts and somatic sensations (more on this later) by systematically switching attention back to the incoming and outgoing breath when he or she realizes concentration has been lost. This requires the client to develop a dynamic awareness of his or her own thoughts, or meta-cognition (Flavell, 1979).

Mindfulness is consistent with Wells' (2002) information processing analysis of mindfulness meditation. Wells argues that:

> the effect of mindfulness strategies on information processing in emotional disorders can be conceptualized in metacognitive terms as (a) activating a metacognitive mode of processing; (b) disconnecting the influence of maladaptive beliefs on processing; (c) strengthening flexible responses to threat; and (d) strengthening metacognitive plans for controlling cognition.(Wells, 2002, p. 95).

In particular, the practice relies on executive functions necessary for the inhibition of automatic evaluative patterns, such as judging a memory or a physical discomfort that has just manifested while observing the breath. Although inhibitory control is as necessary as metacognitive functions, the distinction between the two seems to be both conceptual and neuroanatomical (see Barkley, 1997, for a review). Iversen and Dunnett (1990) assign inhibitory control to the orbital-frontal regions of the prefrontal cortex and its reciprocal interconnections with the ventromedial region of the striatum, whereas processes involving working memory engage the dorsolateral region of the prefrontal cortex and its reciprocal connections to a more centralized area of the striatum (see also Fuster, 1989).

The continuous attempt to improve metacognition and inhibitory control is beneficial for the improvement of self-control, especially with clinically obsessive or intrusive thinking. In a study examining inhibitory control in Obsessive-Compulsive Disorder (OCD), Tolin *et al.* (2002) have shown that obsessive thoughts were more intrusive in participants who demonstrated a reduced ability for inhibition. A more recent study further demonstrated that participants with OCD were more impaired on measures of intentional inhibition (Badcock, Waters, and Maybery, 2007). Moreover, Teasdale (1999) differentiates metacognitive knowledge and metacognitive insight. This dichotomy is an important one because it highlights the advantage of phenomenology, the experience itself, over the rationalization of the experience. It clearly delineates generic/factual knowledge about thoughts (e.g., I know how negative my thoughts are because I can't help thinking about the job I have lost) and online cognitive events (e.g., right now my mind is very agitated, I feel emotional, and my breathing is very irregular when fleeting negative thoughts arise … now it calms down as they are subsiding). Metacognitive insight, traditionally termed "mind awareness" – in the Buddhist traditional teaching of mindfulness – is a skill that facilitates the process of disidentification from ordinary cognitive contents.

Mindfulness through body scanning

The core of the technique requires the client to use these skills to survey the entire body part by part, facing systematically and consistently any physiological manifestation with a neutral, objective, non-judgmental, equanimous attitude (see Stage 1 script in Appendix A). He or she discovers that the simple act of monitoring autonomic physiological activity alone can increase the system's stability.

This widening of focus and orderly scanning of the body is also proposed to be subserved by executive functions, tapping the inhibitory system. What changes is the focus of attention (shifting back to body sensations rather than to the breath). The notion of impermanence (spontaneous change) is also added to the rationale and is consciously experienced by the client. This provides clients with strong ecological validity for the notion that an experience changes if reactions are prevented (extinction procedure). Clients meet their own psychosomatic processes first at a rather gross level of experience (observing normal breath) and progressively, from one day to the next, they discover subtler aspects of experience (e.g., touch of very subtle breath on the skin, and from gross to very subtle body sensations).

The mindfulness approach is essentially based on the core principles of Vipassana or mindfulness meditation (Kabat-Zinn, 1982; see also Hart, 1987, for detailed description), but there exist differences in some technical aspects of implementation depending on the therapist's source of knowledge and training (e.g., trained in Zen, Tibetan, or various Theravada traditions). For example, the Thai and Sri Lankan Theravada traditions focus continually on the breath while neutrally attending to salient body sensations emerging above awareness level (e.g., Bhikkhu, 1982).

In contrast, one of the most practiced Burmese traditions teaches us to scan systematically each body part while neutrally attending to all types of body sensations (whether salient or faint); the breath is preparatory but not central to the technique, as taught by S.N. Goenka (see Hart, 1987, for detail). During formal practice, the former approach deploys attention resources on the breath whereas the latter uses attention dynamically to scan the body for sensations. MiCBT uses this method for both its practical and theoretical strengths.

In terms of clinical benefit, these differences have not been subjected to empirical investigation and may be associated with varying gains. Nevertheless, all these traditions apply themselves to establish and maintain mindfulness in the practitioner (Kabat-Zinn, 2003).

To begin with, with MiCBT, it is suggested that clients focus on areas of five to ten centimeters in diameter, and later decrease the size slightly as practice improves. This narrowing increases concentration but it is also too time-consuming for beginners. Attention should be constantly moving on from a body part to the next (adjacent) body part soon after it has been clearly felt. This will avoid "clinging" to (identifying with) any experience and promote a "letting go" attitude. However, this is very different from avoidance. We move from one sensation to another in a detached manner without desire to avoid something unpleasant. In fact, if a sensation in the body is experienced as very unpleasant, preventing us to focus on more common sensations, we stay focused on this sensation with equanimity for about half a minute (about 2 minutes when some expertise is acquired) in order to promote desensitization. When the sensation becomes sufficiently neutralized, with about 50% decrease in intensity, we can resume with scanning the rest of the body.

Though movement direction is not essential to the results, it is very useful to indicate the movement direction to clients. Most commonly, clients who begin are asked to move vertically (downwards and upwards) rather than horizontally. This is mainly because later scanning techniques will teach rapids "sweeping" scanning techniques that need to be performed vertically, and it is important to be consistent from the start. Refer to the audio recording of Stage 1 or script in Appendix A for detailed application. The important aspect of the movement is its pattern consistency. As trainees cycle their attention through the body several times in their sitting session, if the scanning order is inconsistent and they still experience a fair amount of intrusive thoughts, they often forget which body part they scanned the last cycle. To avoid confusion and possible neglect of some body parts, clients should adopt a preferred scanning order and maintain it.

Whenever an area remains "blank" for a long period or very painful to the extent that attention is automatically drawn to it, the client is encouraged to "work on it" for a minute or two. This involves focusing only on the affected area (e.g., remaining in the very center of the pain if any) while remaining calm and objective, attentive to details of changing phenomena, with equanimity. Otherwise, attentional movement must occur smoothly as soon as a sensation is detected – as long as it is not for the purpose of avoiding an unpleasant experience. With more practice and expertise, this means moving very fast through the body. In fact, as interoceptive capacity and equanimity develop, the client tends to sweep naturally across entire portions of the body (such as a limb) at once because it may feel that sensations in this particular body part vibrate at a high frequency, like a pleasant flow of electricity. However, the entire body should also be scanned, including parts easily neglected such as the armpits and genitals, even though these parts may not (yet) allow the feeling of pleasant "free flow of energy."

Advanced scanning methods

It is important to note that Stage 1 of MiCBT, mindfulness meditation, is an approach that includes numerous sets of skills. Buddhist monks and other practitioners of mindfulness meditation spend years trying to further develop these skills in intensive training courses, some of which last up to 45 days in Vipassana centers, in silence, focusing all waking hours on the breath and body sensations. Among those skills is the ability to scan the body in various ways while remaining aware and equanimous.

The improvement of scanning ability appears in various forms:

1. One is the widening of conscious appraisal of body sensations, by which blank areas give place to salient body sensations. In other words, more of the body becomes prominent, an experience which some teachers of mindfulness have called "opening up."
2. Another form of scanning improvement is an increased subtlety of awareness, which enables conscious detection of very subtle, often tingling, sensations vibrating rapidly throughout large body parts (such as an entire limb).
3. A third type of scanning improvement is the rapidity with which sensations are being felt. We move progressively from local to global awareness.

The rationale for advanced scanning in MiCBT is that it progressively enables clients to detect and address early distress cues, thus enhancing the prevention of relapse. As the task demand imposes more processing from the brain's attention networks in somatosensory pathways, more connections between cells in these regions are being formed. Although the actual regions have not been sufficiently defined empirically, Lazar's *et al.*, (2005) MRI study shows structural evidence that the brain of experienced mindfulness practitioners was thicker than that of the controls in the somatosensory cortex, right anterior insula, and prefrontal cortex. Richard Davidson and colleagues also observed effects of neuroplasticity on the left regions of the prefrontal cortex following mindfulness training (Davidson *et al.*, 2003). A subsequent electroencephalographic study showed high-amplitude gamma synchrony in long-term meditators compared to controls, suggesting "temporal integrative mechanisms and short and long-term neural changes (Lutz *et al.*, 2004).

More recently, using high-resolution MRI data of 44 subjects, Luders *et al.*, (2009) detected significantly larger gray matter volumes in meditators in the right orbito-frontal cortex and the right hippocampus. Both orbito-frontal and hippocampal regions have been implicated in emotional regulation and response control. The authors argue that larger volumes in these regions might account for meditators' singular abilities and habits to cultivate positive emotions, retain emotional stability, and engage in mindful behavior. They further suggest that these regional

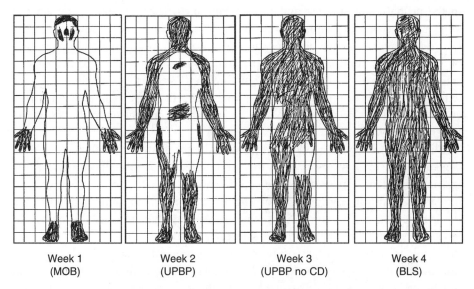

| Week 1 | Week 2 | Week 3 | Week 4 |
| (MOB) | (UPBP) | (UPBP no CD) | (BLS) |

Figure 4. The relationship between the representation of the body in the somatosensory cortex and the progressive ability to feel body sensation using body-scanning techniques in a 42 year-old male (MOB = Mindfulness of breath; UPBP = Unilateral part-by-part scanning; UPBP no CD = Unilateral part-by-part scanning without auditory instructions; BLS = Bilateral scanning).

alterations in brain structures constitute part of the underlying neurological correlate of long-term meditation independent of a specific style and practice.

Schwartz (2003) also provided a strong rationale for "directed neuroplasticity," the notion that directed willed mental activity can generate a force that constructively alters the brain. Since this is a relatively new field of research, studies of neuroplasticity with mindfulness training are scarce, especially when it comes to measuring the effects of scanning techniques.

Figure 4 shows the increase of neuroplasticity in somatosensory networks across the first four weeks of mindfulness training during Stage 1 of MiCBT. In each weekly consultation, the client is asked to color parts of a small silhouette printed on an A4 sheet according to the body areas they can feel. The grid facilitates the quantitative analysis of weekly progressions (see Interoception Forms in Appendix C). Although Figure 4 represents the weekly progression of a forty-two year-old depressed male, it is also representative of most people who adhere to the treatment protocol (about 30 minutes practice twice daily).

Week 1 represents interoceptive ability during mindfulness of breath exercise only. Week 2 involved unilateral part-by-part body-scanning, Week 3 consisted of repeating Week 2 but without the use of audio instructions, and Week 4 introduced Symmetrical (bilateral) scanning (discussed below). Not surprisingly, the baseline in interoceptive ability at Week 1 corresponds to the initial delineation of the body in the primary somatosensory cortex, usually pictorially represented by what is known as the Sensory Homunculus (Penfield and Rasmussen, 1950). Since the face, hands and feet have disproportionately more connections than many other body parts in the brain, these body parts are usually easier to feel at the start of training, even with just mindfulness of breath (Week 1). As practice develops with various body-scanning methods, more connections are facilitated across the entire somatosensory cortex, enabling greater ability to feel sensory cues across the entire body.

Clients who develop good scanning skills in the first two or three weeks are generally able to scan faster than the given (read or recorded) initial learning instructions. This can create some interference that can distract attention and hinder the natural development of clients' scanning ability. Some report that the instructions can be too slow at times (note here that this can also be due to levels of anxiety, especially if this is said early into the training). Therefore, it is preferable to decrease progressively the use of systematic instructions as the skill improves; as instructed on the "Stage 1" training CD. By that time, Stage 2, described in Chapter 7, may be implemented but the client is encouraged to maintain and improve Stage 1. Similarly, Stage 1 continues to be refined and integrated during Stages 3 and 4 as well. Below are some brief guidelines for the advanced scanning stage.

Bilateral (symmetrical) scanning
As scanning the body one part at a time becomes easier and less interrupted by common mental distractions, clients are instructed to scan the body part by part but symmetrically (e.g., both cheeks, both shoulders, both legs, etc at the same time). This constitutes the first level of advanced scanning. At this stage, the brain must activate attention networks from both hemispheres and in equal strength simultaneously.

This hemispheric coupling may have already been experienced naturally in clients whose practice has been very efficient so far (i.e., twice daily for about 30 minutes), but does not come easily in clients who do not adhere to the routine or who may have misunderstood how to practice for some time. Initially, it is possible to feel a little confused by the task if the previous skill (unilateral scanning) was not very developed.

Most clients and colleagues report that their attention is attracted more to one side of the body than the other, sometimes feeling a little disoriented as attention zigzags from one side to the other instead of flowing vertically. This is because of the hemispheric asymmetry in somatosensory networks. We tend to feel more easily the parts of the body to which we pay more attention in daily life. In clients with chronic pain, this is also due to paying more attention to painful areas on one side of the body. Ultimately, this stage also becomes easier with some training. When symmetrical scanning is acquired, the client can scan both sides of the body at once easily, perhaps within five to ten minutes at the most. Then it is recommended to move on to the next level.

Partial sweeping

At the second level of advanced scanning, the notion of "sweeping" the body is introduced. This consists of scanning with a continuous motion in the desired direction (vertically in the beginning). The brain activates large amounts of networks and learns to integrate many more connections and process mass of sensations simultaneously. To borrow from memory research in Cognitive Psychology, sweeping is a way of "chunking" interoceptive information. At this stage, clients are trained to practice "Partial Sweeping" only. They are asked to "sweep" through sets of body parts while trying to feel as many parts as possible with sustained awareness and equanimity towards all sensations they encounter from moment to moment. Clients are generally asked to scan the entire head down to the neck at once, then through both shoulders and upper limbs at once, then go back to the front part of the trunk and sweep through the entire chest down to the abdomen at once, then move up to the upper back and sweep down to the buttocks, and resume in this way with each lower limb down to the tip of the toes.

For clients who do not show much difficulty with scanning, it is suggested that they shift from sweeping the front and the back of the trunk separately to sweeping these sections at once after a few days practice. When Partial Sweeping is easier and faster, with each scan of body length requiring perhaps two to five minutes at the most, it is time to move on to the next step.

Sweeping en masse

The next level of advanced scanning requires attention to move vertically while spreading attention widely through the entire width of the body at once; first at the surface and later in its entire density. To explain this stage to clients, metaphors can be useful. This scanning technique is known as "sweeping *en masse*," as taught by S.N. Goenka (Hart, 1987). During his instructions, Goenka likens the sweeping experience to that of pouring water over our head; so does our attention flow down the entire body, feeling all sensations on the way without any hindrance. Initially, when sweeping is still slow, it seems more like honey running down (and up) along the body.

However, since sweeping methods involve the rapid coverage of very large body parts, practitioners tend to miss parts during scanning. It is important to prevent performance tradeoffs between speed and accuracy. To compensate for missed parts, it is necessary to survey all missed parts separately after each sweep of the entire body.

This stage can be surprising for practitioners. The sense of pleasant physical "dissolution" (i.e., a sense of very low cohesiveness) felt throughout the body can create a genuine experience of oneness with the environment, even with the air surrounding the body. This sense of being physically both "nothing" and "everything" at once is generally pleasant and free from confusion – which is consistent with the fact that the previous steps leading to this more advanced stage are only possible with sustained clarity of mind and equanimity. This experience should not be confused with the experience of avoidance and dissociation. S.N. Goenka describes this experience in the following way:

> Initially it is very gross, solidified, intensified, but as you keep practicing patiently, persistently, remaining equanimous with every experience, the whole body dissolves into subtle vibrations, and you reach the stage of bhanga, total dissolution. (Goenka, 1999, p. 29).

In addition, craving reactions to pleasant body sensations are typical experiences when we have dealt with most of the "gross" (aversive) sensations. By implication, it generally shows signs of progress, but keep in mind that there will be future gross sensations that would not emerge unless the client had experienced "free flow" of body sensations and cravings. Both men and women experience craving reactions, sometimes of a sexual nature, and it is useful to normalize these when you implement sweeping methods by simply letting them know that sometimes people have strong cravings and it is normal to experience them. You certainly want to emphasize this with clients diagnosed with addiction problems. Soon, these clients realize that they are more addicted to craving for body sensations than they are to the actual substance. This realization is likely to help prevent relapse.

The amount and intensity of craving reactions depend on several variables, including genetics, the amount and intensity of past attachment to pleasurable experiences and one's levels of awareness and equanimity. The way to deal with craving reactions is the same as with aversive reactions: remain aware that all body sensations, thoughts and images are impermanent and therefore destined to pass. As such, they can be perceived with a degree of distance from the sense of "I," without the need for attachment, i.e. with equanimity. Just let them pass. You will note that as we let them pass, more tend to emerge. Again, letting these pass is necessary. Slowly, the reactive behavior of craving for what we like weakens. Technically speaking, from an operant conditioning perspective, you may say that your conditioned response is being extinguished due to the prevention of reinforcement.

Transversal scanning
The Advanced Training CD (Cayoun, 2005b) also contains another set of instructions, "Transversal Scanning" (track 8). This is a very advanced level and a further step towards neuroplasticity. Attention is directed part-by-part, as with the first step of body scanning described earlier, but this time it is directed *through* the body rather than maintained at its surface. Attention pierces and penetrates the entire body part by part from front to back, and then from back to front, with sustained equanimity. What is most remarkable is the persistence of this ability following long periods during which training has stopped. In the neuroscience context, this effect is usually termed "between-session plasticity" (Sanes and Donoghue, 2000).

You may recall our discussion of the three common causes of intrusive thoughts in Chapter 2. The co-emergence effect allows schema-based associations to be uprooted and reprocessed equanimously, leading to extinction of the learned response. Because deeper interoceptive awareness takes place during transversal scanning, older memories encoded with their concomitant body sensations can co-emerge and pass away unhindered by a clinging or aversive mind. This is how Buddhist teaching operationalizes the technical aspect of "purification of mind." The benefit of such a deep reprocessing is especially remarkable in individuals with past trauma, as exemplified by the commentaries of ex-clients in Chapter 10.

While such advanced skills do develop in some individuals, MiCBT does not always lead to their attainment. Clients seen in one-on-one consultations tend to develop further advanced skills as the schedule is not always as tightly structured as in groups and more adaptations are possible. Group participants are usually encouraged to follow the group constraints. In addition, because of time constraints in a short therapy system, clients do not generally experience more advanced scanning methods than sweeping *en masse*. Moreover, clients who seek therapeutic care are not necessarily (and often not at all) interested in embracing a meditation course, especially when the targeted problem is resolved.

Although clinicians who employ MiCBT enjoy the use of very advanced methods, they do not attempt to transform clients into Zen masters. If clients show interest in committing to such techniques, there are specialized and well-established meditation centers where they can benefit from a specifically designed context and atmosphere that is more conducive for meditation. The issue of professional roles and boundaries concerning training clients in mindfulness is worth considering given the fast growing interest in professional settings (see Hayes, 2002, for a useful discussion).

Emphasizing the nature of body sensations

Clients benefit from being taught that a body sensation can occur simply because judgmental thinking occurs, and that a body sensation causes a thought to emerge, either below or above awareness threshold. Clients with little practice tend to experience numerous "blank areas" in the body. For most, however, body sensations are detectable when they intensify sufficiently to reach the current threshold of awareness. This is greatly affected by emotional load and stress levels. When body sensations are grossly intensified following contact with an aversive stimulus, it is said that arousal has taken place.

An efficient way of addressing distressing pain, whether physical or emotional, is to focus on body sensations with a non-judgmental frame of mind. Here are some useful steps to demonstrate instant extinction:

- Ask the client to close his or her eyes and breathe calmly and confidently for about 15 seconds.
- Then ask what is (or what was at a time of interest) the client's emotional experience. Ask the client to rate its intensity "out of 10."

- Use open-ended questions to help the client link the emotion to a set of bodily sensations.
- Choose the most intense sensation and ask the client to briefly describe it as objectively as possible, in terms of their basic characteristics (mass, movement, temperature, and cohesiveness). Ask: "You say there is a strong feeling of sadness in your chest, could you describe whether you are actually feeling movement or stillness, lightness or heaviness, coldness or heat, sensations joining and merging together? Try to have a good look at it and tell me as precisely as possible the actual experience."
- Once the client has described the body sensations in objective terms, validate the effort and ask: "Now I would like you to stay in the centre of the sensation of pressure and heat for about half a minute; that means no reaction whatsoever for about half a minute … can you try? I have not come across a client who refused to try – perhaps, validating the previous step brings sufficient confidence.
- Again validate their willingness to try and remind them that they start now for 30 seconds, just after you finish giving instructions.
- After about half a minute: "Keep your eyes closed and describe your experience in this part of the body." Most report a change in one direction or the other, usually a decrease in arousal intensity either in the form of simple decay or in the spreading of the initially narrowly focalized sensation across larger areas surrounding its initial location.

Clients who avoided painful experiences, sometimes by dissociating, will often not experience arousal readily with simple recall of painful experience. Instead, arousal will slowly increase during the exercise, resulting in small increase, rather than decrease, of arousal after 30 seconds. Hence, in case of no apparent change or even an increase in intensity, repeat the procedure, as exposure time may be insufficient.

Occasionally, some clients will not listen to or understand instructions and keep reinforcing the aversive reaction instead, by either suppressing or judging the sensation, or focusing elsewhere or on its periphery (rather than its centre).

- With those situations, after no change has occurred following two 30-second trials, ask the client to describe what other sensations are in the body at this moment. Localize the next most salient and repeat the procedure. Whatever the outcome after 30 seconds, ask the client to return to the initially chosen sensation describe the experience and rate it again out of 10. There is now high likelihood for a decrease in intensity.
- Validate the effort and ask the client to open his or her eyes and ask: "What have you learned from this short exercise?" We are trying to demonstrate the feasibility of extinction; as a principle of "impermanence."

As mentioned in Chapter 2, awareness of both body sensations and reactions varies according to their intensity and the individual's awareness threshold. It

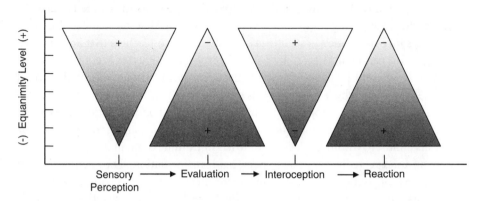

Figure 5. Consequences of increase in equanimity on the overall reinforcement system during mindfulness training. The surface area within each triangular surface represents the amount of attentional processing dedicated to each of the four components as a function of equanimity level.

follows that the more there is stress or mental busyness, the less possible it is to detect subtle sensations. Figure 5 illustrates the typical effects of equanimity on the information processing system.

Recognizing progress

There are three major markers for progress with mindfulness practice. Technically, the most quantifiable and perhaps verifiable is one's **growing ability for equanimity**. At this stage of training, the client has developed an understanding that progress is not determined by the type, frequency or intensity of experience, but rather by the *attitude* toward the experience. In particular, the time it takes to regain calm and emotional stability following a stress response or other causes for emotional imbalance is the most direct measure to gauge improvement. A decrease in the usual time necessary for letting go of reacting to emotional pain signifies progress. From a learning perspective, a decrease in the time to disengage from emotional reactivity also means a shorter reinforcing period. This is a measure of equanimity and self-efficacy.

Another good measure of progress, although less direct, is **whether the person's life is progressively changing across contexts because of increased levels of equanimity**. Admittedly, it is one thing to sit daily in formal practice, and another to apply the skills with common stressors in daily life. Although we do capitalize on the emerging effects of neuroplasticity, significant progress in usually distress-provoking situations takes place when the skills can be de-contextualized from formal meditation practice to a daily application of the skills; when we change from *practicing* mindfulness to *becoming* mindful.

A third measure of progress is the experience of genuine **gratitude toward the teacher** who, by teaching mindfulness skills, took part in that life change. Moreover, as progress increases, one's gratitude is often extended to teachers that are part of a "lineage." This can be illustrated by a brief heart-warming letter I recently received by email. It was sent by the client of a colleague, whom I trained in MiCBT about three years ago and whose gratitude was evident to me and probably evident to his clients as well. This client story is particularly moving, not only because of the client's own results but also because of the transformation that began to take place in the life of his children, whom he decided to teach mindfulness meditation after experiencing an unexpectedly remarkable personal transformation. The client had been incarcerated for many years, with multiple re-incarcerations, as coping within the prison was much easier for him than learning to deal with life necessities and people outside the prison. He had been subjected to much violence, alcohol and drug addictions, and severe anxiety and other mental health difficulties during intermittent journeys outside the prison. His email is included with his permission:

> Hello Bruno, I hope you get to read this in person. My name is [...]. I undertook MiCBT with a Counselor at the Salvation Army in the north of the state about 2 years ago. It is such a big part of each day of my life, it has become my way of life. Every time I meet someone in pain or trauma or addicted to something, I quietly mention mindfulness to them as my way of keeping the balance. I could say a lot but really what I want to say is thank you.

Such gratitude is considered to be both an important marker and a humbling experience in traditional teaching of mindfulness. As an illustration of this point, in traditional Buddhist meditation teaching, the practice often starts with an expression of gratitude to the entire group of teachers (the *Sanga*) who have carefully preserved and passed on the techniques of meditation since they were taught, over 25 centuries ago, and without whom we would not benefit from them today.

Internalizing equanimity

Practice makes perfect. The continuity of practice is one of the two principal factors that enhance the probability of success; the other is quality of practice. Besides the formal practice twice daily, clients are encouraged to live as mindfully as possible from morning to evening. To borrow a term from Jon Kabat-Zinn, this implies "informal" daily practice, whereby clients monitor their body sensations and thoughts in as many situations as possible; as will be discussed below. This helps generalize equanimity.

Use of stage 1 instructions recording

The Stage 1 audio recording format used with MiCBT (Cayoun, 2004) helps clients memorize the technique. It is especially useful in clients with clinical levels of impairment. However, it is important that they learn to practice in silence as soon as possible. They need to decrease sensory input into as many modalities as possible, sufficiently to allow output (intrusive thoughts, images, body sensations and other memories) to emerge for reprocessing. When the CD is used beyond its necessity (learning the task), progress can be delayed. As in all auditory instructions of mindfulness meditation, the author's voice input into the auditory cortex creates interference with outputting ("intrusive") thoughts emerging in the same cortical area when monitoring breath or body sensations.

Psychological science is well acquainted with the principles of "structural interference," which usually refers to the simultaneous processing of two or more stimuli within the same modality (visual, auditory, etc). This has implications which clinicians can easily overlook in their delivery of mindfulness training. For example, providing continuous instructions, using music, counting, mantras, or even the CDs throughout the practice, makes the practice easier because less thoughts can intrude, but inhibitory capacity is not developing as well as it could. This is why some people cling to the CDs and others want to let it go early. A limitation is delayed progress and therefore delayed reward.

In addition, mindfulness skills are most efficient and rewarding when they are made portable, which is hardly possible if the client relies on instructions or the use of background music or mantras, which can inadvertently be used as avoidance mechanisms. In addition, the use of visualization techniques to possibly facilitate concentration is unproductive in mindfulness training because they activate the visual cortex instead of the somatosensory cortex, wherein body sensations are felt and reprocessed neutrally.

Sometimes clients visualize body parts in the hope that it will help to feel more sensations in those parts. This should be avoided because engaging the visual cortex while attempting to feel body sensations will divide attention resources between cortices and delay neuroplasticity in the somatosensory cortex. As explained earlier, more density in somatosensory networks will facilitate the detection of early distress cues and emotional regulation. More connections in visual neurons will not.

Clinicians who use MiCBT tend to encourage the use of recorded instructions for the initial learning period, and then encourage the practice of the same tasks without the CD – though it can be used occasionally during the week to refresh memory and moderate the typical "storm" of intrusive thoughts in clients with severe symptoms, such as OCD or auditory hallucinations.

When mindfulness is perceived as a therapy rather than a healthy and wiser way of life, clients whose recovery is maintained for some time often stop the practice. After having eventually stopped practicing for a few months and stressors reappear, clients can use their CD again on their own and restart practicing to prevent relapse.

Promoting skill transfer

"Informal practice," a term coined by Kabat-Zinn (1990), is an important aspect of mindfulness training. When body sensations are felt in most body parts, generally on week 3 or week 4 of the program, clients are asked to extend the skills they are continuously developing in the formal setting (closed-eyes morning and evening in the sitting posture) to less formal contexts.

As part of homework exercises, they are encouraged to apply their awareness of thoughts and body sensations in as many day-to-day situations as possible. They are encouraged to live mindfully for the entire week. Typically, when walking, they are asked to feel the soles of their feet and the muscle contraction in the lower limbs. When eating, they are asked to slow down and feel the basic flavors and consistencies of foods (salt, sugar, fat, etc), along with the tension in the jaw and the sensations produced in the throat as the foods are being swallowed.

In particular, following psycho-education about the four basic characteristics of body sensations, (see Chapter 2) clients are given the Interoceptive Signature form (see Appendix C) to monitor the emergence of body sensations during stressful situations. The term "signature" is borrowed from Segal *et al.* (2002) because it clearly conveys the idiosyncratic nature of interoceptive cues arising during emotional processing. It proposes that people experience patterns of body sensations which are individual to each person; although body sensations that emerge during certain emotions tend to be experienced with features universally shared (e.g., heat and agitation during anger).

The form also serves to reinforce the more objective nature of mindful observation during formal practice. Clients are reminded to attend to body sensations in terms of the four basic characteristics listed on the form. Additionally, the form can be used in the context of exposure tasks during Stage 2, as described in a later section of this manual.

Thus, an important aim of body-scan techniques is to develop an increasing ability for interoceptive awareness and acceptance in everyday situations, for which skill transfer is essential. The reorganization of brain pathways, or neuroplasticity, in somatosensory pathways which takes place during the formal practice of body-scan techniques facilitates the transfer of interoceptive skills in daily life (Cayoun, 2005a; Kabat-Zinn, 2005; Lazar *et al.*, 2005).

Summary of Main Points

- Proper meditation practice set up enhances commitment and results. This includes using comfortable clothing, finding and maintaining a place and time for practice, and adopting a correct posture for practice.
- Progressive Muscle Relaxation is used only as a preparatory measure for mindfulness of breath. Similarly, mindfulness of breath is used as a preparatory measure for mindfulness of body sensations (body-scanning).
- Mindfulness of breath is used as a means to sustain attention in order to develop three important skills that will subsequently allow efficient body-scanning techniques: First, detecting intrusive thought without identifying with it (i.e., increasing metacognitive awareness). Second, simultaneously preventing the usual reaction to the thought by not engaging with it (i.e., increasing inhibitory

control). Third, reallocating attention to the breath as soon as we have disengaged from the thought (increasing cognitive flexibility), thereby decreasing the probability for the recurrence of ruminative thinking.

- During practice of mindfulness of breath, trainees perceive thoughts as just fleeting mental events, transient vehicles for memories and ideas, and not as containing actual reality.
- There are several ways of scanning the body, delivered hierarchically at weekly intervals. These include (1) unilateral part-by-part scanning, (2) bilateral (symmetrical) part-by-part scanning, (3) partial sweeping, (4) sweeping *en masse*, and (5) transversal scanning. The more complex scanning methods enhance interoception and allow instantaneous appraisal of very subtle sensations through the entire body. One important advantage of this skill is very early detection of distress cues, thereby promoting relapse prevention.
- Body sensations are composed of four basic characteristics: mass, motion, temperature and cohesiveness (sense of density or solidity). Explaining this to clients helps normalizing difficult bodily experiences, such as pain, and prevents catastrophic appraisals of body states, such as visceral symptoms of anxiety.
- Progress with mindfulness training is traditionally assessed on three criteria: life changes, gratitude and, most importantly, the duration of reactivity following encounter with a stressor.
- Informal practice is used to generalize equanimity to multiple contexts.

Chapter 5

Clinical Relevance

It is only in the lonely emergencies of life
that our creed is tested: then routine maxims fail,
and we fall back on our gods.

William James

Confounding Factors

Differences in the operational definition of mindfulness are an important issue in this new line of research and in clinical applications. The construct has been described differently by various authors who tend to emphasize aspects that are more relevant to their own theoretical affiliation. Whereas this may offer a more global perspective on the wider ramifications of the approach, it can also contribute to a difficulty in operationalizing its active components and may create discrepancies in therapeutic applications.

Differences in construct definition: emphasis on cognition versus interoception

Ellen Langer has defined mindfulness with an emphasis on categorization processes (e.g., Langer 1989). Her cognitive modeling describes the mindfulness state as a flexible cognitive style that enables a wider view of a situation. The distinction between "mindfulness" and "mindlessness" is described as follows:

Mindfulness-integrated CBT: Principles and Practice, First Edition. Bruno A. Cayoun.
© 2011 John Wiley & Sons, Ltd. Published 2011 by John Wiley & Sons, Ltd.

Mindlessness can be defined as a cognitive state in which an individual relies rigidly on categories and distinctions created in the past. Mindlessness involves acting based on a formalized set of rules and attitudes. Each new event or situation is classified into a pre-existing category. Based on that category, behavioral and attitudinal responses are prescribed. Mindfulness, on the other hand, can be defined as a state of continuous category formation. A mindful individual creates new approaches to events and situations. He or she is not bound by previously formed rigid attitudes; rather, the mindful person, situated in the present, explores a situation from several perspectives. (Margolis and Langer, 1990, p. 107)

In particular, Langer (1992, p. 289) conceives mindfulness as "a state of conscious awareness in which the individual is implicitly aware of the context and content of information." However, Langer noted that her concept of mindfulness should not be directly compared with the mindfulness approach derived from the non-dualistic description in Theravada Buddhist tradition.

The role of exposure to physiological events and extinction is often secondary to exposure to cognitive events, or even left out of the operational definition in some cases. Wells (2002, p. 96) has described the objective of mindfulness as being a "disengagement of appraisals of stimuli or cognition in order to block ruminative thinking about one's situation." Although this application of mindfulness has significant advantages (e.g., Teasdale *et al.*, 2000), the description focuses mainly on the higher level of cognitive processing, and lacks integration of co-emergent sensorimotor processing.

Accordingly, a number of clinical applications of mindfulness skills emphasize mindfulness of thoughts and overlook the co-emergence of common body sensations. Mindfulness of breath may suffice to regulate the direction of attention and address negative thoughts. In turn, this alone can help prevent depressogenic thoughts and the probability of relapse. It may also help with distancing from the onset of emotions. However, when the processing of information is sub-cortical (emotional) and thoughts are not accessible by conscious awareness (they are "automatic"), focusing mainly on breath may not be very helpful in dealing efficiently with emotions. It can even be a distraction from emotions. This is where body-scanning techniques become crucial since body sensations are always associated with emotional experiences. The more one is skilled in quickly recognizing body sensations and accepting them for what they are, the more efficient they will be in regulating emotions.

A bias towards metacognitive awareness over interoceptive awareness is also likely to limit the efficacy of the intervention to a narrower range of clinical groups or to a narrower range of symptoms within a group. The basis for this claim is the clear shift in mood and coping ability when changing from mindfulness-of-breath to body scanning practice homework. With the latter, more often than not, clients begin to feel a deeper sense of relief.

New delivery models are third- or even fourth-generation adaptations, some of which water down the components according to the characteristics of their client population. For example, a study of the effect of mindfulness on cognitive distortions or symptoms which do not seem to involve aversive body sensations, such as insomnia, rumination, or lack of problem solving ability, may use an adaptation of Segal's *et al.* (2002) Mindfulness-Based Cognitive Therapy (MBCT) model. MBCT is an adaptation of Kabat-Zinn's (1982, 1990) Mindfulness-Based Stress Reduction (MBSR) model, which is also an adaptation from traditional mindfulness meditation "... known as *satipatana vipassana* or insight meditation" (Kabat-Zinn *et al.*, 1985, p.165), tailored for pain patients.

Consistent with the traditional delivery of mindfulness meditation, Kabat-Zinn's (1990, 2005) description of the body-scan technique emphasizes the importance of paying special and systematic attention to body sensations. Its delivery through MBSR (Kabat-Zinn *et al.*, 1998) or a *Vipassana* course format (e.g., Witkiewitz and Marlatt, 2006) usually yields strong benefits for clients in crises, as well as for those in remission attempting to gain relapse-prevention skills (Segal *et al.*, 2002). Yet, scanning the body to reappraise and let go of maladaptive responses to aversive body sensations does not often appear in the method section of published articles that are supposed to be direct or indirect adaptations of MBSR.

In MiCBT, body scanning is the center of the emotional regulation principles. Since emotions manifest themselves in the form of thoughts and co-emerging body sensations, learning to remain at ease with body sensations helps minimizing emotional reactivity during crises. Reading the section on neuroplasticity in Chapter 4 will further illustrate this importance.

When people are locked into processing stressful information in the brain's subcortical areas (especially amygdala and other limbic pathways), redirecting the flow of information to the frontal lobe and regaining objectivity/"rationality" is difficult. However, it is the frontal lobe that allows the re-direction of attention, especially the cingulate cortex and other areas of the prefrontal cortex (Rueda, Posner, and Rothbart, 2005; Tang *et al.*, 2007). Therapy methods which capitalize mostly on "top-down" processing (executive functions in frontal cortical areas), like cognitive methods, are consequently not very efficient on their own during crises (Mohlman and Gorman, 2005) and psychoactive medications are often required to appease the client before they appear effective.

In addition, using a top-down approach, much mental effort will still be required from the client to challenge his or her thoughts/assumptions even after the skills in doing so have been learned. In contrast, mindfulness meditation strengthens, through neuroplasticity, pathways between frontal and limbic areas in a daily practice. This makes it increasingly possible to navigate between the two modalities during the crisis. The brain's emotional centers cannot hijack our attention as easily when the "executive control" centers in the frontal areas of the cerebral cortex are trained to accept co-emerging thoughts and body sensations through daily effort to remain equanimous. Speculatively speaking, this also implies that mindfulness-based methods which do not use mindfulness meditation (especially body scanning methods) will not affect the same pathways and therefore will not benefit from such neurobehavioral flexibility.

Moreover, a number of interventions tend to use a regular but discrete focus on the body, according to whether the salience of some sensations has increased while monitoring ongoing thoughts using the breath as an anchor. By contrast, the systematic scanning of the body taught in the traditional Vipassana method allows increasing sensitivity to subtle sensations, a lowering in the threshold of awareness. As a result, subtler distress cues can be detected consciously and earlier in the sequence of events triggering an emotion, giving the client plenty of time to respond in a conscious and preferred manner.

In a meta-analytic study, Suls and Fletcher (1985) examined the results of several meta-analyses reporting on the relative efficacy of avoidant versus non-avoidant coping styles of people faced with an imminent threat. The main finding was as follows:

- In the short term, avoidance was associated with better adaptation.
- Paying attention with an emotional interpretation, or no particular interpretational type (controls), the outcome was associated with more negative emotions and less adaptability than avoidance.
- However, paying attention with a focus on sensory representation rather than emotional processing led to better outcomes than avoidance.
- For the analysis of long-term effects, avoidance indicated better outcomes initially, but paying attention was gradually associated with more positive outcomes.

The results emphasize the important role of interpretational styles when paying attention during threatening situations. In particular, paying attention with an interpretation based on sensorimotor feedback showed the best outcomes overall. The analyses of these studies provide some evidence that emphasizing interoception during the processing of aversive events constitutes a better coping skill overall.

If studies in the area of mindfulness processing and applications are to base themselves in the essence of the approach, it is crucial that new conceptualizations do not omit the central role of interoceptive awareness and acceptance. Nor should they omit the moment-to-moment awareness that each experience, cognitive or interoceptive, is impermanent and subject to extinction.

Awareness without wisdom

Clinicians often encounter some confusion about the construct of mindfulness and the corresponding tasks they should implement as a priority. As will be emphasized later, this is partly caused by not keeping a regular personal practice. By and large, this is due to the increasing number of authors and trainers who favor some aspects of mindfulness practice over others, sometimes based on theoretical formulations.

One of the common limitations to efficient practice is the understanding that mindfulness is primarily concerned with "bare awareness of experience." However, simply remaining with bare awareness of an experience without developing equanimity does not help to address crisis properly. This is partly because people are not always given a sufficiently realistic or convincing rationale for simply being aware of painful experiences, from which they felt relieved with avoidance behavior.

Many clients with severe or chronic conditions had past experiences with mindfulness and relapsed because they were not taught sufficiently how to reappraise their experiences and thus verify the poor validity of their past unhelpful beliefs about it. In order to address crisis, MiCBT focuses on the problem at hand, including its contributing and maintaining factors.

Based on the theoretical model on which MiCBT is founded (described in Chapter 2), the principal maintaining factor of maladaptive behavior is our reaction to body sensations. Yet the client is not always aware of it because the focus of awareness may have been taught to be equally distributed across perceptual modalities together with giving a sound rationale to the client. Many therapists using a mindfulness-based approach may train clients to give equal importance to paying non-judgmental attention to sight, sound, smell, touch, taste, thoughts, and body sensations. Bare awareness of holding a pen and feeling the sensations may lead to some insight and inspiration, all of which may help prevent relapse, but when the client is about to commit suicide, it is not the most helpful skill to pull out of our clinical tool kit.

Unless clients in crisis operate at the locus of reinforcement and self-desensitize from their aversive experiences, the results are not as productive and may not stick in the long term. One of the best ways to prevent relapse is to deal with crises successfully, which is done effectively when we sustain our focus on the impermanence and impersonality of the painful experience. When impermanence and impersonality of experience is clearly demonstrated to clients, it becomes a very good rationale for letting it go.

This leads to the issue of which modality should attract most effort when addressing crisis. Since the establishment of mindfulness is traditionally applied to four modalities, "body, mind, objects of mind, and feeling," as reflected in the above discussion, should this be adapted when dealing with crisis?

Entrenched in the *Vipassana* tradition of mindfulness meditation, MiCBT teaches to focus on the experience of the client that is within the framework of their body sensations and thoughts, their mind and body. In other words, the principal focus is on the issues that lead clients to trigger or maintain clinical problems. Accordingly, in MiCBT, training modalities such as awareness of images, smells and sounds perceived in the environment, are not given priority unless they are relevant to the problem at hand. Priority of focus is given to learning how to tackle thoughts and body sensations without reacting to them. Minimizing reactivity takes precedence.

During the course of MiCBT, *clients learn that what they are reacting to is not the stimulus; it is not to the person or the external object, but to their own sensations in the body.* Once we get to a stage where increased equanimity is sufficiently helpful in dealing with overwhelming emotions, mindfulness at other modalities can be very useful in transferring the skills to daily life, like walking mindfully. Similarly, there is no urgent need to be aware of the taste of food in their mouth until the crisis is over or unless there is a specific reason for this.

For example, clients with eating disorders benefit greatly from "mindful eating" exercises, but "mindless eating" is not due to being unaware of how the food tastes. If, however, we conceptualize overeating or under-eating in terms of experiential avoidance, then the prioritization of focus on the technique makes sense. For example, if a client overeats to overcome mild anxiety, simply because sensations in the abdomen can mimic degrees of hunger, it is quite understandable for people to confuse the two. In other words, there is a learned association between eating and experiencing anxiety reduction. If clients are taught to delay eating until they have accepted the sensations and let them pass, then the choice of food, as well as the amount, tend to change. The principles of operant conditioning involved in bulimia or anorexia are being addressed and this is precisely because we focus on the locus of reinforcement, people's reaction to body sensations, rather than just the taste of food.

Undifferentiating mechanisms of action in meditative techniques

The word "meditation" can be misleading for some authors, who tend to use the term as if it embodied a set of fundamentally common principles, acting similarly on the practitioner's mental and physical processes. There are two main groups of meditation techniques: concentration meditation and analytical meditation. Concentration-based meditation techniques typically use a mantra (a sound or phrase repeated continually) or a visual object in imagination (light, shape, deity, or scenery). Among these approaches is Transcendental Meditation or "TM." The main purpose of these techniques (but not necessarily the expectation of practitioners) is generally to calm and concentrate the mind by associating with newly created sensory objects. Deep relaxation, with its known benefits (Benson, 1975), can easily be achieved.

By contrast, mindfulness meditation uses already existing and ongoing mental and physical events (naturally arising thoughts, ongoing breath, and ordinary body sensations). Its main purpose is to develop the ability to sustain attention at length and in depth in order to face any *naturally arising* experience (cognitive or somatic) objectively, and accept its occurrence by understanding its impermanent quality.

Based on the co-emergence model of reinforcement underlying MiCBT, mindfulness facilitates extinction by using sustained awareness of, and response prevention toward, automatic responses elicited by naturally occurring pleasant, unpleasant or neutral somatic sensations and their corresponding cognitive networks intruding on the meditative state. This necessarily implies increased awareness of some unpleasant psychophysiological manifestations, some of which have been misinterpreted as "side-effects" of meditation (e.g., Perez-De-Albanis and Holmes, 2000). Consistent with the present conceptualization is Linehan's (1994) description of the active ingredients of mindfulness:

> Part of mindfulness is learning to observe internal and external events without necessarily trying to terminate them when painful or prolong them when pleasant. Rather

than leaving the situation or inhibit the emotion, the individual attends to experience no matter how distressing that attention may be. This focus on "experiencing the moment" is based both on Eastern psychological approaches to reducing suffering as well as on Western theories of non-reinforced procedures as a method of extinguishing automatic avoidance of feared responses. (Linehan, 1994, p. 78)

Similarly, Hayes and colleagues have argued that behavioral disorders, such as those involving anxiety, have a lot to do with experiential avoidance (Hayes *et al.*, 1996). In line with this view and Borkovec's (1994) conceptualization of Generalized Anxiety Disorder (GAD), Roemer and Orsillo's (2002) mindfulness-based analysis of GAD proposes that GAD sufferers use worry to avoid systematically the experience of internal distress. It follows that a form of "experiential exposure" would be adequate to facilitate extinction. Mindfulness training involves precisely this sort of exposure, which may be appropriately termed "generalized interoceptive exposure."

Any method of exposure will, by definition, incur discomfort. It is also likely that a client who is not experiencing some form of momentary discomfort, early or later in the program, is probably not practicing efficiently. It is often unclear to clients, and sometimes to their guides, that mindfulness training "welcomes" discomfort and uses it as "a tool" (the feared or resented stimulus) to desensitize from it. More importantly, we teach the brain to keep processing information in the frontal cortical areas (more rational pathways) during stressful experiences, rather than letting it automatically process the information in limbic areas (emotional pathways). The more discomfort we process while maintaining equanimity, the more the brain learns to process stressful information rationally and with less discomfort.

By contrast, techniques like Transcendental Meditation (TM) tend to be highly relaxing. Similar to standardized relaxation methods, they do not involve the mere observation of the present psychosomatic phenomena, as they arise and vanish, while preventing a response; they do not include an exposure procedure. On the contrary, they wrap the existing psychophysical reality with a shielding sound or visual imagery. This constitutes ongoing sensory data forcing attention networks to process new sensory input rather than processing spontaneously emerging memories and associated sensorimotor information.

Accordingly, what seems a *side effect* in other techniques is generally seen as a *central effect* and an integral part of the extinction process in efficacious mindfulness training (see also Kostanski and Hassed, 2008, for further comments). Even though relaxing is an important means of preventing a maladaptive response, it is certainly not the goal of the mindfulness approach. Nor is mindfulness relaxing in itself. Rather, relaxation in MiCBT is the result of the increasing ability to accept an experience. It is a by-product of equanimity (more on this below).

Concentration methods are indeed very different meditation techniques and reviewers and clinicians ought to acquaint themselves with their fundamental mechanics or, as is often the case, they are likely to misinterpret some unavoidable initial effects as undesirable; just as the ill-informed observer would misinterpret the benefits of interoceptive exposure in behavior therapy (see Barlow, 2002; Craske and Barlow, 1993, for details). Reviews that are most useful take into account the important methodological, goal, and therapeutic differences between meditation approaches. Undifferentiating these aspects between meditation techniques is tantamount to assuming that all Western therapy systems work in the same way, at the same depth, with the same principles and for the same therapeutic goals.

Relaxation and Equanimity

The lack of differentiation between relaxation and meditation techniques is a major hindrance to the understanding of mechanisms of action in mindfulness. For instance, there is an essential difference in contingency factors underlying the processes of relaxation techniques and equanimity. In behavioral interventions, a standard relaxation technique is Jacobson's (1942) Progressive Muscle Relaxation (PMR), as adapted by Bernstein and Borkovec (1973). Control studies have shown that PMR is efficient in treating anxiety (e.g., Borkovec and Costello, 1993). Moreover, for some individuals, the sole implementation of PMR has resulted in various types of improvements, particularly those associated with tension and headaches (Carlson and Hoyle, 1993).

In contrast with mindfulness meditation, PMR does not formally involve awareness of, and response prevention to, continually co-emerging thoughts and body sensations. When used on its own, rather than being adjunct to hierarchical exposure techniques, PMR instructs the individual to create muscle tension and be aware of (artificially produced) body sensations, to stop creating tension. Then they are taught to be aware of the difference between *artificially* created tension and the sensation of relief when tension has stopped. Numerous scripts published for clinical or self-help applications also encourage the client to enjoy the relaxation state achieved through the exercise.

Encouragement, either implicit or explicit, to perceive or develop a preference and enjoyment for relaxed states more than tense states is likely to reinforce the client's habit of reacting with distaste to unpleasant body experiences and with craving for pleasant ones. Are clinicians innocently contributing to the client's lack of objectivity and acceptance in some measures? From a mindfulness perspective, PMR and most other relaxation techniques have to do with stopping an ongoing unacceptable state to create a more acceptable one – the individual changes the reality of the present moment because it is interpreted as unpleasant. This may act as a distraction from the actual, subtler, ongoing psychosomatic processes possibly operating below the current awareness level. It is about creating, controlling, and mastering change, rather than allowing change to operate in its own right, via an acceptance of the experience.

The sense of control derived from the PMR procedure alone may account for some therapeutic gains (Rice and Blanchard, 1982). Nevertheless, it is a limited sense of control because should another type of problem arise, with which relaxation has not been associated, overwhelming powerlessness is likely to recur. A sense of control that provides a more reliable and consistent sense of security is one that is applied and established towards our own reactive habits, and generalized across *all* situations rather than being limited to a set of symptoms and environmental manifestations. It is a function of equanimity.

How reconcilable is this analysis with the evidence that applied PMR has clinically significant benefits in treating anxiety for example, Borkovec and Costello, 1993? In particular, Öst (1988) has shown that PMR can be effective in the treatment of panic attacks, although some studies suggest it is not so (e.g., Barlow *et al.*, 1989). Craske and Barlow (1993) have argued that the mechanisms underlying applied relaxation are still unclear and that perhaps the addition of exposure techniques may further influence the positive effects of relaxation. In effect, Öst's study exposed participants to their feared body sensations whereas Barlow *et al.* did not. There is a similarity between Öst's exposure to interoceptive panic-related cues and equanimity, in that both involve exposure and response prevention.

However, equanimity is applied in a state of deep awareness and automatically creates acceptance of body sensations as they manifest dynamically with co-emerging thoughts to create an experience. This is not limited to panic-related interoceptive cues. It is possible that some individuals asked to relax muscles in a relaxation group find themselves 'unintentionally' developing some equanimity toward the sensations of tensing and relaxing muscles, a skill which, when transferred to daily life, increases tolerance of situational triggers. Hence, psychotherapeutic gains may be less due to the act of relaxing per se than to experiencing the psychophysiological manifestations encountered in the present moment with a degree of acceptance.

For instance, a recent randomized control trial by Michael Posner and his colleagues compared PMR with mindfulness meditation in eighty Chinese undergraduate students (Tang *et al.*, 2007). The forty students in the experimental group attended training in mindfulness meditation and aspects of meditation taught in traditional Chinese medicine, a combination which the authors call Integrative Body–Mind Training (IBMT). Meditation instructions were presented by CD and guided by a skilful IBMT coach.

The two groups were given a battery of tests one week before training and immediately after the final training session. Each person received 248 trials during each assessment session on a standard computerized attention test, the Attention Network Test (ANT; Fan *et al.*, (2002)). The ANT measures the ability to be vigilant, to orient attention, and to resolve conflict (executive attention). It involves responding to an arrow target that is surrounded by flankers that point either in the same or opposite direction. Cues provide information on when a trial will occur and where the target will be. The participants also filled-in the *Raven Standard Progressive Matrix* (Raven, 1938), which is a standard culture fair intelligence test; a self-report questionnaire of mood state, the *Profile of Mood States* (POMS; Shacham, 1983); and undertook a stress challenge of a mental arithmetic task. These assessments were followed by analyses of saliva samples to measure cortisol and secretory immunoglobulin A (sIgA), an antibody that plays a critical role in mucosal immunity. All participants were blind to the experimental condition. Compared with the forty students in the control group (PMR only), the IMBT group showed greater improvement in conflict scores on the ANT, lower anxiety, depression, anger, and fatigue, and higher vigor on the POMS, a significant decrease in stress-related cortisol, and an increase in immunoreactivity.

However, the MiCBT approach places PMR on a "subtlety continuum" of mindfulness exercises, on which it is one of the least subtle, albeit useful, exercises. As implemented in MiCBT, PMR is used as a means, not an end. It is usually implemented for one week, in the very first week, to direct the client's attention toward the body. In addition to increasing interoception, using PMR in the first week can help decrease the client's overall arousal levels and bring about a new sense of control in clients with difficulties such as anxiety symptoms, uncontrolled anger, and other arousal-based manifestations. In clients with difficulties associated with abnormally low arousal, such as depressed clients experiencing flat affect or dissociative symptoms, PMR can help to reconnect with the body and prepares the ground for experiential acceptance, as promoted by mindfulness training in the following weeks.

Control and acceptance in mindfulness training

Another important question is whether control and acceptance are mutually exclusive, as it often appears in popular belief. Mindfulness training demonstrates their interdependence. Clients progressively discover, within the framework of the body, that they cannot control life. Thoughts and body sensations come and go beyond their control. Unpleasant sensations do not pass away at will, and pleasant sensations are seldom present when called upon. In fact, the more we crave for a particular type of sensation (or experience) that does not manifest itself, the more aversive is the experience (Goenka, 1987).

These observations also apply to thoughts. Memories of experiences come and go beyond our control. Any resentment towards an unpleasant memory simultaneously increases the activation of unpleasant body sensations and the subsequent negative mental/behavioral reaction, which in turn serves to reinforce the pattern. In other words, if we are equanimous, we are bound to experience uncontrollable thoughts arising and passing away. In mindfulness training, the only direction for control is towards reactive habit patterns (see Hayes, Strosahl, and Wilson, 1999, for a review related to this principle). "Letting go" without interfering is the mechanism that allows the progressive extinction of these patterns.

Clients further realize that experiencing life within their own mind and body is synonymous with experiencing it in the environment. Some authors have recognized that effective control can be achieved via acceptance (e.g., Hayes *et al.*, 1999; Craske and Hazlett-Stevens, 2002; Roemer and Orsillo, 2002). Inappropriate understanding of what is healthy control is a central feature of most emotional disorders, and is likely to contribute to their maintenance.

The notion of control may also be imparted by the clinician. In some conditions, such as severe depressive episodes, some clients appear insufficiently reactive and clinicians often attempt to invite ventilation (crying). Nevertheless, there is no evidence to date that someone who *appears* numb is not actually in a reactive state. Someone whose reactivity levels are usually normal but decrease significantly during mood disturbance may simply internalize reactions – which may also be suppressed by medication. The act of suppressing emotion *is* in itself a reaction.

The co-emergence model of reinforcement assumes that reactions are either excitatory (overt) or inhibitory (self-suppressing). Accordingly, in some situations, it conceives a "lack of reactivity" as a covert reactive style that reflects the person's resistance to experiencing unpleasant body sensations. However, there is evidence that attempting to change a covert reaction into an overt one (e.g., ventilate) may be useful in reinforcing the clinician's sense of efficacy, but does not necessarily lead the client nearer to self-acceptance (Suls and Fletcher, 1985).

The belief that clients who are encouraged to freely react emotionally have a greater ability to "let go" and maintain recovery in the long-term is not based on evidence. When such "non-reactive" individuals undertake a mindfulness program, paradoxically, they appear to become *more* reactive for some time, despite the fact that emotional reactivity is discouraged. It is possible that reactions become more conscious and externalized because clients are able to relinquish the "second-order reaction" (emotional suppression) and are faced with the "first-order reaction" (the behavior they attempted to avoid, such as a fear response). The process of acceptance is facilitated by their progressive ability to accept the impersonal and impermanent nature of reactions.

Summary of Main Points

- Due to differences in construct definition and operationalization of mindfulness, several confounding factors may ultimately create differences in both applications of mindfulness training and their therapeutic efficacy. These include:
  - undifferentiated mechanisms of action
  - an emphasis on cognition versus interoception
  - the view that mindfulness is, or is not, compatible with traditional CBT
  - the notion that discomfort during mindfulness meditation is abnormal or harmful.
- There is an important difference between relaxation and equanimity. Relaxation induces a sense of relief through avoidance of distress, thereby producing a sense of agency or control over the unpleasant situation. However, this does not bring us any closer to equanimity. Tension remains unacceptable. As such, relaxation techniques can potentially promote experiential avoidance. By contrast, once the experience is accepted during mindfulness meditation, there is nothing to avoid. Relaxation becomes a by-product of equanimity.

Chapter 6

Stage 1 of MiCBT – Part II: Explaining Difficulties and Facilitating Shifts

There was never yet a philosopher
That could endure the toothache patiently.
William Shakespeare

Lost in Thoughts

From the very start of the training, clients report that the mind keeps on being distracted by unwanted thoughts. Despite their attempt to remain focused on the task, their attention "jumps" either to the past (memories) or in the future (expectations, etc), but can hardly rest in the present moment. These "temporal jumps" universally affect everyone attempting this meditation technique, which requires sustained attention to phenomena emerging from moment to moment within the framework of the body and mind. As discussed in Chapter 2, connectionist models of attention can explain temporal jumps in terms of network activation strength competing for access to awareness, which depends on the frequency and/or recency of thought activation, as well as co-emergence factors (encoded cognitions associated with body sensations).

However, this explanation may be too complex for some clients and jargon must be carefully used. Simple concepts, often described through metaphors, are helpful in clarifying thought intrusions. Below is an example of metaphoric explanation for the relentless cognitive flow.

Mindfulness-integrated CBT: Principles and Practice, First Edition. Bruno A. Cayoun.
© 2011 John Wiley & Sons, Ltd. Published 2011 by John Wiley & Sons, Ltd.

"Food for thought:" the fasting metaphor

For most clients, normalizing intrusive thoughts will help. The understanding of extinction in cognitive processes can be enhanced by using the "fasting metaphor" (Goenka, 1987; Hart, 1987). The pattern of activation and decay in neural networks described earlier is synonymous with the principles of fasting, except it involves the cognitive system.

For someone whose physical activity remains more or less constant, losing weight requires a decrease in calories intake. During the diet, the calorie needed to sustain daily activities are no longer found in the food intake, forcing the body to draw on its fat reserves. The less the intake, the more the reserves are consumed.

Similarly, the "mind" also requires some food to sustain its ongoing activity. The activity of the mind is thinking and for thinking to be maintained, it requires more thoughts. If thinking decreases significantly below the usual "amount" of thinking, the mind starts "to starve." Compared to the body, which can withstand long periods of fasting, the mind requires food after just a few moments. The mind is fasting and needs to "consume" its reserves (past thoughts) to survive. In other words, thoughts previously stored in memory are called for processing. Provided no new thoughts are generated as a response to experiencing the memory, older memories are also consumed. This metaphor has proved useful in helping clients understand the frequent overpowering intrusive thoughts during practice, and their decrease with appropriate practice.

If intrusive thoughts are too overpowering, perhaps obsessive, clients may find that using a "three-second rule" helps. This consists of an agreed limited time for the duration of distraction; in this case, three seconds. After three seconds, the client must commit to switching attention back to the breath or body sensations. The discipline involved in this task helps to sustain attention.

Dealing with Pain

Subjectivity and phenomenology

Empirical clinicians have long noticed how depressed or anxious people can perceive their symptoms or situation in a highly exaggerated way, a phenomenon usually termed "catastrophization." New clients starting MiCBT also tend to catastrophize their bodily experiences when they are very distressed. This applies especially in the presence of pain. Pain sensations can emerge for numerous reasons, including posture, old injury, and the like. However, as said the Buddha very economically, "In life, pain is not an option; suffering is."

Especially with clients who present with pain, it is essential to normalize pain. For this, it is useful to remind the client that facing pain by directing attention to the centre of the intense body sensation will first enhance pain and then decreases it as equanimity is applied in the experience. Staying at the periphery of the painful area or trying to move away from it will only appear as though it is strengthened or unchangeable.

It is far more difficult to handle pain when its experience is readily categorized as "pain," a construct to rationalize the intense physical experience, than when it is experienced *as it is*, mere body sensations with the predominance of mass (e.g., pressure), temperature (e.g., heat), and perhaps movement (e.g., throbbing). Thus, the verbal aspect of pain is a significant reinforcer for agitation and other reactivity types such as intolerance (Hayes *et al.*, 1999; Zettle and Hayes, 1986). Below is an extract of Alan Marlatt's first experience with mindfulness meditation, as he later wrote in his journal.

> At one point, the pain became almost unbearable, and I felt compelled to stretch out my legs to release the pressure. The meditation teacher instructed me to resist this strong urge to move my legs, and instead to continue sitting in the same posture while carefully observing the painful sensations I felt in my knees.
>
> At first, the pain seemed solid and unyielding in its aversiveness. After "watching" the pain for several minutes, however, I began to notice small changes. Instead of feeling one solid, unchanging block of pain stimuli, I began to notice that the pain signal changed subtly over time. Instead of one solid block of pain, careful attention showed me that the pain signal pulsed in waves of intensity that went up and down. I began to notice periods of "less pain" between pulses of more intense pain in an "in-and-out" kind of pattern. Once my awareness focused on the spaces of "less pain" that occurred between the more painful pulses, my basic attitude changed as I began to "open up" to the pain experience. Although the pain was still present, it felt less intense, as though my awareness could "see through" the pain to the other side. The spaces between the pain stimuli widened, and I felt my urge to do anything to escape or avoid the pain diminish. The painful sensations rose and fell like waves on the sea, and I was able to find a balance point between the crests of intense sensations. Of course, I was still very thankful when the meditation period was finally over and I could stretch my legs with great relief. (Marlatt and Kristeller, 1999, p. 71).

Besides a general lack of equanimity, another difficulty arises from a fundamental bias in perception that is dependent on the context of the experience, internal or external. We assume that thoughts and body sensations that are not caused by external stimulation are part of the self because they are internally generated, but since other senses, such as olfaction or sight, generally depend on external stimulation in the environment, we usually assume they are not part of the self. We say "I hate *my* thoughts" or "I can't cope with *my* pain," but we do not say "I can't handle my bad smell" when walking in proximity of a broken sewerage pipe, or "I really like my sounds" when hearing our favorite song.

Distraction versus experience

Our role is partly to help the client de-catastrophize by emphasizing the impermanent nature of all sensations. One way to achieve this is to use cognitive therapy skills, such as the Socratic dialogue, in association with behavioral tasks. For example, you can ask how long can they last without feeling pain and without moving while seated comfortably in an armchair watching a good film on TV or at the cinema. Point out that when the mind processes new information there are no aches and pains, even for long periods, whereas when no external input is provided while observing body sensations through body scanning, they can feel discomfort within a short period – sometime almost immediately. You can explain this phenomenon via the lowering of body awareness threshold (increase of awareness level, see Chapter 10). The discomfort was always there but not felt consciously until they started looking at it objectively.

Other Typical Difficulties

Drowsiness

Clients can often feel drowsy, even after a good night sleep. Sometimes this is due to relaxing deeply after some stress; sometimes the room is too warm; sometimes we sit with a full stomach. Sometimes, innocently, clients consume alcoholic drinks before their practice, simply because they practice after dinner, during which they may drink wine. A major problem with alcohol and many other intoxicants is that their action on the brain is diametrically opposite to that of mindfulness. Whereas mindfulness activates inhibitory networks in the frontal lobe, alcohol disinhibits frontal pathways.

If actions are taken to rectify drowsiness but drowsiness persists and seems to occur systematically during practice, it may be worth investigating the possibility of an avoidance mechanism. You may need to discuss it with the client and try to guide him or her in the session so that he or she remains awake for sufficient time to overcome the habit.

When drowsiness is overpowering, strategies offered to clients involve assessing and modifying the external context for practice first, such as increasing light intensity, decreasing room temperature, or sitting in a less comfortable position. It is also necessary to modify the internal context. This is more efficiently done by using a hierarchical approach, so that if an action is not effective, the client tries the next one. The first is to adopt a straighter sitting posture. If this does not improve wakefulness, encourage a slight momentary increase in breath rate and depth. If drowsiness persists, instruct the client to let a small amount of light enter the retina by not allowing sight to perceive more than 2 meters away from the knees. If this is insufficient, practicing while standing up may help. If the pattern persists, the client should go for a short walk and wet his or her face with cold water before coming back and continuing the practice. In any case, drowsiness must be neutralized before moving on to Stage 2.

Agitation

Misunderstanding the technique often leads to some agitation and the desire to distract ourselves, misinterpret the experience, and ultimately stop practicing. Note also that agitation is often an avoidance style for some clients (others prefer to fall asleep). Any reason is a good one: unsatisfactory instructions, background noise, room temperature, lack of time, etc. Often, the client starts practicing well, which results in the manifestation of emotional reactivity and agitation. This is common and expected but tends to be misunderstood by numerous clients, especially already emotionally "fragile" people.

You will note that when this initial difficulty subsides, all the reasons that served to explain agitation disappear: instructions are good, the noise is not so disturbing anymore, temperature is understood as part of the present experience, etc. Sharing your insight and experience in this matter with the client is essential to the continuation of the training.

Emotional reactivity: the "old stock" of past conditioning

Reactivity, of any sort, is precisely what this technique brings into the open. In fact, it is the automatic response we are trying to rectify by giving new parameters to the CNS (i.e., more experiences are acceptable and do not require a response). A reaction is most of the time the reflection of past conditioning, a learned response. You can help the client understand this by using a metaphor: "the stock of reactive habits" (Goenka, 1987; Hart, 1987). They must understand that when a reaction arises and is "observed" with equanimity, more are invited to arise. In other words, the old stock is slowly being eradicated because of the client's ability to be aware and equanimous. However, if they react continuously (as they usually would), the stock multiplies (i.e., their reactive habits are strengthened). At any level of mindfulness practice, there is a golden rule: the more struggling and agitated the mind, the less we can feel subtle sensations. Developing and applying equanimity leads to feeling more sensations in the body.

Moreover, language is a powerful reinforcer. During the practice, words such as "pain," "tearing apart," or other loaded words produce their own unpleasant sensations and tend to reinforce emotional reactivity.

Descriptive (rather than evaluative) words such as heavy-light, hot-cold, movement-stillness, shape-shapeless, dense-loose, etc are based on more neutral perception and minimize the usual aversive response. When clients understand the counterproductive impact that language can have on behavior, their discomfort tends to pass more easily and quickly. The effects of language on behavior and emotional reactivity has been described by Hayes and colleagues through Relational Frame Theory (Blackledge and Hayes, 2001), which serves the authors as a rationale for using mindfulness and acceptance techniques in Acceptance and Commitment Therapy.

Poor interoception

Many clients will have initial difficulties feeling body sensations. This is to be expected. However, some will not progress or even decrease their ability for interoception. This is usually due to a decrease in vigilance during practice. In some cases, clients sit in a "too comfortable" seat or posture, leading to an inability to notice when they are distracted by thoughts. To overcome the lack of sustained attention and interoception, ensure that posture is appropriate (hips slightly above the level of the knees, back and neck straight). Especially in younger individuals, it is useful to ask them to sit on one or two thick cushions on the floor rather than on a chair, as a small degree of discomfort is an advantage in the ability to "stay in the body." Whether sitting in a chair or on the floor, the hips must be slightly above the level of the knees and the back and neck must be kept straight; without straining. Also, applying "absolute immobility" during practice earlier in the program is likely to be helpful.

Confusion and doubt

1. About the technique
    "This is not normal therapy. What am I doing here – closed eyes, watching my breath and feeling sensations? What a waste of time! I expected the clinician to do things for me. …"
2. About others
    "What a strange therapist, teaching meditation … this is not what doctors or nurses do; (in a group) these people are really weird … that's not for me."
3. About oneself
    "Everybody else seems to do it well but I just can't; maybe my pain/problem is much worse than that of others; I'm so useless, I can't even sit quietly with closed eyes. …"

The most efficient way to avoid such doubts is to deliver a good rationale in the first place.

Promoting Adherence

Poor adherence to treatment

Poor adherence to treatment is the greatest cause of therapeutic failure in cognitive and behavioral interventions. Most therapy systems which promote self-awareness and behavior change are likely to produce good results if the client maintains his/her commitment to it. By and large, poor commitment relates to homework exercises. How homework exercises make sense to the client and the trade-off between applied effort and observed benefit are major factors for predicting adherence. Some clients will maintain longer commitment if the therapist-client relationship is nurturing, inspiring and solid, but most clients (especially paying clients) will prioritize the costs-and-gains factor. It is therefore important that the client perceives rapid gains, say within one to two weeks. One significant advantage of mindfulness training is its rapid positive effects on the nervous system, which in turn facilitates behavior change. This is, however, conditional upon the quality of delivery and the therapist's personal knowledge and practice of mindfulness meditation, as will be discussed in Chapter 13.

Factors promoting adherence to MiCBT

The following points are derived from Salmon *et al.,* (1998), who highlighted a number of advantages in the Mindfulness-Based Stress Reduction Program (Kabat-Zinn, 1982, 1990). These also apply to MiCBT, since it is a clearly defined program, both in content and duration (See Chapter 12).

1. Duration of treatment and length of treatment sessions are clearly specified.
2. Psychoeducation and the interactive nature of instructions are designed to evoke active participation and a passion for self-observation, inner exploration, and self-inquiry.
3. The flexibility of tasks (e.g., sitting meditation and generalized informal practice) and schedule (daily practice) is accommodating.
4. High levels of competency, clarity, commitment, empathy, and effective communication are required of instructors.
5. The experience of each patient is genuinely given importance and every attempt is made to honor it explicitly or implicitly.
6. The increase in self-control and self-efficacy due to the nature of the technique is, in itself, motivating adherence.
7. When delivered in a group, the group interventions reinforce the one to one sessions and promote a sense of cohesiveness and community; each is listened to and respected no matter what the experience may be.

Completion of Stage 1

Completion of Stage 1 is determined by increase in two domains: sense of self-control and sense of responsibility. Clients must have developed the ability to feel and withstand body sensations in most parts of the body with some degree of equanimity.

The extent to which equanimity has sufficiently increased is determined partly by the client's descriptions, partly by one or more social network members' feedback, and partly by your professional judgment.

In general, there is an increase in self-satisfaction and self-esteem that are based on greater ability to cope rather than changes with which the client is not directly involved.

Clients must also have developed a sense of responsibility for their experiences. The act of blaming the world for their current and past experiences decreases and a natural reappraisal of their difficult situation increases or starts to emerges. At this stage (generally after about three weeks of committed work with therapy) they are ready to undergo Stage 2, a stage whereby the skills developed in Stage 1 are used to address specific internal and external stressors.

Summary of Main Points

- Learning to practice mindfulness meditation inevitably leads us to encounter experiential difficulties. These include experiencing unwanted thoughts. Thoughts can appear very intrusive and difficult to manage. Clients can be helped by normalizing the process of intrusion using the "fasting metaphor" (this chapter) and explaining the three main reasons for thought intrusion (recency and frequency of neural activation, and co-emergence dynamics. Other expected difficulties include pain, drowsiness, agitation, emotional reactivity, poor interoception (often leading to boredom), and confusion and doubt. Each experience needs to be discussed with the therapist, who will then be able to explain it in terms of "normality" and suggest a useful course of action.
- Promoting adherence to treatment can be addressed in various ways. These include, but are not limited to, using the Socratic Dialogue, providing psycho-education, providing a sound *experiential* rationale, clearly specifying each step of the program and the purpose of each main skill to increase a sense of predictability, conducting the program with a high level of competency and empathy, and proposing a group format when possible if adherence to one-on-one delivery is poor.

Part III

Externalizing Skills

Chapter 7

Stage 2 of MiCBT: Mindful Exposure and Cognitive Reappraisal

You cannot control what happens to you,
but you can control your attitude toward what happens to you.

Brian Tracy

Aim of Stage 2

The principal aim of Stage 2 of MiCBT is teach clients to prevent experiential avoidance that prevents them moving towards their goals or living according to their values. This is achieved by increasing self-confidence in facing challenging situations that the client tends to avoid.

Stage 2 carefully combines core mechanisms of mindfulness meditation with imaginal and *in vivo* exposure methods to desensitize the client from an imminent distressing situation. This is very much in line with one of the primary aims of Acceptance and Commitment Therapy, which is to help clients follow their valued directions (Hayes *et al*, 1999).

Basic Notion of Graded Exposure in Behavior Therapy

Historically, the term "extinction" has been used interchangeably to mean a type of behavioral modification technique, exposure, and the natural change that takes place in a conditioned response which is not being reinforced. The age-old notion of impermanence in mindfulness training is a sophisticated elaboration of the extinction principle. Exposure procedures rely principally on extinction, the law of

Mindfulness-integrated CBT: Principles and Practice, First Edition. Bruno A. Cayoun.
© 2011 John Wiley & Sons, Ltd. Published 2011 by John Wiley & Sons, Ltd.

change. Hence, numerous authors tend to associate mindfulness training with behavior therapy.

Subjective units of distress (SUDS)

The client is asked to list a number of distressing situations (externally or internally generated) on the back page of the SUDS sheet (see Hierarchical Exposure form in Appendix C). The client is required to score the degree of distress in each situation from 1 to 100, and then choose the 5 most significantly distressing ones. These are then written down in increasing order of strength on the front of the SUDS sheet, as explained on the form.

Exposure in Imagination

Research in behavior therapy (especially covert techniques) has shown an equivalence between experiencing in imagination and experiencing in "reality." Both emotional responses and cognitive processing tend to be experienced in similar ways and may differ somewhat in a more quantitative than qualitative fashion. A nightmare may be similarly distressing to a past traumatic event, except perhaps in its intensity. Similarly, the time it takes to walk down a stairway in imagination almost equates the time required in reality. Justifiably, behavior therapists have argued that, provided the client can adequately use imagery, exposure procedures taking place either in imagination or *in vivo* can produce qualitatively equivalent effects (e.g., Cautela, 1967; Spiegler and Guevremont, 2003).

Demonstration of experiential equivalence

Although it may be sufficient to provide psycho-education, it is an advantage to demonstrate this equivalence in that it tends to increase therapist credibility and client motivation. One way of providing such evidence is to compare walking time across the room in imagination and in reality. It is best to use a stopwatch.

Ask your client, or one of the group participants, to stand against the back wall of the room while you set the watch. Ask another group member to verify that the watch is set to zero. Ask the standing person to have a good impression of the distance from where s/he stands to the opposite wall across the room. The client must be told that in a minute, you will ask the client to close his or her eyes and imagine that s/he walks across the room with a normal pace. Then you will ask the client to lift the non-dominant hand (in reality) when the dominant hand touches the wall at arrival (in imagination), and that you will stop the watch then.

When instructions are clear, proceed with the task, then ask another participant to witness (silently) the time on your watch. Write it down. Then ask your walking participant to do the walk for real this time, and time him/her again. Stop the watch and ask your witness what was the "imagery time," which you initially wrote down (s/he must say it aloud to the group), then ask him or her to read the "real time" which you just recorded. Generally, with a 7 to 12 meter-long room, the accuracy with which people match their walking speed is less than one second variance.

Overcoming Imagery Limitations

Individuals differ greatly in their ability to imagine a scene, a scent, a taste, or a sound. Experts in imagery procedures have argued that if a situation in imagination is sufficiently personalized, then anybody is able to use imagery. It is an important issue that needs consideration when implementing Stage 2. The way in which this issue is resolved in MiCBT is by the emphasis on body sensations, which tends to readily personalize the event one tries to elicit. Because both mind and body are involved in the imagery procedure, the clinician can emphasize interoception to compensate for the possible lack of imagery capability.

"Bi-polar Exposure"

Extinction as a consequence of equanimity

In many ways, being equanimous (aware and accepting/non-reactive of body sensations and thoughts) is initially a form of exposure and response prevention.

In the session, the client is asked to close his or her eyes and revisit mentally (visualize, hear, taste or smell, as appropriate) one of the least distressing events from the list made earlier. Once the situation is relatively clear, ask him or her to remember and feel the body sensations associated with the situation and be aware of both, the memory and the body state, while remaining equanimous as much as possible. When this event or situation is easier to manage, the client is asked to move up to the next situation on the list and repeat the procedure, with the same rationale. As practice develops, so does the skill. Sometimes, the distress in all noted situations is being partially extinguished at once because the general level of equanimity is increased.

In traditional systematic desensitization (Wolpe, 1969), clients learn to face a target stimulus while relaxing and preventing the unwanted response. MiCBT requires the client to desensitize from the physical sensations elicited following stimulation rather than desensitizing from the stimulus *per se*. From the start, the client knows that he or she does not desensitize from an external input (e.g., a spider). The mindfulness established during Stage 1 permits a deeper apprehension of experiential phenomena. The client feels where the problem resides and can take

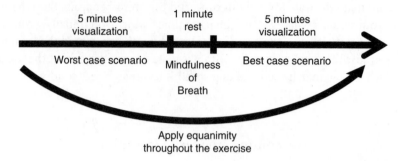

Figure 6. Pictorial representation of the bi-polar exposure procedure.

responsibility. For this reason, there is a reassurance that the client can be in control and feel safe, making the procedure more accessible to more fragile individuals; and hence minimizing dropout rates.

Additionally, the conditioned response is progressively extinguished because equanimity is developed consciously. Clients are asked to use the aversive experience as a tool, a valuable means of exposure, immediate extinction and long-term change. This is done through the repeated application of an equanimous attitude.

Homework for this stage involves desensitization in imagery and subsequently *in vivo* (real life exposure). After each daily seating (mindfulness meditation) session, the client is asked to visualise the *worst* that can happen if he or she confronts the problematic situation, for five minutes. At the same time the client is required to be aware of the body sensations associated with thoughts and to prevent any aversive reaction towards these sensations (i.e., they are encouraged to remain equanimous while catastrophizing the imaginary event). After five minutes, the client has a one-minute break, during which s/he contemplates the incoming and outgoing breath.

The client then resumes by visualizing, this time, the *best* that can happen if he or she confronts the problematic situation. The client is also required to be aware of the body sensations associated with thoughts leading to unrealistic expectations, and to prevent any craving reaction towards these sensations, which are likely to be pleasant. This is repeated several times; often four times or more depending on distress severity. The rationale for this practice is that people are not only disappointed when they obtain what they do not want, they are just as negatively affected when they do not get what they want, however unrealistic and hidden from consciousness this want may be. Figure 6 is a pictorial representation of the procedure.

After several desensitizing sessions in imagery, the client is encouraged to undergo *in vivo* exposure. This can be done with the use of a conventional Subjective Units of Distress (SUDS) sheet (see Hierarchical Exposure sheet in Appendix C). The advantage of this "bi-polar" approach to desensitization resides in its ability to provide coping skills (equanimity) before *in vivo* exposure takes place. All along, clients undergo the procedure with an already internalized locus of control and increased sense of self-efficacy derived from the generalized interoceptive exercises (body scan) required in Stage1.

Once *in vivo* exposure has been carried out successfully, clients are asked how much distress they now believe that this item (issue) is causing them, without reminding them of their first rating. Once the re-rating of the item on the SUDS sheet shows a decrease of distress, they are reminded of the quantitative difference and asked what they think is now different about both the issue and their ability to address it. The therapist carefully attends to the way in which clients spontaneously reappraise their views and encourages them to generalize their insight and skill to the remaining items on the list.

In this procedure, cognitive reappraisal comes from the experience itself, not from the therapist's direct questioning techniques. Technically speaking, we use a "bottom-up" rather than a "top-down" approach. The following section discusses the advantages and disadvantages of a top-down approach, typically used in traditional Cognitive Therapy to help clients reappraise their unhelpful beliefs.

Basic Notion of Cognitive Restructuring in Cognitive Therapy

According to Beck's influential conceptualization of cognitive therapy, "The thesis that the special meaning of an event determines the emotional response forms the core of the cognitive model of emotions and emotional disorders: The meaning is encased in a cognition" (Beck, 1976, p. 52). One asset of such an approach, still widely applied in its original formulation, is its capacity to address directly the evaluative processes, which form one of the four functions (Evaluation) in the co-emergence model proposed by MiCBT. The general emphasis underlying traditional cognitive therapy is on cognitive *content* and how this content is structured in our thinking, whereby reactions (mental, emotional or physical) are generally assumed to emanate from core beliefs activated by current life events (Beck, 1976; Beck *et al.*, 1979, Beck, Emery, and Greenberg, 1985), or by thematic philosophical flaws (Ellis, 1979, Ellis and Dryden, 1987).

Some Limitations

The rationale for cognitive therapy may be explained to anxious or depressed clients by emphasizing that reacting emotionally will only reinforce irrational beliefs and unhelpful thoughts if the reaction contributes to feeling relieved. Whereas mere intellectual understanding provides a sense of direction and motivation, especially in psychologically minded clients, it does not change the reactive habits as readily as initially thought. Beck and colleagues reviewed some assumptions underlying Cognitive Therapy with a more moderate approach on the basis that in endogenous depression, depressogenic thoughts are a characteristic of depression rather than a cause of it (Beck and Haaga, 1992; Haaga and Beck, 1995).

Although rationalizing without fully feeling the bodily experience may have some benefit, research has shown that the verbal modality is often not fruitful in the long term (see Hayes, 1994, for discussion). Some of the inconsistencies in traditional interventions that focus on the content of thoughts have been explicitly expressed by Stephen Hayes and his colleagues (Hayes *et al.*, 1999), and by many more authors since (e.g., Segal, Williams, and Teasdale, 2002).

Dimensional and modality congruence

As mentioned in Chapter 2, John Teasdale and his colleagues make a strong case for the need for dimensional congruence in therapy, which they achieve theoretically through the ICS approach. They propose that a person can experience a great deal of difficulty in attempting to think rationally while at the same time experiencing emotions, because "propositional coding" (as promoted by rational thinking) is incongruent with "implicational coding" (as promoted by schematic models). They argue that processing of information is achieved in various dimensions or "subsystems" of the overall information-processing system (Teasdale and Barnard, 1993; Teasdale, Segal, and Williams, 1995).

With traditional cognitive approaches, the experiential dimension tends to be overlooked. In particular, body sensations are generally left out of the equation unless they become an overt problem, such as symptoms of anxiety, especially those of panic (e.g., Clark, 1986).

In contrast, the co-emergence model of reinforcement underlying MiCBT places Interoception as a crucial element between core beliefs (Evaluation) and emotional reactivity (Reaction). When a core belief is stimulated, a reaction occurs because of the body sensations it creates. Although core beliefs are considered important in both MiCBT and traditional Cognitive Therapy, MiCBT gives equal importance to body sensations on the basis that *they* are the actual consequences of core-belief activation. In MiCBT, we react to those co-emerging consequences; not to the beliefs in isolation.

For a large portion of depressed and anxious individuals, research has shown that traditional cognitive therapy is efficient in helping restructure the *content* of their beliefs, especially after the crisis has passed or with the help of pharmacotherapy. However, it also assumes that a client can use reasoning to address the dynamics of emotional reactivity, i.e., *as it emerges*. This is likely to be a disappointing assumption for distressed clients because the brain functions, or "modalities," involved in this attempt are incongruent. Using neuropsychological testing in a sample of older adults with generalized anxiety disorder, Mohlman and Gorman (2005) demonstrated that participants whose cognitive abilities (executive functioning), located in prefrontal areas of the cortex, were intact could benefit from CBT treatment, whereas participants whose executive functions where less functional did not benefit from CBT. They concluded that executive skills are important for successful applications of CBT.Whereas thinking rationally with factual reasoning requires exerting effort in frontal and prefrontal areas of the cerebral cortex, especially in the left hemisphere, emoting is more associated with activation of sub-cortical (limbic) pathways and right prefrontal areas of the cortex, especially in the right hemisphere (see Davidson *et al.*, 1990, for a review; see also Davidson *et al.*, 2003, for implications of mindfulness training). Hence, we can easily fall in the trap of expecting distressed clients to use a specific modality, the so-called "executive functions" in the frontal lobe, to deal with negative emotions while the brain is processing information in another modality, the emotional brain, where much of the accessible information is experienced through body sensations. The major limitation is that interoceptive information is hardly accessible by executive functions unless one is trained to use the pathways that link both modalities, as taught in mindfulness training.

Accordingly, mindfulness training first addresses the lack of agency over emotions by processing information with immediate reappraisal of the emerging emotional experience. This allows the client's attention to be partly depleted from limbic areas and reallocated to frontal areas. Once the interoceptive aspects of emotion are successfully accessed and handled, attempting to rationalize our way through the conflict is much more likely to succeed. The pathways to the cortex, especially left prefrontal, are more accessible. Then, one can realistically envisage using frontal lobe methodologies, such as the Socratic method, with success.

In summary, one reason for the efficacy of mindfulness training may lie in its "dimensional congruence" with the client's experience and the corresponding modalities activated in the brain. If, for example, the client becomes aware of some anxiety, his or her experience is necessarily and directly linked to body sensations. At the same time, he or she is, more often than not, disconnected from the cognitive dimension when peak intensity is reached. It seems easier to deal with arousal by operating on it directly by remaining aware and equanimous towards body sensations, than it is by operating at a dimensionally incongruent (cognitive) level by trying to access automatic thoughts. Until arousal symptoms subside to a level that is acceptable to the client, the cognitive dimension is hardly accessible – unless the client has progressed in developing equanimity.

Dynamic detection versus retrospective retrieval

In traditional cognitive therapy, each maladaptive response is preceded by distorted automatic thoughts (Beck, 1976). The neurobehavioral model of reinforcement underlying MiCBT is not in full agreement with this proposition. Although MiCBT also places an evaluative system between the stimulus detection and the response (See Chapter 2, Figure 1), it does not assume that evaluations are fully formed thoughts. Empirical research in cognitive psychology has shown the existence of multiple levels of cognition and the need to distinguish between the effects of thoughts and emotions at various levels of the system (Greenberg and Safran, 1984, 1987; Laventhal, 1984; Barnard and Teasdale, 1991; Teasdale and Barnard, 1993).

Accordingly, Williams *et al.*, (1997) have emphasized the need to widen the locus of therapeutic interventions:

> Because of the dissociation that can take place between different levels, there is a danger that therapeutic work at one level will not affect other levels. For example, therapies that operate at the conceptual level cannot necessarily be assumed to have effects at the sensorimotor level. Current 'cognitive' methods of treating depression involve such a complex of component techniques that it is difficult to disentangle scientifically which components are working at which level. We currently need a more varied range of measures relating to the different cognitive levels at which emotional disorders can be manifest." (Williams et al., 1997, p. 13)

The mere fact that a thought pattern has become automatic (i.e., subconscious) suggests that dynamic (immediate) detection is very difficult to achieve, especially during stress or emotional experiences (see Laventhal and Scherer, 1987, for discussion).

The role of automaticity is to increase cognitive efficacy by saving time and mental effort, allowing actions to proceed below the level of awareness while attention resources can be allocated elsewhere. MiCBT proposes that a lower amount of processing networks and co-emergent body sensations are sufficiently activated to trigger a rapid response. Since old habits of responding do not require semantic processing, it seems unlikely that fully formed ideas – as exemplified so often in typical "dysfunctional thoughts records" given to clients – are detectable online. It is far more likely that the "automatic thought" is partially retrieved, or indeed reconstructed by reasoning it out, following the event. For online detection, one has to be mindful of the simultaneity of external and internal phenomena, and such a state of mind is diametrically opposite to an agitated state. Mindfulness and emotional reactivity are mutually exclusive states.

One may ask whether this difference of a few minutes or seconds between the reaction to the event and the thought is of any relevance to the client's understanding and progress. It is very relevant indeed, because between the actual evaluation stage (automatic thought) and the retrieval (or reconstruction) analysis, the reaction has already taken place. If the reaction is destructive, these few seconds or minutes delay become even more relevant.

One may also ask what difference does this make in terms of treatment. It is common to observe friends, colleagues, or clients repeating the same undesired behavior and apologizing for it, but it is often too late. We may be very aware of some of our schemas while remaining incapable of preventing reactive habits, whether cognitive, emotional or behavioral.

This difference is significant for treatment efficacy and duration. First, the client attempting to record dysfunctional thoughts often keeps on reacting negatively and rationalizing the reaction (i.e., when it is too late). Consequently, a recurring outcome in the early stages of traditional Cognitive Therapy is a growing sense that the procedure is either ineffective or too complex, or that he or she is, "once more," unable to achieve even such a simple task. In depressed clients, the typical sense of failure and worthlessness may be reinforced by their inability to prevent their reactions and the possible negative feedback from significant others.

Since therapeutic progress is enhanced by small successes (Larimer, Palmer, and Marlatt, 1999), it is beneficial to prevent reactions by detecting the preceding automatic thoughts *online*. One of the immediate benefits is an increased sense of being in control. One way in which this is facilitated is through the act of attending to body sensations co-emerging with thoughts, as proposed by the mindfulness approach. Dynamic awareness enables earlier detection of psychophysiological changes following stimulation, a short period when the negative experience is sufficiently manageable to enable some inhibitory control over learned reactions.

The Concept of Irrationality

It is because the Western notion of irrationality is dependent upon factors such as personal and cultural values that it cannot be based solely on logic. Should we tell an 82 year-old depressed client who is afraid of dying that his life-long passionate belief in the Bible may be contributing to his irrational fears? Should we ask a 44 year-old depressed client, recently migrated from India with her family, to reconceptualize her sense of injustice and abandonment by the workers' compensation system following her experience of being bullied and rejected at work? A notion of irrationality that is universally valid is often beyond our grasp and attempting to challenge unhelpful views of a situation in the traditional cognitive fashion can push clients further away from their experience, the therapy and the therapist.

From a mindfulness perspective, clinging to any internal event that contributes to suffering, whether a thought or body sensation, is an irrational act, emerging from a lack of mindfulness. Similarly, generating negative thinking that can potentially harm others by its likely manifestation into a verbal or physical response is unavoidably hurting the negative thinker first; it emerges in the form of unpleasant body sensations and aversive reactions. To perpetuate suffering (as experienced via body sensations) while at the same time attempting to escape from what seems to be causing it (e.g., arguing over the selfishness of a partner in order to "change him/her") seems irrational indeed. Put in a different way, mindlessness and irrationality go hand in hand.

Another universally applicable notion of irrationality is the tendency to act (mentally or behaviorally) without taking into account the object of one's action. The action, and even the actor and the object are of changing nature. To the non-practitioner of mindfulness, this may sound more philosophical than based on empiricism, but practitioners will readily grasp daily reality of impermanence. If an experiential approach is the chosen means for learning about oneself, then the notion of irrationality necessarily becomes associated with the notion that people react to unpleasant bodily experience, rather than to the trigger. It is the trigger that provides evidence for irrationality. If irrationality is ecologically grounded in such a way, the client recognizes more easily that it does not make sense to produce and maintain thoughts that generate unpleasant experiences.

Cognitive Reappraisal as a Consequence of Mindfulness

A common feature in traditional cognitive-behavioral models and most mindfulness-based approaches is the attempt to facilitate cognitive reappraisal to decrease unhelpful thinking and emotional reactivity. However, there is an important difference between the traditional context of challenging flawed thinking and the way it is used in MiCBT. This is mainly due to a difference of context from which each approach investigates cognitive flaws.

Reappraisal from experience

Cognitive reappraisal in MiCBT draws from the phenomenology of mindfulness. The problem is not the thoughts, nor their content, but our reaction to the experience of thoughts. It is the reaction to a thought which reinforces the thought. In particular, MiCBT questions the nature of thoughts and their co-emerging body states. Secondly, it focuses primarily on the processing mechanism of thoughts (see Chapter 2), rather than their contents. The primary focus on process pertains to the skills developed with mindfulness meditation, which is the main activity at the start of MiCBT (Stage 1). However, MiCBT does not endorse the view that the two points of focus (content and process) are mutually exclusive and that challenging unhelpful beliefs is not constructive. Rather, MiCBT proposes that cognitive flexibility must be increased sufficiently to allow wider and deeper appraisal of an emerging thought.

For instance, there is a situation very familiar to traditional cognitive therapists in which the client is asked to stay with the breath and observe the changeable nature of thoughts. An important part of the practice is to verify whether a distressing thought is disturbing when observed non-judgmentally. Another is to verify the belief that we have to address its content for it to go away. Clients come to realize that a thought is neither uncomfortable when it is seen for what it is (just a thought) nor permanent if we let it pass.

Furthermore, the reappraisal of physical discomfort encountered during the early stage of body-scanning is achieved in a very similar way. By developing better understanding of the processing of information, the content is easily reappraised because the emotional load usually associated with cognitive content is being addressed with body-scanning techniques. In other words, the view about an issue changes through the experience itself, a process often called "bottom-up" processing, and is not restricted to changing through "top-down" processing, whereby the meaning of the belief is the only focus.

Reappraisal of content

However, with MiCBT, it is sometimes very appropriate to use cognitive restructuring on its own, even though it seems inconsistent with mindfulness training. For example, for some clients, the degree of preparedness for change is not strong enough to overcome the underlying belief that they will not be able to cope with the homework requirement of the 30-minute sitting meditation practice twice daily. In this case, a traditional cognitive approach can be the method of choice, whereby changing the meaning or the belief is assumed to change behavior.

I remember the case of a 10-year old client, a girl who had suffered from Generalized Anxiety Disorder since age 5, about half of her life. The young girl, her mother and I agreed that both of them would practice together twice daily, as per the model requirement. This went very well for the first two weeks. But the mother felt she was too busy to keep up with the rhythm and progressively dropped out of daily practice. The girl continued to practice by herself once a day until our next session. It became obvious that the mother's own stress and anxiety had been reinforcing the child's anxiety and avoidance behavior but I felt at the time that the best I could do was to focus on the child, while making attempts to model change in the mother.

While the mother was in the room with us, I used the Socratic dialogue with the child to help both of them reappraise their views.

THERAPIST: You say it is too hard to get up in the morning to do your practice, even for 10 minutes, because you might arrive late at school, is that right?

CLIENT: Yes, I tried but it doesn't work; I'm too tired.

The mother supported this view, "Yes twice a day is really too much for her ..." reinforcing the child's belief.

THERAPIST: I recall that last week you said that you visited a very nice and very big house and that you were very excited because it has a big pool and lots of space to play. Is that right?

CLIENT: Yes, and Mum and Dad really like it too but they say it is very expensive so I don't know if we'll get it.

THERAPIST: Sounds like a very nice place. You also said that it was a little further out in the country. How far out is it from your current house?

CLIENT: About 20 km.

THERAPIST: And how long did it take to drive back from that big house to your current house?

CLIENT: Maybe 10 minutes?

THERAPIST: So you are saying that if your parents could buy this house you would be happy to live there even though you would need to get up 10 minutes earlier to go to school every morning?

The girl was very smart and began to smile, realizing where I was going with this.

THERAPIST: So now there are no more problems getting up earlier but a minute ago you believed getting up 10 minutes earlier in the morning was too much for you. Do you still believe it would be too much if you were very motivated?

CLIENT: Mmmm, maybe not.

After I asked her what were the differences between the two situations, I used motivational arguments:

THERAPIST: Ok, you say the morning practice is hard but the house would be very fun. That's a good point, but remind me why you're here.

CLIENT: Because I'm afraid of dying all the time and I think there will be terrorists at school and the bridge will break and we will die in the car …

THERAPIST: And do you think you will fully enjoy the new house if you stay with all those fears?

CLIENT: I don't think so.

THERAPIST: Out of 10, how much do you think your life would be happier if you didn't have all those fears?

CLIENT: 10 out of 10!!

THERAPIST: Yes, it would be very different then. And would you say 10 out of 10 even if you stay in your current house?

CLIENT: Yep! Anywhere!

THERAPIST: And if you move to the new house but you can't change your worries and fears, out of 10, how much do you think your life would be happier?

CLIENT: Maybe 5 out of 10?

THERAPIST: Right, so what do you think is the most important to you at the moment, getting up 10 minutes earlier for the new house or for changing how you feel every day?

CLIENT: Changing how I feel.

THERAPIST: Ok, so what would you like to do for the morning practice? Do we give it up or do we have another go and see what happens by next week?

CLIENT: I'll try again.

This client had no problem reappraising her view and her mother eventually encouraged her by finding new strategies. Two weeks later, we agreed on spending 20 minutes in the morning and keeping her 30-minute session in the evening. Four months later, she lost her diagnosis and didn't require anxiolitic medication anymore.

This real case illustrates how it can be very useful to use cognitive reappraisal to help other aspects of treatment. In MiCBT, its use depends on the circumstances and theoretical rigidity can weaken the efficacy of the treatment or even lose the client. There is no need "to throw the baby out with the bathwater." The decision about reappraising content rests on the understanding of context. In the context of formal practice of mindfulness meditation, we ask clients not to confuse content with mechanism. Although the focus should not be on thought content during practice, in daily life, as well as when we discuss issues with clients, there is nothing wrong in challenging the content of a thought, especially when clients are learning that thoughts are not worth clinging to. There is no need for extremes. In MiCBT, we really try to integrate acceptance and change; to find a middle way.

From catastrophic wholes to acceptable parts

A major assumption targeted in traditional mindfulness training is the erroneous notion that emotions are *actual* entities. When a client assumes, "I am justified in being very angry because my wife is so unfair," the traditional cognitive approach is to challenge a number of assumptions, for example the person's views about the expectation that others must be fair. As discussed earlier, the focus is largely on content, with an understanding of the patterns with which the content of cognitive distortion is being processed; e.g., generalizing, minimizing, or personalizing such themes as justice or blame. It assumes that the emotions will change when the meaning on which the thought is based changes.

When using MiCBT, the mechanisms of emotion are also targeted, not just thought content and patterns, which are targeted from Stage 2 onwards. As in the example above, the client would be asked: "How do you know that what you are experiencing is anger, and not joy? What are the experiential differences?" Frequently the therapist asks questions such as "Keeping your eyes closed, can you observe and describe as precisely as possible what anger is made of for you?," or "Where in the body are these sensations located." The client is usually shown how body sensations arise and pass away as a function of the ability to let the blaming thoughts go and of the experiential acceptance of the sensation. The therapist helps the client to experience how body sensations and thoughts continuously interact "in the background," how they are impersonal and impermanent in nature, and how an emotion is actually made of many parts that we can easily learn to handle. In sum, an emotion is the experience of the combination of one or more intense thoughts and associated body sensations.

From an experiential point of view, what differentiates an emotion from a common judgmental thought is the intensity of the thought and body sensations. Thus, it is likely that experiences of "non-emotional" judgmental thoughts and emotions lie on the same continuum, a continuum of experiential intensity. Through the practice of mindfulness (esp. body scanning), the client comes to an understanding that the whole emotion always seems bigger, more intense, and more frightening, than the sum of its parts. The Gestalt notion of whole/parts relationship (that "the whole is greater than the sum of its parts") is a useful one to consider.

The MiCBT approach endorses the Eastern view (and Albert Einstein's view) that wholes exist only conventionally, within the context of the human capacity for sensing and perceiving the world, but do not ultimately exist. Wholes are systems made of interactive parts (Capra, 1997). It is not surprising that trying to cope with the whole of what we call an "emotion" (numerous interactive subsystems) is so difficult for many people.

When learning to practice mindfulness meditation, clients find it easier to cope with a panic attack, intense anger, or even extreme physical pain. They do this by learning to decompose an emotion. They are more able to reappraise the automatic activation of the four main processing components looping rapidly to produce the sense of an emotional entity, such as "a fear" (see Chapter 2).

A client may even realize the crucial role of common language in promoting emotional reactivity; whereas "pain" is not usually acceptable, "heaviness," or "heat" is. Similarly, while "panic" is unacceptable to most, the experience of tingling and other body sensations are acceptable – note that naming such as "pins and needles" also assumes threatening wholes which do not exist: there are no pins and needles in the hands, just sensations of sharpness, motion, etc.

Thus, even the terminology used by clients is challenged to promote more objectivity in order to decrease cognitive distortions such as catastrophization and personalization. This is done via "bottom-up" as well as "top-down" methods. For the client, the increasing ability to investigate and cope with every aspect of an experience is not based on philosophical belief. It is enabled by their daily practice of mindfulness training, during which they discover and learn to accept the co-emerging dynamics of their own mind and body, from moment to moment.

Taking change into account

Additionally, with MiCBT, re-evaluation of thinking and feeling habits takes into account a universal law, the inescapable reality of change (Fleischman, 1986, 1999; Goenka, 1987; Hart, 1987; Kabat-Zinn, 1990; Marlatt, 2002). The basic premise of the mindfulness approach is that the personal realization that this natural law operates within ourselves facilitates change in the foundations of thinking and behavior patterns, so that we begin to processes information according to natural laws, in line with a more objective reality. The notion of intrinsic change is the basis of cognitive reappraisal and reality testing in the MiCBT approach, and is central to the development of equanimity (see Marlatt and Kristeller, 1999, for Marlatt's account of personal experience during Vipassana meditation).

By itself, the understanding that any body sensation is an indication of change (Fleischman, 1994; Hart, 1987) elicits the reappraisal of clients' suffering. When the universal reality of impermanence is *actually* experienced, from moment-to-moment, some form of detachment from worldly matters and from the limited sense of self is a natural consequence. The profound change that often takes place with mindfulness training is not activated by the therapist's philosophical arguments about irrationality or persuasion techniques (see Ellis, 1979, 1991, for details). Rather, change operates naturally with the *experiential* realization that nothing so impermanent can be regarded as an intrinsic entity.

Re-evaluating the Self-Concept

Reappraising the self-concept

Typically, in depression, the reported negative assumptions are abundant in "I" and "My" statements. Assumptions such as "I can only be happy if I please others" can only have a long lasting effect if this sense of self is preserved in spite of its changing nature.

How do we confuse an ever-changing state of being with a fixed identity in the first place? From a perceptual standpoint, the provenance of the stimulus may be central to how people identify with an experience. In the previous chapter, I mentioned that when we experience a stimulus that is generated "externally," outside our body and thoughts, such as smell or sight, we tend not to identify with it. In contrast, when we experience stimulation that originates internally, such as a though or a body sensation, we tend to perceive it as part of our self. We may justified in thinking, "I hate my pain and my negative thoughts," but we rarely think, "I hate my sight" when disliking a visual scene.

Since we are not educated in perceiving the internal context of our experiences equally in terms of perceptual events, we readily identify with the experience. When we train ourselves to perceive thoughts and body sensations less judgmentally and less reactively, they appear increasingly as they are, perceptual information, and we sense them much like other senses perceive odor, taste, sight, etc., with a degree of detachment. Mindfulness leads us to identify less with internal experiences, allowing some distance between painful experiences and the self-concept. It becomes possible to be fully aware of an internal experience while not assuming it is part of our self.

The lack of conscious experience of body sensations, together with a deep-rooted philosophical concept about the sense of self, reinforced by social norms and cultural affiliation, contribute to this costly misconception. It would therefore make sense for an effective therapy system to ensure that its working model does not reinforce the belief in a fictitious sense of self, while remaining sufficiently flexible to avoid aggravation of already disordered thoughts in severe clinical cases. Understandably, the rationale that most of our emotional difficulties are the price we pay for cherishing our sense of self-concept, must be carefully explained and demonstrated through the principles of co-emergence (coupling of evaluation and interoception), as it will help both clients and therapists to stay grounded in the experience – rather than philosophically discussing the ephemeral nature of the self.

Following a sufficient number of sessions (generally 4 to 5 weeks into MiCBT), there is little difficulty for most individuals to understand and experience the impermanent nature of one's sense of self. Typically, clients realize that "If the process by which body sensations and thoughts come and go is beyond my control, they cannot be truly mine," and "If neither my body sensations nor my thoughts are truly mine, then my whole being, including my feelings and physical body, is in a constant state of change and what I call "I" is just as impermanent." Hence, becoming increasingly mindful of "what is," incurs an increased understanding of "what is not." The natural consequence is cognitive reappraisal.

Summary of Main Points

- The principal aim of Stage 2 of MiCBT is to learn to prevent experiential avoidance that stops clients moving towards their goals or living life according to their values. This is achieved by increasing self-confidence while facing challenging situations that they may otherwise tend to avoid.
- This approach carefully combines the core components of mindfulness meditation (experiential awareness and equanimity) with exposure methods well established in Behavior Therapy. In particular, bi-polar exposure (BPE) combines self-guided imagery to avoided situations with equanimity. BPE is typically used in four sequential eleven-minute sessions, placed at the end of each mindfulness meditation practice, before following up with *in vivo* exposure.
- The aim of BPE is to desensitize the client to an imminent distressing situation sufficiently before he or she proceeds with real life exposure more easily, confidently, and skillfully. This method does not necessitate standard graded exposure for each avoided situation, thereby saving a significant amount of time in therapy, while addressing a broad range of issues.
- Therapy systems that do not directly rely on sensory experience are both dimensional and modality incongruent. Dimensional congruence is possible when the therapy method directly addresses the actual experience of the client. For example, attempting to be rational (cognitive dimension) to reduce emotional reactivity (emotional/somatosensory dimension) is using a means that is incongruent with the problem, thereby creating unnecessary complexities in the intervention. Accordingly, incongruent methods use incongruent brain modalities. In the case of standard Cognitive Therapy, the emotional client is expected to use complex analytic skills produced in left and mid-frontal/prefrontal regions of the brain while much of their mental resources are being processed in emotional pathways between right prefrontal and subcortical (limbic) regions of the brain. In contrast, mindfulness-based methods are both dimensional and modality congruent.
- In mindfulness training, cognitive reappraisal takes place as a consequence of experiential insight. MiCBT makes use of both Socratic questioning ("top down") and experiential ("bottom up") means of reappraising unhelpful beliefs.
- Reappraising the sense of self in terms of experience enhances experiential acceptance and promotes flexibility.

Chapter 8

Stage 3 of MiCBT:
Interpersonal Mindfulness

I have striven hard not to laugh at human actions,
Not to weep at them, nor to hate them, but to understand them.
Baruch Spinoza

Human beings do not keep their emotional states to themselves. Whether we feel happy, sad or angry, our experience hardly goes unnoticed. In one form or another, we usually let our emotions permeate through and affect others. In Stage 3, clients are reminded of this unavoidable connection with others, however subtle it may be, and of the potential consequence of unskilled interactions. The ability to direct the focus of attention narrowly inward and take responsibility for our experience during Stage 2 is now expanded outward. Stage 3 is a coherent expansion of the previous stages. Whereas the two previous stages required a predominance of self-observation, Stages 3 and 4 necessitate a skillful decentering of attention from the self and towards others. This chapter first outlines the relationship between interpersonal interactions and the mechanisms underlying suffering. We then look at various ways in which MiCBT integrates mindfulness skills and CBT principles to improve these interactions. We start by drawing on an important theory of how we come to identify ourselves with social categories or groups.

Social Identity Theory

The central tenet of Social Identity Theory (Tajfel and Turner, 1979; Haslam *et al.*, 1996) is that people categorize themselves (self-stereotype) and others into distinct groups: an "in-group" with which they identify and actively favor and an

Mindfulness-integrated CBT: Principles and Practice, First Edition. Bruno A. Cayoun.
© 2011 John Wiley & Sons, Ltd. Published 2011 by John Wiley & Sons, Ltd.

"out-group" which they tend to discriminate against in order to increase self-esteem. This categorization process occurs not only at a social level of abstraction (in-group versus out-group membership), but also at a subordinate personal level, as a single individual (different from other individuals in the in-group), and super-ordinate level (human in-group).

Any rewarding group affiliation can lead to the formation of an in-group (e.g., participating in a new therapy group). The perception of sharing our fate with other individuals is also a powerful catalyst for in-group formation (Horwitz and Rabbie, 1982). For example, someone diagnosed with AIDS may begin to associate his or her fate with that of other AIDS sufferers, associate with them by means of trust associations or foundations, and may even become an AIDS activist. Thus, the new membership of the "AIDS sufferers" group is facilitated by a regrettable fate. The same applies to alcoholism (e.g., Alcohol Anonymous membership), depression and other conditions, as well as social status and socioeconomic background.

Stage 3 and the Theory of Social Identity

The client's discovery that suffering is actually a human condition that no one escapes creates a sense of common fate that is both reassuring and reuniting. As insight increases with mindfulness practice, psychological pain perceived in others develops and creates an interdependence of fate in which everyone joins at a super-ordinate level (a larger in-group), the human group. Rich or poor, intelligent or simple-minded, attractive or not, every human being is seen as being subjected to the inescapable suffering caused by unawareness – despite the countless distractions people use to evade this common fate.

It follows that, since people have a strong experience in common (i.e., mental, emotional or physical discomfort), the probability of interpersonal conflict is reduced. For example, when a depressed son realizes that he and his angry father share the common fate of being caught in the loop of perpetual reinforcement of reactivity (and therefore unhappiness), tension can be more easily defused.

Someone generating maladaptive anger is seen by a mindfulness-trained individual as a person who does not know that reacting to body sensations (such as heat) and anger-perpetuating thoughts can only result in more anger in the future. It follows that it is the angry person who is seen to be the sufferer and the victim of his or her own unawareness-based insecurity and frustration. Having gained this insight, the client does not need to argue or feel victimized. On the contrary, knowing or remembering how costly this lack of understanding had been for him or her in the past, the client can now genuinely generate acceptance and assertiveness. Greenberg has depicted the consequences of acceptance in social settings as follows:

> Change in experience over time is the natural order; stasis is what needs explanation … The more people accept themselves, in their full complexity, the more they change. The affective consequences of acceptance are that people become more understanding

and compassionate, both toward themselves and toward others. When people are aware of whatever feeling or reaction they currently experience, they are unified, integrated beings in that moment. Acceptance of experience thereby enhances internal cohesion and inner harmony. The behavioural consequences of self-acceptance are that once a feeling is fully in awareness, and is fully accepted, then it can be coped with like any other situation. (Greenberg, 1994, pp. 54–55)

As you recall from Chapter 5, Margolis and Langer (1990) define mindfulness in terms of a continuum and its psychosocial implications. They argue that mindfulness is a cognitive state of continuous category formation that enables us to maintain an awareness of the present and create new approaches to situations. We can explore situations from several perspectives, rather than being bound by previously formed rigid attitudes. On the other hand, *mindlessness* is a state of cognitive, emotional and behavioral automaticity in which we rely rigidly on categories and distinctions created in the past. Based on a formalized set of rules and attitudes, we automatically classify each new event or situation into a pre-existing category, a template of how things or people "should" be. As this categorization process is reinforced by our social environment, it increasingly defines our attitudes and behaviors. Inevitably, this has profound interpersonal implications, such as discrimination against one another.

In addition, mindfulness may affect group categorization in other ways. The co-emergence model would predict that perception of threat decreases sensory-perceptual ability and increases evaluative thinking. This would result in preserving detailed discrimination of in-group members (non-threat = greater perception and therefore better recall) and broader or dull discrimination of out-group members (potential threat = lesser sensory perception and poorer recall).

Using Stages 1 and 2 to Understand Others

In Stage 3 of MiCBT, the client learns to extend his or her understanding of him or herself to other human beings, with a focus on significant others. It is a stage of interpersonal facilitation, in which clients are able to decenter their attention from themselves and re-focus on others. This is consistent with John Teasdale and colleagues' view that depression decreases when people decrease their over-focusing on themselves (Watkins, Teasdale and Williams, 2000).

Ultimately, clients completing Stage 2 have acquired a good understanding that everything changes (their experiences as well as those of others). Stage 3 consolidates and expands this understanding in social settings for the purpose of better understanding and improving interpersonal relationships, and help prevent relapse.

Developing "experiential ownership"

Having learned to observe internal events more objectively, clients are now trained to take more responsibility for their unpleasant experiences and their perpetuation (reinforcement through spontaneous reactivity). Reminding the client of the co-emergence model of reinforcement (Chapter 2), the therapist may begin to explain the importance of what I termed "experiential ownership" in the context of interpersonal facilitation. Blunt statements, such as "Unless someone collides with you or otherwise physically touches you, no one can possibly create a body sensation within you; nobody can cause your experience from the outside," can be very effective once the client understands Stage 1 well.

The main home exercise shown to facilitate this skill is as follows: clients are asked to find themselves in a stressful interpersonal situation and first detect and take full responsibility for ("own") their own body sensations within only a few seconds while using their equanimity skills, no matter what is presented before them. Then, they are asked to "disown" responsibility for their interlocutor's experience. They learn to reject responsibility for others' reactivity with a more rational stance, understanding how a person's judgmental thoughts create aversive bodily cues to which they react blindly (co-emergence dynamics). They are asked to think it, but not necessarily express it, with a real understanding of the other's suffering as he or she reacts, thus demonstrating a degree of empathy.

The exercise consists of exposure to at least two potentially stressful interpersonal situations the client expects to encounter in the coming week. Once client and therapist agree on two adequate target situations, the client commits to the task and if possible commits to perform the exercise in as many other contexts as possible for the whole week. Using insight and experiential acceptance, clients learn not to react to others' reactivity.

Hypothesizing about the actual experience of significant others

Understanding that others are also prone to react automatically to body sensations, just as they were before their own training, is a great step towards conflict resolution and empathy. As the client moves further towards an increased ability for interpersonal facilitation, s/he is given tasks which compare the consequences of their usual reactivity to another person with the effects of remaining mindful and equanimous on the interaction they have with that person.

The following exercises are designed to first help the client formulate realistic hypotheses about the internal experience of a significant other when this person entered into conflict with the client or someone else:

- Use an actual event, preferably a recent one, as it is more likely to be intact in memory.
- Question the event in detail. Use imagery to recall it and point out the importance of "owning" and not reacting to the body sensations which co-emerge with the memory of the event. The Diary of Reactive Habits (Appendix C) can be used to facilitate the process:
  - "How did it feel in your body when you were angry at your father because he told you these things in front of your friends? ... Take your time, examine

the predominance of some sensations ... Where is the most unpleasant sensation in your body? ... What is it made of? ... Mass? Temperature? Movement? A shape, a form? A combination of these? ... Take your time and try to be very objective when you describe your experience, keeping your eyes closed."

- Help the client understand how the other's emotion is likely to have produced body sensations similar to those they have experienced with their own emotion:
  - "... Well done, now keeping your eyes closed, try to describe the sensations your father might have felt in his body when he was so angry ... take your time, describe them as clearly and precisely as you did with your experience ... even though you are just trying to guess how it actually felt for him."

This approach requires the client to verify the validity of his/her hypothesis about others' experience and train their ability to remain equanimous and with a degree of empathy if possible. It is essential at this stage that the client sees the benefit of the exercise and the potential long-term benefits in implementing the skills in their day-to-day life. For this, the client is given exposure tasks to perform during the forthcoming week:

- Help the client to fill in the SUDS form (Appendix C) with interpersonal situations he or she would avoid or deal with inappropriately. Sequence the list of items following the instructions on the form.
- Help set up the experiment by simulating and reviewing the two least distressing situations in detail during the consultation. These tend to attract a rating of 20–60% distress.
- Role-play in order to verify their ability to remain aware of, and equanimous towards, body sensations during the challenging interaction. The therapist does not hesitate to be as realistically challenging as possible here, so that exposure, and perhaps some desensitization, can already take place. Clients must feel confident that they can do the task before they leave the session.
- It is also likely that they will need to improve their ability to defuse others' tension using, as a rationale, their understanding that the other person's confrontational attitude is a reflection of the unawareness of his or her reactivity and therefore his or her suffering.
- They must remember from the previous week's exercise their and others' responsibility.
- They are asked to practice the bi-polar exposure skills learned during Stage 2. For this, they are asked to visualize the worst (5 minutes) then the best (5 minutes) that can happen as they undergo *in vivo* exposure to their SUDS items, while at the same time prevent reaction to the body sensations elicited by the aversive (then pleasant) scenarios.
- They are asked to expose themselves to the target in imagery for at least 4 sessions after each mindfulness training session (i.e., two days if they meditate twice daily), and then perform the exposure *in vivo*.

- Immediately after, ideally on the 3rd day following the therapy session, the client is encouraged to start the same schedule with a second SUDS item. This enables the client to expose themselves to two items in the same week, which is most rewarding and self-efficacy enhancing.
- The same type of exposure exercises is given on the following week, except they involve the most distressing items. If time permits, the client can be given a single item with which to work for a whole week, especially if it is likely to be very stressful.

As Stage 3 exercises take place with some success, clients tend to feel relieved by the realization that all human beings suffer the consequence of their lack of self-awareness, including the consequent emotional reactivity. The cognitive restructuring that takes place is facilitated by one's own experience. In clinical and other settings where MiCBT is implemented in this manner, numerous clients perceive deeper and wider aspects of others' experiences, and typically express, "If only Dad knew how to observe his anger more objectively. …"

Brief assertiveness training

Since this stage is can be very challenging for clients who lack assertiveness, it is likely that they will benefit from additional assertive skills. First, brief education of three predominant communication styles (passive, aggressive, assertive) is offered to the client.

The following structure for addressing their interlocutor assertively has produced good results once role-played a few times during the session. One reason for using this 7-step format over others is its inclusion of rewards and acceptance mechanisms. Using the example of a 36 year-old mother of three, married to a neglectful partner who has spent weekends and weekday evenings out of the family home for the last three months, the sequence of the seven statements was as follows:

1. "First, ensure you get (his/her) full attention. Make an appointment if necessary. Avoid engaging the topic while he washes the dishes or watches TV."
2. "State the facts." Here, the client is taught the difference between assumptions and factual information (e.g., "For the last three months, you have hardly been at home on weekends and in the evenings," rather than "You are never here" or "you always prefer the company of your alcoholic friends to spending time with your children!"
3. "State how you feel/felt using an "I" statement." The client is encouraged to use words which describe emotions (I feel sad, hurt, angry, anxious, etc), rather than expressions such as "I feel you don't want to live in this family"). The client is taught to take responsibility for his or her emotions by using "I" statements.
4. "State how you think/thought using 'I' statements." The client is taught to take responsibility for his or her thoughts, trying to link them with the above state-

ment (e.g., "I felt hurt and angry because it meant to me that you didn't care about the family").

5. "Acknowledge the other." This step is a form of disclaimer, demonstrating the client's willingness to take responsibility for their possible misunderstanding of the interlocutor's intent (e.g., "… this is what I thought, but I may be wrong about this, and it is possible that you care very much about the family"…).

6. "State what you want." The client is now required to take responsibility for what he or she wants and state it simply and clearly by linking the "want" statement to the problem to be resolved (e.g., "… but I want a frank discussion about what is the problem").

7. "Reward." It is beneficial for the client and her interlocutor to reward him or her at this stage. If he refuses to cooperate, at the very least she thanks him for having taken the time to listen. This is likely to facilitate future similar requests. If he cooperates, she rewards him for it in order to show her appreciation, how she values his effort, and by the same token enhances future attempts to compromise in future conflicts.

8. "Find a win-win solution." This step is only used if the interlocutor refuses to cooperate. The client is encouraged to negotiate rather than give up and react emotionally. All attempts must be made to promote, at best, a sense of gain for both. Clients in the session write these statements on a pad, keep the notes for rehearsing at home before *in vivo* exposure, and role-play with the therapist.

Interpersonal neurobiology

The study of the relationship between mindfulness meditation and interpersonal competency may lead us to seriously consider the work of Daniel Siegel and his colleagues on the topic of interpersonal neurobiology (e.g., Siegel, 2009b).

Daniel Siegel noted that adults whose middle prefrontal cortex is damaged have significant interpersonal impairments. He also noted the similarities between the attributes of people who have a secure attachment pattern and those who practice mindfulness meditation. He related this to the healthy development of the middle part of the prefrontal cortex. He noted that this part of the brain was impaired in many children who grow with dysfunctional attachment or a significant difficulty to regulate emotions following psychological trauma. He also reviewed the brain research literature and realized that this part of the prefrontal cortex can be notably enhanced by mindfulness meditation. Daniel Siegel's approach overlaps with Stage 3 of MiCBT and is certainly relevant to it.

Summary of Main Points

• The main aim of Stage 3 is to externalize attention toward others and develop better interpersonal awareness and acceptance. It uses an integration of mindfulness and CBT to help prevent reacting to others' reactions, facilitate skillful interpersonal communication and increase interpersonal understanding.

- Through "experiential ownership," clients learn to "own" (take full responsibility for) their current sensory experience and "disown" (relinquish responsibility for) that of another person, while trying to speculate what body sensations the other person is feeling. This method minimizes the probability of reacting to others' reactivity, prevents the occurrence of guilt, and increases assertiveness skills during interpersonal communication.
- Stage 3 paves the way to empathic training. It also serves to prevent relapse by modifying the dynamics of relationships which may be precipitating, maintaining or reinforcing factors for psychopathology.

Chapter 9

Stage 4 of MiCBT: Relapse Prevention with Grounded Empathy

Love and compassion are necessities, not luxuries.
Without them humanity cannot survive.
H. H. 14th Dalai Lama

It is well established in the helping professions involving mental health that a therapist's empathic attitude facilitates the process of therapy and accounts for much of the changes clients are willing to make. Empathy is one of the most important common factors leading to success in therapy. Clients usually rate the therapist's empathy as more important than the technique used.

In psychological interventions, basic empathy may be defined as "the naturally occurring subjective experience of similarity between the feelings expressed by self and others without losing sight of whose feelings belong to whom" (Decety and Jackson, 2004, p. 71). An empathic response typically involves communicating to the client our understanding of their spoken or unspoken dilemma or emotional state.

Empathy operates at various levels of the therapist's experience. We may overtly accept a person's experience and respond with an "empathic" formula (e.g., "this must have been difficult for you") while at the same time feeling rather remote from the person, sometimes because of fatigue, work overload and other factors such as habituation. In addition, empathy does not always involve an explicit response to the emotional experience of a person. We may remain silent while feeling great satisfaction from observing a client relieved from psychological pain, or from watching the success of a family member or colleague.

Mindfulness-integrated CBT: Principles and Practice, First Edition. Bruno A. Cayoun.
© 2011 John Wiley & Sons, Ltd. Published 2011 by John Wiley & Sons, Ltd.

Empathic training, or "Loving-Kindness Meditation," has always been embedded within mindfulness teaching traditions. Empathy is sometimes thought of as being one of the most important human qualities (Hart, 1987). In experienced mindfulness practitioners, empathy, traditionally termed "compassion" (*metta* in Pali language), emanates spontaneously from a profound understanding of personal suffering and its causes, leading the practitioner towards developing more interpersonal acceptance. It incorporates genuine tolerance of others and an understanding that generating acceptance and compassion for oneself and others is an integral part of one's personal growth. Accordingly, empathy has been both a process of learning and a fundamental goal in traditional mindfulness teachings.

Empathy as Part of the MiCBT Model

Stage 4 of MiCBT emphasizes the development of empathy *in the patient* as part of the therapy process. A legitimate question is whether we really need to include empathy in a mindfulness-based therapy model, despite its traditional inclusion in Eastern methods. After hesitating for many years, Kabat-Zinn (2005) proposed, the important advantage of promoting empathy in the client. Daniel Siegel also proposes that the development of empathy helps the brain integrate various modalities that enable healthy interpersonal relationships (Siegel, 2007). I have no doubt that until our ability for compassion increases, mindfulness training remains fruitless.

During the MiCBT program, we capitalize on each stage to move further towards systemic changes – changes that affect not only personal variables but also our relationship with the world. This is because dealing with the social environment, such as family, friends, work colleagues or unemployment agency staff, can interact with future relapses. The "system" in which we live often contributes to the recurrence of events that have consequences on mental health. Though they may be peripheral to a mental health condition, systemic factors often contribute to relapse and remediation.

Stage 3, as you recall, involves the development or improvement of assertiveness skills, the ability to hypothesize about (and tolerate) others' emotional experiences, and the development of an awareness of our responsibility for our experience. Because the insight developed in Stage 3 has already led the client to understand better someone who may have co-created the interpersonal conflict, some form of empathy has already developed. Thus, the empathy training in Stage 4 is the direct and logical following step for clients to acquire a new ability to appraise, understand, and accept the difficulties of others.

An fMRI study by Richard Davidson and colleagues suggests that resilience can be achieved using Loving-Kindness Meditation, as taught in traditional Buddhist teaching (Davidson *et al.*, 2004). During Stage 4 of MiCBT, clients are taught how to make use of their increased self-awareness to pair (or "ground") empathic thoughts with pleasant body sensations.

Consequences of Mindfulness

Experiential consequences of aversion and compassion

We explain to clients that as our capacity to be mindful improves, it becomes increasingly obvious that *we* are the first recipient of our emotions, even though these may be directed to someone else. The extent to which we can ignore this reality when we are not attentive to internal experiences is remarkable. For example, with just a few weeks of mindfulness training, it becomes possible to observe that we are the first to suffer from the heat, tensions and agitation that our anger produces, even though the anger may seem justified and was meant for someone else. Likewise, we note that we are the first recipient and beneficiary of our love for someone. *We* are the generator of the positive thoughts and pleasant co-emerging body sensations and *we* are consequently the ones who are feeling them. In fact, we have no real evidence that the intended recipient actually receives the love we project; despite our assumption that this is the case. The same goes for negative emotions.

Without sufficient insight, our usual tendency is to attribute the cause of our positive and negative experiences to people and external situations – or indeed to ourselves when our sense of self-worth is poor. Mindfulness training helps us reattribute the causes of what we feel and take more responsibility for it. It also helps us develop empathy for those around us who have not had the good fortune to recognize this for themselves.

During Stage 4, clients solidify and apply their understanding that producing a loving and kind attitude creates pleasant and joyful personal experiences, whereas producing emotions such as fear and anger, however justifiable, is associated with unpleasant body sensations and reactions that are often destructive. In daily practice, which will be described later in this chapter, clients also extend their insight to others. Clients discover that people who may react to them negatively are simply unaware that they too merely react to the product of their thoughts: body sensations. In other words, clients learn from personal experience that a person's negativity is the only and true reason for their psychological suffering. In Stage 4, clients learn to accept a person's negative attitude or "forgive" a harmful decision on the basis that they are simply victims of their unawareness – much as they were before mindfulness training. It follows that establishing the practice of such insight and the consequent increase in empathy can help clients prevent relapse into depressive and anxious states and the common co-morbid conditions.

Discovering ethical living

Another effect of becoming more mindful is, of course, a better perception of the consequences of our daily intentions and actions. In fact, there is a strong view among Eastern and Western meditation teachers that a person who does not invest effort to perform behavior that is more ethical will not benefit much from any meditation training. This is partly because human beings are social beings and much of our difficulties either arise from interpersonal experiences or are strongly affected by them. Actions that are harmful to oneself or to others tend to maintain or even reinforce an existing psychological condition and are counterproductive in the course of therapy.

Thus, Buddhist Psychology incorporates ethical guidelines to which mindfulness meditators are usually encouraged to adhere. They are usually known as "the five precepts" of moral life (e.g., Goenka, 1987; Hart, 1987; Hanh, 2007). In Buddhist traditional teaching, taking mindfulness training without initially committing to ethical conduct is simply inconceivable. It is theoretically unsound and technically unsuccessful. The specific inclusion of the five ethical precepts in Western mindfulness-based therapy methods is beginning to emerge. For example, Lynette Monteiro and her colleagues at the Ottawa Mindfulness Clinic (Monteiro, Nuttall, and Musten, 2010) have called these the "Five Skilful Habits" and included them as an integral part of their eight-week program in Mindfulness-Based Cognitive Therapy.

These five ethical principles fit roughly within the Western understanding of "doing no harm" and are usually endorsed for that very purpose. Their simplest description is not lying, stealing, killing, intoxicating, or performing sexual acts without genuine consent traditionally termed "sexual misconduct." It is my opinion that any mindfulness training worth its name ought to help trainees, especially mental health clients, become more aware of their harmful actions and decrease their frequency.

During Stage 4, as "behavioral experiments," trainees are asked to do their best to apply five basic ethical principles in their daily life; usually for a week or two. This is put to them in terms of "ethical challenges" or "ethical experiments." It is important to make clear to clients that committing to these ethical challenges for a week has nothing to do with adherence to a dogmatic morality. After this short period, trainees can choose to adopt whichever ethical principles they have found beneficial during that short trial period and make future attempts at integrating others that are more challenging for them. This alone has transformed the life of many clients and colleagues who took training in MiCBT. The five ethical guidelines or "challenges" are described as follows:

1. With mindfulness training, we become more aware that, as and when we deliberately lie to someone, we also feel accompanying unpleasant body sensations, although this may not be as obvious in the case of pathological lying given the habituation and sense of normality one may have developed from lying continuously. Otherwise, a person's expression of a lie is usually associated with discomfort about his or her truth. If you recall the co-emergence model of reinforcement discussed in Chapter 2, the lie initially takes place within the Evaluation component during the processing of information. The person's automatic or conscious judgment of telling the truth triggers meanings and

expected consequences that are unacceptable to the person (e.g., self-judgment or predicting rejection from others). In other words, the evaluation stimulates negative implications and consequently co-emerges with unpleasant body sensations.

Lying is the person's learned response (Reaction component of the model) that is most likely to help decrease the discomfort. Looking at it from a non-moralistic angle, lying is an important link in the chain of experiential avoidance. People often try to justify lying by weighing the consequences of truth versus those of lies. A strong limitation is that this justification is often based on our limited self-awareness and lack of evidence for the long-term consequences of our choice. As we become less judgmental and self-acceptance increases, it usually seems unnecessary to bend the truth at the cost of our values. To follow our "valued directions," as Stephen Hayes would put it (Hayes *et al.*, 1999), we often need to admit our truth in the eyes of others. At this stage of training, applying this single ethical principle can have enormous positive transformative effects. Note that we also explain to clients that, besides lying, any other form of harmful speech during this exercise is to be prevented.

2. Another instance of what is usually harmful to others and considered unethical is stealing. When clients are asked to prevent taking what is not theirs, they often say that they never steal and this task will not be much of a challenge. This view changes when we specify that this includes actions such as making personal phone calls on the work landline or mobile phone, arriving late at work or leaving early without catching up on the work to be done, calling-in sick when not fully justified, plagiarizing, making a copy of a copyrighted DVD or audio CD without permission, etc. Indeed, stealing can be covertly very entrenched. As in the case for lying, when we steal something it cannot be without a preceding craving towards pleasant body sensations or aversion towards unpleasant ones, to which we react in order to "feel better." Here too, the co-emergence model of reinforcement, discussed in Chapter 2, proposes that we steal to decrease unpleasant body sensations or increase pleasant ones.

3. Intoxication is yet another harmful behavior that relies on unpleasant body sensations, whether aversive or desirable. In addition, intoxication prevents us from paying attention, let alone sustaining attention from moment to moment while remaining equanimous. Intoxication is one of the greatest barriers to mindfulness meditation, which relies heavily on prefrontal activation of neural networks to inhibit our habitual (learned) reactions. When substances disinhibit these pathways, uninhibited, often harmful, behavior follows. When people intoxicate, it is usually to prevent feeling an experience (thoughts and co-emerging body sensations) or to facilitate feeling one that seems more acceptable. In other words, intoxicating hinders experiential acceptance. The abuse of alcohol and other drugs is one of the greatest barriers to using or increasing mindfulness skills. It also decreases the likelihood of committing to other ethical principles.

4. Harming a sentient being voluntarily also obeys the same mode of information processing. For example, before killing voluntarily, we usually feel some amount of fear or anger, which means the presence of very unpleasant body sensations, which we instinctively feel are unbearable. In most situations, killing is the reaction we generate to do away with the unpleasant body sensations. Of course, there are some exceptions, such as severe psychopathy, where the perpetrator's arousal levels are higher prior to a murder and decrease during and just after the murder, as shown by the interesting forensic psychophysiological research by Drs Chris Williams and Janet Haines at the University of Tasmania. However, the bulk of our clients and trainees are not psychopaths and their intent to kill is stressful and usually directed towards insects, such a mosquitoes, ants or cockroaches.

    The hallmark of the 4th stage of MiCBT is the development of compassion for oneself and others. How can we develop compassion while at the same time create suffering to the extent of taking another's life, even that of an animal? Yes, it is also true that someone may kill a few ants while wiping breadcrumbs from the kitchen bench without necessarily feeling like a murderer or even paying attention to it, but this still creates suffering. This may sound a little extreme at times to some clients who have not reached sufficient levels of self-awareness and equanimity. Nevertheless, this non-conscious mode of information processing, often called behaving on "automatic pilot" (e.g., Kabat-Zinn, 2005; Segal *et al.*, 2002), is also what maintains unhelpful behavior that leads to relapse into a psychological condition. When people begin Stage 4, they usually attain sufficient insight to perceive the personal benefit of refraining from killing and often report feeling empowered by their initial effort.

5. The fifth harmful action targeted is performing non-consenting or unintentional sex, for obvious reasons. It is well understood by most that sexual abuse is harmful, often leading people to seek psychological intervention. In a less dramatic context, such as common intimate relationships, an effort to prevent harmful sexual act tends to demonstrate care and respect for one's partner. This is likely to result in more joy when the sexual act is genuinely wanted by both, thereby improving important aspects of the relationship, including creativity, connectedness, and healthy attachment. During one of our recent client groups at the MiCBT Institute, a group participant undertaking Stage 4 said:

> When I told my husband that I had to do an experiment that involved having only intended sex this week, he said that it was going to be difficult but he was prepared to try … because we both thought that nothing would happen on that week. Well, I actually felt like it, so we had sex, and you know what he said? He appreciated so much that he said, "From now on, I want to have only intended sex!"

This was light-hearted and fun and we all laughed joyfully, but it highlighted something very serious about our intimate life. Ethical behavior does not mean living a boring life, suppressing pleasures or disengaging from basic human needs. As presented in MiCBT, it just means preventing harm, not living a life of dogmatic morality.

For instance, we explain to clients and other trainees that if they really "need" to kill (say an insect), they may commit to making an effort to feel the body sensations that just precede the reaction (killing), take full responsibility for it and make an attempt to remain equanimous towards the aversive bodily sensations and prevent the reaction. Of course, this does not make it a "mindful killing" but if they cannot prevent it this time, they may make use of what they learned in the previous reactive experience and try to prevent the next. They are also encouraged to appreciate having saved a life and reflect on the consequence of having coped with an aversive experience without returning to their reactive habit.

Similarly, we explain to clients that if they really "need" to lie or intoxicate, they may commit to making an effort to feel the body sensations that just precede the lying or taking the substance, and take full responsibility for it. They are to make all attempts to remain equanimous towards the aversive bodily sensations and prevent the reaction. As for the previous example, if they cannot prevent lying or intoxication this time, they may make use of what they learn during the reactive experience and try preventing the next. To promote self-efficacy and self-empowerment, they are also encouraged to reflect on the consequence of having coped with an aversive experience without relying on the reactive habit to feel relieved. This, and the therapist's use of Socratic dialogue, facilitates cognitive reappraisal.

Brain changes with empathy practice

Recent functional magnetic resonance imaging (fMRI) research reliably shows that regular practice of Loving Kindness-Meditation, as used in Stage 4 of MiCBT, produces activation in brain cells associated with empathy (Lutz *et al.*, 2008). Antoine Lutz and colleagues established that positive emotion and mental states, such as compassion and kindness, can be learned through regular meditation practice.

Through this and previous research, two main areas of the brain have been identified as particularly relevant to our ability to share emotions and empathy. The insula, a deep brain region close to the frontal lobe, is central to our ability to detect emotions. It also has an essential role in mapping physiological responses to emotions, such as heart rate and blood pressure, and passing on the information to other brain regions. The other region observed to be important in the experience of empathy is the junction between the temporal and parietal lobes in the right hemisphere. This area promotes the processing of empathy, especially our ability to perceive the mental and emotional states of others. A study in 2008 by Lutz *et al.*, shows that these two regions were markedly more developed in expert meditators than in novices.

Should loving-kindness be taught sooner or later?

Various therapy models, and indeed traditional Buddhist approaches, teach Loving-Kindness Meditation earlier in the sequence of mindfulness training; sometimes immediately after commencing training. MiCBT applies the traditional Burmese method, as taught by S.N. Goenka (e.g., Hart, 1987) and his predecessors. This is based on the idea that the capacity for unconditional compassionate love is difficult to produce while judgmental mental contents are still predominant in daily life. Can we genuinely persuade ourselves through affirmations that we are safe while our symptoms of anxiety are still present? Can we truly treat ourselves as our best friend would treat us if self-loathing still pervades our life? Can we authentically wish the very best to our trouble-making neighbor when we are aroused with resentment in their presence? Can we compassionately share our peace and harmony with all beings while our depressed mood reduces our focus to feeling sorry for ourselves?

The analogical rationale is that we need to weed out our garden before planting seeds we want to grow, or weeds can easily swallow up new shoots. Although this makes intuitive sense, there was no empirical evidence for the best type of delivery schedule until a recent study (Barnhofer *et al.,* 2010). Barnhofer and colleagues investigated the differential effects of mindfulness of breath and Loving-Kindness Meditation techniques on prefrontal brain areas using EEG and other measures in previously clinically depressed individuals. Following a 15-minute meditation practice period, the results showed higher activation in left prefrontal areas regardless of the technique used. A very useful finding for clinicians is that responses were moderated by participants' tendencies to engage in ruminative thinking. Those who ruminate responded to mindfulness of breath but not to Loving-Kindness, whereas those low in ruminative thinking responded better to loving kindness than to mindfulness of breath. While both forms of meditation are beneficial, the authors pointed towards "differential indications for offering them in the treatment of previously depressed patients." Although this was a very small study ($n = 15$), it provides the first empirical data to support the hierarchical delivery structure used in MiCBT: implementing mindfulness of breath in the first period of training to address ruminative and other unhelpful thinking processes, and implementing Loving Kindness Meditation in the last period of training to promote compassion after ruminative and other unhelpful thoughts have been neutralized.

Empathy as a Function of "Egolessness"

Before becoming more mindful of what we are and, more importantly, what we are not, our sense of self is maintained through the repeated experience of the four following modalities, to which we continually identify:

(1) perception of sensory stimuli
(2) evaluation of these stimuli with its relationship to deep-rooted belief systems

(3) the sensorimotor experience that derives from this evaluation
(4) the response to the experience, and the feedback or consequence which will determine the appropriateness to the response (see Chapter 2 for a detailed account of the co-emergence model).

For example, realizing and catastrophizing (evaluation) that I am unable to remember much of what I read on a topic (sensory perception) creates unpleasant body sensations (interoceptive experience), which in turn, "make me" feel incapacitated and tense as I anticipate failing the exam (Reaction). Note that my reaction is mental in this case, in the form of a negative thought. As I eventually fail my exam (feedback), I obtain confirmation that I am not good enough for studying, which strengthens a deep-rooted sense of failure as a person. In this example, criticism of the self is limited to one's sense of scholastic achievement and the corresponding schema. In other cases, esteem of the self may rely upon others' recognition for one's creativity at work, ability to raise a family according to social norms, or for physical attractiveness.

As discussed in previous chapters, without sufficient levels of mindfulness, our sense of self is narrow, fragile and vulnerable because it is perceived as being in constant danger of being confronted by our own or others' criticism, or lack of validation. From a mindfulness standpoint, the main problem with over-identifying with worldly matters is that everything changes. Whatever we identify with is bound to change and we feel a deep sense of loss. The resulting psychological pain springs from unawareness.

When mindfulness training starts (Stage 1 of MiCBT), clients progressively realize that all body sensations and thoughts are but transient events, constantly arising and passing away. An understanding that no experience really belongs to them begins to emerge. Even though this is learned at a micro level of experience, clients begin to appreciate that worldly matters are impermanent and therefore cannot be part of a permanent sense of self that we call "I." It becomes clearer with sustained practice that the so-called "I," like its components, is also impermanent, even though this is not the focus or direct intent of Stage 1. The extent to which this realization is achieved depends on the quality and frequency of practice, as well as the person's existing level of equanimity and insight. The more this is realized consciously, the more likely it is that empathic responses will naturally emerge and others' experiences become more accurately perceived when we are not so attached to, and protective of, our sense of self. Being less identified with a "narrow" sense of self enables us to pay more attention to others and generate better an understanding of others.

When the training reaches Stage 3, ego boundaries are more flexible and the sense of self expands to incorporate others, including those who initially seemed so different and threatening. We begin to understand, through experience, that all individuals share the same fate, a legitimate suffering caused by the impermanence of worldly matters, including material possessions, status, family members, the body and its various states of health.

Self-Esteem

If the sense of self is merely a construct (Kelly, 1955), what then is self-esteem? A particular feature of depression is "low self-esteem." The literature related to traditional cognitive therapy advances that the negative self-evaluations that lead to low self-esteem should be the focus of the intervention (e.g., Beck *et al.*, 1979). In other words, the targets are the symptoms. Nevertheless, there is an important distinction to be made between the way in which a person perceives himself or herself (e.g., in low esteem) and the amount of attachment that exists towards the self-concept.

Paradoxically, a person experiencing low self-esteem also generates a tremendous amount of attachment towards the personal aspects he or she dislikes. Inadvertently, this reinforces the devaluing views about him or herself. Hence, attachment to the sense of self and the negative self-evaluations that lead to low self-esteem go hand in hand. The more disliked the self-concept, the more significant it is made, and consequently the more importance it takes in day-to-day life. One remains vigilant, which in time produces and maintains stress.

In severely depressed clients, cognitions commonly involve "I" statements. This has been well documented by Beck and colleagues (e.g., Beck *et al.*, 1979). As briefly described earlier, Beck has shown that negative thought contents are manifestations of deeply rooted assumptions about oneself and the environment one lives in.

Whereas mild depressive symptoms tend to be associated with overt expressions of negative cognitions (e.g., "my husband is unfair"), more severe symptoms tend to be associated with deeper, more "structural" cognitive processing (e.g., "I'll never be happy in my marriage") and deeper, often subconscious, assumptions easily surface (e.g., "I am failing again," "I can't get anything right," "I'm completely useless"). When experiencing low self-worth, people tend to attribute the problem internally. There is the assumption of a relationship between the severity of symptoms and the spontaneous surfacing of "I" statements.

With the sense of self comes the need to present it, protect it, defend it, and "esteem" it. We are continually self-preoccupied and feel more or less in danger of threat to the sense of self. Even though it is our own internal attribution which creates this perception of threat, anything said or done that challenges our sense of self (views, self-image, habits, etc) creates tension. A criticism directed toward this sense of self, and the whole person goes berserk. How can something so ephemeral, so insubstantial, be at the same time so threatened? Human beings seem to be the only organism in which this is so.

On the other hand, it is rather improbable that low self-esteem and the ability to be detached from the self-concept are compatible events. It is far more likely that low self-esteem manifests itself through the magnification of some components of the self-concept that have become predominant in our attention. From a functional point of view, negative self-evaluations in some clients may help preserve a consistent schema, and increase a sense of continuous (permanent) self, at the cost of poor ability for change.

Alternatively, decreasing attachment to a limited sense of self is likely to decrease the fear of criticism, loss, misfortune, loneliness, self-hatred, low self-esteem and any other potential threat to our sense of self. When unpleasant experiences with the sense of self become more agreeable, self-acceptance replaces the need for *esteem* towards the self. In Buddhist Psychology and the viewpoints and observations made with clients in training, a potent common factor in most people's emotional problems *is* an overemphasized (low or high) sense of self. Yet, in the absence of self-loathing, there is no need for self-esteem.

Two Bases for Self-Acceptance

The acquisition of self-acceptance depends on one's ability for self-worth and may be conceptualized as a two-dimensional experience. Clients may learn to accept themselves through external feedback or internal experience of detachment from self and empathy.

External locus of self-acceptance

When a client's sense of self-worth is low because he or she has been invalidated in the past, it is commonly believed that validating the good in them is beneficial. For example, a client diagnosed with a condition currently known as Borderline Personality Disorder (BPD) is likely to present with problems regulating emotions, low sense of self-worth, fear of rejection and abandonment that has been learned from invalidating or otherwise traumatic experiences in childhood. More often than not, consequently, the client seeks reassurance that they will not be criticized or rejected. The need for reassurance can take the form of testing the limits of a friend's or partner's attachment to them or a frank expression of their need for validation.

However, feedbacks, such as praise and verbal reassurance, are all contingent upon uncertainty. None of these can ever be placed under their control. Despite the effort of family members, friends or the therapist in reassuring the client that they are indeed a worthy individual, the need for validation of the self remains unfulfilled and testing the limits of what behavior is acceptable continues to be the main means of measurement for others' acceptance or rejection. More often than not, rejection from others becomes a self-fulfilling prophecy; their need for others' acceptance becomes untenable. One of the client's key difficulties is their inability to be self-reliant for feeling worthy as a person. In other words, the client cannot *internalize the locus of self-worth* and over-relies on external feedback to feel worthy and accept him or herself. The client with BPD may go to great lengths to obtain reassurance. This may include putting others on a pedestal at the early stage of a newly formed relationship, assuming great friendship with someone who seems to appreciate them when the relationship is actually very superficial, blurring boundaries by expressing inappropriate expectation of others, or attempting to over-control situations and relationships. The need for external validation and reassurance expressed through these attempts would be greatly minimized if the client could internalize self-worth, rather than relying on others to feel good about themselves.

Internalized locus of self-acceptance

The second basis for self-acceptance emerges spontaneously from a gain in self-awareness and detachment. Such a basis is not contingent upon "doing" and the appreciation of others it attracts. Rather, we can feel satisfied by "being" more present in any experience, and understand, accept and enjoy it more fully.

Mindfulness training can play an important role in the process of internalizing the locus of self-worth, from which self-acceptance can develop. The mere understanding that "the self' is a construct, that it is just as impermanent in nature as are thoughts and sensations, can decrease the need for external positive feedback. The increasing ability to detach ourselves from the sense of self neutralizes the need for external validation of who we are. We become less dependent on others to feel worthy, acceptable, and connected to others. Paradoxically, self-acceptance and satisfaction in life are enhanced by the ability to let go of our established sense of self.

This way of enhancing happiness is precisely what practitioners of mindfulness discover. Daily training in mindfulness meditation leads to an ability to transfer mindfulness skills to contexts other than the meditation cushion and promotes a sense of self that is more flexible, less vulnerable to change, and therefore requiring less protection and validation. Despite the unpredictability of future events, a sense of safety can be progressively established. It follows that if the sense of self is transformed, so is personality and its expressions. When attachment to an insecure sense of self decreases, the depressive or anxious thoughts it produces also decrease. Established mindfulness skills generate long-term relief and a sense of control in most life domains, from which self-satisfaction naturally springs.

Training in Stage 4

The principles

After each sitting meditation, we proceed for about five minutes of empathic training, making use of body sensations as a grounding modality. This consists of focusing attention on subtle, pleasant body sensations (often in the chest, in the "heart area," or the palms of the hands) in order for the mind to facilitate only positive thoughts. Then, experiencing no tension, clients generate positive thoughts, commonly wishing for themselves to generate peace, compassion for themselves and others, and develop further awareness and equanimity. Given the co-emergence principles discussed in Chapter 2, generating such positive thoughts usually leads to congruent body sensations, such as a flow of warm and tingling sensations in various parts of the body. Once clients have generated benevolent thoughts for themselves for about three minutes, they formulate the wish to share their peace, compassion, and personal merits with others for another three to five minutes (see Grounded Empathy Script (Stage 4) Appendix A, or Track 10 of Advanced CD for complete implementation, Cayoun, 2005b).

The formulation of such thoughts, while attention is "grounded" in pleasant body sensations, creates a powerful and uplifting experience. Some have qualified this experience as "transcendence" (Johnstone and Glass, 2008).

Forgiveness

Stage 4 can be a surprise for clients. Some can be deeply touched and let it show; many shed tears in the first session. Often, genuine forgiveness of self or others involves an emotional experience. Clients who have practiced mindfulness meditation for long periods (including this author) have found that grounding and nurturing empathic qualities tends to foster a secure and satisfying state of mind, a sense of social bonding, and a genuine interest in others' well-being (e.g., Chandiramani, Verma, and Dhar, 1995; Goenka, 1987; Hart, 1987; Kabat-Zinn, 2005).

Implementing Stage 4

The practice of Grounded Empathy in MiCBT follows the Vipassana tradition. It requires the client to have completed a mindfulness (sitting meditation) session and be in a calm and equanimous state of mind. If he or she is agitated, practicing breathing awareness for a few minutes until tranquility returns is recommended. If thoughts are very negative, then the practice of Grounded Empathy is not possible in the current session and it is best left until the next one.

As mentioned earlier, the practice of Grounded Empathy requires us first to focus in the body, wherever there is a pleasant "flow of tingling sensations." Such electricity-like pleasant sensations are usually more common when practicing advanced scanning methods (see Advanced CD, Cayoun, 2005b). However, there are always tingling sensations in the palm of the hands or under the soles of the feet because of the multitude of nerve endings in those parts, even if we are not able to feel them at will. Then we allow these pleasant sensations to "spread" throughout the entire body while generating well-wishing thoughts. Further, we let these sensations "spread out" towards our family and friends (people we love first). After a few minutes, we direct sensations and empathic thoughts towards those with whom we may have had conflicts, with an understanding that the cause of conflict was based on unawareness of what we learned in Stage 1. This stage makes use of counterconditioning principles, whereby a usually aversive stimulus (e.g., the face or voice of someone with whom we were/will be in conflict) is paired with benevolent thoughts and pleasant body sensations.

Since this is not always straightforward to implement for some clinicians, the use of imagery can be included as long as the client's grounding in the awareness of actual body sensations is maintained. The short script in Appendix A illustrates the linkage of imagery and body sensations.

When and how to use Stage 4

When clients are ready for Stage 4, it is important to practice Grounded Empathy with them, whether in a group or in one-on-one sessions, in order to ensure that the process is clear, demystified, and grounded in the "here and now." Then clients are encouraged to practice it after each formal sitting meditation practice, morning and evening, for about five to ten minutes. It is necessary to emphasize the need to relax any possible remaining tension in the body and have clear and positive thoughts first, since we cannot share peace and harmony while having negative thoughts or intense muscle tension.

As is the case for Stages 1 and 3, Stage 4 extends to informal practice applied in daily activities. As clients go about their normal activities, they are encouraged to generate similar thoughts when someone around them generates negative thinking.

Clients are asked to remind themselves that the agitated person is simply unaware of how they perpetuate suffering by generating emotional reactivity. In other words, clients learn to keep in mind that a person with negative thoughts or actions is unaware, but not bad or evil by will. Since this was also the state of unawareness in which clients once were, the conflicting person can be accepted and forgiven there and then (see Grounded Empathy Script in Appendix A). Thus, Stage 4 of MiCBT is conceptualized as a powerful relapse prevention method based on learning existential and altruistic principles.

Reappraising Relapse

Relapse is a significant obstacle to clients' progress in any therapeutic system that promotes behavior change, even when the intervention has been, to some measure, a success (Marlatt and Gordon, 1985). Relapse may be conceptualized as a return to mindlessness. One reason for relapse is the encounter with too challenging, often avoided, experiences, in the face of which one reverts to old habits.

Following some small successes with therapy, the possible sense of failure following relapse can outweigh the relief derived through interoceptive acceptance. In other cases, adherence to the program is threatened; progress may be slower than the client expects and a sense of "laziness" can emerge from the unfulfilled desire for a quick fix. In most cases, non-adherence to the program is mainly a consequence of misunderstanding the technique and its rationale, and tends to occur mostly early in the treatment.

Doubts tend to occur in the first three weeks of the program and vanish as the positive results progressively appear in various areas of functioning. The following comment is from an ex-client with Bipolar Affective Disorder:

> Preventing relapse is a strange feeling, because you are scared of being depressed and scared of being happy all in one, and you are not quite sure which way you should go because if you try to justify either path, neither justification makes sense. So you just have to stop intellectualizing it and meditate! ...then it all makes sense.

The concept of "relapse" needs to be relabeled by the clinician in a non-judgmental way as an "impermanent experience," so that clients perceive the return of symptoms as the emergence of an old response set, a habit, to be observed, accepted, and let go (Salmon *et al.,* 1998). For example, a self-harming young woman, Jane, whose success with MiCBT was rapid and personally very encouraging, felt a deep sense of failure when she self-harmed once more, three weeks into the MiCBT program. Usually, as she explained, the clinicians she saw prior to her present inpatient intake tended to perceive self-cutting behavior as a return to point zero, the sign of a hopeless situation, a chronic case not worth long-term clinical attention. Instead, she was surprised at being told how much she had progressed and how more mindful her state of mind was just preceding the behavior. As she was made to feel successful despite this "set back," she did not lose trust in her ability and continued progressing.

As Jane continued progressing, about two months later she became apprehensive about the recurrence of auditory hallucinations; a friendly male voice that remained silent for a long time re-emerged "out of the blue." Jane was worried that this constituted a relapse. This manifestation was reappraised as "an old habit resurfacing providing the opportunity to desensitize from it." Then she was reminded of her training, whereby thoughts are perceived merely as thoughts (mental events arising and passing) and body sensations merely as body sensations, with the least possible evaluation. She understood that the voice originated from her thoughts and, by remaining in the present moment, she was able to perceive it and let it go immediately each time it emerged. Having not identified with it, she reported its disappearance after only a few practice sessions of mindfulness meditation. The voice never returned.

Jon Kabat-Zinn and his colleagues (Salmon *et al.,* 1998) suggest addressing relapse in mindfulness-based programs in the following ways:

1. By emphasizing the novelty of each moment, including behavior patterns that may seem old and habitual (e.g., breathing, health attitudes, impulses to revert to old habits).
2. By going beyond labels commonly associated with relapse events, such as "backsliding," "reversal," or even "relapse," and treating the experience as an opportunity for renewed focused attention.

3. "Relapses" can be observed as events with familiar features but also with novel and unique qualities that are potent opportunities for growth and change. Psychological and behavioral change always involves a dynamic, non-linear process, with cycles of regression, restructuring, and reintegration.

Summary of Main Points

- As clients progress through the program, they initially develop useful "internalizing skills" by "centering" attention toward, and developing acceptance of, their own sensory processes (Stage 1). They then begin to externalize these skills to address their avoidant behavior and dissatisfying interpersonal interactions by "decentering" from their experience and redirecting attention towards others. As a natural extension, Stage 4 trains individuals to act ethically to better integrate essential notions of compassion and global awareness and connectedness.
- Stage 4 teaches clients to externalize attention to all beings, their rights, their worth, and their significance within the entire system of living beings. Insight develops from the micro to the macro levels of awareness, hence decreasing the likelihood of relapse.
- Clients learn that they are the first recipient of the emotions they generate towards others. Accordingly, producing kind thoughts for themselves and others will produce fulfilling emotional experiences and help prevent relapse.
- Research shows evidence of brain changes taking place in regions associated with emotion regulation when practicing Loving-Kindness Meditation.
- Stage 4 enhances the broadening of our limited sense of self.
- The principles of Loving-Kindness Meditation used in Stage 4 of MiCBT include three steps, each lasting about 2 minutes: Producing kind and loving thoughts for oneself, people we love and care for, and everyone else, while pairing these thoughts with a "free flow" of very subtle, tingling, sensations in the body (see advanced scanning in Chapter 4).
- Relapse needs to be reappraised with acceptance in terms of a momentary occurrence of a familiar, yet different experience, not failure.

Part IV
The Benefits

Chapter 10

MiCBT with DSM-V Axis 1 and Axis 2 Disorders

Just as by one piece of clay everything made of clay may be known –
the modification is merely a verbal distinction, a name; the reality is just "clay" –
so is that teaching.

Chandogya Upanishad

Developmental versus Situational Causes of Psychopathology

The willingness or need to be trained varies from client to client. Some have a specific crisis to traverse. Others have a whole pool of overlapping difficulties which persist across time and contexts, often reflecting a problematic personality. A distinction between these enables the therapist to implement mindfulness training by using either Stage 1 (exposure to the "internal" context) as a main vehicle or by moving earlier on to Stage 2 (incorporating exposure to external contexts).

The problem of diagnosis

One of the continually debated issues regarding the diagnosis of mental disorders is whether a finite classification is better than a continuum-based system. The question is "are mental illnesses truly separate entities?" The DSM uses finite categorical criteria, but warns the clinician against blind reliance on these categories. This issue is even more relevant with categories known as personality disorders. The boundaries are blurred more often than not, and clinicians worldwide are questioning the

Mindfulness-integrated CBT: Principles and Practice, First Edition. Bruno A. Cayoun.
© 2011 John Wiley & Sons, Ltd. Published 2011 by John Wiley & Sons, Ltd.

validity of a strict categorical system with such uncircumscribed sets of emotions, behaviors and cognitions.

Universality versus specificity of psychopathologies

There are not only profound philosophical and practical reasons for educating individuals about natural change within themselves, it is also an aesthetic and sensible way of asserting that extinction (change), rather than avoidance (resistance to change) is the natural order. When clients can easily perceive therapy as a means of facilitating inherent change, the perception of their problem as a "psychopathology" is changed to a notion of "consequences of unawareness" or "mindlessness." In other words, it becomes a matter of development in consciousness, moving along the awareness continuum (see Travis, Arenander and DuBois, 2004, and Pascual-Leone, 2000, for models of awareness continuum).

This alternative view, when expressed by a therapist to his or her client, tends to have a positive effect on the client's self-esteem and increases his or her motivation to work with the therapist. It is accompanied by a more accepting attitude towards both the problem and the therapy (e.g., Kenny and Williams, 2007). A possible reason for this is the understanding that clients suffer from a problem that is universal, since unawareness of change also causes suffering to any healthy person, but for clients this unawareness is more painful and pervasive. By the same token, the therapist does not reinforce the client's identification with their mentally-ill "ingroup" and their sense of separation from more mentally healthy "outgroups" (see Chapter 8).

It is common to hear a client confiding his or her wish that one family member (often the partner or a parent) tries this approach, even though that family member's level of functioning is normally high. This may be an indication that the client perceives his or her condition as more or less normal, increasing the notion of interdependence of fate and the consequent facilitation of reconnecting with social networks. This is of significant help with conditions such as depression and social phobia. Mindfulness training facilitates the practical realization that everything changes, including the person's problems.

Limitations in the research literature

Psychological research in mindfulness is still in its infancy, despite the increasingly large number of studies from various disciplines. For example, there is a need for more outcome studies of mindfulness approaches with conditions such as Post-Traumatic Stress Disorder (PTSD), phobias, and Schizophrenia. Most clinically oriented studies have been focused on reducing symptoms of depression and anxiety.

Similarly, mindfulness research in the areas of personality disorders has been, until recently, mostly restricted to Linehan's (1993) Dialectical Behavior Therapy for Borderline Personality Disorder. Other problematic personality traits have mostly remained unexplored. The very few studies using therapy systems that include mindfulness *principles*, such as Acceptance and Commitment Therapy (Hayes, *et al.,*

1999), have shown positive results in the area of psychotic disorders, but research using mindfulness *meditation* as the main skill is still insufficiently researched.

One of the most difficult aspects of therapy and clinical research is the problem of co-morbidity. Psychologists have adopted the term "co-morbidity" from the discipline of medicine, which means the coexistence of two or more disease processes. Typically, clinicians who engage in the treatment of depression will more often than not have to deal with co-morbid symptoms of anxiety. Among the several advantages already stated in previous chapters, a tight integration of CBT and mindfulness meditation helps address the complexity posed by co-morbidity, as exemplified in the case examples below.

Micro versus macro dimensions

A continuum of "experiential salience" describes well the experience of mindfulness integration. It is convenient to use the notion of "micro-level" (experiential salience) and "macro-level" processing. At a micro-level of processing, muscle tension-related pain, for example, may be perceived as the experience of an intense pressure and heat, moving in wave-like motion in the base of the neck. Information processing at the macro-level, on the other hand, allows the experience to be appraised in its judgmental format: there is pain in the neck; expressed more commonly as: "My neck is so sore!" This is often followed by "implicational processing" (Teasdale and Barnard, 1993): "I'll be sick at work again."

Essentially, processing information about change at the macro level of experience can only be grasped conceptually. In contrast, micro-processing of information allows appraisal of change to become an actual experience. From the experience, clients can derive a re-evaluation of emotional state in a less catastrophic way. This applies across conditions.

Early Cue Detection versus Experiential Avoidance

An important step is to learn how to feel and identify sensorimotor cues as early as possible, when they are still manageable. Since awareness of mental reaction is generally proportional to the intensity of its concomitant body-sensations, an increase in interoceptive awareness also leads to a magnified perception of co-emerging mental events.

It is well documented that "automatic thoughts" accompany or precede initially subtle physical manifestations, which tend to increase in intensity as the thoughts become increasingly intense, as in the typical catastrophic thinking associated with panic attacks. Figure 7 shows the consequence of "high awareness threshold" (low interoceptive awareness) caused by experiential avoidance, and the consequence of lowering awareness threshold (increasing awareness) through mindfulness training.

The early experience of an unpleasant situation is represented in Figure 7 by the thick, curved, double line, showing the onset of sensorimotor stimulation (Time 0 on the X Axis). The subtle interoceptive experience is not salient enough to compete

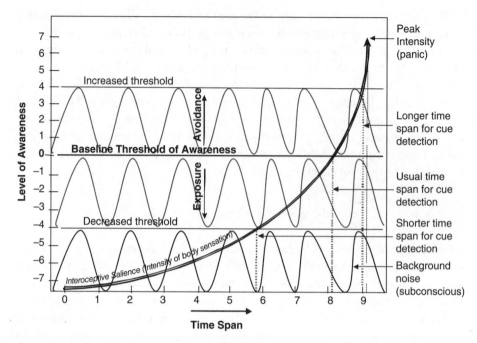

Figure 7. Impact of lowered awareness threshold after mindfulness training. The sine waves indicate areas of unawareness ("background noise"). The lower the level of awareness the higher the threshold.

with the salience of other physiological phenomena (walking, eating, etc) at this stage, and is inaccessible to conscious processing when the mind is untrained for the conscious perception of such subtle stimulation.

With time, interoception intensifies and becomes increasingly accessible to conscious awareness (Y Axis). Without particular training, we become aware when the ascending double line crosses the threshold of awareness. Suppose that a person's usual baseline awareness threshold is represented by 0 on the Y Axis of Figure 7, below which is "background noise," thoughts and sensations of which we are unaware. This threshold may vary slightly in either direction according to factors such as fatigue, time of day, digestion, physical activity, stress, etc. However, people tend to maintain a general level of awareness within a small range spanning below and above the mean (baseline) according to their habitual life style, personality, age, etc.

How widely can the range of fluctuating interoceptive (and metacognitive) awareness span within a person, and from person to person, has yet to be investigated. For the purpose of this discussion, let us assume that a person's baseline of interoceptive awareness is relatively stable when not under great stress. As represented in Figure 7, avoidance of unpleasant experiences is associated with the shift of the threshold upward, so that the unpleasant experience remains unattended, in the background. The successful relief from uncomfortable body sensations is the main reinforcer for this pattern (negative reinforcement).

Strategies such as the consumption of intoxicants, pain-relief and anxiolytic medication, excessive exercising, overeating, self-harm behavior, and all sorts of distractions can be used to elevate the threshold of awareness and "feel better" during an unpleasant experience. They become avoidance strategies that can be learned rapidly if they seem efficient in raising the threshold.

If the problem is addressed and the strategy is no longer needed, the withdrawal of the strategy will allow the awareness threshold to return to its original (or at least a lower) level, allowing us to feel experiences at a subtler level. However, if the problem is not addressed adequately, or not at all, allowing the threshold to decrease without using a new strategy to handle it is likely to be difficult since the unpleasant experience is being re-experienced as soon as the threshold decreases. If I cannot accept the unpleasant body sensations associated with the problem, I am likely to keep using the painkiller, psychotropic medication, or alcohol. In other words, my threshold of awareness will not decrease unless I develop a degree of equanimity. That said, pain relief medication is often a very important part of people's quality of life when they suffer from intense pain. Using it while undertaking MiCBT can be very helpful in alleviating very gross body sensations and enabling people with chronic pain to practice. Usually, pain relief medication can be decreased as equanimity develops.

The tendency of the brain is to adapt, to habituate. As it adapts to the avoidance strategy, the intensity of experience exceeds the new threshold and the unpleasant body sensations are felt more intensely and abruptly as a result. Unless the problem that causes unpleasant body sensations is addressed, the tendency of an avoidant approach to the problem is to change the strategy, in either type or amount, but the habit of avoiding the experience remains unchanged. For example, I will need to drink greater amounts of alcohol to maintain the effect (high awareness threshold), or change my medication schedule to greater amount or with a different "cocktail."

In addition to becoming aware of their symptoms only when they are intense and difficult to manage due to the high awareness threshold, clients who use avoidance strategies are also faced with a detection delay. As shown in Figure 7, the higher the threshold, the less time we have available before the most intense experiences are manifested (e.g., panic attack). Hence, the consequences of "experiential avoidance" (Hayes, *et al.*, 1996) are that the later we become aware of internal states, the less we have time to choose the most appropriate response, and the more intense and least manageable they become.

By contrast, exposure to, and acceptance of, naturally occurring unpleasant body sensations decreases the threshold of awareness. With daily practice of mindfulness of body sensations (body scan), subtler interoceptive cues are being appraised with equanimity. The client can detect and accept to feel subtle discomforts earlier in their manifestation, when they are easier to manage and when there is plenty of time to decide the appropriateness of the response. Thus, detecting the dynamic co-emergence of mind and body earlier during a stressful event helps the client to operate consciously and willingly at a level where thoughts are not yet catastrophic and the accompanying body sensations are still manageable.

From an experiential perspective, it is difficult to conceive that the integration of mindfulness training with CBT, as in the present model, should be restricted only to particular psychological difficulties. The benefits of developing equanimity to increase detection and acceptance of early distress cues and greater response choice would be welcome whatever the disorder may be.

This integrated approach is in line with the self-efficacy literature (Bandura, 1997a, 1997b). No matter what the disorder may be, it is difficult to imagine any case in which the client would not benefit from developing effective coping skills and internalizing the locus of control. This constitutes the main rationale for a non-diagnosis-specific implementation of MiCBT.

Moreover, when mindfulness meditation is carefully integrated with cognitive and behavioral techniques, even clients with complex co-morbid presentations can be helped in the same way as clients with a single condition are helped. Addressing the problem by targeting the context that is internal to the person enables us to modify the mechanisms of reinforcement that maintain conditioned patterns of behavior, whatever the overlapping disorders may be. Below are some of the many examples of these benefits, as experienced by ex-clients of the author.

Case Example 1: Social Phobia

"Danielle" was an undergraduate psychology student in her early 20s. Following her mother's suggestion, she attended six individual MiCBT sessions. Her letter was chosen from among several others describing similar rapid remission because of the peculiar effects of mindfulness practice on her dreams, although the beneficial peripheral effects of mindfulness on sleep patterns is continuously reported by clients.

> I was just emailing because mum thought you would be interested in the change in sleeping pattern I have experienced over the past few months. These days I have at least five dreams a night that I can remember. Sometimes I am scanning (aware of bodily sensations) during the dream (appears as an indistinct mass of subtle sensations).
>
> Usually, I sleep for at least two hours without dreams, then I wake up (and usually go to the loo! [WC]), then for the rest of the night I seem to have a dream, wake up, roll over, have another dream, wake up etc. In some dreams I seem to be able to control my behavior. For instance, someone suggests or does something violent and I'm distinctly aware of something inside me saying that's wrong.
>
> For instance, once I had an adventure type dream that involved me swinging from a chandelier and kicking a guard off a parapet, straight afterwards I was aware that that was wrong. In other dreams I seem to make a choice not to do something. In other dreams something horrible or scary happens, but I seem to be aware that I don't have to become afraid (in some dreams I'm even giving advice to other people not to react to their sensations!).
>
> On another note, there has been almost a complete reversal in my fear of public speaking. Though initially the same sensations may appear, they are certainly not as strong, and each time they appear they are less severe than the last. In a lot of my

practical's I'm actually one of the people that speak the most! I've also seemed to have become more sensitive, or better able to recognize anxiety related symptoms in others. As I'm not anxious anymore (when ever the old sensations arise I literally smile at them sometimes!) I have time to look around me at other people and pick up clues in their behavior that I associated with my own anxiousness. This has actually led to me speaking even more, often in a lighthearted attempt to change their mood. So, thank you very very much for teaching me this wonderful meditation!

Case Example 2: PTSD

"John" was a 42-year old inmate diagnosed with Post-Traumatic Stress Disorder (PTSD), incarcerated about six years ago. He became a client of the author and was treated with MiCBT while incarcerated. His account of mindfulness training in the following letter after six weeks of treatment illustrates both the beneficial effect of experiential awareness and clients' renewal of trust in therapy when rapid results are acquired despite the chronicity of their condition. The identifying parts of the letter have been edited to preserve confidentiality.

I was just an average sort of bloke. I lived in an average house in an average suburb in an average city. I owned and managed an average business. A few years ago my world disintegrated. I was involved in an incident which ultimately resulted in the tragic death of another man. So here I sit in prison.

Have you ever closed your eyes and found yourself engulfed in a swirling darkness that threatens to smother your breath, a darkness so intense you can feel it swelling in your throat and tightening around your chest? I liken it to an immense whirlpool. I would find myself standing on the edge of an unimaginable vortex, trying in vain to maintain my balance. Pieces of my life flash past, disjointed horrible memories that I am unable to make sense of. Memories of accidents from years ago, children, cold and silent, the smell of fuel, blood and the cold night air; flotsam in a raging sea. And then it happens again, and again, and again …

The reason I'm telling you all this is to try and explain how I felt, before I reached out for help. I started speaking with a psychologist and the simple act of sharing my thoughts and fears was like a weight being lifted from my shoulders. In this grey and lonely place I had a friend whom I could talk to. The nightmares didn't stop but I was no longer alone.

Some months ago I was introduced to another psychologist who in turn introduced me to Mindfulness Training. Meeting him was an extremely positive point in my life.

He set about explaining that all emotions were linked to physical sensations within our body. Memories are attached to emotions which are in turn attached to physical sensations. This explains why the thought of something unpleasant can sometimes result in a very real feeling of nausea. In short he described how it was therefore possible to control emotions by controlling our physical sensations. He called this technique "mindfulness." By accepting a sensation at its base level rather than tagging it as either good or bad, by accepting it simply for what it is, the physical sensation can be separated from emotion. Well that's my very basic interpretation of it anyway. To do this one has to listen to one's body and this takes lots of training and practice. But it's worth it!

Suddenly I was in control. Sure, the whirlpool of despair made regular appearances but now I had the power to step back from the edge. I have been able to re-visit a lot of the horrors from my past and examine them as exactly what they are, memories from the past. I have been able to accept the physical sensations associated with these memories. The memories have now lost their terrible power; they no longer fill me with dread. I have accepted them. I made the choice.

But even more than this I have been able to use this technique in dealing with the present. The biggest difference I can attest to now, after practicing the mindfulness technique, is that I no longer react. I respond. There is a huge difference. In responding I have made a considered decision as to the course of action rather than an emotive reaction.

I feel calmer and more in control of my everyday experiences. As corny as it sounds, I feel like I'm in touch with the real me. I haven't had a nightmare in ages, and the negative thoughts that used to plague me through each day have just faded away.

Please don't misunderstand what I am saying here. I still have some issues in my life, and I still have some problems but I believe that I am now far better equipped to deal with life thanks to this training.

I sit here in prison, deprived of my family, my friends, my liberty, but still I can find something to smile about every day. I have been given the opportunity to make a choice every morning when I wake. The first option is to run around in ever decreasing circles crying out "why me, why me" and searching for non-existent answers, wishing I could turn back time. The second choice is to accept the current situation for what it is, and then move on.

What good can possibly come from the former option? I therefore choose to accept and look forward instead of behind. I'm not advocating that acceptance of a given situation means giving up hope. I am simply saying that the mindfulness technique has proved to be a very powerful tool that helps me accept the reality of life.

Have you noticed that the recurring theme of my little account is "acceptance?" To me, acceptance is the key.

I'm still just an average bloke but now I have a degree of skill and knowledge that helps me cope when real life is anything but average. And if Mr Average can do it, anyone can!

Case Example 3: PTSD and Dysthymic Disorder

Katherine" is a highly educated 49-year old woman who sought support, direction and skill to proceed with a marital separation, which she had been avoiding for about three years. Inspired by the results of MiCBT with a work colleague in similar circumstances, she decided to address her situation using the same approach. Katherine met her husband at age 17. She lived with him since and they had two daughters who are now young adults. She had been very dissatisfied with her love life, feeling a sense of emptiness and disconnection. On assessment, she presented with Dysthymia, moderate symptoms of clinical anxiety, hyperactivity and avoidance of certain topics characterized by attempts to control the direction of our interaction. She also reported dissociating during sexual experiences for as long as she could remember. After several sessions of mindfulness meditation, Katherine experienced increasingly clear memories of violent sexual abuse from several family members and was subsequently diagnosed with late onset Post-Traumatic Stress Disorder (PTSD). In the following letter, written after about eight weeks of treatment, Katherine illustrates the beneficial effect of mindfulness practice on her sensory perception and insight.

> Last week I tasted an apricot for the first time. Of course I've had lots of apricots in my life, but this one exploded its way throughout my entire body until my breath was taken away. Like in the movies in the scene where someone says, "I'll have what she's having …" In the same week, I remembered I had been raped by my father.
>
> In regaining my ability to feel sensations I had to own all the experiences of my childhood. Over the last twelve months I have been working with Bruno on Mindfulness Training. I have gradually revisited painful memories of ongoing emotional and physical violence, sexual abuse at the hands of three men and now rape.
>
> I had blocked out my memories as a way of surviving. And I did survive. I worked until there was no space left in a day; ate myself into fat, drank madly at times and gave my energies to protecting my children. I lived in a constant state of anxiety.
>
> By spending time each day in Mindfulness Training, I gradually came to be able to feel my body. By following Bruno's advice – wise, patient, knowledgeable advice, I have come to care about myself. Enough to start a whole new life. At almost fifty.
>
> The only way I can see to explain it to those who haven't experienced PTSD is to say that I have lived my life in my shadow. A life where I thought I was feeling what others were experiencing, but it wasn't the real thing. My senses had been numbed. I didn't taste in the same way as others, feel music, love or sex in the same way as others and I made no time for consideration of my own needs – if I had any.
>
> I'm not magically cured. And it wasn't just Mindfulness. It was being able to talk to a person I trusted, exercising daily, timing in my life, support of friends and being born with a strong spirit.
>
> I couldn't have got there without this unique combination of forces. I still have a long way to go. But I am optimistic. I have started a novel, I pay attention to my sensations and I stop to savor moments. And some of the time, even though I know there are so many things that are not yet right in my life, I feel that illusive feeling I have come to know as happiness.

During treatment, Katherine was able to leave the marriage, purchase a new house and begin a new and fulfilling relationship. One of her most peculiar experiences was the discovery of her sensuality, which she expressed in a few words: "It's hard to handle feeling like a teenager at 50."

Case Example 4: PTSD and Major Depressive Episode

"Sue" was 31 when she came to the Psychology Center referred by her GP for Major Depressive Episode. She had previously been diagnosed with Bipolar Affective

Disorder and subsequently PTSD. She presented with severe depressive symptoms, including persistent suicidal ideation. A few weeks earlier, Sue attempted suicide by overdosing on medication. Sue had been a clerk in a local Government office for about three years. Before this, she had been a security officer in the female section of a high security prison for several years. During that time, she repeatedly witnessed several prisoners committing suicide. On one such occasion, she found a prisoner hanged. She described her experience as shocking and traumatic. Throughout her work at the prison, she was also a victim of continuous bullying by other female custodians. These kinds of stressful experiences would trigger panic attacks, flashbacks, nightmares and avoidance of traumatic cues with regard to the witnessed suicides. The flashbacks decreased to some degree when she left the prison but recurrent severe episodes of depression began to emerge. She undertook the MiCBT program, which she completed within eight sessions. The following is a letter she sent just over one year following discharge from the program.

It's been a long time since I last saw you and I really wanted to give you an update on how I have progressed since you first saw me twelve months ago after my GP referred me to you.

I am ever so grateful to you for teaching me mindfulness and cannot express enough how much more rich my life has become! In a nutshell I shall try and condense the last few months since I saw you last. [...] The biggest news of all is:

Last week I had two major flashbacks to my past and I survived with NO ILL EFFECTS or traumatic response AT ALL!

The second event is much more momentous:

Late last week I went to a party plan party at a friend's place with my sister. I walked in the room and registered that a lady had visibly tensed when I had entered the room. I didn't recognize her so did not take any notice. A few minutes later I looked at her and thought "I think I should know her?" She appeared quite uncomfortable in my presence, which naturally piqued my interest in her. I had been sitting opposite her for about half an hour when I suddenly realized that it was one of the women who had bullied me and been quite horrible to me whilst I was at the Women's Prison. Apart from a momentary quickening of my heart beat and a second of tenseness, I had no other reaction. I was so proud of myself! She was clearly way more uncomfortable than me. I did not pity her, but I did think that it was sad that she looked so old and bitter and unhappy.

It did give me a whole lot of satisfaction to have turned the tables and have her see how strong and happy I am and that she did not destroy me as she had set out to. What a feeling of empowerment that was! It wasn't until after I got home that I realized the importance of this occasion and the fact that I had no traumatic response. I am just so proud of myself and the fact that I had no bad reactions to these events.

I feel as if I could climb a mountain - well maybe not, but I know that I can cope when events from the past come into the present. I am constantly astounded at the progress I have made and find it hard to believe that just over twelve months ago I had overdosed on anti-depressants. I remember sitting in your office, crying and saying that I was sick of being unwell and telling you how it was such hard work to stay on top of everything. I really was on a downhill spiral to nowhere. Yes, staying well does take a bit of work – but it is much easier to be mindful than it is to be depressed.

Mindfulness is now a part of my whole life it is something that I practice from the moment I wake until I go to sleep. Yes, I do have slip ups and catch myself at times being "not mindful" but it is not hard to bring myself back to reality. I am a much more calm and peaceful person now and so much happier than I have ever been. As a matter of fact my GP took my blood pressure a couple of months ago – 92 over 84, how relaxed is that?!

Thank you so much for teaching me! You did ask me at our last session if I would be interested in writing down my experiences to share with others. We can call this email the first installment if you like, I give you permission to use this email as you like. If my experiences can help turn someone else's life around then I am all for it! I think it has taken the two recent events to prove to myself that mindfulness does work and it has changed my life – this is concrete evidence …

Case Example 5: PTSD and Gambling Addiction

"Jacqueline" is a 51-year old woman who was referred to a government-funded MiCBT group for gambling addiction facilitated by the author. Like other participants, Jacqueline had multiple difficulties and her gambling addiction had been a way to handle her elevated stress levels for several years. Being in a group situation was initially very difficult and in the first few group sessions, she had at least one mild panic attack. She explained that she had avoided being in situations where there would be strangers.

Jacqueline married at 18 to a man whose sexual sadism led to Jacqueline being the victim of continual severe sexual abuse, including regular gang rape with extreme violence for about ten years. During that time, she fell pregnant and experienced a stillbirth, delivered by her partner at home, as she was forbidden to leave the house. For over two years prior to attending the group, she nursed her second husband who had been diagnosed with a terminal illness. The principal diagnosis was PTSD and her grief was immense. Several years in counseling had helped her gain insight and decrease the frequency of gambling, but the bulk of the problem remained. In the letter below, Jacqueline described some of her experiences with MiCBT.

> I am a 51-year old woman who has a 2-pronged problem that I received counseling for: gambling and post-traumatic stress following severe physical, sexual and psychological abuse over a period of 10 years. There was a break of 18 years until I sought help for my gambling and repeated flashbacks.
>
> I was approached to do a course in mindfulness training. When the technique was initially explained to me I was only skeptical. It appeared a too simple approach for a too complex problem.
>
> The fact that I was willing to go into a group situation is testament of my desperation. I didn't, and still don't to some extent, trust anyone and was somewhat hypervigilant in strange surroundings. Opening up to a group of strangers was my idea of hell. Bruno's gentle yet determined teaching methods overcame my wish to escape the group situation.

Making time to do my practice was very difficult as I am the primary carer to my seriously ill partner. As I made time to do the initial stage of the treatment I felt (much to my amazement) that it actually helped.

Although the flashbacks continued, the training helped focus my mind to be able to dissect the flashbacks and deal with the feeling and actual truths that these were only a memory that couldn't actually harm me.

The advanced techniques enabled me to go to a space in my mind that is safe, calming and that allows me to deal with the stresses of living with a terminally ill partner. The flashbacks still occur but much less frequently and with less impact on my life. The gambling has really decreased due to my ability now to deal with stress …

Towards the end of treatment, Jacqueline was able to use make-up, after over 20 years of being unable to do so due to flashbacks. She had preciously kept a bag of make-up at the back of her dresser draw for the last 10 years, just in case she would be able to wear some one day. As part of Stage 2 of MiCBT, we used graded exposure which required her to put make-up on. Jacqueline's sole pleasure in life was singing in a choir. She reported that her voice had become deeper and expressed: "Now I can really feel what I am singing about instead of worrying about the technique. I feel so much closer to myself and to God when I sing."

Case Example 6: Chronic Pain

When it comes to dealing with chronic pain, the issue of interoceptive avoidance versus acceptance is even more noticeable. The following letter is from an ex-client of the author. She addressed it to a colleague of the author who inquired about some difficulties his client had been having when using mindfulness skills. "Julia" is a 46 year-old single mother who has had repeated disappointments with relationships and had come to rely solely on herself for everything, no matter how strenuous certain physical tasks may be. She underwent the MiCBT program in both group and individual session formats.

I was checking on the mindfulness.net.au website today when I came upon your communication with regard to your client who is suffering chronic pain. After reading your report, I feel compelled to offer my own experiences in managing chronic pain as, hopefully, a point of both encouragement and perhaps some insight.

In 1986, I was hit by a car. I was on a bicycle. The result of this incident was six months in traction, a cornucopia of drugs, and a sense of despair … not to mention agony. Over the years, my spinal injuries have caused me countless hours of grief while the drugs have brought about more problems due to their side effects, one of which was bouts of anxiety and depression. I can honestly say that I have tried countless approaches to relieving my situation but none had any "staying power" … except this one; Mindfulness.

Over a year ago I had two series of one-on-one sessions (2 × 6) with you and have also participated in an eight-week Mindfulness Therapy group. I am not looking back. I sit twice a day and do the practice of body sweeping/observing sensations. When I first started, the pain seemed intolerable. I went into involuntary convulsions and often wanted to vomit. With your guidance, I learned to stay with the pain to the point of non-reactiveness. What I then discovered is that what had seemed like agony was in fact measurable by the degree I reacted to it. I didn't realize it before, but I had been in a viscous cycle of ignoring my body because the pain was so bad, and because I was ignoring my body I wasn't able to "catch the cues" before things escalated out of control. Then, on to the drugs and an even greater lack of awareness. Because of Mindfulness I am increasingly aware, enough to note the sensations in my body, and relax; let go before I am in trouble. Now I might have an occasional headache and the odd day out, which are hardly worth mentioning compared to what I used to suffer through. As for the drugs. ... I have not had to resort to numerous painkillers (Tramal, Celebrex, and codeine tablets) ... or the Emergency Unit ... at all.

Now for the first time in years I feel happier and confident about having my life back. Where last year I was flagged as "Highly Disadvantaged" by [the employment services], I now feel so good that I have committed myself to a pretty tough study course to go back to work ... and am loving it. Oh, and by the way, ... the other nice thing about Mindfulness is a better developed sense of discernment, detachment, and discipline. I have a private joke about the "3D effect" as I quite definitely have a much better perspective of life. These skills have impacted every aspect of my life in a very positive way. I remind myself of this on those days when I feel lazy and the half hour practices seem like "too much" (we are all human after all); but the rewards are too great to be missed.

I learned my lesson about that when I was on holiday over last Christmas. I stopped practicing Mindfulness, got sloppy, and BANG! the pain and confusion returned. Never again ... The interesting thing is that although I was beating myself up for this at the time and thinking that I had put myself back to "Square One," in reality I had charged up the batteries enough due to diligent practice previous to my "wobble" that I got back on track pretty quickly.

This has been, and is, a life-changing point for me. I feel so much calmer and things are going well ... still have the challenges but I am riding the waves of life with a greater sense of trust and happiness, plus I am making better decisions these days.

Do feel free to contact me anytime via return email. I am always happy to answer any questions you may have, and you have my permission to share this information with other clients if it is of service.

Julia has not returned for further sessions since.

Case Example 7: Chronic Pain, Chronic Depression, OCD and Panic Disorder with Agoraphobia

After attending a two-day MiCBT workshop, a Health Psychologist from a local pain clinic asked me if I would be willing to demonstrate how to implement MiCBT with one of his "most complex clients." He explained that his team uses evidence-based therapy for pain treatment, mostly, but not only, standard CBT, but this case was difficult because of the substantial problem of co-morbidity. "Jill" was in her mid-forties and was one of about ten for whom there were very few good results. She did not respond to relaxation. Any attempt to relax led her to experience moderate to severe symptoms of anxiety. Accordingly, her habit was to keep busy, at the detriment of her already damaged vertebrae. In the past ten years, she had been hospitalized once to twice monthly because of her difficulties to cope with flare-ups. It was agreed that I would introduce the client to the various stages of MiCBT and my colleague would supervise her practice within each stage. About two years later, she wrote this letter, as part of a book she began to write soon after we began with this treatment.

A car accident thirteen years ago took its toll on my body, forcing me to deal with a series of life-changing events. As mother of three children aged five and under, trying to cope with Post-natal Depression and building a new home meant an already difficult and stress-filled life was about to turn into a living nightmare. Now my world was collapsing around me. My close and loving family became nothing more than a blurry memory and any attempt to interact socially would often render me incapable of even the ability to speak.

Years of medical intervention followed, including all sorts of procedures from x-rays to major operations. The frustration I felt when relating to every different doctor and nurse my story over and over again was enough in itself to send me completely mad. Eventually I suffered a complete breakdown. Constant and unrelenting pain had taken its toll on body and mind. Unaware of the unrelenting pressure my extended periods of hospitalization had on my loves ones, the lowest of times came when I attempted to end it all. This was followed by confinement within private psychiatric facilities. Imagine becoming so lost within your own mind that you couldn't even recognize your own children.

Once back on track psychologically, a battle with chronic pain, more hospitalization and more procedures continued. Assortments of pain relieving medications were trialed, and I began feeling like a laboratory experiment. Often my body rejected a new drug and I became increasingly desperate. Also, the psychological complications of Post Traumatic Depression and Obsessive Compulsive Disorder added to the dilemma. It seemed to me that if I could have some relief from the pain, then my psychological problems would be a lot less or go away completely. Adding to this the surgeons would only operate if my mental faculties were in order.

Some relief from the medical roundabout came when I had spinal fusions in my lower back. After this came some respite, but I was still left with a lot of referred pain. Later another diagnosis of Regional Complex Pain Syndrome was treated with the implantation of a Spinal Column Stimulator. This successful procedure even gave me the opportunity to go back to work for a short time. However, I would have to muster as much strength as possible to get through the days without loosing the plot completely and bursting into tears. After most shifts I sat in my car, shook uncontrollably and often had panic attacks. Life was exhausting.

As the months turned to years, once again I found myself in a very dark place psychologically, as pain increased, influenced also by arthritis. Higher up in my spine my cervical vertebrae were under pressure and another big operation was being discussed. The psychological aspect of my health and well being, especially the OCD was making it difficult to relax. I cleaned the kitchen benches and picked up dust off the floor, robotically pushing all my physical boundaries, seemingly unable to stop hurting myself. None of the known psychological approaches helped. Even hypnosis couldn't break my relentless routine.

A breakthrough came in October 2005 when a different Psychologist introduced me to "Mindfulness-integrated Cognitive Behavior Therapy." The radical approach used by this therapy was unlike any of the previous procedures. Instead of using relaxation to take my mind off the pain, this therapy required me to direct my thoughts straight at the pain, with a detached and accepting attitude. Initially I admit to being extremely skeptical and doubted that I would ever be able to focus on the task at hand and set aside the time required for the daily training. In the early days I dreaded the sessions, as I would develop panic attack symptoms, cry, and feel out of control. But, as the days went by something must have clicked because it gradually became easier. There were daily feedback forms to fill out to keep track of my progress between sessions. As difficult as it was to add meditation time into what I thought was already a busy daily schedule, I had nothing to lose.

My self-esteem gradually improved and I gained the skills to enable me to cope with day to day events. By February 2006 I looked back on the forms I so loathed filling in and could see in black and white just how far I had come in a few months. I could now go to the supermarket, buy a magazine at the news agency, or go to the hairdressers without suffering any anxiety symptoms. A far cry from parking outside of the salon and being too scared to leave the safety of my car. Gaining the confidence to leave the house to go to the letterbox was a significant breakthrough.

Now, in November 2007, chronic pain is still a big part of my life, and I take strong daily medications. Nevertheless, I haven't been as in control for a long, long time. This year I took a huge step and enrolled in an Arts degree at the University of Tasmania as a part-time student. Overcoming crowded lecture theatres and new places has given me an immense personal boost. The confidence to attend University, make new acquaintances and do well in my studies has inspired me to continue in 2008. I am also hopeful of publishing my recently completed manuscript of a life-changing journey. Life just keeps on getting better.

The experience of this client no longer meets the DSM-V criteria for Dysthymic Disorder, Panic Disorder with Agoraphobia, or OCD, and relaxation-induced anxiety has completely subsided. In addition to the gain in quality-of-life, the cost incurred by frequent hospitalizations has decreased. Jill has been hospitalized only two or three times in the past two and half years, and this for less time and more superficial interventions. About a month ago, she sent me a copy of her completed and self-published book about her painful journey through pain and depression and her remarkable transformation. This achievement further empowered her and reinforced her new sense of self-efficacy.

Case Example 8: General Anxiety Disorder, Connective Tissue Disorder and Osteoarthritis

When she presented at my rooms for the first time, this 55-year-old woman had both hands in plastic wrap, hidden by thin white gloves. The extremely dry, cracked and discolored skin made her hands appear very red. Her initial description was as follows: "I have pompholyx breakouts on my hands and feet and my hands are like two lumps of meat at the end of my arms." She reported having regular infections around the fingernails, extreme itchy rashes, painful blisters, and difficulties finding cool enough places for her feet and hands. I recall switching the heater off during our sessions so she would not feel apprehensive about the air being too dry. She would drink about half a liter of water during the session. She also developed strong dermatological reactions to heat and fluorescent light.

She described experiencing "orgasmic scratches" during which she would scratch her hands until she damaged her skin. She had been treated with steroid medication, PUVA therapy (up to three Rx weekly), topical ointments and emulsifiers. She experienced continuous worry and other symptoms of generalized anxiety , aggravated by having to deal with a daughter diagnosed with Borderline Personality Disorder and a son who showed little respect for her, and by whom she felt continually used and verbally abused. Her mood was markedly low. Since she thought that her severe dermatitis was associated with stress, she obtained a referral from her GP to receive psychological treatment which could help decrease stress. She underwent the standard 4-stage model of MiCBT. It was only towards the end of the program that she admitted abusing alcohol to self-medicate. She had been consuming between 1 and 2 standard (750 ml) bottles of wine per night for several years and had been skilled at not letting it show. She wrote the following letter soon after she completed therapy.

At age 48 and getting by ok. At that time, my eventful life became overwhelmed with additional stressors – all-surrounding stressors – on the work front, hideous peri menopause symptoms, these on top of connective tissue disorder, osteoarthritis and general anxiety disorder. My "at-home" son reached adolescence, my "away from home" daughter's borderline personality disorder's behaviors were most distressing, hurtful and infuriating. My frail, ageing parents needed lots of support. As I struggled to stay functioning, my body could not cope.

In the summer of 2003, I experienced the onset of dermatitis pompholyx, unfortunately misdiagnosed, delaying treatment, all adding to anxieties. It was 3 months before I came under the care of a dermatologist, thus starting PUVa therapy, corticosteroid therapy, antibiotic therapy, applying topical ointments and emulsifiers around the clock. I developed contact allergies, rarely problematic before, as well as painful sensitivities to pressure, heat, and fluoro lighting especially.

Initially, my feet responded to treatment over a period of months, but my hands remained two lumps of meat at the ends of my arms, often too sore to use dressings or wear protective cotton gloves. As months turned to years, I swung through cycles of "a little better" to "horrid" pompholyx which could flare for weeks, exacerbated by stress which, in turn, was exacerbated by the physical symptoms of the disease and anxiety disorder. I used alcohol daily to help relieve the physical pain, emotional pain and anxiety symptoms – all too much to cope with.

In May 2005, I resigned my (then new) clerical position as my damaged hands were constantly pummeled by paper handling, filing, pen writing and typing (I did become adept at typing with fingernails!). Pompholyx and anxiety dictated my life. My general functioning deteriorated: household / gardening activities, leisure activities, even reading books and practicing piano, all declined or stopped.

In subsequent work placements over the next 2 ½ years, I managed selected office tasks with layers of gloves over various dressings and coatings of ointments, countering regular skin infections with courses of antibiotic, and treating full body flares with courses of Prednisolone. All medications came with side effects. Anxiety remained high. It was impossible to find comfortable, cool places to rest my feet and hands in bed. Quality-of-life was cruelly compromised – I thought I'd done my best adapting to the chronic pompholyx and living with anxiety disorder. Whilst remaining hopeful of remission from the dermatitis, I nevertheless hated the appearance and uselessness of my hands. I'd spent thousands of dollars and hundreds of hours on conventional treatments and alternative remedies, but I was still burdened by the condition – the infernal itch, the pain, the misery. Over a period of 6–7 months my moderate alcohol consumption increased to heavy drinking – from early evening until bed time – when I just wanted to slip into sleep and oblivion. I knew drinking was detrimental and irresponsible, but it was one of my crutches and I didn't want to let go.

In Nov 2007, I commenced MiCBT. For me, learning mindfulness practice has been challenging. With your support and guidance, I am persevering with it. I see mindfulness practice as my best ally. My well-being has improved so much. I am more resilient. I feel closer to full recovery from dermatitis. Even in early stages of mindfulness practice, I experienced something wonderful and curious – "nothing of consequence" in my hands.

I can't help feeling delighted with improvements in myself and the dermatitis: now only occasional pompholyx in my feet; my hands are greatly improved – minor flares with quicker recovery; my fingers and hands are useful again – I can tackle manual tasks; I am able to better rest my hands day and night; the itch is reduced, so scratching and damage to skin also reduced; and much less inflammation and redness of hand tissues.

I even recently experienced the sensation of cold hands - first time in 4 ½ years. In July 2008: I haven't used steroids or antibiotics for 3 months now. I use less and fewer ointments; I ceased PUVA therapy, there are far less appointments to attend – more time for me. And, until now, I couldn't imagine reaching the turning point which had to come, living without excessive drinking – I couldn't attempt sobriety. This was one of my challenges. Mindfulness practice lessened the need to feel numbed by alcohol. Mindfulness is my key tool for moving ahead. I feel that my presence is back in my home, with energy and momentum. I feel more confident and competent, better prepared for whatever is ahead. I'm planning lots …

MiCBT has benefited me in many ways, including improved sleep, improved pain management, generally better ability to recognize and manage anxiety symptoms, especially agitation and panic episodes, and recognize my thought patterns and challenge them.

I am most grateful for the opportunity to learn MiCBT. I am so thankful to you Bruno for your teachings, patience, guidance and support. I acknowledge the wisdom of your own teacher, and, wherever possible, I happily and respectfully pass on the merits which have been shared with me through my practice of Loving Kindness.

Case Example 9: Chronic Depression, General Anxiety, Binge Eating and Diabetes

This lady was in her late 40s when she decided to travel about 4000 km from Perth (Western Australia) to Hobart (Tasmania) and undergo the MiCBT program for a two-month period to address her chronic depression and anxiety. Her sister had recovered from long-lived PSTD using this method a couple of years earlier and she had been thinking about undertaking it herself for some time. On assessment, she described she had been consuming about 500 g chocolate daily compulsively for years! She was also unemployed and unhappy with her relationship.

Next Monday I will get up and go to work in the first day of my new full time job as a University Lecturer. Yesterday I rang my Mother without being left feeling wrung out and guilty. Last night I slept soundly and deeply and woke fresh in my own little house on which I have a manageable mortgage. Today I bought steak and salad to cook for my dinner. I also had a shower with lovely pampering products and got dressed in clothes I like, did my make up and hair and went into the city to see my GP. I got test results that said my blood sugar is being well managed (I have diabetes), my cholesterol is under control and I have lost around 13 kg since August.

It all sounds rather normal doesn't it, bordering almost on boring? To me though, living this life is little less than a miracle. In May last year (9 months ago) I could not go to work, was not looking after myself and could not afford my mortgage. I slept fitfully and was constantly exhausted. I was incapable of clear thought and my short term memory was shot to pieces. Meals were haphazard and, not being able to remember if I had taken medication or not, my blood sugar was out of control and my cholesterol was through the roof. My GP told me that if I continued this way I would die – sooner rather than later. In addition to diabetic medication I was taking 52 units of insulin a day and 80 mg of prozac daily for diagnosed chronic depression. I weighed 105 kg and felt constantly unwell. There could be days on end where I did not shower or get dressed. Of course I was very skilled at hiding this from "the world" so no one would have ever dreamt of the daily pain I fought.

I was offered my dream job; working with an Aboriginal community in a rural town to address the issues of suicide and self harm experienced there. I had been approached by Aboriginal people to do this work. I spent one week there and "hit the wall." I knew that I couldn't sustain this work, couldn't work with people and was incapable of the level of patience required to work collaboratively within a diverse community. Tearfully I resigned and retreated into my own self.

Not only was my home sold by then, I had no idea where I might live or how I would be able to afford to live anywhere once settlement happened. I was in tears often, regularly angry and felt numb the rest of the time. I avoided people; couldn't answer the phone and did not mix socially with anyone. Fear and anxiety were insidiously dictating the way I spent my days. I was so ill that Social Security staff actually directed me to apply for a Disability Pension and it was granted without question.

I became physically ill, a viral infection of some kind that left me even more exhausted. I stopped even testing my blood sugar … it was too demoralizing to see the constant high readings. I was eating anything up to 4 family blocks of chocolate a day – self medicating the pain. I was staying with a friend in her tiny spare room. I slept almost constantly for the first two weeks there. My body said "enough." It was like being a totally lost and spent soul that felt worthless and hopeless and incapable.

With my house sold I had a little money in the bank and decided to visit family in Tasmania for a couple of weeks. My sister had seen Dr Bruno Cayoun, a Clinical Psychologist in Hobart, and her life had turned around in an amazingly short time and her health improved exponentially. Before flying to Tasmania I emailed him and asked if he would see me. I didn't see how it might work but I didn't want to feel this way anymore and thought maybe he could help. He agreed and I made 2 appointments for the period of my stay.

Counseling wasn't going to be new for me. I first saw a Psychologist 24 years ago and have been in and out of counseling ever since. Years and years of one-on-one work, group work, residential workshops, diaries, art therapy, writing, rebirthing, rethinking, rehashing and reliving. In retrospect it was probably those years of work that had kept me functioning at as high a level as I had managed. But the pattern was I did some counseling, felt better, worked hard, anxiety would rise, I would burn out and become depressed. Nothing really changed inside, it was a treadmill.

I saw Bruno my first morning in Hobart in early August. I liked what he seemed to offer and I was desperate to feel better. There and then I decided to return briefly to Perth, sort out my things and fly back to Tasmania to live in my sister's spare room for as long as it took. My health and well being were going to be my priority – and they were. I flew back to Western Australia in early November, after six more sessions using Mindfulness-integrated Cognitive Behavior Therapy with Bruno. I came home a different person to the one that sat in the little room in Princes Street with tears in her eyes as Bruno said, "I think I can help."

What had changed? Well, everything really. Within 3 weeks of starting the exercises my blood sugar dropped so rapidly that I was having hypos in the middle of the night and halved the amount of insulin I was taking. The amount of prozac was now 20 mg per day instead of 80 mg. I was sleeping like a log. I had found joy in living and the butterflies in my tummy (my anxiety) were stilled. I was consuming no more than 40–50 mg of chocolate per day – and it had to be darned fine quality too! I had lost around 10kg of my excess physical baggage and an untold quantity of my emotional baggage.

It is hard to put into words the enormity of change and the simplicity of the process that led to that change. Because it is a simple process – simple but not easy. What led to the dramatic turnaround in my life was half an hour twice a day. ... Doing the exercises set by Bruno. And this was unlike any counseling I had ever done; no mind bending gymnastics required to change thinking, no copious piles of tissues as I rendered my heart and soul bare and raw and bleeding. This was gentle, kind, respectful and totally empowering in every way.

Bruno questioned my diagnosis so I went to see a psychiatrist for the first time – and she took a thorough history and gave an accurate diagnosis of Anxiety Disorder with many aspects of PTSD. Oh, the release and power of an accurate diagnosis is indescribable in itself.

Mindfulness changes everything – in all areas of my life. I am more loving and accepting of so much in my life. Anxiety is something I now notice but don't have to react to. I can have full-on days and, with some mindfulness practice, a walk with my dog, have a cuppa on my front porch watching the trees, I am back in a place of equanimity.

I am by no means the "perfect practitioner" (whatever that looks like). I have days where I miss my practice ... and my physical and emotional health reflect that almost instantaneously. I still sometimes react from habit and I quite often forget to treat myself with loving kindness. But I now have the tools to deal with that. Sometimes the experience isn't pleasant – but it still beats the pain of life without the practice.

And chocolate? I rarely eat it and never crave it.

Mindfulness is blissfully portable – and cheap! I can practice for free as often as I want. I have practiced on planes, on trains and in public meeting places and waiting rooms. I don't need a PhD, special music track or blissful place or private health insurance to access it. All that is needed is a desire, a little courage and commitment … all available to anyone.

Mindfulness is a precious gift, one that I am extremely grateful for. I could wax lyrical about mindfulness for volumes and could tell you more of my personal story and background. But I think you get the point; mindfulness works and I am the living, breathing, walking proof of that. So, to my wonderful sister who gave me a safe home to live in and was the best ever "mindfulness police" in the early days – thank you! And to Bruno who gives so freely to so many – God Bless You! I can now delight in the joy of doing what was unthinkable only a few months ago – cooking a meal, walking my dog, sleeping and a full time professional job, love and joy … and more. My story doesn't end here. In so many ways it is just beginning.

Case Example 10: Borderline Personality Disorder

The following are two letters from the same client treated by the author in a private psychiatric hospital. "Jenny" was a 30-year-old client diagnosed with Borderline Personality Disorder. Jenny had a difficult childhood, remembering only some of it (e.g., having been sexually abused by her father and living on the streets for some time as an adolescent). When we met, she had partly recovered from a dissociative identity disorder but still experienced severe dissociative symptoms, along with severe self-mutilating behavior (including body parts amputations) and severe depression.

The pervasiveness of her long-term condition has led to a separation in her relationship, following which she was denied custody of her children. Jenny's social network was limited to very few individuals, upon whom she felt emotionally dependent. She described a long list of psychotherapies (including standard CBT) that failed to help deal with her condition. Following six weeks of MiCBT, Jenny reported clear improvement. She was discharged from the inpatient program and admitted as an outpatient. As I mentioned to her that her rapid change would be a good example to cite for educational purposes, Jenny kindly decided to write the following letters reflecting her experience.

> I came here two months ago with three aims: to try to find out who I was, to be able to feel emotions, and to become more "real" rather than switching constantly from role to role. I was unable to feel strong emotions and was often unaware of the less intense emotions as well. To control the sensations that emotions produced in me I was using controlled dissociation, suppression and various distraction behaviors.
>
> Over the next six weeks, I changed my perspective from being event-focused to focusing on my reactions to events. This meant that instead of trying to deal with the event itself, which wasn't the problem, I could start to deal with my reactions and responses at the basic level. This will enable me to deal with any stressful event as it happens, rather than having to cope with each new event as a separate problem or just suppressing any reaction to it.

As my awareness of myself increased, I realized that my sense of identity was caught up in *doing* rather than *being*, so as I became more aware of my bodily and emotional reactions, and more able to just *be*, my sense of self increased naturally.

Then I realized that there were a number of things about the "real" me that I didn't like and couldn't accept in myself, and this led me to some dissociative episodes and some self-injurious behavior. It took me some time to be able to accept that it was "normal" to be ambivalent about oneself – that there are parts of everyone that they find harder or easier to accept (Some cognitive work had just taken place at this stage – author's addition). I was then able not only to be aware of myself but also to come to some acceptance of myself.

After discharge, I continued to become more and more aware of my reactions, feelings and thoughts. A few days ago I experienced a very negative reaction to a trigger and felt so much emotional pain that I reacted out of habit rather than my new training and self-harmed again. Afterwards I felt very negative and depressed, but instead of burying these emotions, I was able to stay with them and struggled to accept them until they passed. When they did, I looked back and realized that I had become the "emotional wreck" I had always wanted to be. (i.e. "I'd rather feel miserable than feel nothing" – author's addition) I knew that to experience life fully meant experiencing the "negative" emotions and reactions as well as the "positive" ones, but I hadn't realized how painful they could be.

Looking back however, I can appreciate the experience, because I really did experience it, and that was my goal, after all. I finally was able to be "emotional" and even though I felt awful and hated every minute of the negative feelings, being emotionally unstable was a great experience!

Jenny's discovery of a clearer, more authentic and more consistent sense of self, and a shift from external to internal locus of control were not due to traditional cognitive restructuring methods, which had been offered to her for many years without lasting benefit. In fact, she reported to be "very good at using the mind to rationalize and avoid the pain." Hence, the working assumption that merely changing thoughts is sufficient to change emotions and behavior is yet another limitation of traditional CBT.

Six months later, Jenny enrolled in a science degree at university and wrote the following letter. The last two paragraphs reflect the sense of self-control and self-efficacy necessary to prevent relapse.

Now that the initial excitement of being well has worn off, after such a long period of time being sick, I can look at my life more objectively and evaluate how things are for me now. Firstly, things are not perfect, but that is now a given fact of life, rather than a cause for despair. I try not to catastrophize the things that happen now. Instead, I have the tools to grow and learn from the challenges that present themselves, if I choose to use those tools.

There is still a small part of me that would rather go back to the old, familiar ways of coping but as these new skills become more ingrained the old pathways grow weaker. They still show themselves in little ways – sneaky, repetitive thoughts and sudden cravings, but I am much more adept at breaking them down into basic sensations, which are much easier to deal with. In my case, the "whole" really is greater than the sum of its parts. Taken together it is still easy to get overwhelmed by thoughts and cravings. Individually, they are just sensations. A feeling of tenseness here? Let's see how long it lasts. A recurring thought? Just wait, no reaction, and it will pass. I can still hear my therapist saying: "That is their nature – to arise and pass away." And they do so more quickly than ever now.

Sometimes I wonder what will happen if I relapse. One component of my depression is genetic. Medicated and mindful, I am much less likely to allow myself to be dragged under again, but there is still the possibility that it may recur. Even if it does, I will never be the same person that I once was. I can't unlearn all the new skills I have; they are too deeply ingrained for that. If I do get sick again, I will try to do it mindfully. I have already experienced that acceptance is a powerful weapon against depression and the more adept I become at not reacting to periods of being "down," the less likely I am to perpetuate that state.

So now the future looks livable. Actually, it is only in the last 6 months that I have been able to envision a future for myself at all. Before, it was all I could do just to survive from one day to the next. "Living" is more challenging, but also far more rewarding than simply surviving."

About 18 months following the end of MiCBT treatment (20 months after her last hospitalization), Jenny was on the university campus and came to my office to say hello. She proudly showed me her new ring and announced she was engaged and planned to get married in the following month. She described what seemed to be a healthy relationship, a possibility she could hardly envisage when we met. We laughed at the thought that her past cravings for self-harm did not succeed in depriving her from what is now the most important finger of her left hand. Indeed, Jenny had tried to amputate it twice, but never really succeeded. She said she was still practicing her mindfulness exercises but only intermittently, mostly when stress gets the best of her.

The new activities of Jenny and her beloved partner appeared in a long article of a local newspaper. The article described how the two benevolent individuals had been successful in attracting financial assistance to help people with drug and alcohol problems, especially the homeless. Their main operations consisted of supporting these people by providing information and act as a go-between with appropriate agencies. As part of the motivation for their altruistic operation, there was a very brief note saying Jenny had been able to recover from past psychological difficulties and was very familiar with the problems these people encounter with the current mental health system.

The Issue of Personality

The positive outcome resulting from an informed and skillfully delivered mindfulness-based program is made possible through a gentle detachment from the self-concept that starts at the perceptual level (shapes and colors, sounds, tastes, etc), extending to ways of thinking, body sensations, and the way in which we react.

When all these four primary factors of reinforcement are targeted, identification to each becomes a conscious process, placed under more control of the individual. Disidentification from these parts of the self-concept is thus made possible, which in turn allows cognitive reappraisal to be generalized across *all* situations in daily living, rather than being constrained to specific schemas and their situational manifestations. Attachment to what the self represents pervades all associations with the self-concept, maintained over time in accordance with the reinforcement pattern that operates through the four functional components of the reinforcement system (described in Chapter 2). When an emotional difficulty appears, the tendency is inadvertently to identify with evaluative thoughts and co-emerging body sensations. As a result, the strength of identification with the experience maintains the symptoms far longer than they should (e.g., *my* feelings, *my* depression, *my* anxiety symptoms, *my* heart pounding, *my* addiction, etc). When attachment to a problematic behavior is sufficiently maintained to allow long-term identification with it, the behavior is incorporated into the sense of self and letting go of it can be as psychologically painful as the loss of a body part. The more "fixed" or "rigid" is the attachment to the self-concept, the longer it takes for personality to change.

Summary of Main Points

- Human suffering can be "legitimate" on the basis that we are insufficiently cognizant of the ever-changing nature of all phenomena; including our possessions, health, wealth, appearance, emotions, reputation and relationships. When we expect these to remain how we believe they should be, unwanted change creates unhappiness. Acceptance of change will moderate the amount of suffering. Some psychopathologies, such as Adjustment Disorder (with or without depression or anxiety), typically embody the lack of acceptance and adaptability to one or more significant life changes.
- Based on the co-emergence model of reinforcement, MiCBT operates below the overarching verbal determinant of experience, at the locus of reinforcement (reaction to body sensations), and is consequently able to target a wide variety of conditions.
- Advanced scanning methods promote a large and rapid decrease in threshold of awareness and a resulting skillful detection of distress cues, sufficiently early in the sequence of an event to let us choose an appropriate response; instead of allowing an automatic reaction.
- The clinical results from mindfulness-based interventions challenge the traditional view that chronic conditions are difficult to resolve and that personality does not change. When therapy addresses directly the locus of behavioral reinforcement, behavior change takes place regardless of the type of mental health condition.

Chapter 11

Evaluation of Mindfulness Training

If something exists, it must exist in some amount.
If it exists in some amount then it is capable of being measured.

René Descartes

Based on Beck's differentiation between a system of psychotherapy and a cluster of techniques, it is apparent that MiCBT fits the format of acceptable psychotherapy systems more than that of mere techniques. Beck pointed out:

> A system of psychotherapy provides both the format for understanding the psychological disorders it purports to treat and a clear blueprint of the general principles and specific procedures of treatment. A well-developed system provides (a) a comprehensive theory or model of psychopathology and (b) a detailed description of and guide to therapeutic techniques related to this model. (Beck, 1976, pp. 306–307)

Beck also proposed a set of useful standards for evaluating theories of psychopathology and systems of psychotherapy. As described below, both mindfulness meditation and the theory on which it is based in MiCBT fulfill these standards.

Evaluating the psychotherapy system

1. The therapeutic system of MiCBT is well defined, including standardized scripts. It is described clearly and explicitly in both a traditional way (e.g., Hart, 1987) and in a theoretically and empirically based manner (Cayoun, 2003; Lindsay, 2007; Roubos, Cayoun, and Hawkins, 2010).

---

2. The general principles of the treatment are sufficiently articulated so that different therapists dealing with the same problem among similar clients can use similar techniques.
3. There is empirical evidence to support the validity of the neurological, cognitive and behavioral principles underlying the MiCBT therapeutic system, as mentioned in previous chapters.
4. Mindfulness training has been shown to be efficient, either as a stand-alone system (Kabat-Zinn, 1990) or when associated with a cognitive-behavioral approach, as in the case of Mindfulness-Based Cognitive Therapy (Segal *et al.*, 2002; Teasdale *et al.*, 2000; Williams *et al.*, 2000) and Dialectical Behavior Therapy (Linehan, 1993, 1994; Linehan *et al.*, 1999).

Evaluating the theory of psychopathology

1. The co-emergence model of behavior maintenance (see Chapter 2) which underlies MiCBT is parsimonious (simple yet sufficiently complex to explain the phenomena). It involves the recognition that all aspects of an experience (mental, physical and emotional, as well as the stimulus itself) obey the same fundamental law; they are all impermanent and therefore of impersonal nature. Whereas low experiential awareness leads to behavioral automaticity (identifying with an experience that precedes a learned evaluation and response), higher experiential awareness leads to choice and self-efficacy (preventing identifying with the experience, which allows the reallocation of attention from established schematic models to the processing of sensory stimuli. Applying equanimity (exposure and response prevention) to these sensory aspects leads to extinction. It also has a high ecological validity due to its ability to explain reinforcement and extinction principles with minimal complexity and because it is grounded in experience.
2. Its theory of psychopathology, based on disequilibrium in information processing, is sufficiently related to its allied therapeutic training so that it is obvious that the therapeutic principles are logically derived from the theory.
3. The model of reinforcement underlying MiCBT provides the basis for understanding the effectiveness of its derived therapeutic application through mindfulness training.
4. The theory is sufficiently flexible to allow for the development of new techniques while preserving its essence, as exemplified by other authors' adaptations of mindfulness training to suit various disorders and clinical populations.
5. The main assumptions underlying the MiCBT approach have been clearly spelt out and can be tested through systematic empirical investigations. They are derived from, but not limited to, a larger experiential system, mindfulness meditation, supported by twenty-five centuries of anecdotal accounts and increasing empirical evidence. The model of co-emergent reinforcement also integrates well-documented cognitive, behavioral, and ecological principles.

Measuring Efficacy of Mindfulness-based Treatments

Dimidjian and Linehan (2003) pointed out that a priority for mindfulness researchers should be able to construct and apply reliable and valid methods of measuring core components of mindfulness.

Early questionnaires

There exist various measurement tools for the mindfulness construct. One is the Freiburg Mindfulness Inventory (FMI). The instrument is a 30–item self-report questionnaire constructed by Buchheld, Grossman, and Walach (2001), primarily to evaluate empirically the construct of mindfulness within a multifactorial framework and operationalize mindfulness in a sensitive, valid and reliable manner. This was done with a pre- and post-mindfulness training design. Tests over two sessions ($n = 115$) support the validity and reliability of the measure, despite some instability in the factor structure between pre- and post-training experience.

Interestingly, it appears that ten items (a third of the total number of items) may be associated with equanimity. For example, in Factor I, "I remain present with sensations and feelings even when they are unpleasant or painful," "I notice that I don't need to react to whatever pops into my mind;" in Factor II, "I can accept unpleasant experiences," "in difficult situations, I can pause without immediately reacting;" and in Factor III, "I experience moments of inner peace and ease, even when things get hectic and stressful."

The first factor emphasizes disidentification, and instances of Egolessness (e.g., "I watch my thoughts without identifying with them," "I know that I am not identical to my thoughts"). Moreover, at least three items reflect the notion of impermanence (e.g., "I observe how experiences arise and fade away," "I observe how my thoughts come and go"). This indicates the importance of notions of *impermanence* and *egolessness* in mindfulness training, as emphasized in MiCBT. Buchheld, Grossman, and Walach, recently produced a shorter (14–item) version for individuals completely new to meditation, the FMI-SF. There is now a French version available (Trousselard *et al.*, 2010).

The Mindfulness Attention Awareness Scale (MAAS; Brown and Ryan, 2003) is a 15–item self-report questionnaire which assesses individual differences in the frequency of mindful states over time. In contrast with the FMI, the MAAS emphasizes the construct of presence, rather than that of acceptance and equanimity.

Another instrument designed to measure the mechanisms underlying mindfulness is the Kentucky Inventory of Mindfulness Skills (KIMS; Baer, Smith, and Allen, 2004). These authors identify four mindfulness skills based on discussions in the current literature: observing, describing, acting with awareness, and accepting without judgment. The data show a clear factor structure, good internal validity and test-retest reliability. Ruth Baer and colleagues included a fifth factor, a "non-reactivity" component to their construct of mindfulness, which is consistent with the notion of equanimity, a core mechanism of mindfulness in the MiCBT model. This led to the development of the Five Facet Mindfulness Questionnaire (FFMQ; *Baer et al.,* 2006), which is gaining popularity.

Some words of caution. A recent study clearly confirms that our self-report of personal mindfulness skills is extremely sensitive to our ability to be mindful. Van Dam, Earleywine and Danoff-Burg (2009) found that non-practitioners of mindfulness meditation understood the items of the FFMQ very differently than did mindfulness meditators. Indeed, how can we understand a question asking directly about a mindfulness skill unless we already understand how mindfulness is supposed to be experienced? This poses a serious challenge to authors of mindfulness scales. For example, a group of adults, naive about mindfulness qualities and skills, might perceive their ability to be experientially aware and accepting to be fairly high. However, as their mindfulness training takes place, they are likely to become more aware of the extent to which they are *not* so aware and accepting of their experiences. Accordingly, *because* of their increased mindfulness skills, they are likely to rate their levels of mindfulness as being lower than it was before training started. As a result, a more mindful individual can sometimes score lower than a less mindful person on the same mindfulness scale. The principal author, Nicholas Van Dam, later mentioned in a public email through the Kent University Listserve Mindfulness Digest forum, that in the absence of mindfulness, mindfulness cannot be detected and that the more mindful the individual, the more likely they are to actually notice lapses in mindfulness.

We, and some of our students, often notice this bias emerging in the data when using mindfulness scales that includes mindfulness-specific items, in both clinical and non-clinical populations. Other have also expressed concerns and the need for caution (e.g. Davidson, 2010; Heidenreich, Ströhle, and Michalak, 2006; Wells, 2011).

In addition, some scales are clearly not appropriate for clinical settings and clinicians and researchers intending to use a mindfulness scale in psychiatric settings need to choose the most suitable instrument. Some authors are currently developing instruments that contain items that may fit better one population of clients than another.

The Mindfulness-based Self Efficacy Scale (MSES), on the other hand, was precisely constructed for a general clinical population (Francis and Cayoun, 2011). This is reflected in items such as "I am aware when I am about to do something that could hurt me or someone else" or "I avoid feeling my body when there is pain or other discomfort." The MSES is a 35–item self-report questionnaire destined to measure self-efficacy before, during, and following therapy across seven subscales (Behavioral, Cognitive, Interoceptive, Affective, Interpersonal, Avoidance and Mindfulness). Each subscale comprises five items, some of which are presented in reverse order (see Appendix B for a copy of the MSES client form).

Hunsinger (2006) compared the MSES with other mindfulness measures in 1250 university students. The MSES was found to have good internal consistency (Cronbach alpha = 0.86), good concurrent validity when compared to the FMI ($r = 0.62$), the KIMS ($r = 0.49$), and the Mindful Attention Awareness Scale (MAAS; Brown and

Ryan, 2003) ($r = 0.57$). Another study ($n = 163$) recently confirmed the internal consistency (Cronbach alpha $= 0.86$) and validity of the MSES with respect to the FMI ($r = .62$), KIMS ($r = .67$), and MAAS ($r = .57$) (Francis and Cayoun, 2010).

A number of authors (e.g., Wells, 2010; Husinger, 2006) and several data sets which we collected in routing clinical practice from various mental health organizations over a five-year period (e.g., Bilsborrow and Cayoun, 2008) also show strong negative correlations between MSES scores and measures commonly used in clinical treatments (e.g., Depression Anxiety and Stress Scale; Lovibond and Lovibond, 1995). From these observations, four ranges were proposed as a tentative rough clinical guide as to levels of self-efficacy: 0–34 = poor, 35–69 = weak, 70–104 = moderate, and 105–140 = good. Although they are useful ranges, however, they should be used cautiously until more empirical evidence from normative data substantiates these cut-off points.

Measuring equanimity

A mechanism of mindfulness that is worth measuring is equanimity. At present, however, there is no existing tool for the specific measurement of equanimity known to the author. Since it is proposed that equanimity is a core component in mindfulness training, a measurement system that could evaluate a person's general ability for equanimity would provide a number of assessment and therapeutic advantages. When equanimity is assessed in a mindfulness questionnaire, it tends to appear through items that measure "non-reactivity" to common situations. However, priority in most instruments seems to be given to elements of self-awareness and acceptance.

Measuring therapy progress and self-efficacy

In accordance with the self-efficacy approach (Bandura, 1977a; 1997b), MiCBT promotes self-control and self-efficacy, rather than just a decrease in symptomatology. Accordingly, outcome measures will show data that are more meaningful if they include scales assessing these psychological qualities.

The common view in the self-efficacy literature is that general scales are not as useful as those designed to measure specific areas. For this reason, the *Short Progress Assessment* (SPA) has been constructed (Cayoun and Maeder, 2011). We also conceptualized the MSES with this in mind.

The SPA (see Form 1 in Appendix B) is a self-report questionnaire destined to measure progress during the course of therapy. One of the peculiarities of the SPA is its use of both pre-post and "post-then-pre" scores. Post-then-pre scores are pre-treatment scores that clients are asked to rate weekly during the course of therapy. They are retrospective scores, based on the client's current perception of "what it was like" before therapy started. This has a great advantage over simple pre-post questionnaires, especially when it comes to measuring the therapeutic effects of mindfulness training. It has the capacity to offset the problem highlighted by Van Dam and his colleagues, mentioned above. It may be possible to use the same method for mindfulness scales (along with collecting pre-post data, simply asking the client how they *now* perceive their mindfulness skills *before* the program started, and this on each item of the scale and at each assessment time).

The SPA consists of four scales, Symptom Severity, Symptom Manageability, Perceived Improvement, and Satisfaction with Therapy, each comprising five items to be rated on a 5-point scale. The severity scale serves to assess the respondent's severity of symptoms, whereas the manageability scale helps assess his or her sense of self-efficacy acquired during therapy. Impairment is the sum of severity and (lack of) manageability scores across five life domains, behavioral, cognitive, interoceptive, affective, and interpersonal. The SPA also provides percentage improvement scores across the five domains from one week to the next and is rapidly implemented – about 2 to 3 minutes (see Appendix B for a copy of the SPA forms).

Data Collection: A Non Diagnosis-Specific Analysis of MiCBT

The clinical data presented below may be interesting in showing the convenience of MiCBT in its ability to address crisis and co-morbidity. They were obtained from an 8-week MiCBT group conducted by Cayoun, Sauvage and van Impe (2004) in routine clinical practice at a private psychiatric hospital in southern Tasmania.

Participants

The 15 participants were 5 inpatients and 10 outpatients: 73% females, 27% males, age range was between 26 and 67. About 80% were in crisis situations. Based on DSM-V criteria, all were diagnosed with a chronic condition: 3 with Bipolar Mood Disorder (2 had psychotic experiences), 3 with Post-Traumatic Stress Disorder (2 chronic pain, 1 anger problems, 2 severe binge drinking, 1 with OCD symptoms, 2 depression), 1 with Panic Disorder With Agoraphobia and Major Depressive Episode, 5 with Chronic Depression (2 binge drinking), 2 with Generalized Anxiety Disorder, and 1 with Borderline Personality Disorder (self-harmed).

Measurement

Each client was asked to fill in self-report questionnaires weekly, just before the start of each session. Three measurement tools using a Likert-type scale were used, the *Symptom Checklist-90 Revised Edition* (SCL-90-R) (Derogatis, 1994), the *Depression Anxiety and Stress Scale* (DASS; Lovibond and Lovibond, 1995), and the *Short Progress Assessment* (SPA; Cayoun and Maeder, 2010).

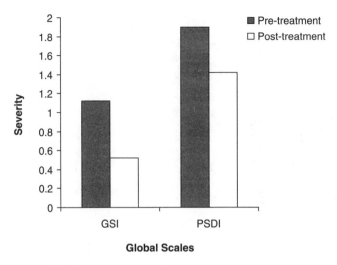

Figure 8. SCL-90-R global scores at pre- and post-treatment.

The SCL-90-R is a self-rated questionnaire, which assesses symptomatology on 10 psychiatric scales, Somatization, Obsessive-Compulsive, Interpersonal Sensitivity, Depression, Anxiety, Hostility, Phobic Anxiety, Paranoid Ideation, Psychoticism, and Additional Items.

The DASS also assesses symptomatology from the client's perspective, focusing on three clinical scales (Depression, Anxiety and Stress). The SPA is a self-rated questionnaire which provides broad scores on four main scales, Symptom Severity, Symptom Manageability (self-efficacy), Perceived Improvement, and Satisfaction with Therapy. Clients rate the severity and manageability of their symptoms, on five subscales (Behavioral, Cognitive, Somatic, Affective, and Interpersonal).

Results

The Global Severity Index (GSI) and the Positive Symptom Distress Index (PSDI) of the SCL-90-R are displayed in Figure 8. These represent the global psychiatric measures at pre- and post-treatment. On the GSI, there was a statistically significant decrease in symptom severity from pre-treatment to post treatment. Similarly, the PSDI measure reflected a significant decrease in symptom distress from pre-treatment to post treatment.

The differences in the severity of symptoms from pre to post treatment across all psychiatric measures are displayed in Figure 9. The results showed a statistically and clinically significant decrease in most scales, despite the variety of diagnoses across participants. The clinical significance was high overall, as reflected by the effect sizes displayed in Table 1.

The DASS self-reported measures at pre- and post-treatment are displayed in Figure 10. As with the SCL-90-R data, the participants rated the severity of their

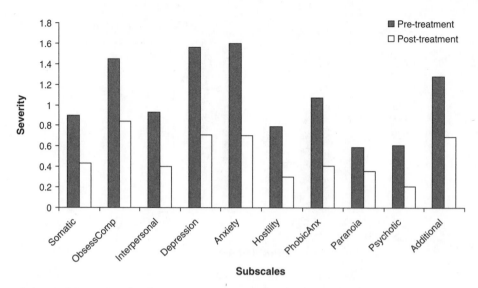

Figure 9. SCL-90-R subscale severity scores at pre- and post-treatment.

Table 1. Effect size for each scale of SCL-90-R (T-test subjected to Boneferroni adjustment).

Scale	Cohen's d	t-test
Somatic	1.11	$p < .05$
Obsessive Compulsive	0.83	$p < .05$
Interpersonal Sensitivity	0.94	
Depression	1.18	$p < .05$
Anxiety	0.99	$p < .05$
Hostility	0.76	
Phobic Anxiety	0.82	$p < .05$
Paranoid Ideation	0.48	
Psychoticism	1.09	
Additional Items	0.91	$p < .05$
GSI	1.27	$p < .05$
PSDI	1.14	$p < .01$

symptoms significantly lower at post-treatment than at pre-treatment on the three clinical scales.

The results were statistically and clinically significant. Table 2 shows the treatment effect sizes for each scale.

The percentage of change on each clinical scale of the SPA is calculated by adding the severity and manageability scores (not shown here) and then by calculating the

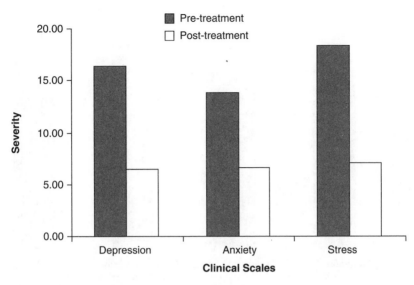

Figure 10. DASS-42 severity scores at pre- and post-treatment.

Table 2. Effect size for each scale of DASS-42 scales.

Scale	Cohen's d	t-test
Depression	1.00	$p < .05$
Anxiety	0.92	$p < .05$
Stress	1.28	$p < .01$

percentage difference between pre-and post-treatment scores on these tow scales. The scores showed an overall 66.04% improvement.

The satisfaction scores are displayed in Figure 11. Satisfaction with therapy was calculated by the "absolute percentage" (where "Not at all satisfied" = 0%, and "Extremely satisfied" = 100%). The participants rated an overall 80.92% satisfaction with therapy. The high statistical significance on the one-sample t-test for each scale score shows that patients were overall very satisfied.

Some observations at post-treatment

- None of the clients abused alcohol (not substituted with drugs). Two separated from their partner.
- Self-harming behavior had stopped.
- All could manage pain better
- All wanted to decrease medication (about 1/3 withdrew all medications)

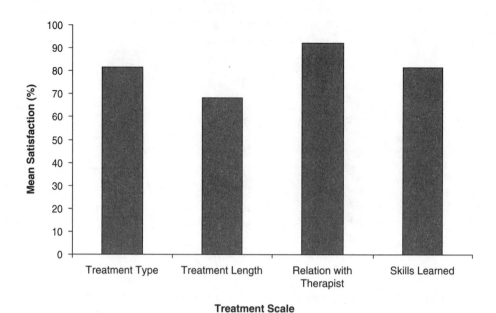

Figure 11. SPA percentage satisfaction with the therapy process.

Concluding comment

Based on the three measurement tools used, the results of this outcome analysis demonstrate a statistically and clinically significant improvement across a number of life domains after an 8–week MiCBT intervention. Although the results must be considered cautiously due to the lack of control condition, they call for attention in the newly emerging field of mindfulness research and therapy. While most mindfulness-based therapy models address homogeneous diagnostic clusters, such as people recovered from major episodes of depression (Segal *et al.,* 2002) or Borderline Personality Disorder (Linehan, 1993), more comprehensive and controlled studies may show the general efficacy of MiCBT in addressing crises across a broad range of conditions.

Effects of MiCBT on Health Behavior of People with Type 2 Diabetes

The empirical data presented below were obtained from a quasi-exploratory feasibility study of the MiCBT 8–week program as a method of improving health behavior in people with Type 2 Diabetes. The study was conducted by Melanie Lindsay as partial requirement of her Masters Degree in Health Psychology at the University of Auckland (Lindsay, 2007). The study used quantitative, qualitative, and single case methodologies.

Participants

At the Auckland Diabetes Centre, 184 patients with Type 2 Diabetes were approached. Of these, 17% ($n = 32$) were eligible to participate. They were aged over 25, had Type 2 Diabetes for over 1 year. They experienced difficulty managing their blood glucose levels and would like to feel more confident about it, less distressed by self-judgments, and wished to feel more self-kindness. Out of these, two male and eight female patients were able to participate and were pseudo-randomly assigned to either the MiCBT group ($n = 6$), aged 43–68, or to a "standard care group" ($n = 4$), aged 45–71. Due to time constraints, the first 6 participants who returned their baseline questionnaires were allocated to the MiCBT group and the last 4 to the control group.

Measurements

Eight self-report measures were used: Ruth Baer's Five-Factor Mindfulness Questionnaire (FFMQ; Baer *et al.*, 2006), The Mindfulness-based Self Efficacy Scale (MSES; Francis and Cayoun, 2010), the Self-Compassion Scale (SCS; Neff, 2003), the Diabetes Self-efficacy Scale (DSES; Toobert and Glasgow, 1994), the Rosenberg Self-Esteem Scale (RSE; Rosenberg, 1965), the Hospital Anxiety and Depression Scale (HADS; Zigmon and Snaith, 1983), and the Short Progress Assessment (SPA; Cayoun, 2003).

Behavioral measures were Diabetes Profiles, which were compiled by a diabetes clinic registrar after the research was completed, and the Summary of Diabetes Self-Care Activities (SDSCA; Toobert and Glasgow, 1994).

The physiological measure was Glycosylated Hemoglobin (HbA1c), which is a generic marker for average blood glucose levels over a 6 – 8 week period. It is used as an indicator of the diabetes patients' self-management of daily blood glucose levels.

Intervention

Participants were assigned to either a "standard care group or a MiCBT group in a pseudo-randomized fashion. The intervention consisted of the four stages of MiCBT (with minimal alterations) administered during one 2–hour group session per week for 8 weeks and one 30–minute individual weekly session for each participant between group sessions. Participants in the MiCBT group were asked to maintain a daily practice ($\times 2$) using the Stage1 and Advanced Practice CDs.

Results

The Mann-Whitney U test was used to analyze differences between the MiCBT group and the control (standard care) groups on all measures across time, except home practice frequency and duration. Results show that, compared with the standard care group, the MiCBT group had greater increases in four facets of mindfulness (Observe, Actaware, Nonjudge, and Nonreactive, but not Describe), greater mindfulness-based global self-efficacy, self-compassion, diabetes self-efficacy, and diabetes self-care behaviors such as general and specific diet, and exercise. Further, frequency of home mindfulness practice was associated with greater HbA1c reductions. The effects were maintained, and some further improved, at 6–week follow-up.

Participants reported an overall reduction in global impairment, which includes a reduction in severity of symptomatology in five domains (various unwanted behaviors, unpleasant thoughts, unpleasant body sensations, unpleasant feelings, and unpleasant relationships with others) and an increase in ability to manage symptoms. Therapist mindfulness experience was identified as an important aspect of supporting participants in their development of equanimity as awareness of their body-states increased. Based on SPA data, the MiCBT group reported large perceived improvement in their ability to control their unwanted behaviors and were highly satisfied with the MiCBT program.

Preliminary evidence indicates the MiCBT program may be a useful training program for supporting people with diabetes to develop greater generalized self-efficacy, self-compassion, and improvement in diabetes self-care. More research is necessary to replicate these promising results.

Mindfulness and Western Therapies

This book proposes a rationale and a set of practical methods to enable a tight integration, rather than juxtaposition, of CBT principles with mindfulness training. This type of integration has already shown to produce better outcomes than CBT alone in the treatment of a broad range of psychological disorders.

However, empirical comparisons between mindfulness-based therapies are quasi-inexistent to date and there is no real basis for the claim that a mindfulness-based CBT would be more effective than another mindfulness-based approach.

To date, there are no studies comparing MBCT, MBSR, MiCBT, ACT, DBT, a Mindfulness-based Rational Emotive Behavioral Therapy, a Mindfulness-based Schema Therapy or a Mindfulness-based Dynamic Therapy in approaching particular difficulties. We will benefit from Abraham Maslow's reminder that if the only tool we have is a hammer, every problem begins to look like a nail. Provided that the clinician and client understand the micro-level of experience and work at it with an accepting attitude, it seems that whatever therapy type is adjunct to mindfulness, desirable change is a likely outcome. Just as important is the anecdotal evidence that the skills employed for centuries by meditation masters from various Buddhist orientations were predominantly behavioral in their formulations to pupils, as mentioned in the introduction of this volume. The integration of traditional CBT and mindfulness seems a natural consequence of the congruence between the two approaches.

Summary of Main Points

- According to Beck's (1976) standards, mindfulness training integrated with CBT qualifies as a psychotherapy system, rather than a set of therapeutic tools to be used eclectically. It is sufficiently flexible for clinicians to make alterations and rests on a sound theoretical framework that enables the testing of predictions.
- Measuring the efficacy of mindfulness is currently done via self-report questionnaires, including the FMI, KIMS, MAAS, FFMQ, MSES and others. The research literature shows recent criticism of such self-report questionnaires, on the basis that the respondent's responses are limited by their own self-awareness. The argument is that we must first be sufficiently mindful to know how much we are mindful. Thus, meditators may rate their skills as average based on their expert evaluation, whereas novices may rate their skills as high because of lack of self-awareness or their lack of familiarity with the construct of mindfulness, creating differences in the understanding of the questions. Accordingly, choosing questionnaires well and using them with caution is recommended.
- To prevent the measurement confounds mentioned in the previous point, measuring therapeutic progress with MiCBT is best done with measures of self-efficacy and standard well being and quality-of-life measures, rather than merely relying on mindfulness questionnaires. These measures are best chosen according to the proposed mechanisms of action (sensory awareness and equanimity), as well as the therapeutic goals initially stated by the client during the goal-setting process.

Part V
Teaching and Training

Chapter 12

Weekly Implementation Protocol

The future is not some place we are going to,
but one we are creating. The paths to it are made, not found,
and the activity of making them changes both the maker and the destination.

John Schaar

Our current research shows that group delivery of the MiCBT program improves client engagement, especially their commitment to daily practice of mindfulness meditation. On the other hand, individual delivery allows for a more specific focus on the peculiarity of the client's issues (Roubos, Cayoun, and Hawkins, 2010). Each group participant clearly benefits from the stories and weekly feedback of the other participants. This benefit is often in the form of motivation from hearing others' effort and benefit, and the spontaneous normalization of their difficulties by listening to those of others. On the other hand, despite the short individual sessions provided to participants between group sessions, the therapist does not have sufficient time for in-depth follow-up in each session, as the focus is on the development of skills. Traumatic and psychodynamic issues emerging spontaneously or progressively through the stages (especially through spontaneous memories emerging during mindfulness meditation) are better addressed in one-on-one sessions.

Expected Skills Acquired with the Program

- Clinically significant increase in self-efficacy
- Clinically significant increase in sense of self-control
- Greater degree of equanimity

Mindfulness-integrated CBT: Principles and Practice, First Edition. Bruno A. Cayoun.
© 2011 John Wiley & Sons, Ltd. Published 2011 by John Wiley & Sons, Ltd.

- Increased ability to discern, understand and tolerate emotions and body sensations associated with them
- Increased ability to understand, interrupt, and shift focus from ruminative and other unhelpful thoughts as they arise
- Increased ability to prevent relapse or get assistance before relapse occurs.

Contact Hours for the 8- to 12-Week MiCBT Program

- A 30-minute standardized pre-group interview per participant (including assessment and signing informed consent). The mindfulness literature indicates that a pre-intervention assessment before participation in a mindfulness-based treatment is important (Bonadonna, 2003; Grossman *et al.*, 2004). In fact, for any form of well-structured cognitive-behavioral intervention, it is recommended to begin with a "therapy contract." In MiCBT, a four-step therapy contract is used and discussed in the following order:

   1. Formulating the "targeted problems." This is not an expression of the client's desired outcomes, as the first step is the client's open acknowledgement of his or her difficulties. This is in line with the Eastern traditional establishment of mindfulness, during which the student experiences consciously the first "noble truth:" life brings legitimate suffering.
   2. Proposing the MiCBT 4-stage model and expected duration to address these problems. With some clients, eight weeks will not suffice to address the crisis and teach MiCBT relapse-prevention techniques. For example, clients with a problematic personality, severe trauma or very well-established dissociative habits, will often require ten to twelve sessions to acquire reliable and generalizable skills. Others will need more.
   3. Formulating "success indicators." These must be real, day-to-day, observable and measurable changes. If the client's formulation of expected change is, "I'll be happier within myself," it needs to be clarified. For example, the therapist may ask, "How will you know that you're happier within yourself? What will your daily life be like when you feel happier? How could we observe this in terms of changes in your behavior?" The client may answer, "I'll be more motivated to do chores, go out and socialize, smile more," etc. Writing a list of these into the therapy contract can then constitute a form of personalized self-efficacy scale, perfectly designed for the client's situation and need.
   4. Setting a date for review. The review focuses on how close the client's daily experiences are to those success indicators.

   Including this agreement in the pre-intervention assessment helps formulate realistic expectations for both client and clinician. The client comes to address certain difficulties, which are perhaps not the ones the therapist would prioritize or even address. It also provides a personalized set of markers against which to compare outcomes.

- A weekly 2-hour group session (including weekly assessment) for 8 to 12 weeks, as appropriate.
- A weekly 30-minute 1:1 session
- Three 2-hour follow-up sessions spread over the year following the program for chronic conditions.

Structure of Facilitator Handouts

The following protocol applies to both group and one-on-one sessions, except that one-on-one sessions allow for more flexibility in the delivery of each task. It is formatted in the order of delivery. The therapist is encouraged to revisit and revise the topics in the sections of the book before each weekly session.

Aim

The aim for each week and the reasoning that led to the content and method of delivery appear in this section.

Method of delivery

The method of delivery for each week appears in this section of the handout. Week 1 contains more information and requires more sound understanding and memory of content than other weeks. This is partly because of the amount of topics and information to cover, and because most, if not all, are unfamiliar with the approach and hence some may carry a degree of insecurity and perhaps skepticism. The first session helps remove possible doubts and build rapport, for which the facilitator must be knowledgeable, confident, and most of all, equanimous.

Homework

This section lists the client's homework. Calling it "home exercises" may prevent unnecessary reactions associated with unpleasant memories of schoolwork.

Variation

This section provides an alternative delivery method (a 1-week delay), relevant for clients with varying degrees of distress, abilities or adherence to treatment. It is also relevant for group versus one-on-one delivery styles. One-on-one delivery of

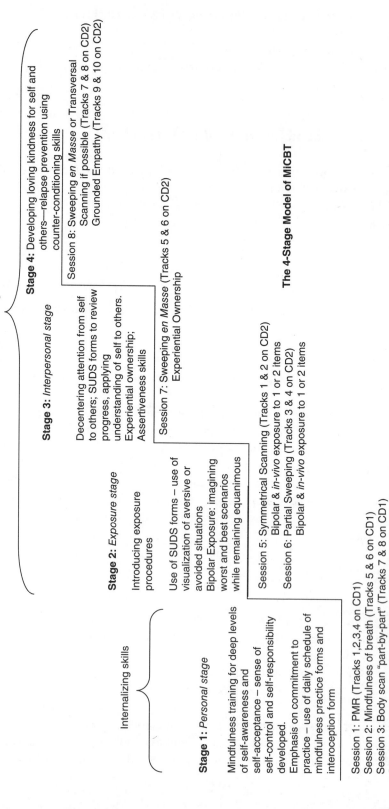

Figure 12. The main roles and components of the four hierarchical stages in MiCBT (crisis intervention structure).

MiCBT allows more flexibility and can be more easily adapted to the client's needs and state. Clients in crisis may need longer program duration. If you use the variation in Week 1, continue with ensuing variations. More delay may be necessary if the client has difficulties in engaging in the required daily practice, or is unable to feel body sensations sufficiently before starting Stage 2. This is often the case with dissociating clients. The program is *not* a one-fits-all system. It is most productive when it is flexibly delivered, according to client's situation and presentation.

Summary of the 4-Stage Model

Figure 12 shows the four stages of MiCBT based on the "Variation" delivery for crisis. Clients begin to internalize attention and the focus of effort is at the personal level. This is Stage 1. Clients develop greater ability for self-awareness, self-acceptance and a greater degree of equanimity.

This allows them to externalize personal skills to various contexts in Stage 2 by first learning to address avoidance-provoking situations. During the second stage, clients learn exposure skills that help the processes necessary to face difficult situations. Once clients feel more confident with their ability to face, rather than avoid difficulties and resolve problems, they engage further into externalizing skills in Stage 3.

Stage 3 is for developing interpersonal skills that better enable clients to understand others better and the dynamics of interpersonal relationships. These skills naturally lead to the fourth stage of the program, the empathic stage.

In Stage 4, clients realize that they are the first beneficiaries of the emotions they produce and therefore learn to reduce the duration of negative emotions and increase the duration and frequency of positive ones.

Whereas the first two stages help address crisis, the last two help prevent relapse by normalizing and accepting the "legitimate" reasons for human suffering. They promote one's ability to direct attention both inwardly and outwardly toward others and their situation with genuine intention to understand and accept others. These stages produce further insight and greater ability for forgiveness and empathy.

Week 1

Aim   Session 1 introduces MiCBT and aims to establish commitment to daily practice. The first session provides sufficient understanding of the principles of mindfulness and a sense of direction for clients. There is more material to cover in this session than during all subsequent ones because there is no practice feedback to discuss and participants tend to benefit from more information and practice.

Materials   White board and markers, Stage 1 training CD for daily practice, CD player, Daily Record of Mindfulness Practice and Daily Schedule of Mindfulness

Practice forms (in Appendix C), and assessment forms for baseline data when necessary. Pen and paper for clients.

Method of delivery

- Set the chairs in a full or ¾ circle. This helps everyone to see and hear each other easily, which in turn will facilitate group cohesiveness. Keep your preferred setting for the entire program.
- Introduce participants to the program (in order of delivery): First, mention the three ways of learning: devotional, rational/intellectual, and experiential, and the differential personal involvement and responsibility with each; most involvement being with experiential learning (see Introduction of the book).
- Then, briefly introduce participants to the concept of mindfulness. Start with writing a definition on the white board with an emphasis on the internal context of experience (see Chapter 1). Explain that mindfulness training and CBT are evidence-based approaches, which the program integrates into one therapy system to address both content and process of information processing. Briefly and simply mention the difficulties associated with the lack of integration of propositional (rational/neutral) and implicational (judgmental/schematic) processing, and that mindfulness establishes a balance between the two types of processing, facilitating the ability to let go of emotional reactivity.
- Briefly describe the four stages to be covered during the eight-week (or longer) program:
  (1) mindfulness training to acquire very deep levels of self-awareness and acceptance,
  (2) exposure to the difficulties for which the client came to the program,
  (3) improving relationship with others, and
  (4) using grounded empathy to consolidate progress and prevent relapse.
- Explain the main structure of weekly sessions. In order of delivery: group practice, participants' feedback on the past week, the topic of the week to learn, explanation of "home exercises" (rather than "homework"), and weekly measurement of outcome (e.g., SPA).
- Emphasize the need for three main commitments:
  (1) Attending each session
  (2) Doing home practice (reiterate making time rather than trying to find time). Make a point that the greatest benefit of the program will come from home exercises.
  (3) Commit to confidentiality about, and respect for, other group participants.
- Use the white board to set goals. Brainstorm first and then condense clients' overlapping goals into more generic ones so that there are at least five goals and not many more than fifteen.
  - Ask the group what each would like to change/improve through the program and tally each person's endorsement of a proposed improvement on the white board (e.g., if a participant says "I want to feel less angry," ask if this goal

would apply to other participants by show of hand, count the people concerned and report the number on the board next to the item).

  ○ Record the list of goals and the number of participants who endorsed each of them on a note pad to allow future comparisons in week eight.
- Group practice of mindfulness training (Stage 1): MiCBT uses the traditional Burmese Vipassana method, the delivery of which is different from the methods in MBSR/MBCT. Guide the group into mindfulness of breath using Track 6 of the Stage 1 CD or the script in Appendix A.
- Offer a rationale for practicing mindfulness with breathing.
- Briefly explain the practice and rationale for PMR in the 1st week.
- Explain setting-up for home practice of Stage 1.
- Distribute the Daily Record of Mindfulness Practice and Daily Schedule of Mindfulness Practice forms (Appendix C) and your own outcome questionnaires (if needed). Collect their goal scores.

Homework
- Listen to introductory tracks (1, 2, and 3) on Stage 1 CD (Cayoun, 2004) once or twice. People have consistently reported benefitting from listening to the short rationale on Track 2.
- Practice PMR and Mindfulness of breath (MOB) *twice* daily using tracks 4, 5 and 6 on Stage 1 CD if available, or provide your own recording of PMR and your own recording of MOB from the script in Appendix A.
- Explain the likelihood of feeling very relaxed after PMR and consequently drowsy during the mindfulness of breath exercise. Point out ways to overcome drowsiness and other difficulties (see Chapter 6).
- Emphasize commitment to daily practice for the entire week. Stress that they don't need to commit for weeks or months, but rather agree to commit fully for one week and see what sort of benefit they derive from this initial full commitment. Asking clients to commit one week at a time helps prevent fear of failure. It can reassure the client and enhance his or her sense of control and choice.
- Clients fill in all assessment and practice forms (as appropriate) and are told by the therapist that next week is an important week and they must do all they can to attend even if a crisis has emerged.

Variation   If group members (or clients in one-on-one sessions) are experiencing moderate to severe symptoms because of a current crisis, you may consider the following variation:

- The rationale delivery may be swapped for the rationale for body scanning. Limit the home exercise to PMR, i.e., delay mindfulness with breathing and the rationale for it until the following week, but ask participants to try to remain aware of body tensions and relax them as often as possible outside their formal practice of PMR.

- As above, emphasize commitment to daily practice for the entire week and fill in all assessment and practice forms, as appropriate.

Week 2

Aim   Session 2 introduces participants to the most important mechanisms of MiCBT, the co-emergence model of reinforcement and equanimity. These are necessary topics because better understanding at this stage increases the likelihood of practice (in contrast with Eastern countries where devotion is often sufficient). A good understanding of the co-emergence model of reinforcement will direct clients to take more responsibility for what they think and feel, and for their reactions. A good understanding of equanimity will help their levels of acceptance to internal contexts and promote further success in becoming more aware and comfortable with common triggers this week.

Materials   White board and markers, Stage 1 CD and CD player, Daily Record of Mindfulness Practice, Daily Schedule of Mindfulness Practice, Diary of Reactive Habits and Home Practice Feedback forms (in Appendix C). Outcome measures questionnaires (if needed).

Method of delivery
- Conduct a short (about 5 min) group practice of mindfulness with breathing conducted with the CD (track 6) if available or using the script in Appendix A. This is provided they trained with it for the past week. In case you used the variation of delivery mentioned on the previous page (i.e., only PMR), delay the group practice with track 6 till after you deliver the rationale for it, following the feedback period.
- Distribute the Home Practice Feedback form (Appendix C). Clients fill it in and return it with all other forms. Use it as additional information during feedback time.
- Welcome feedback on the home exercises set last week and clarify points as they arise. Invite everyone to share their experiences sequentially and avoid conversations (they are time consuming and not very productive). Ask them also to share how the week was in general. Did they notice anything different this week? Notice, value and validate little changes. This helps reinforce their practice.

Describe the internal causes of intrusive thoughts and their extinction (Chapter 2).

(1) Explain and normalize distractibility during practice via the "fasting metaphor" (see Chapter 6).
(2) Then describe neural networks competing for access to the level of conscious awareness. Relate to and complement last week's rationale. Mention briefly the

three causes of high network activation: frequency, recency and co-emergence effects (see Chapter 2). This is rather a topic for experts in cognitive neuro-science, so part of your challenge is to simplify sufficiently while preserving the important points.

(3) Explain thought suppression. As an illustration, you can do "the bear experi-ment:" Ask everyone to close their eyes, visualize a white bear as vividly as possible for about thirty seconds, then ask them "Now try *not* to think about a white bear" for about fifteen seconds. Ask for feedback and explain why the thought of the bear keeps on intruding in terms of the strength of neural network activation. The more intensely they activated networks to think about the bear, the more intrusions.

- Deliver the rationale for body scanning. It is useful to revise this in Chapter 3. On the white board, reproduce the five components of the co-emergence model (see Diary of Reactive Habits in Appendix C). The group setting does not facili-tate an experiential delivery format unless the facilitator is experienced and confident. The experiential delivery is best provided during the next one-on-one consultation. Meanwhile, it is sufficient to explain the principles on the board by illustrating the five components with a real experience one of the participants has had this week or recently. Ask someone to volunteer a challenge in the last week. Write his or her challenging situation in the upper-left box (Stimulus), the modality with which they perceived it in the next box (Sensory Perception), and continue completing the form (as per the co-emergence model). Show how reinforcement takes place when the mode of coping (written in the Reaction box) provides relief.
- Explain the omnipresence of change or *impermanence* in all aspects of our life, and its extinguishing consequence on thoughts, body sensations and behavior. Emphasize the need to remain aware of impermanence while practicing, espe-cially with very pleasant or very unpleasant experiences.
- Discuss equanimity, its role in developing self-acceptance. Explain that self-acceptance starts with acceptance of our own thoughts and body sensations.
- Conduct a group practice of body-scanning for about thirty minutes using tracks 7 and 8 of Stage 1 CD (if available) or as time permits using a shortened version of the body-scan script in Appendix A. *If you use the delivery variation, group practice involves only mindfulness of breath. When finished, answer ques-tions and clarify points.
- Distribute two copies of the Diary of Reactive Habits (Appendix C) for home-work and explain they will need to use it to record two stressful experiences in the way you demonstrated on the white board today. This task will enhance *online* awareness of co-emergence.

Homework
- Withdraw PMR and mindfulness-of-breath exercises and practice the "part-by-part" (unilateral) body-scanning technique using tracks 7 and 8 on Stage 1 CD

(if available), or the script in Appendix A. Emphasize that the practice schedule is *twice* daily and that they make a strong effort to make time for it. Mention that long-lived reactive habits will not go away after just a couple of practice sessions and the more we practice the better the results. Mention that in the next week or two you will discuss the effect of sufficient practice in giving new parameters to the brain (neuroplasticity), which will help establish new habits.

- From this point onward, in addition to their formal half-hour practice twice daily, clients learn to remain aware of sensations in their body (without scanning) and equanimous in bed for a few minutes before they fall asleep, and again when they wake-up before getting out of bed.
- Ask clients to record two stressful events with the Diary of Reactive Habits.
- Fill in all assessment and practice forms (see Materials section).

Variation (following Week 1 variation)   Withdraw PMR and practice mindfulness of breath *twice* daily. The 5-minute pre- and post-sleep practice is with the breath, not body sensations. While all discussions of the co-emergence model take place, delay the task with the Diary of Reactive Habits until next week.

Week 3

Aim   Session 3 deepens the participants' understanding of interoception and equanimity.

Materials   White board, Stage 1 CD and CD player, Interoceptive Signature-Pocket Form, Home Practice Feedback and Daily Record of Mindfulness Practice forms (Appendix C). Outcome measures form.

Method of delivery
- Conduct a 15-minute group practice of part-by-part body scanning (or 5 minutes breath awareness if variation is used) using your own guidance or a shortened version of the body-scan script in Appendix A. Keep a realistic timing between your instructions, guiding clients' attention through the body and the time it takes for new trainees to scan body-parts.
- Distribute the Home Practice Feedback form (Appendix C). Clients fill it in and return it with all other forms. Use it as additional information during feedback time.
- Feedback on the home exercises set for the week. Clarify points if necessary. When these are incomplete or not done, remain equanimous while explaining the notion of prioritizing. You may explain that people do first what will be most rewarding or least punishing and this is why we prioritize activities the way we do. This week was not different. Use the Socratic dialogue or other useful questioning methods if necessary.
- Discuss pain, agitation, doubts and other difficulties (see Chapter 6) using the examples of group participants willing to volunteer their experience.

- Explain that, from now on, the practice will be with complete immobility, thereby increasing awareness of subtle physical changes (often discomfort, which needs to be normalized) and decreasing experiential avoidance. Explain that this commitment leads to much greater levels of equanimity and enhancement of inhibitory networks which will help prevent learned reactions to aversive experiences. Link this with the notion of creating change (e.g., changing posture because of pain) versus acceptance (e.g., immobility despite physical pain while accepting the experience), and how changing a situation can mean avoiding the problem and reinforcing avoidance now and in the future in painful contexts.
- Discuss the hedonic continuum with three main ways of experiencing body sensations (pleasant, unpleasant, and neutral) and the four basic characteristics of body sensations (see Chapter 2). Use the white board and draw each continuum.
- Describe "informal practice" and its role in generalizing the skills to multiple contexts. Mention the importance that informal practice helps move from only *practicing mindfulness meditation* twice daily to *becoming mindful in daily life*. This can mean looking at the face of a friend or neighbor, hearing a piece of music, or tasting a familiar dish, non-judgmentally, as if it were for the first time. This can also be a useful means of decreasing calorie intake for people who overeat.

Homework
- Daily practice of part-by-part (unilateral) scanning in silence, i.e., *without* the CD or any other audio instructions. The client practices in "strong determination," i.e., with a commitment to physical immobility throughout each practice session.
- Informal practice (ask clients to fill in the Interoceptive Signature-Pocket Form at least 5 times during the week), and pre- and post-sleep awareness of body sensations.

Variation (following Week 2 variation)
- Conduct in-session group practice of the body-scan (track 8). Cover all other topics
- Homework: Withdraw breath awareness (track 6) and practice body-scan using the CD (track 8) if available (see script in Appendix A).

Week 4

Aim Session 4 introduces Stage 2, some of the CBT components of MiCBT, and the notion of neuroplasticity through the introduction of advanced scanning methods.

Materials White board, Advanced Training CD (Cayoun, 2005b), CD player, Home Practice Feedback, Exposure to Target Events (used as "SUDS"), and

Interoception Forms (all in Appendix C). Your own outcome measure forms, as appropriate.

Note: There are no transcripts for advanced scanning methods, and that you will need the auditory instructions henceforward from the Advanced Training CD.

Method of delivery

- Conduct a 15-minute group practice (scanning the body part by part), even if your clients have used the variation schedule. This time, do not guide clients through the body parts. Rather, give brief and assertive instructions such as "start scanning the entire body part by part, remaining alert, attentive, and very equanimous no matter what you experience ..." Provide intermittent reminders: "Remain aware, attentive and keep moving through the entire body ..."
- Distribute the Home Practice Feedback and Interoception Forms, front and back (Appendix C). Clients fill them in and return them with all other forms. Use them during feedback time.
- Facilitate feedback on the homework set last week. Point to best measure of progress.
- Discuss the notion of skill transfer through neuroplasticity.
- Group practice of symmetrical scanning (tracks 1 and 2 of Advanced Training CD).
- Describe awareness thresholds in detail using the white board. Draw the graph of awareness thresholds as a function of an avoidance-exposure continuum. It is recommended that you train yourself to draw the graph rapidly while explaining it aloud.

Introduce Stage 2 (Chapter 7)

1. Link mindfulness training to CBT by pointing out that so far we have been working on the internal context, the experiential aspect of the difficulties that brought clients to therapy, and that they are now ready to use these skills to address the external aspects of their difficulties (it is not helpful to mention disorder or psychopathology).
2. Distribute the Exposure to Target Events (SUDS) form and ask clients to fill it in using concrete issues; offer help.
3. Explain "experiential equivalence" between imagery and *in vivo* stimulation. To illustrate experiential equivalence, conduct the timing experiment (if time permits).
4. Explain "Bi-polar exposure." Distribute the Bipolar Exposure form (in Appendix C). To facilitate understanding of the task, it is useful to draw the graph on the board while explaining the principles of the exercise.
5. Target exposure: ask clients to choose two mildly to moderately distressing items for this week's exposure tasks. They will first use Bi-polar (imaginal) exposure to the item and then, after four sessions (2 days), they expose *in vivo* to the item. They start to work with the second item on the 3rd or 4th day and

repeat the task with the same schedule. Reiterate the central role of equanimity towards body sensations in achieving full desensitization.

Homework
- Symmetrical scanning for 30 min twice daily (track 2 on Advanced Training CD)
- Informal practice
- Pre- and post-sleep body awareness
- "Bi-polar" and *in vivo* exposure to two SUDS targets.

Variation Clients who cannot feel sensations in most body parts, as reflected by the coloring of their Interoception Form, will have difficulties feeling both sides of the body at the same time and should delay symmetrical scanning by a few days. They should focus on the breath for about ten minutes before scanning the body in a unilateral manner (as per last week), but *without* using the CD. Delay also the explanation of awareness thresholds until next week, when participants are more aware of body sensations.

Week 5

Aim Session 5 continues with Stage 2 at a more challenging level and introduces Stage 3, another integration of mindfulness and CBT, which addresses interpersonal dimensions.

Materials White board, Advanced Training CD (Cayoun, 2005b), CD player, SUDS and Home Practice Feedback forms, Interoception Forms (in Appendix C). Your own outcome measure forms.

Method of delivery
- Conduct a 15-minute group practice of symmetrical scanning (track 2 on Advanced CD).
- Distribute the Home Practice Feedback and Interoception Forms (Appendix C). Clients fill them in and return them with all other forms. Use them during feedback time.
- Ask participants to re-rate each item on their SUDS form following exposure ("… % Distress 2") and start the feedback session on the homework set last week.
- Target exposure: from the SUDS sheet, ask clients to choose the two most severe items for bi-polar and in vivo exposure, as implemented in Week 4.

Introduce Stage 3 (Chapter 8)

1. Explain Experiential Ownership: taking full responsibility for our thoughts and body sensations and disowning those of others.

2. Discuss hypothesis about others' body states. Explain that more often than not, people react to the reactions of others. When remaining aware of a person's suffering (unpleasant body sensations) and equanimous towards our own, the person's level of arousal is more likely to diffuse rapidly than if we feed the cycle of reactivity. However, participants must verify this "diffusion" hypothesis for themselves this week. Perhaps the exposure tasks required to complete Stage 2 (exposure to the two most distressing items) will provide a context to test this hypothesis. If not, encourage clients to find themselves in two stressful inter-personal situations, practice experiential ownership and allow diffusion to occur.
3. Conduct a 15-minute group practice session to introduce the partial-sweeping method of body scanning using track 4 of Advanced Training CD.

Homework
*   Partial sweeping for 30 minutes twice daily (track 4 on Advanced Training CD, the instructions last for 16 minutes then an additional 14 minutes is spent in silence).
*   Informal practice
*   5-minute pre- and post-sleep interoceptive awareness
*   Bi-polar and *in vivo* exposure to the two most severe targets on the SUDS form.

Variation
*   Clients who cannot yet scan symmetrically will have difficulties with partial sweeping and should delay partial sweeping by a few days. They should focus on the breath for about ten minutes before scanning the body during those few days and make a genuine effort to focus.
*   With the SUDS exposure tasks, if a client is certain they will not be able to cope with two greatly distressing items, they should delay the process and expose to only one; but choose the one which causes the most impairment. This also applies when the obstacle is only organizational.

Week 6

Aim   Session 6 continues with Stage 3 at a more challenging level by introducing Assertiveness skills and in-session role-playing as means of exposure.

Materials   White board, Advanced Training CD (Cayoun, 2005b), CD player, SUDS and Home Practice Feedback forms, (in Appendix C). Outcome measure forms, as appropriate.

Method of delivery
*   Conduct a 15-minute group practice with partial sweeping (track 4 on Advanced CD).
*   Distribute the Home Practice Feedback form (Appendix C). Clients fill it in and return it with all other forms. Use them during feedback time.

- Ask participants to re-rate each item on their SUDS form following exposure ("… % Distress 2") and start the feedback session on the homework set last week.
- Feedback on the homework set last week (re-rate SUDS items following exposure).
- Discuss assertiveness and the fact that most people who are depressed, anxious, angry, or highly stressed tend to be either passive, aggressive or both, but rarely assertive. Getting what they want comfortably with people, at home, work or with family is often very difficult. Using the white board, write the seven assertive statements: stating with the fact, how "I" feel, how "I" think, acknowledging the other, what "I" want, how to reward cooperation or compromise for a win-win solution.
- Ask clients to fill in another SUDS form with at least four items related to inter-personal conflicts or avoidance of conflict. Then ask clients to pick the two most distressing or otherwise incapacitating items for exposure. Remind clients to practice bi-polar exposure before *in vivo*, using the same task schedule as last week. In addition, encourage clients to integrate experiential ownership within the exposure task.
- Role-play with a volunteer client, using one of their moderately rated items, is an effective communication style. If time permits, have the whole group form pairs and practice the statements using one of their items for a few minutes. Remember, this can be fun.
- Conduct a 15-minute group practice session to introduce the sweeping-*en-masse* method of body scanning with track 6 of Advanced Training CD. Mention that sweeping *en masse* can be deeply satisfying and that becoming attached to the sensations will bring disappointment because this experience is impermanent as well, and when it passes, we feel disheartened.

Homework
- Sweeping *en masse* (track 6 Advanced Training CD)
- Informal practice
- 5-minute pre- and post-sleep interoceptive awareness
- Bi-polar and *in vivo* exposure to using assertive statements with two items.

Variation
- Clients who cannot yet sweep partially should delay sweeping *en masse* for a few days and use the breath a few minutes pre-scanning. With the exposure task, follow last week's direction.

Week 7

Aim Session 7 introduces Stage 4. Having first learned to center on themselves with more objectivity and responsibility (Stages 1 and 2), then to de-center and look outward at others' sufferings and responsibilities (Stage 3), participants' attention has been shaped to attend to both internal and external contexts simultaneously with greater understanding and acceptance of themselves and others. Stage 4 further shapes and consolidates thought towards empathy using body sensations as an anchor and a grounding, powerful encoding of positive thought.

Materials   Advanced Training CD (Cayoun, 2005b), CD player, Home Practice Feedback forms, (in Appendix C), your own outcome measure forms, as appropriate.

Method of delivery
- Conduct a 15-minute group practice with sweeping *en masse* (track 6 on Advanced CD).
- Distribute the Home Practice Feedback form. Clients fill it in and return it with all other forms. Use them during feedback time.
- Feedback on the homework set last week (re-rate SUDS items following exposure).
- Describe transversal scanning (track 8 of Advanced Training CD) as a very advanced level and a further step towards neuroplasticity. Schema-based associations are more easily uprooted due to the co-emergence effect of deepened interoceptive awareness.
- Conduct a 15-minute group practice with the transversal scanning method.
- Describe the five ethical challenges (preventing lying, killing, stealing, intoxicating, and non-consensual sex). Revising Chapter 9 will help linking your discussion to the practice of interoceptive awareness.
- Introduce Stage 4 (Chapter 9). Discuss how developing empathy benefits the therapeutic relationship, yet clients are scarcely taught empathic responses to improve their relationships. Explain the rationale for Stage 4 (see Aim section on this page) and the counter-conditioning effect of pairing an aversive stimulus with an agreeable body state. Explain how empathizing for oneself and others can help decrease reactivity and prevent relapse.
- Implement a 5-minute group practice of the sweeping *en masse* method, followed by 10 minutes of Loving-Kindness Meditation (track 10 of Advanced CD or script in Appendix A).

Homework
- Practice transversal scanning (or sweeping *en masse*, as appropriate)
- Informal practice
- Adopting five ethical challenges
- 5-minute pre- and post-sleep body awareness
- A 5- to 10-minute practice of Loving-Kindness Meditation twice daily following each scanning practice session, once using track 10 of Advanced Training CD and once without using clients' own thoughts and formulations.

Week 8

Aim   Session 8 consolidates Stage 4 and serves to recap the entire program, including an assessment of results according to clients' initial expectations.

Materials   White board and markers, pen and paper, a standard "Certificate of participation" for each client (if possible), and your own outcome measure questionnaires (if data is needed).

Method of delivery
- Conduct a 10-minute group practice with sweeping *en masse* (no instruction) followed by a 5-minute Loving-Kindness Meditation; either in silence, using the script in Appendix A, or your own formulation.
- Conduct the feedback session on the homework set last week without Home Practice Feedback form. Validate better coping styles and discuss the yardstick for progress.
- Do a program revision by summarizing the most important points of MiCBT and provide relapse prevention guidelines.

Assess goal achievement using the white board.

1. Before starting the session or during the break, list on the board all initial generic goals and write the number of participants who endorsed them in session 1 (from the copy you kept).
2. Go through each item listed on the board and ask participants who has been able to improve their skills with each issue by show of hand. You are measuring their sense of self-efficacy.
3. Copy the results on paper for your records

Conclusion
- Explain post-treatment evaluation and propose follow-up sessions to consolidate and further develop the skills.
- Deliver a "Certificate of Participation" to each participant. This can act as a positive reinforcer for attending follow-up sessions, which in turn stimulates the consolidation of skills.
- If appropriate, encourage the possibility of joining or forming a regular mindfulness practice group. This maintains group cohesiveness, maintenance of sitting practice, and fosters social networking.
- Fill in last outcome assessment forms if data are needed.

Concluding Comment

The above delivery structure is only a guide. A longer delivery format for the same content can be used where there is less limitation in the service and more opportunities to spend more time with complex or challenging clients, including those with poor adherence to practice requirements. If there is a need for a longer delivery period than the above schedule, it is recommended that the client using the MiCBT audio CDs practices one task (breath awareness or one of the scanning methods) with the CD for one week and in silence the following week. Each type of skill can be acquired more slowly and easily. Such a schedule would be especially appropriate for children, older adults, avoidant or dissociating clients, intoxicating clients and those with adherence difficulties.

Follow-up Sessions

Follow-up sessions have been shown to promote the continuity and further integration of practice, thus increasing the prevention of relapse. Based on this author's observations, a useful schedule involves four sessions spread over a year following the end of therapy. Clients may be invited to attend the first follow-up session one month following the end of the program, and the subsequent sessions three, six, and twelve months following treatment.

Outline for the MiCBT Follow-up Groups

Proposed contact hours with clients

- A 2-hour session repeated over the year, at month 1, 3, 6, and 12 following the group program. Each session is approximately identical in structure but may vary slightly in content according to participants' needs and issues. Validation of small changes is essential.

Program structure and content for each follow-up session

- Welcome and assessment forms.
- Group practice of mindfulness training for 15 to 20 minutes (1/3 = breath awareness, 2/3 = body scan).
- Feedback on practice and general functioning since the group ended.
- Assess the level of maintenance of achievements by writing on board the participants' goals initially set on Day 1 of the group and rate each goal. See list of actions below:
  1. List initial goals and their initial ratings on board.
  2. Ask each participant to rate (/10) the extent to which they have maintained their achievement.
  3. If low rating, ask to rate (/10) the extent to which they invested an effort.

    4. List post-treatment ratings (scored on week 8 of the group program) and compare with present coping level.
- Clarify specific issues of information processing
- Role-playing with equanimity for interpersonal issues. Use assertive statement equanimously.
- Reiterate the significance of impermanence
- Discuss and process short-, medium-, and long-term goals:
  1. Reality testing of goals as initially presented.
  2. Bi-polar visualization of goal achievement.
  3. Realistic goal setting by next session (in 2 months from now). Ask them to rate /10 how realistic the goals are and question feasibility.
  4. Visualize realistic short-term goals
- Practice of Stage 4
  - Reiterate the importance of practicing Stage 4
- Reiterate the possibility of (but not encourage) joining another (same) group if needed, or a more advanced group.
- Encourage weekly/fortnightly support group
  - Ideally, the group would involve 50% practice and 50% catching up and discussion.
- Close session (reminder of next session)

Last follow-up contact

- Celebrate and deliver certificate at the end of the session.

Summary of Main Points

- The MiCBT weekly implementation protocol is flexible, adaptable to the situation and client group. It can be as short as a six-session program or as long as one needs to acquire the personal, exposure, interpersonal, and empathic skills needed.
- The protocol proposed above is based on a standard eight- to ten-week intervention, easily extendable to twelve weeks when treating clients in crisis.
- The standard delivery format is organized in order of task difficulty, so that easier skills are taught first and more complex ones later in the program.
- It is recommended that clients be offered follow-up sessions.

Chapter 13

Professional Training

Physician, heal thyself.
Aesop

The Importance of Therapist Variables

It is well documented in the research literature that the therapeutic relationship is the greatest determinant of success or failure in therapy. The amount of variance accounted for by the relationship between client and therapist varies between 40% and 60%. Therapeutic technique tended to account for not much more than about 15% of change in clients – albeit, none of these studies included mindfulness-based therapies. Admittedly, even if there were such a thing as a best approach for everyone, clients need to be able to trust the therapist enough to engage in it and not drop out of it when therapeutic challenges arise or when results are slow.

Indeed, the therapist's show of interest, concentration levels, genuine empathy, and ability for patience, interpersonal awareness and mindfulness of their own processes as a clinician are all significant common factors affecting the therapeutic relationship, and consequently the client's progress. Accordingly, a therapy approach that requires the clinician's improvement of those common factors is likely to increase its likelihood for therapeutic success. Such therapy would not be limited to an impact of 15% probability of outcome variance. Since it increases the chances for optimum client-therapist relationship, as well as providing its technical tools, such therapy may be responsible for up to 75% of the betterment clients experience at post-treatment; at least in theory. Sound research is needed in this area.

Mindfulness-integrated CBT: Principles and Practice, First Edition. Bruno A. Cayoun.
© 2011 John Wiley & Sons, Ltd. Published 2011 by John Wiley & Sons, Ltd.

Effects of Mindfulness on Therapy Outcomes

Recent research indicates that therapist variables are significantly improved with mindfulness training. For example, a randomized, double-blind, control trial in Germany investigated whether promoting mindfulness in Psychotherapists-in-training influences the treatment results with their patients (Grepmair *et al.*, 2007). Patients treated by the more mindful therapists reported more appreciation of the therapy process, gaining better perspective and problem-solving ability, and greater symptom reduction overall.

Moreover, the levels of mindfulness in the therapist are associated with his or her own coping abilities. For instance, May and Donovan (2007) explored the relationship between mindfulness, wellbeing, burnout and job satisfaction of 58 individuals working as therapists. The results indicated that higher levels of mindfulness are associated with cognitive and emotional wellbeing, work satisfaction, and less experiences of burnout. Similarly, a prospective randomized control pilot study showed that health care professionals who participated in an 8-week mindfulness-based intervention experienced reduced stress, increased quality-of-life, and increased self-compassion (Shapiro *et al.*, 2005).

Additionally, the emerging picture from the literature is that clinicians who implement mindfulness-based programs for clients with a chronic condition or a personality disorder tend to be enthusiastic about the data they report.

The Importance of Professional Training

As with any comprehensive therapy model, MiCBT requires comprehensive training, supervised by competent clinicians. The effort for clinicians to learn this complex approach, added to the expectation that they themselves practice mindfulness skills (e.g, Kabat-Zinn, 2003), may initially lead to hesitations for colleagues who are not "introspection-minded."

Nonetheless, because mindfulness training is largely a skills-based intervention that addresses our experiences, it is important that therapists who implement it in their work engage in their own regular practice. This has also been recommended by others (e.g., Kabat-Zinn, 2003; Kostanski and Hassed, 2008; *Segal et al.*, 2002).

Even though there is a lack of replicated empirical evidence to claim superior clinical gains when clinicians undertake their own practice, there are some obvious potential dilemmas when the experience of mindfulness is unknown to the clinician. For example, imagine that a client with Panic Disorder experiences early signs of an attack in the session room. To what extent should the clinician allow the client to experience the symptoms? Should she or he revert to traditional treatments if there is a doubt that what was recommended is effective? For the therapist who has not experienced equanimity and the reality of "impermanence" at the level of body sensations, it is difficult to ask the client to attend to sensations of physical and emotional discomfort confidently and equanimously. Doubts are likely to remain. The only way to dispel doubts in the clinician is to practice.

More importantly, a therapist teaching mindfulness meditation who does not practice it personally is not likely to value and emphasize personal practice in the trainee, who will then not be able to develop the desired skills, as produced and maintained by neuroplasticity. This was also pointed out by Kabat-Zinn (2003) with regard to MBSR; and consequently MBCT. A lack of actual experience will lead to distortions and problems with replication of problem-solving skills.

Training standards

In a recent article addressing the topic of professional training in the UK, Crane, Kuyken, Hastings, Rothwell and Williams (2010) suggested a set of professional training guidelines and a sound rationale for their proposed structure. Their view is that implementing a mindfulness-based therapy without engaging personally in a regular practice is unproductive and should be discouraged.

The MiCBT Institute is an Australian Registered Training Organization that offers a Vocational Graduate Diploma in MiCBT. It is a one- to two-year long course nationally accredited in Australia, which is based on competencies and structured in a way that fulfills Crane *et al.'s* recommendations. Trainees first undertake an eight-week introductory course to learn and implement MiCBT skills in their personal life much like clients do. Once this is completed and their personal daily practice of mindfulness meditation is established, trainees can undertake the intermediate eight-week course, which requires them to implement each step of MiCBT in their client population, in individual or group format, under the supervision of a qualified trainer. The third level of direct contact training is undertaken via an intensive residential five-day retreat, which includes silent mindfulness meditation practice and discussion of ways to address complex cases (e.g., trauma, addiction, personality factors, etc) with MiCBT. There are ten training modules, each requiring specific *in-vivo* or filmed demonstration of competencies.

Following 8-week applied courses in MiCBT, some therapists send feedback by email at the MiCBT Institute. The following are common examples of therapists' professional and personal experiences with the program (reported with permission).

Case Example 1: Needle Phobia

MiCBT is working well for my clients at least partly because I am also keeping engaged in practice and can talk with clients about my own practice methods and what difficulties I have experienced. It is so much more than applying theory … You might recall that one of my anxiety reduction projects was to be able to give blood. Well, I had 5 phials of blood taken for medical reasons – AND I WATCHED THEM ALL. Still felt light headed and queasy in the tummy – but I was scanning as best as I could. I was sitting up but did not faint. Hours later I still feel a bit weak but composed and practicing non-judgment and breath awareness …

Case Example 2: Pain, Gambling Addiction and Anxiety

I completed the 8-week MiCBT workshop for professionals in Launceston, Tasmania, in April 2008. Mindfulness has become a part of my life now and many issues, both professionally and personally relating to confidence and anxiety have now been resolved. My development in MiCBT continues today and I am now achieving professional and personal goals that I considered to be some years away. I now also understand the relationship between Equanimity and Happiness.

Equanimity is continually replacing reactive behaviors, promoting a near con-stant state of happiness for me. I now love every aspect of my life. Prioritizing has become much easier and a number of chores I once viewed as essential, now have no meaning for me. The following is one of many examples:

> My wife casually asked me about 3 weeks ago, "Have you put our Tatts [lotto] in this week?" I looked at her with a blank look, as the gravity of realism sunk in. (I had not bothered to check our numbers for approximately 2 months. I had also not bought a ticket in that time). I recall feeling absolutely nothing, complete non-reactivity. I also recall thinking that this feeling was in stark contrast to the level of anxiety experienced in the past if I were to miss just one week of entering my numbers. It was around 30 seconds before I realized that mindfulness had freed me from the shackles of an unhealthy gambling addiction. I quickly passed this information onto my wife, who responded by saying, "You mean to tell me that all these years of screaming and cursing over the absence of a ticket come Saturday night and you are no longer interested in Tattslotto?" I could see the disbelief on her face, and to demonstrate my genuine-ness I threw the Tatts plastic card in the bin while scanning and monitoring by body sensations in total neutrality. I had never viewed Tattslotto as a gambling activity and had "normalized" this activity as something that was socially accept-able, and therefore could not be classed as gambling. "Everybody does it, don't they?"

My training in mindfulness has certainly provided a level of clarity I have not experienced before. I now see, and more importantly, understand, that I had fallen into the trap of relying on a lucky Tatts win to bring me happiness. I really don't think that I would have ever won, but my behavior was negatively reinforced for years. The relief from anxiety that I felt every time I bought a ticket reinforced the action of obtaining one, at any cost. I now have an extremely deep understanding that happiness can only be found from within.

Prior to MiCBT training, I had read a great deal of books on Buddhism and had adopted several views of Buddhism; however, I had never applied the meditation as experiential learning. I also strongly believe that I would never have given mindfulness the serious consideration it deserves without the "westernized" rationale provided in MiCBT.

I also feel I need to share this life changing experience: In 1994, I was involved in an industrial accident resulting in a spinal fusion of three vertebrae. Bone grafts, metal rods and screws were used to stabilize the spine. As a result of this, I have experienced chronic pain for the past fourteen years. Over this time, I have tried many therapies, techniques and medications to deal with the pain. In 2002 I began full-time studies and entered into the Health and Human Services industry. In order to perform at any reliable level I required 119 tablets per week, beginning with 7 tablets first up in the morning.

Approximately, three weeks into the MiCBT training, I began forgetting to take morning medication, which was significant in itself, as my mobility was usually difficult in the morning and therefore the reminder had always been there to take my medication. At this stage of the training, we had not discussed the positive outcomes in terms of chronic pain so this came as a huge surprise. I then found the confidence to experiment with my medication and plan a withdrawal process. I experienced no additional pain during this withdrawal period and am now using 14 tablets per week and am currently working on reducing this further. I no longer perceive chronic pain in terms of pain. I have developed sufficient equanimity to be more objective about how body sensations really feel, such as mass and temperature, and find that these sensations are acceptable and will pass, and therefore they dissipate quite quickly.

My wife and I have travelled, and seen most of Australia and have for years wished to travel in Asia. Unfortunately, my fears around carrying the amounts of medication into other countries required for chronic pain have prevented us from doing this. We are now planning a trip to Thailand and Vietnam. I cannot begin to express the freedom mindfulness has provided to me.

(A few weeks later ...)

... Mindfulness continues to be a positive routine for me in both personal and professional terms and my mindfulness practice is now as much a part of life as eating. In addition to the positive experiences I have previously shared with you, I have now lost 15 kilograms of weight since beginning MiCBT and feeling great ...

Regards

(The following week ...)

... I am now having quite a bit of fun with MiCBT and have taken it to a physical level in terms of equanimity. I have for years reacted to anybody in the household turning the hot water tap on while I am showering, which in turn, causes the shower to get cold without notice. I am deliberately turning the hot water tap off, in short bursts while showering and observing any reaction. I have now desensitized myself to this. In addition to working with individual clients using MiCBT, I am now delivering MiCBT to a group of 15 ...

Case Example 3: Pain

Do you remember how I said that I had been able to alleviate pain in my hip? Since then, I began to doubt that I achieved very much at all, because I have had a whole lot of pain that I could sense acutely, but not register as anything other than pain.

Well, the doctor has confirmed that indeed my hip is a problem. I have to have a new one! It is bone to bone, the cartilage is too damaged, and I am limping.

I also think I have trouble in L1-L4 in the spine, which is where the femoral nerve branches from. I am reasonably sure that this complicates things with referred pain from the spine at various points in the leg, particularly the knee and just above the ankle. As referred pain, it is different, I think, to usual range of sensations (mass, movement, etc).

I have a complicated relationship with my hip and leg. My mindful attitude to the hip seems to act as an anesthetic, but the other pain sensations test me.

I have been reading about arthritic pain and how symptoms can actually cause further arthritis, mediated through pain channels that pass on inflammation. I presume that if one can redefine the pain mindfully, it may also deal with secondary inflammation.

Also been reading about the medial pain system, that part of the total pain circuitry that processes pain emotionally. If pain is interpreted through fear and distress it heightens the pain. Mindfulness allows me to travel with pain as sometimes an unpleasant traveler, but not an enemy. Cheers.

Case Example 4: Distressing Situation

I have been practicing MiCBT [...] and co-facilitating MiCBT groups for 2 years as a Counselor in an Australian non-government / non-profit organization. I wish to pass on an experience I recently had while facilitating a MiCBT group at week 3.

I had been visiting my father in hospital interstate, he was having serious health problems, and there was concern from my family that he might not last too much longer. When visiting I was comforted by the medical specialist indicating that if my father continues as he is, they will be able to perform an operation that might solve all his health problems. But his condition was so weak; it was only possible if he remained stable. My father was in a positive frame of mind, and I left him after 4 days to return home and to my work.

On the next day back at work, and 20 minutes before the MiCBT group was to start, I had a strong urge to text my sister in New South Wales to ask how our father was. She immediately replied "Not good at all." This news hit me hard. I realized this might be his last hope fading. I felt very emotional at this point. I also realized the mistake I had made, texting family just before the start of the group, and how I was not in a good frame of mind to facilitate a group. It was too late to make other arrangements.

I quickly decided to sit down in a quiet room and meditate on the situation. Using my learnt MiCBT practice, I centered myself on my breathing and body sensations, then focusing on my father, I gently placed this situation to the side (like on a shelf in my mind) and focused on the group, my role in the group, and how I intend to spend the next 2 hours there with them. Then, after the group, I picked up on my father's situation – making phone calls, booking flights etc.

This seemed to help tremendously. I felt immediately focused, went into the training room, and for the next 2 hours I was able to stay focused. Feedback from my co-facilitator (who was unaware of my earlier dilemma) was that I had performed very well. I also felt I had taught well; I was totally focused on the course and the needs of the participants. My father died 4 days later.

Case Example 5: ADHD

Post comment by an MD on Radio National's (ABC Radio) Health Report talk show:

Thank you for your very helpful presentation. The association between ADHD and drug addiction is well known in the ADHD community. Some studies have found undiagnosed or undertreated ADHD in up to 65% of drug addicts. Medical and scientific studies of ADHD generally focus too much on genetics, neurotransmitters, and pathways, and have too little to say about experience. For ADHD sufferers, life is a continuous series of failures, mistakes and embarrassments. Inevitably, the individual's evaluation of and unskillful response to the situation makes it worse. The resort to overuse of drugs and alcohol is best viewed as an attempt at self-medicating by a highly stressed person.

Our stress is made worse by all the ignorant commentators in the press who insist on saying we are just undisciplined. In my now quite extensive experience, repeated exposure to that sort of attitude is one of the essential preconditions for ADHD to arise. The best management of the problem will combine all understandings.

Current mindfulness based treatments actually deal very directly with extinction of persistent unwanted responses and development of equanimity. I would especially recommend the variant called Mindfulness-integrated CBT, developed by Bruno Cayoun, a Psychologist from the University of Tasmania. This short, but intense program can produce dramatic improvements in as little as 8 weeks for a wide variety of psychological problems.

My personal experience was a very late diagnosis of ADHD, at age 46. I experienced great benefit from treatment with dexamphetamine but when that was combined with training in MiCBT, my requirement for medication collapsed. The current usage is now minimal, and not every day, and continuing to decrease.

Psychological therapies, in my opinion, have spent too much time talking about the bad stuff. As "neurons that fire together, wire together," the catch with that approach is that it is bound to reinforce the memory of the experience.

Additionally, as stimulants enhance learning (well proven), they are an obvious candidate to be used as an adjunct to mindfulness training for ADHD in my opinion.

Recommendations for Clinicians

It is necessary that professionals willing to implement MiCBT undertake proper training with a qualified MiCBT trainer. Since a number of professionals trained in cognitive and behavioral approaches are also mindfulness meditators, the structure and content of this approach are likely to be familiar and therefore more easily applicable. For those, the following recommendations are highlighted.

Before implementing MiCBT, it is recommended that they practice sitting mindfulness meditation if they have stopped for some time or are not very experienced, for at least 30 minutes once daily for a whole week – twice daily is best. Beside the importance of being consistent (practicing what we preach), it is essential that clinicians know experientially what exercises their clients undertake.

The audio recording of the standardized script "Mindfulness Training - Stage 1" (in Appendix B) can be used. The recording of mindfulness with breathing lasts about 18 minutes (track 6) and mindfulness of sensations (unilateral body-scan) lasts about 30 minutes (track 8); but relaxation beforehand is recommended when stress levels are high. There is a progressive muscle relaxation (PMR) instruction on track 4, which lasts 17 minutes. The rationale for the use of PMR in clients is described in Chapter 4.

When the clinician's practice improves, a few minutes of mindfulness of breath before body-scanning will keep the mind focused and more able to detect subtle body sensations with scanning techniques. Clinicians who maintain a personal practice are likely to find it beneficial both personally and professionally (Connelly, 1999).

Summary of Main Points

- Therapist variables are significant contributors to therapy outcome. This is even more relevant when implementing a mindfulness-based approach.
- Research shows empirical evidence that clients treated by a therapist well trained in a mindfulness-based therapy who practices mindfulness meditation regularly are more benefitted by therapy (i.e., mindfulness-based practitioners who meditate may be more effective therapists).
- Appropriate professional training delivered by expert and accredited trainers is essential.
- As is the case for MBCT- and MBSR-trained therapists, professionals who implement MiCBT are required to undergo accredited training and keep a regular personal practice, and maintain good levels of equanimity.
- Much like their clients, professionals who undergo the MiCBT program as a professional training often report important, sometimes life-changing, personal benefits.

Chapter 14

Frequently Asked Questions

To be wise, one must remain a student.
Aristotle

This chapter regroups questions by clients, clinicians and researchers, addressed to me over the past nine years, which I answered to the best of my ability. This chapter can be a useful resource for clinicians and other teachers of mindfulness given that the majority of the questions discussed are likely to be asked by their clients or students at some stage of their training. Since the exchanges with clients and colleagues were in simple conversational language, this chapter preserves the same simple conversational style. When communication was via email, the email is directly quoted, although most greetings and unrelated comments have been erased to prevent unnecessarily long text sections. Any information that could possibly identify the person has been removed or sufficiently changed to ensure full confidentiality. Since it was not possible to list all questions and answers exchanged, only those associated with themes that recurred several times over the years are included.

Common Questions about Mindfulness Meditation

My mind wanders when I don't use the CD

Question: Do people notice that the quality of their meditation session changes when they begin meditating without the CD as a guide? I think that my mind may tend to wander more. The CD and headset helped muffle outside noises.

Mindfulness-integrated CBT: Principles and Practice, First Edition. Bruno A. Cayoun.
© 2011 John Wiley & Sons, Ltd. Published 2011 by John Wiley & Sons, Ltd.

Answer: This is a common and expected experience, except when the trainee is encouraged to use the teacher's instructions continually. When we start practicing in silence, an increase in what is initially perceived as distractions is understandable in many ways. From a neurocognitive point of view, listening to auditory instructions interferes with thoughts that would otherwise "intrude" into conscious awareness. Instructions act as imposed "external distractions" from our spontaneous "internal distractions." It is well established in decades of cognitive research that when two stimuli of the same type are processed in the same modality in the brain, they compete for access to consciousness and the stronger one wins. In this case, since you tended to focus attention on the verbal instructions on the CD, the words of the teacher interfered with verbal processing in your auditory cortex, from where many of your memories would otherwise intrude in consciousness because they have been recently or frequently created or re-activated. Technically, this is called "structural interference." There are reasons for which externally-generated sounds tend to be perceived as louder that internally-generated ones (such as our thoughts) in the auditory system of the brain. Hypothetically, from an evolutionary point of view, we best survive if the brain is efficient in responding spontaneously to cues of potential threats. It makes evolutionary sense that even subtle sounds, such as the crackling of branches in wood, can capture our alertness effortlessly and interrupt the flow of our self-talk. It is likely that we are well equipped to capture interruptive external stimuli – though this may depend on the extent to which we are in the presence of potential internal threat, such as the cue of a heart attack, which would override the otherwise inherent tendency of attention to be directed externally. Hence, we can inadvertently become dependent on a teacher's voice and instructions because they may not only be inspiring, but also appear to make concentration easier. However, there are at least two limitations with over-relying on external instructions. First, we cannot always use teacher's instructions when we most need the practice to work. If the practice is not portable – e.g., someone who feels very anxious when going to the supermarket cannot listen to the CD to calm down – it doesn't serve its intended purpose. Second, the purpose of mindfulness training is not just concentration. It is supposed to produce wisdom through the insight one gets when realizing that every thought and accompanying body sensation, even the most distressing one, is impermanent and impersonal, and there is therefore no need to be distressed. Learning to remain equanimous while thoughts keep on arising is part of the training, which can be delayed, or even limited, by the use of auditory aids, such as music or instructions, when the practice is already learned. The same reasoning applies to the use of mantras. We produce our own verbally-generated interference, the mantra, which will help us focus attention by blocking the natural emergence of memories, the so-called intrusive thoughts. This would be a great choice of technique for the purpose of developing concentration, but certainly not for the purpose of reprocessing schema-based judgmental thoughts with more neutrality and acceptance, since processing the mantra interferes with these thoughts and thus cannot be permitted to emerge.

Is there an ideal size with which to apply attention?

Question: The intro CD says to scan with about two to three inches (6 to 10 cm) diameter spots of attention. Sometimes, I scan in much smaller areas. Is it important how big is the size of the body part we are scanning at a time?

Answer: Yes, the size for the spot of attention you use when scanning is best when it is not too small and not too large. If it is too small, say one or two centimeter diameter spots of attention with which to scan, it will take a very long time to feel the entire body, especially when you are not yet experienced. If it is too large, say whole body parts, such as the whole face or forearm, you are likely to miss many parts. If you recall the first skill you developed when you practiced mindfulness of breath, you were asked to focus on a small triangular area of the face, starting below the nostrils, above the upper lip (moustache area), extending throughout the inner walls of the nostrils. If you draw a rough circular shape around this area, you will find that it is a spot of about six to ten centimeters. Since we already shaped our attentional focus on this approximate size, people tend to find it familiar and often easier to scan the rest of the body using the same size. In contrast, with the second CD ("Advanced Scanning"), you will train to widen the focus of attention increasingly. This can start only once you can feel at least about 90% of the body when you scan, otherwise you will find these scanning methods too difficult. Their purpose is twofold. On the one hand, we produce rapid neuroplasticity to detect earlier cues of distress effortlessly, which helps preventing relapse. On the other hand, we learn to approach very pleasant, rapidly oscillating, subtle body sensations, sometimes called "free flow," without attachment to it or craving for it. We can discuss the relevance of these advanced scanning methods later on, when we get to this stage.

Why scanning in an order?

Question: You said in the group last week that it is important to follow a particular order for scanning the body but I was sitting behind everybody and didn't hear your answer clearly. The CD is very specific about scanning vertically, one part after the other. Can you clarify why we need to scan the body in that particular order? I find it easier to scan the parts that are most obvious, than surveying all parts, especially since I can't feel any sensation in some body parts.

Answer: Scanning in order appears more difficult at the start, but it also helps to not forget which body parts have been scanned during a sitting practice and those that have not. This is the main purpose. If you don't scan with a systematic order, you are likely to scan some parts more than others, because you feel them more easily, and neglect "blank spots." Yet, body parts in which you can't feel anything early in your practice are important tools to work with. The task is to stop scanning at each blank spot and focus on it calmly and equanimously (smilingly!) for about half a minute and then (or earlier if a sensation emerges earlier) move on to the adjacent part, and continue scanning. Sustaining neutral, non-reactive attention to blank spots in the body produces neuroplasticity (increased connections or connection strength) between the neurons responsible for making us feel these body parts, in the somatosensory cortex. If you pass your attention only through more obvious, gross, intense sensations, you won't develop the ability to feel very subtle body sensations. In turn, you won't be able to develop the ability to detect very subtle changes in the body that take place very early in the sequence of emotional experience. This skill is an important one because early-cue detection of distress allows us to choose our response when encountering a stressor, when it is still easy to deal with it comfortably. Later detection of distress-cues more often than not implies stronger emotional emergence, during which we tend to react automatically.

I find it difficult to scan the body by myself

Question: Without the CD, I find it difficult to move fluidly through the body scan. Sometimes, the exercise feels choppy for me. I try to keep a "vertical order" but run into problems when I reach my arms and legs. Is there a trick to scan the body more smoothly?

Answer: Your difficulty is common. Patience and persistence will help. It takes time to master the techniques. In the meantime, try to address the "blanks," especially in your arms and legs, by focusing for up to about half a minute on the body parts you can't feel. Stay there calmly, patiently and equanimously for this small period (about 4 to 6 breaths) every time you cycle through these body parts. If you don't react during the process, you are likely to feel sensations everywhere on the body sooner than later.

I am distracted by my own sensations

Question: If I am scanning and I notice a sensation elsewhere, do I turn my focus to that spot or try to ignore it and stay with the order?

Answer: Choose the middle way. Neither react to it, nor ignore it. Since it enters your sensory perception, just acknowledge and accept its presence and switch your attention back to the part you were scanning. If you follow every sensation popping up here and there in the body, you reinforce your distractibility instead of enhancing your ability to choose your response (which is to focus) by developing "response inhibition" in the frontal lobe.

Can I create body sensations?

Question: During body scan, I feel that I might create a sensation just by focusing on a certain spot. It feels somewhat like a nervous twitch that is created simply by focusing. Is this normal?

Answer: Yes and no. We can imagine a body sensation, we can produce a thought that then co-emerges with a body sensation, but we cannot technically create a body sensation just by focusing on a body part. Usually, because subcortical firing during emotions hijacks our attention, the more we crave the experience of a body sensation, the less we can feel common sensations. However, we do increase the ability to feel body sensations via neuroplasticity, which *is* the result of focusing on body parts with an intention to feel them. Best practice is to remain clear about what we truly feel and what we don't, accept, and move on to the next part without concern.

What do I do when I feel very tired?

Question: When I practice in the morning, I wonder if I may be drifting off into sleep while I'm meditating. I usually feel increasingly alert when I meditate and enjoy starting my day this way, but sometimes I wake up very tired and it's challenging.

Answer: The first step is to assess and modify the environment in which you practice, such as increasing the light, reducing the temperature of the room, sitting in a less comfortable chair or modifying your posture to keep our neck and back straight and the knees below the level of the buttocks. If drowsiness persists, try to breathe slightly deeper for a minute or so, feeling the touch of the breath within and below your nostrils. If drowsiness is still present, you can open your eyes to let a small amount of light enter the retina to wake the brain. Rather than fully opening your eyes, open the eyelids just enough to let you see the floor, not further than between two and two and a half meters away from your knees. If this is insufficient to reduce drowsiness, practice standing up for a few minutes. If this is still insufficient, go for a short walk and perhaps wet our face with cold water and return to continue the practice. Train yourself not to give up. I would also look at ways of reducing your morning fatigue.

Can I practice open eyes?

Question: Should I ever meditate with eyes open? I have done this on occasion and find that I can concentrate and focus well, but your manual indicates that eyes should be closed.

Answer: Yes, open is OK but only for very short periods to overcome drowsiness when it is present. Usually a couple of minutes suffice and we resume the practice closed eyes. The main reason for closing our eyes is to reduce the chances of being distracted by visual stimuli. We do our best to minimize externally-generated sensory inputs and the distractions they produce, in order to allow internally-generated outputs, such as thoughts and body sensations, which we then reprocess equanimously and in doing so neutralize the emotionality attached to thoughts.

Can I relieve myself from discomfort during practice

Question: Should I re-position myself if my leg falls asleep? It has happened and I have left it, but it's hard to get moving once my session ends!

Answer: Good work! It sounds like your equanimity is improving. It will be less hard with time. Your body slowly gets used to sitting immobile in that posture and you won't be disturbed by it anymore. This was my experience many years ago and is a very common experience in new trainees. I would recommend that you ensure your initial posture is comfortable to begin with.

How do I deal with interruptions?

Question: I remain completely still during the meditation, but have had to stop a couple of times because someone entered the room accidentally. Should I begin again or just continue?

Answer: Just continue from where you stopped when you were interrupted. Try to switch your attention back to it flexibly, without frustration or other kind of reactivity. Try smilingly! This is good training.

My mind wonders

Question: When my mind wanders, I try to use the "3-second rule" you suggest in the book but I may have wandered more than 3 seconds before I remind myself of the rule. Is this a problem?

Answer: It takes time for the brain to learn a new routine. Persevere! The 3-second rule is a helpful technique to learn progressively to inhibit more rapidly our tendency to identify with the thought and react to it by thinking it. It is not a rigid technique. If you can inhibit your response after a few more seconds, you are still doing very well.

Where should I refocus?

Question: When I get distracted by a thought, should I return my attention to my breath or to the part I was scanning in my body?

Answer: Refocus your attention to the body part you were scanning just before being distracted. You would reallocate attention to the breath if you were practicing mindfulness of breath. However, if you experience intrusive thoughts that are so distracting that you can't focus elsewhere on the body, then practicing mindfulness of breath for a few minutes will help. Sometimes, intrusive thoughts are so over-powering, and equanimity only mildly developed, that it is better to practice only mindfulness of breath and resume with body scanning when the mind settles.

Stomach tension during practice

Question: Sometimes I notice a tension in my stomach during meditation. Does this have to do with posture as I am holding my back straight and engaging the stomach muscles?

Answer: This could be due to many things, including visceral symptoms of anxiety. Standard practice is to keep a comfortably upright posture and remain equanimous to all sensations, keeping in mind that they are all impermanent and therefore impersonal. If the tension becomes so intense that it prevents you from focusing on other parts of the body, then better work on it a little. Working on a sensation means focusing on it for about a minute or so while remaining as equanimous as possible using discomfort to develop equanimity is the wisest form of coping.

The introduction CD was too slow for scanning

Question: I found that the body scan using the CD moved very slowly. If there was no sensation, I started to become impatient and wanted to move on. Any suggestion?

Answer: The first CD ("Stage 1") introduces various mindfulness meditation skills, as taught in the Burmese Vipassana tradition. Scanning the body, in this very ancient tradition, has a very specific purpose: surveying each body part indiscriminately in a systematic order to develop somatosensory awareness and equanimity (i.e., non-reactivity through experiential acceptance). Different people feel body sensations, move through the body and learn at a different pace, so the delivery involves instructions that are slow enough to accommodate for the large majority of trainees. Of course, we can scan faster as the skills are learned, and this is usually when practicing without the CD, on the second week of body-scanning exercises. During the second week, practicing without instructions, in silence, you are encouraged to move at your own pace. However, your comment also suggests that you became impatient. This is common in people who begin to learn the practice. There is an implicit expectation that the instructions "should" follow *our* pace, while we know that these are only a fixed recorded set of words on a CD that will not change pace and content according to our progress with practice. This is clear when we think about it, open eyes, unengaged in practice. However, the practice context changes our perceptions in various ways. If you recall the theoretical framework of MiCBT, especially the co-emergence model of reinforcement, every "implicational" thought co-emerges with its concomitant body sensation(s). The intensity and pleasantness of the body sensation(s) are functions of the importance of the meaning and the level of agreeableness of the thought. This twofold interactive relationship between mind and body also works in the opposite direction. When you scan the body, feeling certain kinds of sensations will lead thoughts that were associated with these sensations during their initial encoding in memory to co-emerge spontaneously. Accordingly, many (if not most) of our spontaneous cognitive and emotional experiences are based on our memories, our past, which we "project" in the present. In doing so, our tendency is also to attribute the experience to external factors, such as a trigger of some sort , so we can make sense of it. In this case, "someone is slowing you down." This is how, in a nutshell, this theoretical framework partly conceptualizes the behavioral perpetuation of our schemas and why well-established schemas can be so persistent when the therapy approach used to address them does not take somatosensory concomitants into account. This is principally why mindfulness training is a central part of MiCBT. You could find it interesting to link your experience of impatience to your beliefs, just out of interest perhaps. As far as the practice is concerned, it would be productive to perceive your impatience more perceptually, in terms of thoughts about how things *should be* (and are not) and their co-emerging unpleasant body sensations. Try also to pay close attention to how feeling unpleasant sensations in the body can trigger disagreeable thoughts. Then you will realize that you are only reacting to your own experience (body sensations), not to the trigger (CD instructions). Using "impatience" as a tool, developing equanimity to body sensations associated with the experience of impatience will help you deal with future experiences of impatience. See it as a form of exposure and response prevention. Try not to miss the current opportunity given that you will soon be practicing without the CD and won't need to work on this challenge. You can "invest" your discomfort or waste it.

The pace on the advanced CD was too fast

Question: I found that the advanced body scan using the CD moved too fast sometimes, especially with the most advanced one, Transversal Scanning. Have others mentioned this as well? I just moved throughout the body at my own pace. I hope it is ok.

Answer: The scanning instructions on the CDs are based on traditional teaching in the East, which is where I learned many years ago, and the delivery style and pace are "standardized" according to the large majority of thousands of people whom I taught over the years. Accordingly, it will not be the best fit for everyone. The suggested speed of scanning will also fit a person differently according to their current skills and how they progress. Sometimes we need to scan slowly. Sometimes we can move faster. Since you already know the basic elements of this practice, just adapt the practice to your best scanning speed each time. The CD is just a guide.

I feel bored during the practice

Question: I haven't practiced much of the body-scanning method this week [...] I find the practice terribly boring when I don't use the CD, so I am not feeling very motivated. What do you do with patients who can be so unmotivated to make them practice?

Answer: Your experience is a common one. In the West, we are not used to doing nothing, just witnessing the passing moment. When we experience a lack of sensory stimulation, our common habit is to "feel bored." But what is boredom? How do we experience it? We must *think, judge,* that our experience is boring and then make it our reality. So boredom comprises a judgmental thought about an experience, usually an unpleasant one. When prompted, people report either having an experience they don't want or not having an experience they want. In sum, we feel bored when our expectations are not met. When it comes to mindfulness meditation, this usually translates in terms of being unable to focus on body sensations (either of the breath or by scanning) and/or having too many thoughts despite our attempts to direct attention on the body. I see "boredom" either as a misinterpretation of an unpleasant experience or as a reaction towards it. This may include impatience and resentment. Our lack of insight and practice skills can sometimes result in interpreting our practice difficulties via boredom. We basically try to make sense of our experiences with external attributions – and think the practice is boring. When clients' sense of self-worth is low, they tend to attribute the difficulties internally, thinking the method might be very good and the problem is due their uselessness or failure. We first normalize the perception of boredom and investigate the skills with which they are having difficulties. We explain that thoughts of boredom are also just thoughts that need to be recognized and that they need to refocus on the body without further judgment and with more acceptance. We remind them that they could use this unpleasant experience as a tool to develop more equanimity. If this is insufficient to help them move on, we use the Socratic dialogue to demonstrate that their meditative experience is but a reflection or extension of their daily life, and that boredom can be an issue in their life, whether they meditate or not. Are they easily bored unless they keep their mind busy? Are they filling up their free time with mental or other activities? Is their life organized around sensory stimulations? Would they like to be able to be able to not depend on these to feel comfortable alone or with others? These are useful questions to ask and link to the practice. The fact that you feel bored mostly without listening to the CD suggests that you may be over-focusing on my voice on the CD when you use it, which results in dependence on it. I recommend that you practice one third (10 minutes) of your sessions using mindfulness of breath and two thirds (20 minutes) of body-scanning for each session. This will help you keep your concentration sharp before you start scanning. Please remember also that this practice requires a real mental effort during which you do all you can to focus attention, in the present experience, or boredom will persist.

I can't feel body sensations but I see colors

Question: I'm a very visual person and I used to practice meditation techniques that teach to visualize on different chakras and different patterns of colors, so I see different colors when I scan different parts of my body, but I can't feel sensations. Is that ok?

Answer: It might be useful to look at two important aspects for the practice in a therapy context. One is the aim – the development or improvement of equanimity through experiential awareness and experiential acceptance by remaining non-reactive with every experience in order to regulate attention and emotions. The other is the process by which this is achieved – feeling sensations in the body and its reliance on accurate brain pathways. The reason for this is that we cannot regulate emotions effectively unless we can feel them, and to feel them requires feeling sensations in the body, as emotions can only exist through their manifestation in the form of somatosensory stimulation (interoception); otherwise they are just thoughts or behaviors, not emotions. Accordingly, training ourselves to feel *all* possible sensations while becoming increasingly non-reactive towards them and eventually comfortable with any kind of sensation will result in what we call "skill transfer." This means feeling more comfortable with emotional experiences and detecting them earlier, when they are still manageable. Visualizing colors might have its own benefit but is not part of this practice and doesn't serve the therapeutic purpose we set out with a mindfulness approach. For this reason, we need to activate the somatosensory cortex and therein produce neuroplasticity; not the visual cortex. Your past training in visualization may have trained brain cells in the visual cortex to activate easily when you are closed eyes while awake. Since you are trying to develop a different set of skills while closed eyes, this automatic activation of visual pathways is now a distraction from the *feeling* task. This is a classic example of how neuroplasticity is not working in our favor. A useful way to go about it is to treat your intrusive images as intrusive thoughts. They are just momentary and impersonal mental activations that arise and pass away. Do your best not to reinforce them by engaging with them, and nerve cells that subserve these images will progressively decrease their activation strength and let you focus on other modalities. This might take a few weeks if you practice twice daily, as per the standard practice schedule.

I feel sensations only in few body parts

Question: I practiced every day twice a day for the past week and I can only feel about 20% of my body so far. Most others in the last class shared that they were able to feel much more. Am I doing something wrong or is there something wrong with me?

Answer: Our ability for interoceptive awareness, the ability to feel body sensations, depends on the amount and strength of neural connectivity in the brain's somatosensory cortex. These can be enhanced with sufficient frequency and quality of body-scanning practice. You already have a great commitment to the preferred practice frequency (twice daily). The quality of practice largely depends on your level of equanimity with which you scan the body. The highest likelihood of increased ability to feel body sensations is when we are least reactive towards our experiences, and most accepting of them. The more stressed we are, the less we can feel. There is a good reason for this, which you can review in the book section covering the co-emergence model of reinforcement. When we are stressed, once alerted by some right prefrontal areas of the brain, the processing of information is switched from the somatosensory cortex (where we feel body sensations when scanning) to the subcortical areas of the brain, in the limbic or emotional parts of the brain. Feeling common sensations becomes difficult until we calm the mind and regain a degree of equanimity. Then we are often surprised as to how much we can feel.

My beliefs interfere with my practice

Question: I have been experiencing some distress by some activities we've been doing in the course and was hoping you may be able to offer some strategies I can use to bring down my distress. I have a very strong link (have had since a very young age) between anxious thoughts and feelings and a specific core belief (which is a negative interpretation of me for having such thoughts and feelings). I am also coming to realize through more self-awareness over last week that other situations and thoughts and feelings (e.g., loneliness, boredom, failing at tasks) very quickly arouse that same core belief and others. And I now see very clearly all the negative feelings and avoidance that goes with these thoughts. But find I don't know what to do now to move forward from that. I have had cognitive therapy in past but it was not helpful in changing my core beliefs. I want to be able to feel like I can bring the distress down and others seem to be able to do this in the class exercise we had on Saturday, but instead it is having the opposite effect on me and my mind quickly sees it as proof for my defectiveness, which is the category of my core belief. I didn't give the bi-polar exposure a go straight away, as soon as I do the self-guided imagery I have strong emotions and my reaction to emotions comes up and it takes me some time to come down from this. I find that I am most afraid of thoughts and feelings associated with feeling useless, like if there's something wrong with me, a failure, and I have difficulty bringing the distress down to continue with the exercise. It takes some time to pass through and is often very intense. I think my focus is on learning to deal with strong beliefs, fear, and high anxiety with mindfulness at moment. Any strategies you can give would be most welcome.

Answer: It sounds like one of your challenges has a metacognitive basis, leading you to worry about your thoughts. Try to note every thought of that kind and treat them as mere thoughts, mere mental events. Even your negative interpretation of your thoughts and feelings are *only* thoughts, mental events, not truths, which you usually endorse and have learned to make yours. Now they appear to be part of you. This is the very pattern of identification we are training to change through mindfulness practice. Accordingly, do your best to not "waste" the opportunity to use these thoughts in terms of their *process*, not *content*, as part of your training. Every time such a thought emerges in consciousness, make a simple mental note that this too is just a thought that will pass given time. Very importantly, note the sensation in the body co-emerging with the thought, note what is the most predominant basic characteristic activated in the most intense sensation (mass, motion, temperature or density), accept it, and reallocate your attention to the target, which is the body part you were scanning before this thought emerged. I think it's ok to take time to practice a skill well before moving on to another and I wouldn't worry about where the others are at – especially since such worry would feed your failure schema. We can discuss this further on Saturday's class, as a group or privately if you want.

Reply: Thanks for your email. The core belief is in the defectiveness category. I have been having some times of intense emotion, thoughts and body sensations. It has been very uncomfortable at times. I am going back into mindfulness of breath and trying to sit through intense emotions I have and using mindfulness through it. It takes some time to pass through and is often very intense. I didn't give the exposure a go straight away, as soon as I do imagery, I have strong emotions and my reaction to emotions comes up, and it takes me some time to come down from this. I think my focus is on learning to deal with strong beliefs, fear, high anxiety with mindfulness at moment. I would prefer not to share with the class. Thanks for the explanation, which I will not mention in the group either. I think it's ok to take time to practice a skill well before moving on to another. I would also recommend that you take into account the co-emerging body sensations of your beliefs and their manifestation into negative self-talk. Without this multi-level appraisal of your experience, changing well-established significant schemas can take a very long time, even with a good therapist or therapy – including a mindfulness approach. I trust that you are doing you best and remain available in case you want to discuss this further outside the course times.

Compatibility with Pharmacotherapy

Is my antidepressant medication a problem?

Question: I am taking an antidepressant called Lexapro. Is it going to interfere with the meditation?

Answer: Lexapro is a medication of the SSRI family. These medications are usually not a problem with the program. Provided they are dosed appropriately, they often help people concentrate better by reducing their distressing symptoms. However, stopping suddenly is likely to produce withdrawal symptoms that can interfere with the practice.

My client feels sleepy when he meditates

Question: I started to implement Stage 1 of MiCBT, the mindfulness of breath exercise, and my client feels very sleepy when he meditates. He thinks his Valium contributes to his drowsiness. Is it possible? He asked me if he could reduce it while doing this training. Do you think this is a good idea?

Answer: It is possible that Valium can cause drowsiness and your client might need to discuss this with his GP or whoever prescribed the medication. Valium is habit-building and it is not advisable to change the dosage without medical supervision. However, drowsiness is also a common experience when we start practicing mindfulness meditation. It can be due to our unfamiliarity with deep relaxation. Given that Diazepam is usually used to reduce anxiety, I gather your client is anxious. People with ongoing anxiety tend to really relax only when they are asleep. They are not used to being relaxed when awake. As they sit closed eyes and begin to relax, they can inadvertently associate this with sleep and feel drowsy. There are also typical concomitants of drowsiness that many meditators encounter. These include practicing too late, when feeling too tired, practicing with a full stomach, practicing in a room that is too hot or too dark, practicing after consuming alcohol or other drugs, or while being otherwise intoxicated. Have a look at the various waking strategies proposed in the book chapter on "addressing difficulties and facilitating shifts."

Unexplained Experiences with the Practice

My body feels weird when I meditate

Question: I have recently felt very strange in my body during my sitting meditation. While I was scanning my body, it felt like I lost my sitting posture and my body was lying on the floor, on my right side. Then I opened my eyes and I was sitting up perfectly straight. Has this happened to you or to other people? What do you think happened?

Answer: People commonly report this kind of experience. While practicing crossed-legged on the floor, I have also personally experienced feeling that my knees were not aligned with the abdomen and the rest of the trunk while I was sitting up straight. I have never been able to explain this strange perception, but it has passed a long time ago. Try to remain "perceptual" about it, try to tolerate it and remain patient with it, and it will pass, soon or later. Being aware of it is useful but wanting it to be different is not. I would treat it just as any other experience, with detachment and an understanding of its essential impermanence and impersonality.

My hands lift up when I practice

Question: I have a weird experience when I meditate and I don't know if it happens to others. My hands feel extremely light and when I open my eyes I notice that they are both slightly raised up in the air without my choice or effort. They are just doing this by themselves.

Answer: I haven't experienced this personally. Whereas experiencing extreme lightness in the body is expected with more advanced levels of practice, "partial levitation" is not. I would just allow it without reacting to the experience and minimize my assumptions about what this means. If it becomes a source of too much distraction for you, despite having worked on increasing and applying your equanimity, try to position your hands comfortably held together in a way that may help prevent them to rise – though this would be my last choice.

My fingers rise when I practice

Question: Last week, during my practice, my thumbs raised all on their own, even though I didn't chose to move them. I find this very strange and inexplicable. Have you heard of this kind of experience when meditating Bruno?

Answer: Yes, I have heard of this kind of experiences, but they are uncommon. A colleague in Canada who practiced advanced scanning methods reported having her hands rising up on their own. I think her experience passed over time. You will find that if you just let it happen and don't react to the experience, it will change for you too. I recommend using this experience as a means of further developing your equanimity.

Adherence to Therapy

Poor adherence to practice

Question: The group is going well and some participants are starting to feel the entire body when they scan and feel generally less reactive. I also see that some prefer to practice 15 to 20 minutes at a stretch instead of the 30 minutes suggested in the MiCBT protocol. Some choose to practice only once a day, either because they are too busy or they are benefiting enough with one session per day. Does this happen a lot in your clinical work?

Answer: Regarding your question about shortening time on task, there is a cost. Less neuroplasticity means less ability for clients to generalize their new skills (attention and emotion regulation) easily across multiple contexts. All become a bigger effort and often require a mental effort. I think that shorter sessions are best negotiated on a case-by-case basis and we need to work on the client's believed limitations.

The Socratic Dialogue is the main method used in MiCBT. Changing the protocol is good when we have a good rationale for it (e.g., severe symptoms making practice unproductive), but if we buy into people's belief that their limitations reduce their ability to choose and prioritize, we reinforce it both in the client and ourselves with future clients … and the efficacy of the method decreases. We find that a very good way of addressing lack of commitment is to use standard CBT tools (Socratic Dialogue, behavioral experiment, reinforcement methods, etc) combined with motivational interviewing skills. I am aware that you are currently limited under the supervision of someone unfamiliar with MiCBT and I can detect the limitation of the traditional (usually cognitive) mindset. However, pleasing the client is a Western thing that is ineffective in the long term because we, as therapist, inadvertently model avoidance by making less effort when a task seems too hard. Instead, using MiCBT, we normalize the difficulty and teach the importance of using the difficulty as an opportunity for self-discovery and experiential acceptance. We also model this as a therapist by not shying away from carefully investigating the client's difficulty instead of avoiding it by changing our approach because we may find it too hard to be kind and simultaneously assertive with clients. Contrary to what is becoming a Western myth, mindfulness meditation is hard work. When it comes to the crunch, our existing or new ability for hard work makes the difference. The sooner clients experience this, the quicker their sense of self-efficacy and self-confidence improve, and progress on other measures soon follows. Please do not hesitate to let me know whether you need to discuss this more practically. You can organize supervision through the MiCBT Institute. It is great that some of your participants can now experience sensations throughout the body and are learning to detect early cues of distress, showing your good implementation skills.

Trauma

Can MiCBT address trauma symptoms?

Question: I work with humanitarian workers, often providing psychosocial support and coping strategies in sessions that are geographically located within the environment that they are working. Some of the vicarious trauma that they experience (including putting people back together surgically as well as medically) can be considerable and they find a number of ways to cope. I imagine that working with survivors of domestic violence is similar. At the workshop, will you be able to cover how one can provide a realistic framework for MiCBT for crisis intervention in such instances? How does one safely support such clients to increase sensitivity to their thoughts and feelings whilst also strengthening their ability to remain equanimous?

Answer: Yes, MiCBT can provide a useful framework for people continuously exposed to traumatic contexts and I can cover this in detail in the forthcoming 3-day workshop or via supervision. One important point to remember about MiCBT is that it is not confined to implementing mindfulness meditation. It carefully integrates mindfulness with CBT techniques that work well with trauma. The first thing to clarify is your question about how we could help clients to "increase sensitivity to thoughts whilst also strengthening their ability to remain equanimous." We want to do the exact opposite; *decrease* sensitivity to thoughts and feelings by *increasing* awareness and equanimity. Regarding the elements of mindfulness that would help, one is attention regulation (trained via mindfulness of breath), which helps people becoming more aware of their thoughts, while training to disengage from their grip, and reallocate attention to the intended task or action. This would include the ability to stop ruminative thoughts or intrusive images. Another important mechanism of action is emotion regulation through scanning the body with equanimity in order to teach the brain that all body sensations are acceptable and impermanent – whether they are part of an emotion or not. In particular during "Stage 2" of MiCBT (the exposure stage), we would discuss clients' aversive reactions (e.g., avoidance behavior) to various levels of trauma exposure while applying "Stage 1" skills and teach them Bi-polar Exposure (sometimes called "Balanced Exposure" by colleagues) to the avoided or otherwise resented situations (first in imagery, then *in-vivo*). This would include the ability to feel the bodily experiences of the emerging emotion while perceiving it less judgmentally and more perceptually, i.e., in terms of their basic characteristics [mass, motion, temperature, and cohesiveness (solidity)], and observe them progressively change. This requires regular personal practice.

Passion

The sadness of my passion is overwhelming

Question: I've been doing the loving kindness during the week and it's been fine – until this morning. As soon as I got to the part on the CD where you say "concentrate on parts of your body that vibrate with peace, free flow of sensations" (this is where I often feel the "glitch") I felt consumed with agitation, loneliness, despair and burst into tears that won't stop. I know my boyfriend is playing me like a cat plays with a mouse. I'm tormented by my yearning to find a way through with him, I'm distraught he can walk away without any apparent feelings of remorse, just move from one love(r) to … find another, a fresh start that doesn't remind him of who he is – yet. I believe there is a lot that is worthwhile for us to work through and deepen, we've been presented with an opportunity, it's a blessing; for me it is sacrilegious to give up on that. There is something he is obviously wanting to hold onto to. I think we share a similar yearning, and there is certainly similar attitudes and beliefs around life and spirituality, and similar life lessons. Why be alone in this, when we can be companions? He tells me he loves me, and sometimes, in our intimate moments I both see and feel his sincerity – there is a longing and vulnerability behind it. This, along with his texts that keep coming, even when he asks me to let him go, connecting with my yearning – these are what feed my hopes. And yet, so much of the time he is distant, secretive, defensive, disrespectful, rude, hurtful, everything that my body yells "get out, you don't want this, this is toxic." I feel trapped and I don't know my way out. Maybe I'm afraid to leave because then I would enter into the void of loneliness, a bleak and barren place. To think of it brings up fear, fear of the loneliness, of being cut off from love, of never being able to love or trust in love again. All I have is my anguish, the intense feelings of unrequited love and all the tensions and hopelessness that goes with it. This is going on for a long time, the yearning, the sadness, confusion, and pain is relentless. Never been so distraught over lost love like this before, I'm surprised at myself and humiliated. I know this has gone into a therapy session but writing it in my diary wasn't enough, speaking with a friend wasn't either, telling my boyfriend is useless, bashing a pillow only makes it worse and the CD just brings on the tears. I don't know what to do any more.

Answer: [...] I understand this situation is very painful for you. We have discussed the co-dependent nature of your relationship, the unhealthy attachment involved, and how better boundaries could help a number of times in the past and you showed good understanding. I also note that facing the difficulty is important to you and that you are making effort by practicing Loving Kindness. This is painful but it is great that you are trying. I would be happy to discuss all this further in our next session tomorrow, as emailing is not the ideal medium for therapy. In the meantime, try to limit the practice of Loving Kindness meditation to times when you feel less emotionally reactive, so that you prevent reinforcing your reactivity and suffering. It would also be very beneficial if you used this emotional pain "as a tool," by focusing on the body sensations associated with your distress with as much equanimity as possible, and as frequently as possible throughout the day, when you get caught in such unhelpful thoughts. Try to decompose the sensations in their most basic parts (mass, motion, temperature and density/solidity), as we discussed previously. This can help you be more objective about what you actually feel and help you stay more in the present reality of the experience – rather than giving in to the temptation of ruminating over the past and worrying about the future. Try to have a real go at it. I look forward to our session tomorrow ...

Can mindfulness coexist with romantic love?

Question: During your professional workshop in Auckland, I understood that in reducing the negative evaluation/sensitization to some thoughts, mindfulness aims for neutrality. Is there a space for building positive emotion within mindfulness and/or how and where does positive emotion fit? A possible, but not necessarily common, emotion is love. If one is "in love," can one be "in love" mindfully?

Answer: When we can increase "neutrality" of our response (equanimity) to events and prevent reactions such as craving and aversion, what emerge are usually kindness, love, friendliness, acceptance, and a sense of being connected within ourselves and to others. Along with it, fear of love is minimized and we tend to feel freer to love less conditionally. Whereas the state of romantic love, its maintenance really depends on how much it relies on cravings. Clients and colleagues who have become more mindful have consistently reported encountering fewer conflicts with their love life, but none has ever reported feeling less passion. I guess they simply feel more in control of their passionate reactions. My consistent observation has been that when people begin to practice body-scanning methods and become more aware and equanimous, they become increasingly able to *inhibit their habitual inhibitions* and allow themselves to feel and act more authentically, often with passion and creativity. Interestingly, I have observed a number of women who practiced advanced scanning, which often produces a pleasant bodily experience, returning for their next therapy session better groomed, putting on make-up, reporting feeling more energy and a renewed interest for intimacy. For others, people tend to report that their loving experience transforms into a less conditional love and they are happy to restrict sexual activity to when both partners are genuinely interested, often for the first time in their married life. Mindfulness meditation helps prevent reactivity without promoting nihilism. It helps to find a middle way. Sometimes it is useful to conceptualize "falling in love" as a *collapse* of ego boundaries, and more genuine, voluntary love as an expansion of ego boundaries. Falling in love, however important and useful it may be, is usually followed by "falling out of love," because the quasi-egoless state of feeling in love is based on a strict condition produced externally to ourselves; we feel that it is the *other* who makes us feel in love. I really relate to Psychiatrist Scott Peck's definition of genuine love in his best seller *The Road Less Travelled*: "Genuine love is the will to extend oneself for the purpose of nurturing one's own or another's spiritual growth." A well-implemented training in mindfulness helps us extend our limitations as we become more interpersonally aware, accepting, patient, tolerant, caring, empathic, and connected, without disregarding our and others' boundaries, to include more people and phenomena within our sense of self. The love we feel is then not strictly limited to one person with whom we are "in love." Accordingly, I not only believe that we can feel much love mindfully, I also believe that our ability to love genuinely is a function of the degree to which we are mindful. Love starts with attention and depends on it.

Pain

Pain during practice

Question: How do I help my client with strong pain? She also worries about her heart rate during the practice.

Answer: I would recommend that she stays in the heart area, on the most unpleasant area for half to one minute, calmly, equanimously (with acceptance and without reaction), with a degree of curiosity, and this in your presence so she knows it is safe. Ask her to describe the sensation in detail in terms of 4 characteristics:

temperature, mass, movement, and cohesiveness (ie, whether the sensation has a shape, a form). Before she starts, ask her to rate her worry about it out of 100. After about half a minute exposure to it, ask her if it is "the same as before" (without leading too much) or did things change, and then ask her to re-rate her worry about it out of 100. During exposure, break the silence every 15 seconds with a gentle voice reminding her not to get caught in thoughts and continue visiting the physical area in a "scientific" manner, taking note of all the different sensations she comes across "in this area of the body," rather than "in your heart." If the words you choose are neutral, rather than words that have personal implications (e.g., "the pain in your heart") there is more chance for her to remain equanimous. If she remains equanimous during the interoceptive exposure, the experience is likely to change. If the change leans toward greater intensity, it is either because she is now becoming more aware of the sensation that she usually avoids, or because she catastrophizes during the exposure process – consciously or not. You need to explain that this is normal because she became more aware of the sensation and ask her if she would be alright to try again, but now she should come back to the sensation as soon as she is aware a thought arises, calmly, equanimously. It is useful to start your sentence with "keeping your eyes closed …" This is because opening her eyes will distract her, which is likely to cause arousal to decrease without her effort. She needs to be reminded that "this sensation will also change" if she stops reacting to it (reinforcing it). It is good to remind her that her past attempts to avoid the experience have not been helpful since she still can't cope with the problem. She will also benefit from the reminder that the essential skill to develop in the face of unpleasant body sensations is equanimity rather than "making the discomfort go away," however painful the discomfort may be.

MiCBT for Children

How do you use MiCBT with children?

Question: I'm a Zen-practitioner and do sitting meditation every day. That's why I'm so interested in the application and theoretical background of MiCBT. My life has tremendously changed since I m practicing zazen. What I've read about the theoretical basis of MiCBT has really impressed me. The described model of cognitive processing within the concept of equilibrium in your manual is fascinating and I'm excited at the prospect of reading your book. Is there any information about your MiCBT treatment model for children with behavioral problems available? I'm a cognitive behavior therapist for children in Germany and many of my clients are children that are diagnosed with ADHD. In my opinion it must be a good service to teach those children in mindfulness meditation techniques. Eventually they get used to those techniques and are in charge of their awareness and therefore can better control their attention. So I'm actually very interested in your set of exercises, explanations, homework tasks, etc. What are your experiences with the children?

Are they willing to do the exercises and do they appreciate the breath techniques? What did you tell them in the beginning about the goal and the content of the treatment? How do you motivate the children? I hope you will appreciate my interest in your work and find time to answer my questions.

Answer: One of the most challenging aspects of teaching mindfulness to children with behavioral and/or attention problems is how we can help the parents practicing with the child – given that parental modeling and support are essential to the child's practice. Most of the time, when the child doesn't practice, it is because the parent stopped practicing. In my experience, this is one of the trickiest aspects in implementing any mindfulness approach with behavior-problem children. Children often end-up practicing such challenging tasks on their own for a while and soon after they give up too. To help prevent this, it has been essential to have a clear (and strict) agreement with the parent(s) from the start. Another important aspect is that the therapist must practice. In contrast with some mindfulness–based interventions (they crop-up like monsoon frogs these days), the MBSR, MBCT and MiCBT approaches capitalize on daily practice of mindfulness meditation and are good candidates to produce productive neuroplasticity. I am sending you a protocol we use flexibly to adapt the adult model for children with behavior problems (not just ADHD). It explains why children need to "shape" attention with various intermediate techniques to bring it to a sufficient level of efficacy that enables the child to start with the adult model within a few weeks. The proposed approach offers one way that makes this possible and relatively easy; though it still requires mental effort. In a nutshell, we teach the child breath-counting techniques that initially require only little attention, and we progressively increase the complexity of the task, while each effort is rewarded by the parents or guardian and by the very attention they direct to the child for a few minutes daily. Once the child's ability to sustain attention develops sufficiently, we start using the CDs as we would with an adult.

Reply: [...] I'm already using this protocol for implementing mindfulness training with two boys, 12 years old and diagnosed with ADD; and in another group consisting of two boys at the age of 14, suffering from anxiety disorders. I had interviewed the parents and children to find out about their motivation taking part in the training. They will support their children by their homework. I'm glad that I have asked you about the difficulties. Now I'm looking forward to my first session.

Can MiCBT help with ADHD?

Question: I have a genuine interest in learning on how mindfulness has scientifically proven that it can help treat ADHD. I have ADHD and I would say that I continually practice mindfulness, but have the playfulness to go out of my mind ... not all that different. Bizarre. And I reached great heights, though I never have seen scientific evidence of improving the actual deficit in attention, which everyone else seems not to have. It's not so much only about outward behavior seeming less abnormal. I'm not in desperation, curious about the papers, and whatever else that would be conducive to understanding mindfulness as your collective presents it. Obvious question: Is this related to Buddhism? ... I find interesting, the difference between the physical dart of pain, and mental one ... Healthcare is very expensive here, in the United States ... So that puts me at a disadvantage in my stunted experiences in treatment medicines. It's like I know I need to try new things, but there's no support which allows me to do it, in the USA.

Answer: Hi [...]. Sorry this is not Dr Bruno Cayoun here. Bruno has asked me to reply to your email given his current workload and because of my own interest in the use of mindfulness in managing my own ADHD and that of my patients. I will be perfectly upfront with you. I am a family physician in Melbourne, diagnosed with ADHD almost 2 years ago at age 46. I have classed myself a Buddhist since my early 20s, and soon after starting treatment for my ADHD became aware that my response to stimulants was highly variable, but often excellent. I started to ask myself why this was so and realizing the applicability of Buddhism to the problem, immediately began the task of breaking down inattention to its "component things" to use a little Buddhist terminology. I also realized that the description of suffering (or *dukkha*) in Buddhism is very much analogous to the processes in ADHD. Indeed Alan Wallace also makes this observation in his book "The Attention Revolution." I developed a process of mindfulness of action as a sort of self-treatment, and became progressively more aware of all the little things that impaired my attention. Just asking myself before every act "How alert am I? Can I improve my alertness?" made me focus on the little things like physical discomfort or hunger that interfere with my attention, and the bigger things like tiredness, sleep deprivation, anger and worry. That is when I discovered Bruno's MiCBT. MiCBT starts with mindfulness of the breath and then uses that single pointed attention to closely examine body sensations in increasingly subtler and revealing ways. As we progress in other stages, we use this while learning to visualize difficult situations and imagine good and bad outcomes while we become aware of the intensity of our emotional reactions and learn to prevent the reactions. We become aware that we often react in haste because of the unpleasantness of anger or fear, and that often we act unskillfully. We also learn that the overreaction is quite unnecessary because if we learn instead to minutely examine the nature of these body sensations, they will fall away by themselves. MiCBT requires about 8 weeks of two 30-minute practice sessions each day. It needs supervision. I did the training in a group of 14 people. My wife and I are both family physicians, the remainder were counselors and psychologists. To my eye, every one of us personally benefitted greatly from the course. My requirement for stimulants simply collapsed in the last 2 weeks of the course, and I now use them only infrequently, and almost never more than once a day. My marriage has been taken to a new level and both my wife and I find it a pleasure to help people learn such a positive and simple technique. It is derived from Buddhism, but has been modified so that people of any religious tradition, or none, may feel comfortable using it. MiCBT is also strongly grounded in neuroplasticity theory. Specifically, it trains the mind in development of single pointed attention, impulse control, interior perception, metacognition and ultimately in equanimity. We need to understand the importance of neuroplasticity theory in modern psychological treatment, namely that virtually any psychological quality is able to be developed if we pay enough attention to defining our terms and work closely with the individual to ensure he engages with the technique and remains motivated to persevere in treatment. Bruno did present a number of case histories at the Mind and Its Potential Conference in Sydney at the start of December 2009. I will search these up for you and ask at our extra training session tonight whether there are any more papers that would be applicable. I am happy to correspond further if you wish. I think this is a wonderful technique and the good news about it needs to be spread about. I personally am so much happier to be out of the ADD state. It really was pretty unpleasant. I remain simply amazed at the ongoing improvements in our lives that my wife and I continue to experience since doing the MiCBT training.

I'm losing hope with my child's progress

Question: I'm afraid my optimism of two weeks ago when we spoke about my daughter's progress is being tested. Alice is starting to suffer performance anxiety about Body-scanning (CD1, Tracks 7 and 8) in particular and Mindfulness practice in general. My wife and I are concerned that insisting on the body-scan and breathing practice is becoming counterproductive for Alice, as she starts to punish herself for her self-perceived inability and lack of success. We (separately) have tried coaching her through a practice CD without success. She misses preparing for the focal point of her sessions with you (as well as the personal contact with you). We are however finding that Alice likes the Progressive Muscle Relaxation CD track, and are hoping to establish some continuity with it. She has mentioned more than once that she feels unable to tell you when she can't do something for fear of disappointing you, and not being able to live up to your belief in her. My wife has observed that Alice seems to have inherited her father's tendency to paint rosy pictures about his progress when in therapy, and that this might be misleading you as to how she is progressing. Would you please be able to suggest a strategy that would in the meantime keep her calmly in touch with Mindfulness practice at the same time helping to keep her anxiety about it in check? I also wonder whether during this period of Mindfulness training we should abandon her extra-curricular music lessons. Can you please let us know what you think about the music lessons as well?

Answer: Thanks for the detailed explanation. I had suspected that Alice tried to impress me at the cost of trust in my ability to accept that she finds the practice difficult at times; which she sees as failures. I would first "normalize" her difficulty. Please let her know that learning often starts with difficulty, that difficulty is also a valuable experience that can be used to develop great levels of equanimity, and that the best quality of practice is achieved while experiencing difficulty. This is because increasing our ability to accept our experience of difficulties requires more skill than accepting our experience of ease. Once a kind of difficulty becomes more acceptable, we are changed by both the effort we produced and the realization of our achievement. This applies very much to learning the practice of mindfulness meditation.

Learning to accept an intense body sensation, the inability to feel a body part, a flood of intrusive thoughts preventing us to focus, the lack of time for practice, all these and other difficulties are excellent platforms and opportunities for developing greater levels of equanimity. Let's use them, or they will be wasted! Of course, all this in a language that is more accessible to a 10-year old. Based on your information, I suggest she practices 1 session of PMR (AM or PM), 2 short sessions of breath counting and 2 short sessions (5 minutes each) of mindfulness of breath without counting (AM or PM) daily until we meet again. I also suggest she practises awareness of body sensations during daily activities, but not in sitting practice at this stage, while remaining equanimous. Please reiterate that what determines her success is her very acceptance of the experience of difficulties. I will try to direct the next session towards Stage 2, gently bringing exposure tasks to reduce her fears of being in the bedroom alone while awake, which have led her to develop OCD. She now needs to relate her practice more to external issues and see how her internal work affects her experience of external contexts as soon as possible. This will help reinforce her motivation, effort and enthusiasm for her training. Last, I am also suspecting that she might feel over-monitored or scrutinized by her parents during her practice, and that her performance anxiety may also comes from this. You are both highly regarded teachers who sometimes need to express high expectations of university students. You have also been both my clients for the treatment of anxiety and know well what it takes to practice effectively to overcome continuous worry. It is possible that you inadvertently convey to Alice an expectation that she should be up to standard with my expectations. Naturally, she would assume the expectation to succeed with the training is mine. This is only a hypothesis but just in case this is what is occurring, and to prevent escalation of anxiety, I recommend that she practice on her own until our next session. I also suggest you verbally express trust in her ability to practice at the level she can at present and let her know that it is good enough and you are proud of her. If her extra-curricular music lessons provide something "special" for her, I think it would be better to preserve the routine. If it adds stress and the perception that she has to please you or perform at that level to feel worthy, then having a break for a while during our work could help, but it needs to be presented sensibly. Some children are under the impression that parents validate who they are based on their special talent. If this is the case for Alice, you would need to ensure she is validated for adhering to her mindfulness training routine, not just for the results she gets with it. We can review the situation when you all return for the next session.

Conducting Groups

Conducting groups for drug and alcohol consumers

Question: I have also been approached to facilitate a MiCBT group with recovering Drug and Alcohol users. I have not committed to this at this point in time. Do you have any thoughts or advise for me around this Bruno?

Answer: I think you would do well with the recovering drug and alcohol users, but I think having some supervision during this would be a good idea, particularly if your clients present with high co-morbidity, if they tend to relapse often or are ambivalent about their conviction to change. It is also important for group implementation of MiCBT that consumers also receive individual weekly sessions, each lasting between 30 and 60 minutes (20 minutes at the very least). People in crisis don't do as well when therapy is limited to group interventions. Can the logistics for this be handled well? I would collect data on weekly changes in consumption, using either a standard questionnaire for alcohol/drug consumption or, at least, by recording carefully the amounts consumed by participants weekly. I would also collect data on emotion regulation, severity of dependence and locus of control, much as we do in our research at the University of Tasmania. I am happy to discuss this further if you need.

Contraindications

Are there contraindications for MiCBT?

Question: I am writing to get your opinion on the suitability of MiCBT for a recently referred client. This man has few options left and possible contraindications, so your opinion would be invaluable: He is mid 40s. Normal developmental history, then work-related stress became a diagnosis of Major Depressive Disorder (MDD) with psychotic elements. 10 years of psychiatry, heavy pharmacotherapy, and inpatient stays has left him with the label "treatment-resistant." He is cognitively impaired. It is a heart-wrenching story. His primary concerns at present are verbal aggression (sudden onset, explosive, quickly forgotten), and intrusive negative thoughts (e.g., "you're hopeless") that have led to attempted suicides. What's next for this man? One saving grace is his dedicated and stressed partner. I know you are busy, so I hope this request doesn't add a burden.

Answer: [...] I reply to your questions within your text. I hope it helps.

Question: I suspect that PMR may assist by reducing bodily tension (one possible contributor to his outbursts). It would be straightforward enough for him to do.

Answer: I agree.

Question: Also, Mindfulness of breath (MOB) is simple enough, might give some calm and mastery over attention and possibly a generalized sense of having some control?

Answer: I agree that it would help, but not that it is simple enough. Given his impulse-control problem, he is likely to experience difficulties accepting the frustrations most people experience when focus is not developed and thoughts are difficult to tolerate. Regarding gaining sense of control, yes but your emphasis on equanimity all the way through is crucial. You need to ensure that you deliver the rationale for the co-emergence model of reinforcement in an experiential format, as proposed in the manual.

Question: Can a simple scanning technique reveal some ability to detect early or moderate signs of tension that may be antecedents of problematic behavior?

Answer: Yes, that's the idea! But again, you need to ensure that you deliver the rationale for the co-emergence model experientially.

Question: I wonder whether he would come to see that intrusive negative thoughts will pass, and he does not need to act on them. This may get him past the impulsive timeframe in which he self harms. What do you think?

Answer: Remember that when you use MiCBT and the theoretical framework on which it is based, you need to consider, and emphasize with the client, that people react to the body sensations their thoughts (overt or covert, conscious or automatic) create. One important implication of this understanding is the emphasis on body-scanning techniques and the necessary effort to develop equanimity towards body sensations. From a learning theory perspective, this constitutes a habituation/desensitization procedure to internal cues (including those of anger). Accordingly, the focus of the "response-prevention" strategy is best directed to the somatosensory experience of thoughts, not to the cognitive one. Since both are intimately coupled, becoming comfortable with body sensations makes thoughts ineffective in producing further arousal.

Question: Do you have a confident stance on the merits of trialing MiCBT with such a presentation (I would include both partner and client)?

Answer: Yes. MiCBT is designed to be non-diagnosis specific. Well delivered (no short cuts) and well received, it will help anybody to recreate a healthy balance in the allocation of attention during a stress response. While experiencing the intense body sensations associated with high arousal (in your client's case), people can produce a simultaneous response tapping the so-called executive functions, thereby allowing a greater degree of rationality and self-control while emoting. This is because they have trained the brain to routinely learn not to react to arousal-based sensations.

Question: Are there contraindications you have found to be relevant?

Answer: None that is immediate in this case, except for psychotic features. Usual potential avoidance/dropping out when the therapist is unable to provide sufficient validation for small results, lack of assertiveness with practice requirements, and (most importantly) lack of empathy, may lead to poor outcomes. If the client's experience during his practice of mindfulness doesn't allow him to have some control of the direction of his attention and he is caught-up in thoughts that produce, maintain or increase anxiety or depression, it is prudent to alter or interrupt his practice. People who don't understand the practice can make things worse by reinforcing their response and thereby increase their distress. As for any exposure method, attempts to desensitize can turn into reinforcement if the person doesn't change the response. Here, the stimulus is an internal cue (body sensation or thought or both) but the rule remains the same: expose and prevent the response. When this is not possible, stop the practice until the crisis has decreased sufficiently to enable the person to practise productively. There are no strict rules applicable to particular disorders, but if the person reports increased anxiety with the practice, you need to investigate thoroughly the way they understand the practice and the way they practise it. For example, if he ruminates during practice, while closed eyes, it is not a good sign. He could try to practice with eyes slightly open for a few minutes and then retry closed eyes, and continue with intermittent periods with eyes open. In other cases, practicing 10 to 15 minutes several times daily might be a "softer" approach for a period, until the main symptoms subside. Poor insight in the client can often be remedied by revisiting the co-emergence model of reinforcement experientially. There's a good paper by Paul Chadwick and colleagues (2005) in the UK, showing good results using mindfulness *very cautiously* with psychotic patients (e.g., using short sessions and eyes open). I can send you the reference. If poor results persist and you already investigated his practice, I suggest a pause for a week or so, which gives you time to query the matter with an experienced colleague. Of course, the usual precautions, such as knowing whether the client had a sudden change in their medication intake, etc, are also important.

Which clients can use MiCBT?

Question: I am very excited by the idea of integrating mindfulness and CBT with some of my clients and wonder whether I should not use it with some clients. Do you have any advice?

Answer: The MiCBT program is usually safe and non-intrusive. However, people who practice mindfulness meditation on their own during very distressing experiences can sometimes feel worse. People with lack of insight or poor understanding of the techniques who cannot handle distressing thoughts can sometime ruminate while being under the impression that they are practicing the skills – and then think the practice "makes them" feel worse. At this early stage of research in this area, it is not recommended to practice standard mindfulness meditation while experiencing psychotic states (e.g., delusions, hallucinations, paranoia), manic states (e.g., extreme anxiety or anger, uncontrollable agitation or impulse), or suicidal intent or states in which the person may be at risk. This is even more important if the clinician is not experienced in mindfulness applications and in treating these conditions.

Summary of Main Points

- Progress starts with difficulty. Difficulty is also a valuable experience that can be used to develop great levels of equanimity, and the best quality of practice is achieved while experiencing difficulty. This is because increasing our ability to accept our experience of difficulties requires more skill than accepting our experience of ease.
- Once the difficulty becomes more acceptable, we not only feel relieved. We are changed by both the skill we developed through the effort and the realization of

our achievement – a greater sense of self-efficacy. This applies very much in mindfulness meditation.

- Learning to accept an intense body sensation, the inability to feel a body part, a flood of intrusive thoughts preventing us to focus, the lack of time for practice, and other difficulties, are all excellent platforms and opportunities for developing greater levels of equanimity.

- Despite the cultivation of emotional detachment during mindfulness meditation training, mindfulness facilitates, enhances and sometimes leads to genuine loving states. Indeed, love starts with attention and depends on it. When our attentiveness is replaced by assumptions, our love is filled with expectations. When negativity is targeted successfully, what remains is a greater ability to switch to positive states of mind.

- Invest challenging experiences into a learning experience or they will be wasted! In any case, as Aristotle said, "There is either a solution to the problem and therefore it is pointless to worry about it, or there is no solution to the problem and it is pointless to worry about it."

Love starts with attention and depends on it.
When our attentiveness is replaced by assumptions,
our love is filled with expectations.
May we learn to attend to ourselves and to each other.
                              Bruno Cayoun, 2011.

References

Allen, N., Chambers, R., Knight, W., and Melbourne Academic Mindfulness Interest Group. (2006) Mindfulness-based psychotherapies: A review of conceptual foundations, empirical evidence and practical considerations. *Australian and New Zealand Journal of Psychiatry*, 40, 285–294.

Axiom Australia. (2002) *Buddhist parables: Tales to illuminate*. Axiom Publishing, Stepney, Australia.

Badcock, J.C., Waters, F.A.V., and Maybery, M. (2007) On keeping (intrusive) thoughts to one's self: Testing a cognitive model of auditory hallucinations. *Cognitive Neuropsychiatry*, 12, 78–89.

Baer, R.A. (2003) Mindfulness training as a clinical intervention: A conceptual and empirical review. *Clinical Psychology: Science and Practice*, 10, 125–143.

Baer, R.A. (ed.) (2006) *Mindfulness-based treatment approaches: Clinician's guide to evidence base and applications*. Academic Press, Elsevier, London.

Baer, R.A., Smith, G., and Allen, K.B. (2004) Assessment of mindfulness by self-report: The Kentucky Inventory of Mindfulness Skills. *Assessment*, 11, 191–206.

Baer, R.A., Smith, G.T., Hopkins, J., *et al.* (2006) Using self-report assessment methods to explore facets of mindfulness. *Assessment*, 13, 27–45.

Bandura, A. (1977) Self-efficacy: Towards a unifying theory of behavioral change. *Psychological Review*, 84, 191–215.

Bandura, A. (1997) *Self-efficacy: The exercise of control*. Freeman and Company, New York.

Barkley, R.A. (1997) Behavioral inhibition, sustained attention, and executive function: Constructing a unifying theory of ADHD. *Psychological Bulletin*, 121, 65–94.

Barlow, D.H. (2002) *Anxiety and its disorders: The nature and treatment of anxiety and panic* (2nd ed.) The Guilford Press, New York.

Barlow, D.H., Craske, M.G., Cerny, J.A., and Klosko, J.S. (1989) Behavioral treatment of panic disorder. *Behavior Therapy*, 20, 261–282.

Mindfulness-integrated CBT: Principles and Practice, First Edition. Bruno A. Cayoun.
© 2011 John Wiley & Sons, Ltd. Published 2011 by John Wiley & Sons, Ltd.

Barnard, P.J., and Teasdale, J.D. (1991) Interacting cognitive subsystems: A systematic approach to cognitive-affective interaction and change. *Cognition and Emotion*, 5, 1–39.

Barnes, J. (1995). *The Cambridge Companion to Aristotle*. Cambridge University Press, Cambridge.

Barnhofer, T., Chittka, T., Nightingale, H., *et al.* (2010) State effects of two forms of meditation on prefrontal EEG asymmetry in previously depressed individuals. *Mindfulness*, DOI 10.1007/s12671-010-0004-7.

Beck, A.T. (1976) *Cognitive therapy and the emotional disorders*. International University Press, New York.

Beck, A.T., and Haaga, D. (1992) Perspectives on depressive realism: implications for cognitive theory of depression. *Behaviour Research and Therapy*, 33, 41–48.

Beck, A.T., Emery, G., and Greenberg, R.L. (1985) *Anxiety disorders and phobias: A cognitive perspective*. Basic Books, New York.

Beck, A.T., Rush, A.J., Shaw, B.F., and Emery, G. (1979) *Cognitive therapy of depression*. Guilford Press, New York.

Bennett–Goleman, T. (2001) *Emotional Alchemy: How your mind can heal your heart*. Rider Books, London.

Benson, H. (1975) *The relaxation response*. William Morrow, New York.

Bernstein, D.A., and Borkovec, T.D. (1973) *Progressive relaxation training*. Research Press, Champaign, Illinois.

Bihikkhu, B. (1982) *The A, B, C of Buddhism*. Bangkok, Thailand: The Sublime Life Mission.

Bilsborrow, G., and Cayoun, B.A. (2008). [*Discrimination between clinical and nonclinical samples with the MSES*]. Unpublished raw data.

Bishop, S.R. (2002) What do we really known about Mindfulness-based stress reduction? *Psychosomatic Medicine*, 64, 71–84.

Bishop, S.R., Lau, M., Shapiro, S., *et al.* (2004) Mindfulness: A proposed operational definition. *Clinical Psychology: Science and Practice*, 11, 230–241.

Blackledge, J.T., and Hayes, S.C. (2001) Emotion regulation in Acceptance and Commitment Therapy. *Journal of Clinical Psychology / In Session*, 57, 243–255.

Bonadonna, R. (2003) Meditation's impact on chronic illness. *Holistic Nurse Practice* 17(6), 309–319.

Borkovec, T.D. (1994) The nature, functions, and origins of worry. In G.C.L. Davey, F. Tallis (eds.), *Worrying: Perspectives on theory, assessment, and treatment*. Wiley, New York, pp. 5–34

Borkovec, T.D., and Costello, E. (1993) Efficacy of applied relaxation and cognitive–behavioral therapy in the treatment of Generalized Anxiety Disorder. *Journal of Consulting and Clinical Psychology*, 61, 611–619.

Bouton, M.E., Mineka, S., and Barlow, D.H. (2001) A modern learning theory perspective on the etiology of Panic Disorder. *Psychological Review*, 108, 4–32.

Bower, T.G.R. (1977) *The perceptual world of the child*. Harvard University Press, Cambridge, Massachusetts.

Breslin, F.C., Zack, M., and McMain, S. (2002) An information processing analysis of Mindfulness: Implications for relapse prevention in the treatment of substance abuse. *Clinical Psychology: Science and Practice* 9, 275–299.

Brown, K.W., and Ryan, R.M. (2004). Fostering healthy self-regulation from within and without: A Self-Determination Theory perspective. In P.A. Linley and S. Joseph (eds.), *Positive psychology in practice*. Wiley, New York, pp. 105–124.

Brown, K.W., and Ryan, R.M. (2003) The benefits of being present: Mindfulness and its role in psychological well-being. *Journal of Personality and Social Psychology*, 84, 822–848.

Buchheld, N., Grossman, P., and Walach, H. (2001) Measuring Mindfulness in insight meditation (Vipassana) and meditation-based psychotherapy: The development of the Freiburg Mindfulness Inventory (FMI). *Journal of Meditation and Meditation Research*, 1, 11–34.

Bykov, K.M. (1957) *The cerebral cortex and the internal organs*. Chemical Publications Company, New York.

Capra, F. (1997). *The web of life: A new scientific understanding of living systems*. Anchor Books, New York.

Carlson, C., and Hoyle, R. (1993) Efficacy of abbreviated progressive muscle relaxation training: A quantitative review of behavioural medicine research. *Journal of Consulting and Clinical Psychology*, 61, 1059–1067.

Carlson, L.E., Ursuliak, Z., Goodey, E., *et al.* (2001) The effects of a Mindfulness meditation-based stress reduction programme on mood and symptoms of stressing cancer outpatients: 6-month follow-up. *Supportive Care in Cancer*, 9, 112–123.

Cautela, J.R. (1967) Covert sensitization. *Psychological Reports*, 20, 459–468.

Cayoun, B.A. (2003) Advances in mindfulness training integration: Towards a non-dualistic Cognitive Behaviour Therapy. *Newsletter of the Australian Psychological Society (TASAPS)*, 2, 6–10.

Cayoun, B.A. (2003). The Short Progress Assessment. Unpublished questionnaire.

Cayoun, B.A. (2004) *Mindfulness training: Stage 1*. Audio CD, Hobart, Australia, MiCBT Institute. Available from web: http://www.mindfulness.net.au (accessed 6th November 2010)

Cayoun, B.A. (2005a) *From co-emergence dynamics to human perceptual evolution: The role of neuroplasticity during mindfulness training*. Keynote address presented at the 2005 National Conference of the New Zealand Psychological Society, Otago University, Dunedin, New Zealand.

Cayoun, B.A. (2005b) *Mindfulness training: Advanced scanning*. Audio CD, Hobart, Australia, MiCBT Institute. Available from web: http://www.mindfulness.net.au (accessed 6th November 2010).

Cayoun, B.A. (2010) *The dynamics of bimanual coordination in ADHD: Processing speed, inhibition and cognitive flexibility*. Lambert Academic Publishing, Saarbrücken, Germany.

Cayoun, B.A., and Maeder, S. (2011) Measuring progress with therapy: The psychometric properties of the *Short Progress Assessment*. Manuscript in preparation.

Cayoun, B.A., Sauvage, V., and van Impe, M. (2004) *A non diagnosis–specific application of Mindfulness-based Cognitive-Behaviour Therapy (MCBT): A pilot study*. Annual report to The Hobart Clinic, Rokeby, TAS, Australia.

Cayoun, B.A., Tayler, M.A., and Summers, J.J. (2001) The role of attention in stabilizing interlimb coordination dynamics. *Australian Journal of Psychology*, 53(Suppl.), 43.

Chadwick, P., Newman-Taylor, K., and Abba, N. (2005) Mindfulness groups for people with psychosis. *Behavioural and Cognitive Psychotherapy*, 33, 351–359.

Chandiramani, K., Verma, S.K., and Dhar, P.L. (1995) *Psychological effects of Vipassana meditation on Tihar Jail Inmates: Research report*. Vipassana Research Institute, Igatpuri, India.

Clark, D.M. (1986) A cognitive approach to panic. *Behaviour Research and Therapy*, 24, 461–470.

Cohen, J.D., Dunbar, K., and McClelland, J.L. (1990) On the control of automatic processes: A parallel distributed processing account of the Stroop effect. *Psychological Review*, 97, 332–361.

Connelly, J. (1999) Being in the present moment: Developing the capacity for mindfulness in medicine. *Academic Medicine*, 74, 420–424.

Corsini, R., and Wedding, D. (2005) *Current psychotherapies.* 8th ed. F.E. Peacock, Itasca, Illinois.

Crane, R., Kuyken, W., Hastings, R.P., *et al.* (2010) Training teachers to deliver Mindfulness-based interventions: Learning from the UK experience. *Mindfulness*, 1, 74–86.

Craske, M.G., and Barlow, D. (1993) Panic disorder and agoraphobia. In D. Barlow (ed.) (2008), *Clinical handbook of psychological disorders: A step-by-step treatment manual.* 2nd ed. The Guilford Press, New York, pp. 1–47.

Craske, M.G., Hazlett-Stevens, H. (2002) Facilitating symptom reduction and behavior change in GAD: The issue of control. *Clinical Psychology: Science and Practice*, 9, 69–75.

Dalai Lama-Gyatso T. (2008). *Handbook for the spirit: Love, compassion and tolerance.* R. Carlson, and B. Shield (eds.). New World Library, Novato, California.

Davidson, R.J. (2010). Empirical explorations of mindfulness: Conceptual and methodological conundrums. *Emotion*, 10, 8–11.

Davidson, R.J., Kabat-Zinn, J., Schumacher, J., *et al.* (2003) Alterations in brain and immune function produced by mindfulness meditation. *Psychosomatic Medicine*, 65, 564–570.

Davidson, R.J.; Ekman, P., Saron, C.D., *et al.* (1990). Approach-withdrawal and cerebral asymmetry: Emotional expression and brain physiology I. *Journal of Personality and Social Psychology*, 58, 330–341.

Decety, J., and Jackson, P.L. (2004) The functional architecture of human empathy. *Behavioral and Cognitive Neuroscience Reviews*, 3, 71–100.

Denckla, M.B. (1996) Research on executive function in a neurodevelopmental context: Application of clinical measures. *Developmental Neuropsychology*, 12, 5–15.

Derogatis, L.R. (1994) *Symptoms Checklist-90-R: Administration, scoring, and procedure manual.* 3rd ed. National Computer Systems Inc, Minneapolis.

Descartes, R. (1644). *Les Principes de la philosophie.* Miller, V.R., and R.P., trans., (1983). Principles of Philosophy. Reidel, Dordrecht, Holland.

Dimidjian, S., and Linehan, M.M. (2003) Defining an agenda for future research on the clinical application of Mindfulness practice. *Clinical Psychology: Science and Practice*, 10, 166–171.

Doshi, J. (1989) Vipassana and psychotherapy. In Vipassana Research Institute (ed.), *Vipassana: Addiction and health.* Vipassana Research Institute, Igatpuri, India, pp. 11–17.

Ellis, A. (1979) The practice of rational-emotive therapy. In A. Ellis and J.M. Whiteley (eds.) (1982), *Theoretical and empirical foundations of rational-emotive therapy.* Brooks/Cole, Monterey, California, pp. 61–100.

Ellis, A. (1991) Using RET effectively: Reflections and interview. In M.E. Bernard (ed.) (1991), *Using rational-emotive therapy effectively.* Plenum, New York, pp. 1–33.

Ellis, A., and Dryden, W. (1987) *The practice of rational-emotive therapy.* Springer, New York.

Fan, J., McCandliss, B.D., Sommer, T., *et al.* (2002). Testing the efficiency and independence of attentional networks. *Journal of Cognitive Neuroscience*, 14, 340–347.

Fan, Y., Tang, Y., Ma, Y., and Posner, M.I. (2010) Mucosal immunity modulated by integrative meditation in a dose-dependent fashion. *The Journal of Alternative and Complementary Medicine*, 16, 151–155.

FitzGerald, M.J.T., and Folan-Curran, J. (2002) *Clinical neuroanatomy and related neurosciences.* 4th ed. Saunders, London.

Flavell, J.H. (1979) Metacognition and cognitive monitoring. *American Psychologist*, 34, 906–911.

Fleischman, P. (1986) *The therapeutic action of Vipassana and why I sit.* Buddhist Publication Society, Kandy, Sri Lanka.

Fleischman, P. (1989) The experience of anicca through Vipassana meditation and the maturation of personality. In Vipassana Research Institute (ed.), *Vipassana: Addiction and health.* Vipassana Research Institute, Igatpuri, India, pp. 11–17.

Fleischman, P. (1994) *The experience of impermanence.* Vipassana Research Institute, Igatpuri, India.

Fleischman, P. (1999) *Karma and chaos: New and collected essays on Vipassana meditation.* Vipassana Research Publications, Seattle, Washington.

Follette, V., Palm, K.M., Pearson, A.N. (2006) Mindfulness and trauma: Implications for treatment. *Journal of Rational-Emotive and Cognitive-Behavior Therapy*, 24, 45–61.

Francis, S., and Cayoun, B.A. (2011) Measuring mindfulness skills in clinical populations: A preliminary study of the *Mindfulness-based Self-Efficacy Scale.* Manuscript sent for publication.

Fuster, J.M. (1989) *The prefrontal cortex.* Raven Press, New York.

Genther, H.V., and Kawamura, L.S. (1975) *Mind in Buddhist psychology.* Dharma Publishing, Emeryville, California.

Goenka, S.N. (1987) *The discourse summaries: Talks from a ten-day course in Vipassana Meditation condensed by William Hart.* Vipashyana Vishodhan Vinyas, Bombay, India.

Goenka, S.N. (1999) *Discourses on the Mahasatipatthana Sutta.* Vipassana Research Institute, Mumbai.

Goleman, D. (1977) *The varieties of meditation experience.* Dutton, New York.

Greenberg, L. (1994) Acceptance in experiential therapy. In S.C. Hayes, N.S. Jacobson, V.M. Follette, and M.J. Dougher (eds.), *Acceptance and change: Content and context in psychotherapy.* Context Press, Reno, Nevada, pp. 53–67.

Greenberg, L.S., and Safran, J.D. (1984) Integrating affect and cognition: A perspective on the process of therapeutic change. *Cognitive Therapy Research*, 8, 559–578.

Greenberg, L.S., and Safran, J.D. (1987) *Emotion in psychotherapy: Affect, cognition, and the process of change.* Guilford Press, New York.

Grepmair, L., Mitterlehner, F., Loew, T., *et al.* (2007) Promoting mindfulness in psychotherapists in training influences the treatment results of their patients: A randomized, double-blind, controlled study. *Psychotherapy and Psychosomatics*, 76, 332–338.

Grossman, P., Niemann, L., Schmidt, S., and Walach, H. (2004) Mindfulness-based stress reduction and health benefits: A meta-analysis. *Journal of Psychosomatic Research*, 57, 35–43.

Haaga, D., and Beck, A.T. (1995) The future of cognitive therapy. *Psychotherapy: Theory, Research, Practice, Training. Special Issue: The Future of Psychotherapy*, 29, 34–38.

Hanh, T.N. (2007) *For a future to be possible: Buddhist ethics for everyday life*. Parallax Press, Berkeley.

Hart, W. (1987) *The art of living: Vipassana meditation as taught by S.N. Goenka*. Harper and Row, San Francisco, California.

Haslam, S.A., Oakes, P.J., Turner, J.C., and McGarty, C. (1996) Social identity, self–categorization, and the perceived homogeneity of ingroups and outgroups: the interaction between social motivation and cognition. In R.M. Sorrentino and E.T. Higgins (eds.) (1996). *Handbook of motivation and cognition: The interpersonal context*. Guilford Press, New York.

Hayes, S.C. (1994) Content, context, and the types of psychological acceptance. In S.C. Hayes, N.S. Jacobson, V.M. Follette, and M.J. Dougher (eds.) (1994), *Acceptance and change: Content and context in psychotherapy*. Context Press, Reno, Nevada, pp. 13–32.

Hayes, S.C. (2002) Acceptance, Mindfulness, and science. *Clinical Psychology: Science and Practice*, 9, 101–106.

Hayes, S.C., and Wilson, K.G. (2003) Mindfulness: Method and process. *Clinical Psychology: Science and Practice* 10, 161–165.

Hayes, S.C., Bissett, R.T., Korn, Z., *et al.* (1999) The impact of acceptance versus control rationales on pain tolerance. *The Psychological Record*, 49, 33–47.

Hayes, S.C., Follette, V.M., and Linehan, M.M. (2004) *Mindfulness and acceptance: Expanding the cognitive-behavioral tradition*. Guilford Press, New York.

Hayes, S.C., Strosahl, K., and Wilson, K.G. (1999) *Acceptance and commitment therapy*. Guilford Press, New York.

Hayes, S.C., Wilson, K.W., Gilford, E.V., Follette, V.M., and Strosahl, K. (1996) Experiential avoidance and behavioural disorders: A functional dimensional approach to diagnosis and treatment. *Journal of Consulting and Clinical Psychology*, 64, 1152–1168.

Hayes, S.C. Barnes-Holmes, D., and Roche, B. (2001) *Relational Frame Theory: A Post-Skinnerian account of human language and cognition*. Plenum Press, New York.

Hebb, D.O. (1949) *Organization of behavior*. Wiley, New York.

Heidenreich, T., Ströhle, G., and Michalak, J. (2006) Mindfulness: Conceptual aspects and results of the Freiburg Mindfulness Inventory. *Verhaltenstherapie*, 16, 33–40.

Herring, D. (2005) *Using mindfulness-based approaches with persons who have severe and persistent mental illness*. Paper presented at the 2005 Annual Conference of the Center for Mindfulness, University of Massachusetts Medical School, Worcester, Massachusetts.

Horowitz, M.J. (1975) Intrusive and repetitive thoughts after experimental stress. *Archive of General Psychiatry*, 32, 1457–1463.

Horwitz, M., and Rabbie, J.M. (1982) Individuality in membership in the intergroup system. In H. Tajfel (ed.) (1986). *Social identity and intergroup relations*. Cambridge University Press, Cambridge.

Hunsinger, M. (2006) *The relationship between social cognition and Mindfulness meditation*. Doctoral Dissertation. University of Massachusetts, Amherst.

Ivanovski B., Malhi G.S. (2007) The psychological and neurophysiological concomitants of mindfulness forms of meditation. *Acta Neuropsychiatrica*, 19, 76–91.

Iversen, S.D., and Dunnett, S.B. (1990) Functional organization of striatumas studied with neural grafts. *Neuropsychologia*, 28, 601–626.

Jacobson, E. (1942) *You must relax*. McGraw-Hill, New York.

Johnstone, B., and Glass, B.A. (2008) Support for a neurological model of spirituality in persons with traumatic brain injury. *Zygon*, 43, 861–874.

Kabat-Zinn, J. (1982) An outpatient programme in behavioural medicine for chronic pain patients based on the practice of Mindfulness meditation: Theoretical considerations and preliminary results. *General Hospital Psychiatry*, 4, 33–42.

Kabat-Zinn, J. (1990) *Full catastrophe living: The programme of the Stress-Reduction Clinic at the University of Massachusetts Medical Center*. Delta, New York.

Kabat-Zinn, J. (1994) *Wherever you go, there you are: Mindfulness meditation in everyday life*. Hyperion, New York.

Kabat-Zinn, J. (2003) Mindfulness-based interventions in context: Past, present, and future. *Clinical Psychology: Science and Practice*, 10, 144–156.

Kabat-Zinn, J. (2005) *Coming to our senses: Healing ourselves and the world through mindfulness*. Piatkus, London.

Kabat-Zinn, J., Lipworth, L., and Burney, R. (1985) The clinical use of Mindfulness meditation for the self-regulation of chronic pain. *Journal of Behavioral Medicine*, 8, 163–190.

Kabat-Zinn, J., Massion, A., Herbert, J.R., and Rosenbaum, E. (1998) Meditation. In J.C. Holland (ed.), *Psycho-oncology*. Oxford University Press, New York.

Kabat-Zinn, J., Massion, A., Kristeller, J., *et al.* (1992) Effectiveness of a meditation-based stress reduction programme in the treatment of anxiety disorders. *American Journal of Psychiatry*, 149, 936–943.

Kelly, G.A. (1955) *The psychology of personal constructs*. Norton, New York.

Kenny, M.A., and Williams, J.M.G. (2007) Treatment-resistant depressed patients show a good response to Mindfulness-based cognitive therapy. *Behaviour Research and Therapy*, 45, 617–625.

Kornfield, J. (1979) Intensive insight meditation: A phenomenological study. *The Journal of Transpersonal Psychology*, 11, 41–58.

Kostanski, M., and Hassed, G. (2008) Mindfulness as a concept and a process. *Australian Psychologist*, 43, 15–21.

Koster, H.W., Rassin, E., Grombez, G., and Näring, G. (2003) The paradoxical effects of suppressing anxious thoughts during imminent threat. *Behaviour Research and Therapy*, 41, 1113–1120.

Kutz, I., Borysenko, J.Z., and Benson, H. (1985) Meditation and psychotherapy: A rationale for the integration of dynamic psychotherapy, the relaxation response, and Mindfulness meditation. *The American Journal of Psychiatry*, 142, 1–8.

Langer, E.J. (1989) *Mindfulness*. Addison–Wesley, New York.

Langer, E.J. (1992) Matters of mind: Mindfulness/mindlessness in perspective. *Consciousness and Cognition*, 1, 289–305.

Larimer, M.E., Palmer, R.S., and Marlatt, G.A. (1999) Relapse prevention: An overview of Marlatt's cognitive-behavioral model. *Alcohol Research and Health*, 23, 151–160.

Lau, M.A., and McMain, S.F. (2005) Integrating mindfulness meditation with cognitive and behavioural therapies: The challenge of combining acceptance and change-based strategies. *Canadian Journal of Psychiatry*, 50, 863–869.

Laventhal, H. (1984) A perceptual-motor theory of emotion. In L. Berkowitz (ed.) (1985), *Advances in experimental social psychology*, Vol. 17. Academic Press, New York.

Laventhal, H., and Scherer, K. (1987) The relationship of emotion and cognition: A functional approach to a semantic controversy. *Cognition and Emotion*, 1, 3–28.

Lazar, S.W., Kerr, C.E., Wasserman, R.H., *et al.* (2005) Meditation experience is associated with increased cortical thickness. *Neuroreport*, 16, 1893–1897.

Lindsay, M. (2007) *Mindfulness-integrated Cognitive Behaviour Therapy: A pilot programme for developing mindfulness-based self-efficacy and self-compassion for people with Type 2 Diabetes Mellitus.* Masters Dissertation. University of Auckland, New Zealand.

Linehan, M. (1993) *Cognitive-behavioral treatment of borderline personality disorder.* Guilford Press, New York.

Linehan, M. (1994) Acceptance and change: The central dialectic in psychotherapy. In S.C. Hayes, N.S. Jacobson, V.M. Follette, and M.J. Dougher (eds) (1994), *Acceptance and change: Content and context in psychotherapy.* Context Press, Reno, Nevada, pp. 73–86.

Linehan, M.M., Schmidt, M.A. III, Dimeff, L.A., *et al.* (1999) Dialectical behavior therapy for patients with borderline personality disorder and drug-dependence. *The American Journal on addictions,* 8(4), 279–292.

Lovibond, S.H., and Lovibond, P.F. (1995) *Manual for the Depression Anxiety and Stress Scale.* 2nd ed. Psychological Foundation Monograph, Sydney, Australia.

Luders E., Toga, A.W., Lepore N., and Gaser, C. (2009) The underlying anatomical correlates of long-term meditation: Larger hippocampal and frontal volumes of gray matter. *NeuroImage,* 45, 672–678.

Lutz, A., Brefczynski-Lewis, J., Johnstone, T., and Davidson, R.J. (2008) Regulation of the neural circuitry of emotion by compassion meditation: Effects of meditative practice. *PLoS ONE,* 3, e1897.

Lutz, A., Greischar, L.L., Rawlings, N.B., *et al.* (2004) Long-term meditators self-induce high-amplitude gamma synchrony during mental practice. *PNAS* 101, 16369–16373.

Mahoney, M.J. (1974) *Cognition and behavior modification.* Ballinger, Cambridge, Massachusetts.

Margolis, J., and Langer, E. (1990) An analysis of addictions from a mindful/mindless perspective. *Psychology of Addictive Behavior,* 4, 107–115.

Marlatt, G.A. (1994) Addiction, Mindfulness, and acceptance. In S.C. Hayes, N.S. Jacobson, V.M. Follette, and M.J. Dougher (eds) (2005), *Acceptance and change: Content and context in psychotherapy.* Context Press, Reno, Nevada, pp. 175–197.

Marlatt, G.A. (2002) Buddhist philosophy and the treatment of addictive behavior. *Cognitive and Behavioral Practice,* 9, 42–50.

Marlatt, G.A., and Gordon, J.R. (1985) *Relapse prevention: Maintenance strategies in the treatment of addictive behaviors.* Guilford, New York.

Marlatt, G.A., and Kristeller, J. (1999) Mindfulness and meditation. In W.R. Miller (ed.) (1999), *Integrating spirituality in treatment: Resources for practitioners.* American Psychological Association Books, Washington, DC, pp. 67–84.

Marlatt, G.A., Witkiewitz, K., Dillworth, T., *et al.* (2004) Vipassana meditation as a treatment for alcohol and drug use disorders. In S.C. Hayes, V.M. Follette, and M.M. Linehan, *Mindfulness and acceptance: Expanding the Cognitive-behavioral tradition.* Guilford Press, New York.

Martin, J.R. (1997) Mindfulness: A proposed common factor. *Journal of Psychotherapy Integration,* 7, 291–312.

Mason, O., and Hargreaves, I. (2001) A qualitative study of mindfulness-based cognitive therapy for depression. *British Journal of Medical Psychology,* 74, 197–212.

May, S., and O'Donovan, A. (2007) The advantages of the mindful therapist. *Psychotherapy in Australia* 13, 46–53.

McClelland, J.L., Rumelhart, D.E., and The PDP Research Group, (1986) *Parallel distributed processing: Explorations in the microstructure of cognition* (Vol. 2). Bradford Books/MIT Press, Cambridge, Massachusetts.

McLaren, N. (2006) Response to "Mindfulness-based psychotherapies" (2). *Australian and New Zealand Journal of Psychiatry*, 40, 818–819.

McMillan, T., Robertson, I.H., Brock, D., and Chorlton, L. (2002) Brief Mindfulness training for attentional problems after traumatic brain injury: A randomized control treatment trial. *Neuropsychological Rehabilitation*, 12, 117–125.

Meichenbaum, D. (1977) *Cognitive–behavior modification*. Plenum, New York.

Mohlman, J., and Gorman, J.M. (2005). The role of executive functioning in CBT: a pilot study with anxious older adults. *Behaviour Research and Therapy*, 43, 447–465.

Monteiro, L., Nuttall, S., and Musten, F. (2010) Five skilful habits: An ethics-based mindfulness intervention. *Counseling et Spiritualité*, 29, 91–104.

Narada, M. (1968) *A manual of Abhidhamma*. Buddhist Publication Society, Kandy, Sri Lanka.

Neff, K.D. (2003). Development and validation of a scale to measure self-compassion. *Self and Identity*, 2, 223–250.

Orsillo, S.M., Roemer L., and Barlow, D.H. (2003) Integrating acceptance and mindfulness into existing cognitive-behavioral treatment for GAD: A case study. *Cognitive and Behavioural Practice*, 10, 222–230.

Öst, L.G. (1988) Applied relaxation vs. progressive relaxation in the treatment of panic disorder. *Behaviour Research and Therapy*, 26, 13–22.

Parrinder, G. (1992). *Collins dictionary of religious and spiritual quotations*. HarperCollins, Glasgow, UK.

Pascual–Leone, J. (2000) Mental attention, consciousness, and the progressive emergence of wisdom. *Journal of Adult Development*, 7, 241–254.

Penfield, W., and Rasmussen, T. (1950) *The cerebral cortex of man*. MacMillan, New York.

Perez–De-Albaniz, A., and Holmes, J. (2000) Meditation: Concepts, effects and uses in therapy. *International Journal of Psychotherapy*, 5, 49–59.

Phaf, R.H., van der Heijden, A.H.C., and Hudson, P.T.W. (1990) SLAM: A connectionist model for attention in visual selection tasks. *Cognitive Psychology*, 22, 273–341.

Posner, M.I., and Raichle, M.E. (1997) *Images of mind*. Scientific American Library, New York.

Pralhad, P. (1950) *Abhidharmasamuccaya*. Santiniketan, Visva Bharati.

Pridmore, S. (2006) Response to "Mindfulness-based psychotherapies" (1). *Australian and New Zealand Journal of Psychiatry*, 40, 818–818.

Ramel, W., Goldin, P.R., Carmona, P.E., and McQuaid, J.R. (2004) The effects of Mindfulness meditation on cognitive processes and affect in patients with past depression. *Cognitive Therapy and Research*, 28, 433–455.

Raven, J.C. (1938) *Progressive matrices: A perceptual test of intelligence*. H. K. Lewis, London.

Razran, G. (1960) The observable unconscious in current Soviet psychophysiology: Survey and interpretation of experiments in interoceptive conditioning. *Progress in Clinical Psychology*, 4, 1–31.

Razran, G. (1961) The observable unconscious and the inferable conscious in current Soviet psychophysiology. *Psychology Review*, 68, 81–147.

Rice, K.M., and Blanchard, E.B. (1982) Biofeedback in the treatment of anxiety disorders. *Clinical Psychology Review*, 2, 557–577.

Roemer, L., and Orsillo, S.M. (2002) Expanding our conceptualization of and treatment for generalized anxiety disorder: Integrating Mindfulness/acceptance-based approaches with existing cognitive-behavioural models. *Clinical Psychology: Science and Practice*, 9, 54–68.

Roemer, L., Orsillo, S.M., and Barlow, D.H. (2002) Generalized anxiety disorder. In D.H. Barlow (ed.) (2002), *Anxiety and its disorders: The nature and treatment of anxiety and panic.* 2nd ed. The Guilford Press, New York, pp. 477–515.

Rosenberg, M. (1965). *Society and the adolescent self-image.* Princeton University Press, Princeton, New Jersey.

Rosenzweig, S., Greeson, J., Reibelc, D., *et al.* (2010) Mindfulness-based stress reduction for chronic pain conditions: Variation in treatment outcomes and role of home meditation practice. *Journal of Psychosomatic Research.*

Roubos, L., Cayoun, B.A., and Hawkins, R. (2010) A comparison of group and individual implementations of Mindfulness-integrated Cognitive Behaviour Therapy (MiCBT): A naturalistic efficacy study. Manuscript sent for publication.

Rueda, M.R., Posner, M.I., and Rothbart, M.K. (2005) The development of executive attention: Contributions to the emergence of self regulation. *Developmental Neuropsychology*, 28, 573–594.

Salmon, P.G., Santorelli, S.F., and Kabat-Zinn, J. (1998) Intervention elements promoting adherence to Mindfulness-based stress reduction programmes in the clinical behavioral medicine setting. In S.A. Shumaker, E.B. Schron, J.K. Ockene, and W.L. McBee (eds.), *The handbook of health behavior change.* Springer, New York, pp. 239–266.

Saltzman, A., and Goldin, P. (2010) Mindfulness Based Stress Reduction for School–Age Children. In S.C. Hayes and L.A. Greco (eds.), *Acceptance and mindfulness interventions for Children, adolescents, and families.* Context Press/New Harbinger Publications, Oakland, California.

Sanes, J.N., and Donoghue, J.P. (2000) Plasticity and primary motor cortex. *Annual Review of Neuroscience*, 23, 393–415.

Schaar, J. (1981). *Legitimacy in the modern state.* Transaction Books, New Brunswick, US.

Schwartz, J.M. (2003) *The mind and the brain: Neuroplasticity and the power of mental force.* Regan Books, New York.

Segal, Z.V., Williams, J.M.G., and Teasdale, J.D. (2002) *Mindfulness–based cognitive therapy for depression: A new approach to preventing relapse.* Guilford Press, New York.

Sekuler, R., and Blake, R. (1994) *Perception.* 3rd ed. McGraw–Hill, New York.

Shacham, S. (1983). A shortened version of the Profile of Mood States. *Journal of Personality Assessment*, 47, 305–306.

Shah, I. (1969). *Tales of the dervishes: Teaching-stories of the Sufi Masters over the past thousand years.* Dutton and Co, New York.

Shapiro, S.L., and Carlson, L.E. (2009) *The art and science of mindfulness: Integrating mindfulness into psychology and the helping professions.* APA Books, Washington, DC.

Shapiro, S.L., Astin, J.A., Bishop, S.R., Cordova, M. (2005) Mindfulness-based stress reduction for health care professionals: Results from a randomized trial. *International Journal of Stress Management*, 12, 164–176.

Siegel, D. (2007) *The mindful brain: Reflection and attunement in the cultivation of wellbeing.* Norton, York.

Siegel, D.J. (2009a) *Mindsight: Change your brain and your life.* Scribe, Melbourne.

Siegel, D.J. (2009b) Mindful awareness, mindsight, and neural integration. *The Humanistic Psychologist*, 37, 137–158.

Skinner, B.F. (1953) *Science and human behavior*. The Free Press, New York.

Solé-Leris, A. (1992) *Tranquillity and insight* (1999 ed.). Buddhist Publication Society, Kandy, Sri Lanka.

Solomon, P. (2006) *Psychotherapists who meditate: A phenomenological study*. Master Thesis. Auckland University of Technology, New Zealand.

Speca, M., Carlson, L., Goodey, E., and Angen, M.A. (2000) A randomized wait-list controlled trial: The effect of a Mindfulness meditation-based stress reduction programme on mood and symptoms of stress in cancer outpatients. *Psychosomatic Medicine*, 62, 613–622.

Spiegler, M.D., and Guevremont, D.C. (2003) *Contemporary behavior therapy*. 4th ed. Wadsworth, Belmont, California.

Suls, J., and Fletcher, B. (1985) The relative efficacy of avoidant and nonavoidant coping strategies: A meta-analysis. *Health Psychology*, 4, 249–288.

Summers, J.J., and Ford, S. (1995) Attention in sport. In T. Morris and J. Summers (eds.), *Sport psychology: Theory, applications and issues*. Wiley, Brisbane, pp. 63–89.

Swanson, J., Posner, M.I., Cantwell, D., *et al.* (1998) Attention-deficit hyperactivity disorder: Symptom domain, cognitive processes and neural networks. In R. Parasuraman (ed.), *The attentive brain*. MIT Press, Cambridge, Massachusetts, pp. 445–460.

Tajfel, H., and Turner, J.C. (1979) An integrative theory of intergroup conflict. In W.G. Austin, and S. Worchel (eds.) *The social psychology of intergroup relations*. Brooks/Cole, Monterey, California.

Tang, Y., Ma, Y., Wang, J., *et al.* (2007) Short-term meditation training improves attention and self-regulation. *PNAS Proceedings of the National Academy of Sciences of the United States of America*, 104, 17152–17156.

Taylor, C. (2010) *Enough! A Buddhist approach to finding release from addictive patterns*. Snow Lion Publications, New York.

Teasdale, J.D., and Barnard, P.J. (1993) *Affect, cognition and change*. Local Education Authortiy, Hove, Sussex, UK.

Teasdale, J.D. (1999) Metacognition, Mindfulness, and the modification of mood disorders. *Clinical Psychology and Psychotherapy*, 6, 146–155.

Teasdale, J.D., Segal, Z.V., and Williams, J.M.G. (1995) How does cognitive therapy prevent depressive relapse and why should attentional control (Mindfulness) training help? *Behaviour Research and Therapy*, 33, 25–39.

Teasdale, J.D., Segal, Z.V., Williams, J.M.G., *et al.* (2000) Prevention of relapse/recurrence in major depression by Mindfulness-based cognitive therapy. *Journal of Consulting and Clinical Psychology*, 68, 615–623.

Temprado, J.J., Zanone, P.G., Monno, A., and Laurent, M. (1999) Attentional load associated with performing and stabilizing preferred bimanual patterns. *Journal of Experimental Psychology: Human Perception and Performance*, 25, 1579–1594.

Tolin, D.F., Abramowitz, J.S., Przeworski, A., and Foa, E. (2002) Thought suppression in obsessive-compulsive disorder. *Behaviour Research and Therapy*, 40, 1255–1274.

Toneatto, T., and Nguyen, L. (2007) Does mindfulness meditation improve anxiety and mood symptoms? A review of the controlled research. *Canadian Review of Psychiatry*, 52, 260–266.

Toobert, D.J., and Glasgow, R.E. (1994). Assessing diabetes self-management: The Summary of Diabetes Self-Care Activities Questionnaire. In C. Bradley (ed.), *Handbook of psychology and diabetes research and practice*. Harwood Academic, Berkshire, England, pp. 351–375.

Tracy, B. (2010). *No excuses!: The power of self-discipline*. Vanguard Press, New York.

Travis, F., Arenander, A., and DuBois, D. (2004) Psychological and physiological characteristics of a proposed object-referral/self-referral continuum of self-awareness. *Consciousness and Cognition*, 13, 401–420.

Trousselard, M., Steiler, D., Raphel, C., *et al.* (2010) Validation of a French version of the Freiburg Mindfulness Inventory – short version: Relationships between mindfulness and stress in an adult population. *BioPsychoSocial Medicine*, 4–8.

Van Dam, N.T., Earleywine, M., and Danoff-Burg, S. (2009) Differential item function across meditators and non-meditators on the Five Facet Mindfulness Questionnaire. *Personality and Individual Difference*, 47, 516–521.

Varela, F.J. (1999) Steps to a science of inter-being: Unfolding the Dharma implicit in modern cognitive science. In G. Watson, S. Batchelor, and G. Claxton (eds.), *The psychology of awakening*. Rider, London, pp. 71–89.

Voronin, L.G. (1962) Some results of comparative-physiological investigations of higher nervous activity. *Psychological Bulletin*, 59, 161–195.

Watkins, E.D., Teasdale, J.D., and Williams, R.M. (2000) Decentring and distraction reduce overgeneral autobiographical memory in depression. *Psychological Medicine*, 30, 911–920.

Wells, A. (1997) *Cognitive therapy of anxiety disorders: A practical manual and conceptual guide*. John Wiley and Sons, Chichester, West Sussex, UK.

Wells, A. (2002) GAD, metacognition, and Mindfulness: An information processing analysis. *Clinical Psychology: Science and Practice*, 9, 95–100.

Wells, A., and Matthews, G. (1994) *Attention and emotion: A clinical perspective*. Erlbaum, Hove, UK.

Wells, L.L. (2010). *Associations between mindfulness and symptoms of anxiety*. Dissertation. East Tennessee State University, USA.

Whitfield, H.J. (2006) Towards case-specific applications of mindfulness-based cognitive-behavioural therapies: A mindfulness-based rational emotive behaviour therapy. *Counselling Psychology Quarterly*, 19, 205–217.

Whitmont, E. (1969). *The symbolic quest*. Princeton University Press, Princeton.

Williams, J.M.G. (1984) *The psychological treatment of depression: A guide to the theory and practice of cognitive-behaviour therapy*. Croom Helm, London.

Williams, J.M.G, Teasdale, J.D., Segal, Z.V., and Kabat-Zinn, J. (2007) *The mindful way through depression: Freeing yourself from chronic unhappiness*. Guilford Press, New York.

Williams, J.M.G, Teasdale, J.D., Segal, Z.V., and Soulsby, J. (2000) Mindfulness-based cognitive therapy reduces over general autobiographical memory in formerly depressed patients. *Journal of Abnormal Psychology*, 109, 150–155.

Williams, J.M.G., Watts, F.N., MacLeod, C., and Mathews, G. (1997) *Cognitive psychology and emotional disorders*. 2nd ed. Wiley, Chichester, West Sussex, UK.

Wilson, N. (2006). *Aesop: The Complete Fables*. Penguin Books, New York.

Witkiewitz, K., and Marlatt G.A. (2006) Mindfulness-based relapse prevention for alcohol and substance use disorders: The meditative tortoise wins the race. *Journal of Cognitive Psychotherapy*, 19, 221–228.

Wolpe, J. (1969) *The practice of behaviour therapy*. Pergamon Press, New York.

Woodward, F.L. (1939) *Some sayings of the Buddha*. Oxford University Press, London.

Wuyts, I.J., Summers, J.J., Carson, R.G., *et al.* (1996) Attention as a mediating variable in the dynamics of bimanual coordination. *Human Movement Science*, 15, 877–897.

Yates, A. (1970) *Behaviour therapy.* John Wiley and Sons, New York.

Zettle, R.D., and Hayes, S.C. (1986) Dysfunctional control by client verbal behavior: The context of reason giving. *Analysis of Verbal Behavior*, 4, 30–38.

Zigmond, A.S., and Snaith, R.P. (1983) The Hospital Anxiety and Depression Scale. *Acta Psychiatrica Scandinavica*, 67, 361–370.

Glossary

Note: Terminology specific to MiCBT is marked by an asterisk ("*").

Awareness threshold*: The level of intensity of a phenomenon at which one begins to perceive an experience. In the context of MiCBT, the experience is *interoceptive* (see below).

Bi-polar exposure*: An exposure technique involving repeated voluntary experience of imagined unpleasant and pleasant outcomes in the anticipation of *in-vivo* (real life) exposure to a feared or avoided forthcoming event. Since bi-polar exposure requires the client to visualize best and worst case scenarios while remaining *equanimous* (see below), it is a task that can be implemented only in Stage 2 of MiCBT when the client has developed sufficient ability to perceive common body sensations through body-scanning techniques during Stage 1.

In addition to being used to desensitize the client to the experience, or internal context, of a stimulus prior to in-vivo exposure, bi-polar exposure can be used as a separate tool to desensitize from situations where using *in-vivo* exposure would be too difficult (e.g., fear of flying, of being harassed, various sexual difficulties, etc).

Cartesian dualism: According to the French philosopher René Descartes (1641), the mind is a nonphysical substance. This philosophy clearly identifies the mind with consciousness and self-awareness and distinguishes this from the brain, which was believed to be the seat of intelligence. Ideas on mind/body dualism originate at least as far back as Plato and Aristotle and deal with speculations as to the existence of an incorporeal soul which bore the faculties of intelligence and wisdom. It was believed that people's "intelligence" (a faculty of the mind) could not be identified with, or explained in terms of, their physical body. However, few

---

Mindfulness-integrated CBT: Principles and Practice, First Edition. Bruno A. Cayoun.
© 2011 John Wiley & Sons, Ltd. Published 2011 by John Wiley & Sons, Ltd.

if any neuroscientists would consider taking such a position. As a simple example of the difficulty in assuming dualistic views today, just think of the significant effects of psychoactive drugs, whether illicit or not, on people's mental states.

Classical conditioning: A method of learning by association that requires the pairing of a neutral stimulus with a stimulus that evokes a response. If a stimulus that results in an emotional response is repeated alongside another (neutral) stimulus which does not cause an emotional response, eventually the second (neutral) stimulus will cause the same emotional response. The neutral stimulus has become a conditioned stimulus, and emotional response to it has become a conditioned response.

Co-emergence*: The "coupling" or simultaneous manifestation of judgmental thought and body sensation.

Co-emergence dynamics*: The non-linear simultaneous interaction of judgmental thought and body sensation. A direct correspondence between thoughts that evaluate a phenomenon and body sensations can be observed on two dimensions: hedonic tone and intensity. To the extent that the thought is agreeable, the sensation(s) in the body will be pleasant. The same goes for the unpleasant end of the hedonic tone continuum. Similarly, to the extent that the thought is intense, the sensation(s) in the body will be intense. Note also that this principle applies from body to thought. A strong pain is likely to attract both an intense and disagreeable judgment.

Counterconditioning: A behavior-modification approach by which a particular response to a certain stimulus is replaced by a new response. This new response is supposed to deter the person from the stimulus. For example, a person may feel cravings towards the experience of smoking. Through a counterconditioning approach, he or she could learn to feel negatively about their smoking by pairing it with an aversive experience in imagery or in real life. Moreover, it also attempts to replace an undesired emotional response to a stimulus with a more pleasant, adaptive one. For example, pairing a fear of traumatic memory (learned avoidance) with laughter in order to unlearn the avoiding behavior and replace it with a more helpful one.

Dimensional congruence*: The similarity of pathways, dimensions, or philosophical orientation between the way in which a maladaptive thought, behavior or emotion is experienced and the treatment used to address it. For example, whereas the experience of thoughts and co-emerging body sensations during a panic attack is not dimensionally congruent with a treatment which attempts to rationalize the experience, it is congruent with a treatment which directly addresses thoughts and co-emerging body sensations, such as mindfulness. It operates change within the cortical pathways in which the experience arises. There is no detour via "incongruent" pathways.

Egolessness/selflessness: These terms are translations of the Pali (ancient language of popular India) word *anatta*, which also means the substanceless and ephemeral nature of all phenomena, including the experience of the self, in Buddhist psychology. Along with the natural and omnipresent reality of impermanence of all phenomena (*anicca*) and the suffering (*dukkha*) which derives from being unaware of selflessness and impermanence, it is one of the basic characteristics of all phenomena taught by Buddhist teachings.

Equanimity: In brief, it means neutrality of response. It is a state of conscious awareness in which the response to a stimulus is neither an aversion towards the stimulus nor a desire for more stimulation. It is particularly used to summarize what could be described as "experiential awareness and acceptance". In Buddhism, equanimity has the effect of preventing the arising of negative thoughts and emotions.

Equanimous: An active, rather than reactive, attitude. To be qualified as equanimous, the attitude must also be grounded on awareness and acceptance of internal states.

Experiential ownership*: Both a complex exposure technique and a desired skill within the MiCBT approach. As a skill, experiential ownership is the ability to fully own one's experience and disown that of others while remaining equanimous. As an exposure technique, it requires the client to position him or herself in stressful interpersonal situations, take full responsibility for the immediate internal experience, apply equanimity to the experience, hypothesize about the other's experience of unpleasant body sensations and their consequent tendency to react due to unawareness, foster an understanding of the other's suffering and their responsibility for it, and generate empathic thoughts or supportive behavior. To a degree, experiential ownership integrates what the Buddha, and subsequent Buddhist teachers, called "profound understanding".

Functional equilibrium*: The hypothesized balanced distribution of attention across the four components of the information-processing system that helps regulate emotions and maintain a healthy degree of objectivity in everyday life.

Grounded empathy*: Both a meditative technique and a desired skill within the MiCBT approach. The traditional (Pali) term in Buddhist psychology is *metta*, usually translated as "loving kindness". As a skill, it usually requires practitioners to generate selfless love and good will towards oneself and others while experiencing unhindered "flow" of pleasant body sensations. Empathy is thus "grounded" in bodily experiences. As a skill, it is the ability to experience unconditional love, good will and forgiveness independent of the context.

Impermanence: Omnipresence of change in all phenomena, a natural law. In Pali (the language spoken in ancient India) it is called *anicca* (pronounced "anitcha"). In many respects, impermanence is the most important characteristic of phenomena in Buddhist psychology because of its consequences on phenomena: If all is impermanent, in a perpetual state of change, then so is the self, and our ignorance of this natural law leads to unrealistic expectations (e.g., "I should remain healthy all my life", "I shouldn't feel pain" or "I shouldn't experience loss") and ultimately disappointment and suffering.

Impersonality: Another term for the more traditionally used words *egolessness* and *selflessness* (see above).

Interoception: In brief, the perception of internal states. In particular, it is the ability of perceiving body sensations.

Interoceptive acceptance*: The ability to "accept" bodily experiences, especially in reference to those involved during emotions.

Interoceptive awareness: Present moment awareness of body sensations.

Interoceptive cue: A specific cue experienced within the body.

Interoceptive exposure: In its simplest form, body scanning. In the context of a consultation, it is common in MiCBT to ask the client to close their eyes and immediately identify the body sensations that are co-emerging with the memory of an event or corresponding to a schema. Typically, the therapist may use the so-called "downward-arrow" technique, traditionally used in cognitive therapy to unravel a (maladaptive) core belief, while asking the client to identify the corresponding body sensations and remain *equanimous* towards them for about half to one minute.

Note that the term "interoceptive exposure" was originally coined by David Barlow and Michelle Craske to describe a different technique to desensitize from panic cues. This involves the artificial production of bodily experiences that are sufficiently similar to panic cues while learning to prevent the usual aversive reaction.

Interoceptive signature*: A specific pattern of body sensations that is experienced in direct relation to emotions such as anger or fear, or associated with more global experiences such as the onset of depression. The term "signature" was originally coined by Jon Kabat-Zinn. Within the MiCBT approach, it distinctively specifies a value on four continua, each representing a fundamental characteristic of experience within the body (mass, temperature, motion and cohesiveness).

In vivo: Traditionally used Latin term for live, real, to mean exposure to a real situation. Typically, a client may be asked to perform a task in a feared environment, in contrast with exposure in imagination.

Metacognition: Thinking about thinking, or knowing about knowing.

Metacognitive: Pertaining to Metacognition.

Metacognitive awareness*: Awareness of the experiential process of thinking. See also Metacognitive Insight.

Metacognitive insight: Experiencing thoughts as mental events in the field of awareness. This term was initially coined by John Teasdale, who found it important to differentiate metacognition and metacognitive insight.

Mindfulness: In Western psychology and other disciplines, mindfulness is usually summarized as a voluntary and sustained non-judgmental attention to an experience. As taught by Buddhist schools, this would be insufficient to qualify as mindfulness. As described in the Buddha's discourse on the "Establishment of Mindfulness" (*Satipatthana Sutta*), it is necessary to have a "profound understanding" (*sampajanna*) of the experience. In other Buddhist texts, mindfulness works to keep the mind focused on the chosen object of meditation. While sustaining non-judgmental attention to an experience, the trainee must also hold in mind its impermanent and impersonal nature, and the consequence of this on the totality of the human phenomenon. To a degree acceptable in Western cultures, MiCBT attempts to foster this profound understanding in its delivery of mindfulness meditation.

Neuro-phenomenological: Phenomenon or evidence that pertains to the combination of neurological structure and function during immediate experience.

Neuroplasticity: The ability of the brain to adapt to new effort or environmental demands. For example, neural connections that sub-serve a new behavioral or cognitive task increase when the repetition of the task is consistent and regular.

Nihilism: A philosophical doctrine holding that all values are baseless and that nothing can be known or communicated. It is also an extreme form of skepticism that denies all existence.

Operant conditioning: A learning principle that relies on consequences to modify the occurrence and form of behavior. Each past consequence "operates" on the subsequent response. Hence, reward can be used to generate reinforcement of a desired response, whereas punishment can be used to generate extinction of an undesired response.

Phenomenological: Phenomenon or form of evidence which pertains to immediate and personal experience.

Phenomenology: The doctrine which argues that psychological science should be based on the immediate and personal experience of an event or occurrence. It is the reflective study of the essence of consciousness as experienced from the first-person point of view. Phenomenology takes the intuitive experience of phenomena as its starting point and tries to extract from it the essential features of experiences and the essence of what we experience. It encompasses our understanding and experience of "being" itself. Thus, phenomenology is also taken as the method of the study of being: ontology.

Sensory perception: Perception of the five senses (hearing, seeing, tasting, smelling, and touching), and of the two internally-generated senses (interoception and metacognitive awareness; see above).

Social identity: A theorized system of group identification whereby individuals self-categorize into a social group according to the various positive features they assign to this group. Thus, they belong to their "in-group" and tend to discriminate against "out-groups" in order to reinforce their sense of identity and preserve or improve their self-esteem. The group becomes progressively "part of" the individual self. Rituals, such as wearing uniforms or the t-shirt of the preferred football team, are reflections of self-categorization to groups.

Vipassana: Word from the Pali (ancient Indian language dating over twenty-five centuries) that means insight. In particular, "insight into the nature of reality".

Vipassana meditation: Often referred to as "insight meditation" in English, *Vipassana* meditation aims at developing profound understanding of the nature of reality by focusing sharply on physical and mental processes. It has been, and still is, traditionally used for the attainment of Enlightenment (*Nirvana*). Mindfulness of breath is usually the preparatory technique used for Vipassana meditation, which gives more importance to the processes underlying emergence of body sensations (*Vedana*).

List of Appendices

APPENDIX A
Mindfulness with Breathing Script (Stage 1)
Part-by-Part Body Scanning Script (Stage 1)
Grounded Empathy Script (Stage 4)

APPENDIX B
The Short Progress Assessment (SPA)
The Mindfulness-based-Self-Efficacy Scale (MSES): Client Form and Scoring Sheet

APPENDIX C
Practice Feedback Sheet
SUDS Sheet
Diary of Reactive Habits
Daily Schedule of Mindfulness Practice
Daily Record of Mindfulness Practice
Interoceptive Signature
Interoceptive Signature – Pocket Form
Interoception Form
Bi-polar Exposure Exercise Form
What is MiCBT (Client handout)
Dealing with Difficulties in Mindfulness Training (Client handout)

Mindfulness-integrated CBT: Principles and Practice, First Edition. Bruno A. Cayoun.
© 2011 John Wiley & Sons, Ltd. Published 2011 by John Wiley & Sons, Ltd.

Appendix A – Scripts

Guidelines for Scripts

The following two scripts are approximate transcripts of the author's recorded instructions on the Mindfulness Training "Stage 1" CD (Cayoun, 2004), which clients listen to during daily practice. These instructions are adapted from those of Eastern teachers of the Burmese Vipassana tradition, such as Sayagyi U Ba khin, Mother Sayamagyi and S. N. Goenka during intensive 10-day courses. For a detailed implementation protocol, see Chapter 12. Note that instructions are given once the client is relaxed. These instructions are given in a slow and peaceful but assertive manner by a trained professional. Note also that "…" means pause (varying from 3 to 10 seconds), that "…" means a pause about twice longer, and that a half-minute pause is denoted by "_". These pausing notations appear at the end of the word just preceding the pause. In any case, pauses should be sufficiently long to enable the client to scan the targeted body part. Some words are italicized, marking an emphasis. The client hears all instructions in each script below with closed eyes, sitting up with neck and back straight.

Mindfulness with Breathing Script (Stage 1)

Script duration is about 18 minutes including silences

In this set of exercises, you will learn to relax and concentrate on your breath without stretching any muscles. The following exercises pertain to mindfulness training and are limited to developing mindfulness of breathing. These are important exercises that will prepare you for mindfulness of body sensations. They will also help you relax further without any stretch, wherever you are, at work, with your family, alone, even in bed. You will learn to become aware straightaway of all conscious and perhaps subconscious activities in the mind, which often affect our breath. Being able to observe the breath and have a degree of control over our reactivity or attitude towards the breath is important because it teaches us self-control, not just relaxation. These exercises will also help in developing a degree of concentration. Often our mind is busy, stressed, and ruminative, which means that we repeat over and over negative or unhelpful thoughts. This exercise will help you focus and remain focused.

So let us start now with the practice … Sit comfortably cross-legged on the floor, if you are used to sitting that way, or on a chair without leaning against the back of the chair. Your knees should be lower than your buttocks so you might need to sit on top of one or more cushions that you can place on your chair. Your neck and back must be kept straight. Neck straight, back straight, comfortably seated, focus all you attention at the entrance of your nostrils. Be aware of the breath coming in, going out … simple breath … non-controlled breath … natural breath … breathe as you need to breathe, without controlling the breath_.

If the air in the environment is very warm or very cold, you may feel the temperature of the air, touching the outer ring or the inner walls of the nostrils, and at other times you won't. That's ok. Then be simply aware that the air is flowing continuously at the entrance of your nostrils … Notice if it comes more though the left or right nostril …if it is deep or shallow … fast or slow_. When you are aware of the incoming and outgoing breath, there is no past or future … you are in the present moment, from moment to moment … Time almost doesn't exist_ _.

Your mind is not used to staying in the present moment. It is used to wandering in the past … wandering in the future … but very rarely staying in the present moment … There are reasons why this occurs. When parts of the brain are constantly activated, by habit or because there is a memory that is more or less stressful, the strength of this activation in the brain is such that we tend to repeat the thought or the memory. And because of this repetition, these pathways in the brain are facilitated and the thoughts related to these pathways keep on intruding. They keep on intruding over and over and over again, until you stop nurturing them by not *thinking* them … Your big challenge during this exercise is to withdraw your attention from an ongoing thought, understanding this is *just* a thought_.

Keep breathing consciously_. Very alert, very attentive ... Every time a thought arises, see it for what it is, just a thought. Not the truth, not you ... Although there may be true issues within that thought, the thought is just a thought ... Learn to see thoughts for what they are. Practice now for a few minutes, to see thoughts for what there are, without reacting or engaging with them, without identifying yourself with them ... with a degree of detachment. And look at the incoming and outgoing breath, as it comes in, as it goes out. Do your best_ _ _ _.

Keep on focusing steadily on the in and outgoing breath... trying to sustain your attention towards your breath for as long as you can_ _ _. There is no need to count or to put any strategy into your mind because you would focus on the strategy and forget about the breath ... You might start saying "one two, one two" or "in out, in out" and forget all about what you are actually doing ... So just *observe* what actually happens rather that *thinking* about what happens_. Learn about your or mind by focusing on your breath, from moment to moment, without judging, evaluating, or reacting to the experience ...

Keep practising. The longer you practise, the more changes you will notice in your daily activities or you will be able to focus better, gain time on the job, be less bothered by intrusive thoughts, and develop a degree of self-confidence and self-control_ _.

Keep practising steadily, focusing on your incoming and outgoing breath ... Every time your mind wanders, do not feel disappointed or defeated. Bring it back smilingly to the awareness of respiration, at the entrance of the nostrils ... and keep on developing your awareness of breath ... mastering your own mind, bit by bit, progressively ... Keep practising confidently_ _ _.

You may be able to feel a sensation of cold on the inner walls of the nostrils as you breathe in, and maybe a little sensation of warmth on the inner walls of the nostrils as you breathe out, and maybe a little feeling of the air touching the skin below the nostrils on the area above the upper lips, on the area of the moustache ... If you don't feel anything, breathe slightly harder for a few seconds just to feel the touch of the breath and then quickly come back to normal breathing, natural breathing. Remember we are not trying to regulate the breath, we are just observing and accepting it as it is_ _.

Sometime your mind will wander because it doesn't like to stay in the present moment; it is not used to it ... It will wander either in the past or in the future. Bring it back to the present moment ... smilingly ... without resenting the fact that it has wandered despite your effort to keep it steady ... Each time it wanders, gently bring it back to the awareness of respiration_ _.

Keep on focusing on the in and outgoing breath, trying to sustain your attention for as long as you can_ _ _.

Keep breathing consciously ... very alert, very attentive ... Every time a thought arises, see it for what it is, just a thought ... in the present moment, from moment to moment ...

Some of you may already feel sensations somewhere around the nose perhaps, on the face, or elsewhere on the body. This is normal. Whether they are pleasant or unpleasant, feeling these sensations is absolutely normal … The more relaxed you are, more sensitive to your processes you become, because you are not distracted …

Very alert, keep on focusing consciously on the in and outgoing breath for as long as you can_. Now you can stop the CD and continue practicing without the CD for another 10 minutes. The more you practice, the more benefits, immediate benefits.

Part-by-Part Body Scanning Script (Stage 1)

Script duration is about 30 minutes including silences

Now that you are very relaxed, consider that changing the reality of this moment, which is what we often try to do when we try to relax, is quite different from accepting the reality of this moment. When you feel anxious … depressed … or when you experience any unpleasant emotion, you can't always change the unpleasant reality in your mind and body. In fact, trying to do so is often impractical or it can even make things worse … The answer is acceptance. When you are able to accept an unwanted experience, it doesn't bother you that much anymore. Since this is not easy to do without good training we are now going to learn a technique which, if practiced properly, will help you to develop the skills to accept events which occur from moment to moment within yourself. You will learn to look and accept things at the deepest level of your experience, and the deepest level is the level of body sensations, from the most obvious to the subtlest …

The purpose of this next exercise is certainly not to relax. Relaxation has its own purpose. The purpose is to develop self-awareness, awareness of thought, awareness of body, and equanimity, which is the term that means balance of the mind, equipoise, composure, equilibrium. It means not reacting, either with craving for what is pleasant, or aversion for what is not pleasant. It means a form of acceptance, unconditional acceptance … The purpose of the following exercise, commonly called body-scan, is to develop acceptance of one's own experiences. It is not a way of getting rid of unpleasant sensations. It is not a way of attracting pleasant sensations or pleasant experiences. It is a way of learning to accept whatever is arising, and get on with life. Relaxation becomes a by-product of that, because when acceptance is increased, you relax. So let us make sure that you understand what this technique is about. And it is certainly not to fall asleep, have a better sleep. It is to remain awake and attentive all along. So keep your eyes closed, keep breathing peacefully, calmly and attentively_.

Start by focusing all your attention on your nostrils and focus on the incoming and outgoing breath, as it comes in … as it goes out … without changing anything this time … we are not changing the reality of this moment … We are not judging whether this moment is pleasant or unpleasant … This is very different to retraining the breath to relax. We are learning to be equanimous, non-reactive, neutral_.

Now shift *all* your attention, *all* your attention to the top of your head, to the top of your head, and observe whatever sensation you feel at the top of your head ... You may not feel any sensation yet ... Certainly you will not feel the subtle ones, even though there are millions of sensations on top of your head, but your mind hasn't been trained enough, it is not concentrated and subtle enough to feel them ... In time, this will become easier if you persevere ... For now, you may feel perhaps some gross sensations like itching or like ants crawling, pressure, and temperature of some type ... anything ... or maybe you feel nothing. It doesn't matter as not feeling anything is still an experience, therefore just observe... No reaction. Stay there at the top of your head ... As you observe the top of your head, if you feel nothing, you may feel something somewhere else on your body ... don't allow yourself to be distracted. *You* are "the master of the house"... therefore *you* decide where you put your attention ... At this moment, you are in control of your attention ...

Having made sure that there are no more sensations to perceive on top of your head, start moving further and survey the entire scalp area, bit by bit, part by part ... If you feel you have difficulties feeling any sensation at all, then use larger parts of your head, so you may feel something if you scan a larger portion at a time ... maybe three to four inches diameter area at a time. If you stay in an area and you feel nothing there for about half a minute, then move further and as soon as you feel a sensation, again move further straight away ... avoid getting stuck with *any* sensation, whether pleasant or unpleasant ...

If any thought overpowers you, maybe a recurring thought, then go back to the awareness of breathing in and breathing out for a few seconds, even half a minute if you can. If it is still overpowering, breathe slightly harder, not too hard, just slightly harder or you might hyperventilate ... and then as soon as you are aware of your breathing again, and the thought is gone, then start slowing down your breathing and go back to the body sensation where you left off and continue scanning the entire scalp area ...

Now move to the forehead and survey the entire forehead area. Survey the eyebrows start with one, continue with the other ... Move then to the nose look at any sensation on the nose ... Move further down to the mouth and survey the lips for any sensations ... feel the tongue, any sensations on the tongue? ... Of course your mouth is closed or the lips gently parted, but you are breathing through the nose ... Move to the chin for any sensation in your chin ... Move up to the left cheek and then move aside to the right cheek ... If you have any sensation, avoid getting attached to it in any way, just move further ... Move up to the left ear and then move to the right ear ... Now survey the throat area, any sensation in the throat area? ...

It can be anything, pain, strain, tingling sensation, itching sensation, pulling, throbbing, sweating ... any sensation is an experience, therefore we just observe it ... objectively ... without judging it or reacting to it ... It is not *yours*, it is not *you*.

It merely arises to pass away, *just* to pass away … It is the same with your thoughts, they arise and pass away if you don't nourish them, feed them with more thoughts …

When you finish surveying the throat area, keep moving and survey the entire neck area … any sensation in the neck? … Keep moving and try to feel sensations on your left shoulder … part-by-part, not reacting to any type of sensation whether subtle, gross, pleasant or unpleasant … If you feel any discomfort it is absolutely normal, so just observe smilingly, peacefully, progressively moving down to the left arm, surveying the entire left arm and left elbow … Patiently and calmly, survey the entire left wrist and left hand …

… Then move up to the right shoulder, the *right shoulder* and survey the *entire* shoulder, moving as soon as you feel a sensation … If there are no sensations for about half a minute, then move further anyway … Maybe when you go back to this shoulder in the next round you might feel something there… There is no need to feel defeated or annoyed by what you experience. The whole exercise is to develop equanimity, balance of the mind, the opposite of reactivity …

Now move down to the right arm and the right elbow_. Move to the right forearm and down to the right wrist and the right hand_. Then move up to the chest, from the upper chest to the lower chest area, and try to feel sensations in this area part by part … Try to scan in the vertical order _ _. Keep the same order of scanning each time you scan your body parts …

If you feel your heart beat and you interpret it as your heart beat, then you are not simply feeling sensations, you are *interpreting* sensations. It is important that you try to remain with the task of *pure* observation … *no* evaluation … *no* interpretation … *just* observation. It is a *very* specific task … *mere* observation. The basic *experience* of the heartbeat is just a body sensation … Pleasant or unpleasant makes no difference, try to just observe … If you are not evaluating it, then it is bound to subside progressively although it may increase at first, simply because you are aware of it … in fact it doesn't really increase, it is your awareness of it which increases … The sensation will subside and then pass away, however long it takes, because this is the nature of *all* sensations … As soon as it is reinforced, as soon as it is reacted to, when the next similar sensation arises you will react to it similarly or even more strongly … So we start learning not to react to sensations, even benign sensations, or even pleasurable sensations … no reaction and your mind will get very skilled at this … and this skill will be transferred in your daily life, but first you will need to train very seriously …

Now move down and survey the entire abdomen area, part by part, without any reaction whatsoever … try not to miss any part, including genitals_ _. Now move up to the upper back area, the upper back area and feel any sensation you may come across in your *upper back area* … always very calmly, equanimously_ _. Then move down to the lower back area_.

Try not to get caught in your thoughts … as soon as you think something, and this is bound to happen over and over, quickly go back to the awareness of any sensation you were looking at and *move* further … maybe you haven't felt a sensation for some time, so, in a manner of speaking, the mind gets bored ... Try to remain optimistic, this is just your beginning but you will get better at it with practice ...

Now keep moving down to the buttocks and survey the entire buttocks area. Start with the left and once it is surveyed move to the right buttock_ _. Move down to the left thigh and survey the entire *left thigh*, part by part down to the left knee_ _. Now move down to the left leg, the *left leg* ... Even though there may be some gross sensations, like pressure, tension, or even pain perhaps, especially if you are sitting crossed-legged on the floor, try to be very still, accepting *every* experience ... Within the most painful sensations, in case you encounter any today or another day, you will find there is an underlying current inside that sensation ... it is like an underlying sensation in which there is no pain ... a flow of very tiny sensations running through ... so always try to remain very still and attempt to feel this underlying current_.

Now move your attention down to the left ankle, and the entire left foot, to the tip of the left toes, the left foot to the tip of the toes_. Now go up to the right thigh, the *right thigh* and survey the entire right thigh, part by part, in the same way_. Keep moving down to the right knee, the right leg, the right ankle and the right foot_ _.

You have now surveyed the entire body, from the top of your head to the tip of your toes. Now start from the tip of your toes and move back up to the top of your head. Start from the left foot and move up to the left leg, left thigh and left buttock _. Similarly, from the right foot, move up progressively to the right leg, the right thigh and survey the right buttock_.

Continue scanning your body calmly and equanimously, focusing on the lower back ..., followed by the upper back_ _. Now survey the entire abdomen and chest areas, patiently and calmly_ _. From the upper chest move up to the throat area ... From the left hand move up to the left shoulder ... From the right hand then move up to the right shoulder ... Survey then the entire neck area and then the face ... part by part ... and then do the same with the entire scalp area_ _.

And again from the top of the head go down to the tip of your toes and scan your body entirely, as long as you can give it time ... As you practice correctly, your mind will become increasingly and profoundly detached, at the level of body sensations ... Remember, the most important thing to keep in mind is that all body sensations and all thoughts are impermanent by nature ... The impression that they remain is because we react to them, we reinforce them ... Each time you come across a sensation, especially those that are very pleasant or very unpleasant, just remember their nature, their *impermanent* nature. Reacting to it only increases the reinforcement of our habits in daily life ...

What you do during this training will be reflected in your daily life ... it is a very effective technique... Of course, sometimes you will react during your practice, but watch that you react less and less and the results in daily life will be surprising ... Now you can stop the CD and practice without the CD if you have some time ... the more you practice the more you will benefit_.

Script Example for Stage 4

Script duration is about 8 minutes including silences

This script represents approximately the instructions given by this author to clients, who learn to practice the principles of this technique in their daily practice. These instructions integrate creative visualization with the technique of loving-kindness meditation (Metta Bhavana), as taught during intensive Vipassana Meditation courses.

Note also that "…" means pause (varying from 3 to 10 seconds) and "……" means about twice longer pause, and a half-minute pause is denoted by "_". These pausing notations appear at the end of the word just preceding the pause. Having ensured that the client is relaxed and following some explanations of the purpose and process, and working out the sort of fruitful thoughts that may be used, the clinician may start by saying:

… Now, focus all your attention on the heart area …, the *heart* area … Each time you breathe in, breathe as if your breath enters through your heart area, feeling subtle sensations over there … and each time you breathe out, let your heart area expand slowly throughout your entire body, feeling all the sensations spreading into all parts of your body, each time you breathe out_. Now generate good thoughts, thoughts of peace, harmony, love and success for yourself_.

(After about ½ a minute, model the process by verbalizing your own aloud)

… May I be peaceful and balanced in my life …, may I be successful in what I do …, may I be understanding and patient with myself …, may I generate love *(or compassion)* and happiness in my life_.

Keep breathing in through your heart … but now, as you breathe out, let your heart expand towards others … starting with your friends and family, letting all the subtle sensations flow out of your body towards those you care for and love … Generate positive thoughts for them_. Now let your good thoughts and pleasant sensations spread further to all human beings, including those who have not had the chance to develop in Mindfulness … those who may have been in conflict with you_. Just imagine how different it would be if they were developing awareness of body sensations and equanimity … You can make a wish that they do so one day and benefit as you do_.

(After about ½ a minute, model the process by verbalizing your own aloud :)

May I share my peace and equanimity with all beings … May I share my success and my merits with all … May all beings be happy … May all be peaceful … May all be free from reactivity_ _.

Take a few conscious breaths and in your own time, open your eyes.

Appendix B – Assessment Tools

Mindfulness-integrated CBT: Principles and Practice, First Edition. Bruno A. Cayoun.
© 2011 John Wiley & Sons, Ltd. Published 2011 by John Wiley & Sons, Ltd.

Short Progress Assessment (SPA)/Pre-Assessment Form

SPA© - ASSESSMENT BEFORE THERAPY	Actual	FORM 1

FULL NAME:.. DATE............................

How strong or upsetting were your ⬇

Circle one number in each column in the section below according to **how strong or upsetting your experiences** were <u>**IN THE PAST 7 DAYS, INCLUDING TODAY**</u>

	Not at all or a little	Moderate	Strong but bearable	Sometimes unbearable	Unbearable most of the time
UNWANTED BEHAVIOURS/ACTIONS	0	1	2	3	4
UNPLEASANT THOUGHTS	0	1	2	3	4
UNPLEASANT BODY SENSATIONS	0	1	2	3	4
UNPLEASANT FEELINGS/EMOTIONS	0	1	2	3	4
UNPLEASANT RELATIONS WITH OTHERS	0	1	2	3	4

How manageable were your ⬇

Circle one number in each column in the section below according to **how you coped with the above experiences (how manageable were they)** <u>**IN THE PAST 7 DAYS, INCLUDING TODAY**</u>

	Easily manageable	Moderately manageable	Managed with difficulty	Sometimes unmanageable	Unmanageable most of the time
UNWANTED BEHAVIOURS/ACTIONS	0	1	2	3	4
UNPLEASANT THOUGHTS	0	1	2	3	4
UNPLEASANT BODY SENSATIONS	0	1	2	3	4
UNPLEASANT FEELINGS/EMOTIONS	0	1	2	3	4
UNPLEASANT RELATIONS WITH OTHERS	0	1	2	3	4

SPA© - ASSESSMENT BEFORE THERAPY   Retrospective   FORM 2

FULL NAME:..   DATE.............................

Circle one number in each column in the section below according to **how strong or upsetting your experiences** were **BEFORE YOUR FIRST THERAPY SESSION**

How strong or upsetting were your ⬇

	Not at all or a little	Moderate	Strong but bearable	Sometimes unbearable	Unbearable most of the time
UNWANTED BEHAVIOURS/ACTIONS	0	1	2	3	4
UNPLEASANT THOUGHTS	0	1	2	3	4
UNPLEASANT BODY SENSATIONS	0	1	2	3	4
UNPLEASANT FEELINGS/EMOTIONS	0	1	2	3	4
UNPLEASANT RELATIONS WITH OTHERS	0	1	2	3	4

Circle one number in each column in the section below according to **how you coped with the above experiences (how manageable were they)** **BEFORE YOUR FIRST THERAPY SESSION**

How manageable were your ⬇

	Easily manageable	Moderately manageable	Managed with difficulty	Sometimes unmanageable	Unmanageable most of the time
UNWANTED BEHAVIOURS/ACTIONS	0	1	2	3	4
UNPLEASANT THOUGHTS	0	1	2	3	4
UNPLEASANT BODY SENSATIONS	0	1	2	3	4
UNPLEASANT FEELINGS/EMOTIONS	0	1	2	3	4
UNPLEASANT RELATIONS WITH OTHERS	0	1	2	3	4

SPA© - ASSESSMENT DURING/POST THERAPY				FORM 3

FULL NAME:...DATE..........................

How strong or upsetting were your ⬇

Circle one number in each column in the section below according to **how strong or upsetting your experiences were IN THE PAST 7 DAYS, INCLUDING TODAY**

	Not at all or a little	Moderate	Strong but bearable	Sometimes unbearable	Unbearable most of the time
UNWANTED BEHAVIOURS/ACTIONS	0	1	2	3	4
UNPLEASANT THOUGHTS	0	1	2	3	4
UNPLEASANT BODY SENSATIONS	0	1	2	3	4
UNPLEASANT FEELINGS/EMOTIONS	0	1	2	3	4
UNPLEASANT RELATIONS WITH OTHERS	0	1	2	3	4

How manageable were your ⬇

Circle one number in each column in the section below according to **how you coped with the above experiences (how manageable were they) IN THE PAST 7 DAYS, INCLUDING TODAY**

	Easily manageable	Moderately manageable	Managed with difficulty	Sometimes unmanageable	Unmanageable most of the time
UNWANTED BEHAVIOURS/ACTIONS	0	1	2	3	4
UNPLEASANT THOUGHTS	0	1	2	3	4
UNPLEASANT BODY SENSATIONS	0	1	2	3	4
UNPLEASANT FEELINGS/EMOTIONS	0	1	2	3	4
UNPLEASANT RELATIONS WITH OTHERS	0	1	2	3	4

Name: _____

Date of Birth: _____

Today's Date: _____

Date at start of therapy: _____

DIRECTIONS

Below is a list of five areas of life in which people can experience improvement (behaviours, thoughts, physical sensations, feelings, and relationships). Please circle one number in each column in the section below according to **HOW MUCH IMPROVEMENT** you have **experienced in each of these five areas.**

Please ask your assessor if you need more detail.

Try not to spend too long on your answers. There is no right or wrong answer.

How do you perceive your improvement with	Have worsened	No improvement noted	Small improvements	Clearly visible improvement overall	Significant improvement, goal reached
UNWANTED BEHAVIOURS/ACTIONS	0	1	2	3	4
UNPLEASANT THOUGHTS	0	1	2	3	4
UNPLEASANT BODY SENSATIONS	0	1	2	3	4
UNPLEASANT FEELINGS/EMOTIONS	0	1	2	3	4
UNPLEASANT RELATIONS WITH OTHERS	0	1	2	3	4

Name: _____

Date of Birth: _____

Today's Date: _____

Date at start of therapy: _____

DIRECTIONS

Below is a list of five areas related to therapy. Please circle one number in each column in the section below according to **HOW SATISFIED YOU ARE** with **each part of the therapy you have had**.

🗣 Please ask your assessor if you need more detail.

🕐 Try not to spend too long on your answers. There is no right or wrong answer.

How satisfied are you with	Not at all satisfied	A little satisfied	Moderately satisfied	Very satisfied	Extremely satisfied
TREATMENT TYPE	0	1	2	3	4
TREATMENT LENGTH	0	1	2	3	4
RELATIONSHIP WITH THERAPIST	0	1	2	3	4
THE SKILLS YOU LEARNED	0	1	2	3	4
COST (IF APPLICABLE)	0	1	2	3	4

MINDFULNESS-BASED SELF EFFICACY SCALE© (MSES)

Bruno A. Cayoun & Janet Freestun,
University of Tasmania

NAME……………………………….......…………. DATE……………….... Session/Week No……..

Circle one number in the shaded column according to how much you now agree or disagree with each statement below, using the following scale:

Not at all	A little	Moderately	A lot	Completely
0	1	2	3	4

Try not to spend too much time on any one item. There are no right or wrong answers.

1.	I am able to think about what I am about to do before I act	0	1	2	3	4
2.	When an unpleasant thought enters my mind, I can cope with it	0	1	2	3	4
3.	When I relax, I can feel sensations in my body	0	1	2	3	4
4.	I get easily overwhelmed by my emotions	0	1	2	3	4
5.	I find it difficult to make new friends	0	1	2	3	4
6.	I try to avoid uncomfortable situations even when they are really important	0	1	2	3	4
7.	I am aware when I am about to do something that could hurt me or someone else	0	1	2	3	4
8.	Stopping myself from engaging in unwanted or hurtful behaviours is very difficult	0	1	2	3	4
9.	I know that my thoughts don't have the power to hurt me	0	1	2	3	4
10.	When I am stressed, I am aware of unpleasant body sensations	0	1	2	3	4
11.	When I feel very emotional, it takes a long time for it to pass	0	1	2	3	4
12.	I feel comfortable saying sorry when I feel I am in the wrong	0	1	2	3	4
13.	It is ok for me to feel strong emotions	0	1	2	3	4
14.	It is often too late when I realize I overreacted in a stressful situation	0	1	2	3	4
15.	If something needs to be done, I am able to complete it within a reasonable time	0	1	2	3	4
16.	I get so caught up in my thoughts that I end up feeling very sad or anxious	0	1	2	3	4
17.	When I have unpleasant feelings in my body, I prefer to push them away	0	1	2	3	4
18.	I believe that I can make my life peaceful	0	1	2	3	4
19.	I can resolve problems easily with my partner (or best friend if single)	0	1	2	3	4
20.	I can face my thoughts, even if they are unpleasant	0	1	2	3	4
21.	I am tolerant with myself when I am repeating old habits that are no longer helpful	0	1	2	3	4
22.	My actions are often controlled by other people or circumstances	0	1	2	3	4
23.	I get caught up in unpleasant memories or anxious thoughts about the future	0	1	2	3	4
24.	I can deal with physical discomfort	0	1	2	3	4
25.	I feel I cannot love anyone	0	1	2	3	4
26.	I am often in conflict with one (or more) family member	0	1	2	3	4
27.	I avoid feeling my body when there is pain or other discomfort	0	1	2	3	4
28.	I find it difficult to accept unpleasant experiences	0	1	2	3	4
29.	I do things that make me feel good straightaway even if I will feel bad later	0	1	2	3	4
30.	When I have a problem, I tend to believe it will ruin my whole life	0	1	2	3	4
31.	When I feel physical discomfort, I relax because I know it will pass	0	1	2	3	4
32.	Even when things are difficult I can feel happy	0	1	2	3	4
33.	I can feel comfortable around people	0	1	2	3	4
34.	Seeing or hearing someone with strong emotions is unbearable to me	0	1	2	3	4
35.	If I get angry or anxious, it is generally because of others	0	1	2	3	4

Table of results

Subscale	Item No.	Items to reverse	Raw Score	Scale Score
Behavior	1.			
	8.	Reversed		
	15.			
	22.	Reversed		
	29.	Reversed		
			DSE =	
Cognition	2.			
	9.			
	16.	Reversed		
	23.	Reversed		
	30.	Reversed		
			DSE =	
Interoception	3.			
	10.			
	17.	Reversed		
	24.			
	31.			
			DSE =	
Affect	4.	Reversed		
	11.	Reversed		
	18.			
	25.	Reversed		
	32.			
			DSE =	
Interpersonal	5.	Reversed		
	12.			
	19.			
	26.	Reversed		
	33.			
			DSE =	
Avoidance	6.	Reversed		
	13.			
	20.			
	27.	Reversed		
	34.	Reversed		
			DSE =	
Mindfulness	7.			
	14.	Reversed		
	21.			
	28.	Reversed		
	35.	Reversed		
			DSE =	
Name:		Date:	GSE =	

Appendix C – Client Forms

Mindfulness-integrated CBT: Principles and Practice, First Edition. Bruno A. Cayoun.
© 2011 John Wiley & Sons, Ltd. Published 2011 by John Wiley & Sons, Ltd.

Home practice feedback

Were you able to practice the Mindfulness Training? YES / NO
   If yes, score the extent to which you practiced in the last week on the scale below (circle the number of times).

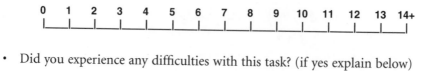

- Did you experience any difficulties with this task? (if yes explain below)

_____

_____

_____

   Score below the extent to which you could feel body sensations

Could not feel   Could feel them
them at all   throughout

- After practicing for a week / few days, how did you feel at the end of your practice session?

_____

_____

_____

- What did you observe about your body sensations and associated thoughts?

_____

_____

_____

- Score below the extent to which you feel to have benefited from practising mindfulness.

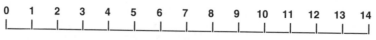

No observed   Extremely
benefit   beneficial

Hierarchical exposure to target events/subjective units of distress (SUDS)

Write down 10 events or situations that are distressing and that you are likely to avoid on a piece of paper. Then, in the space below, list the 5 most relevant situations in order of difficulty, with the most distressing and least manageable situations last. Write the date in "Date1" only, and the amount of distress they cause you from 1 to 100 "in distress1 only" (other dates and percentage of distress will be used after the issues have been targeted).

Date1:............Date2:............Date3:............Date4:............
SITUATION 1 (distress1....%) (distress2....%) (distress3....%) (distress4....%)

_____

_____

_____

Date1:............Date2:............Date3:............Date4:............
SITUATION 2 (distress1....%) (distress2....%) (distress3....%) (distress4....%)

_____

_____

_____

Date1:............Date2:............Date3:............Date4:............
SITUATION 1 (distress1....%) (distress2....%) (distress3....%) (distress4....%)

_____

_____

_____

Date1:............Date2:............Date3:............Date4:............
SITUATION 1 (distress1....%) (distress2....%) (distress3....%) (distress4....%)

_____

_____

_____

Date1:............Date2:............Date3:............Date4:............
SITUATION 1 (distress1....%) (distress2....%) (distress3....%) (distress4:....%)

_____

_____

_____

DIARY OF REACTIVE HABITS

Fill in the boxes each time you encounter a situation that evokes an emotional or stressful experience

EVALUATION

SENSORY PERCEPTION

BODY SENSATION

REACTION / RESPONSE

SITUATION
INTERNAL / EXTERNAL

DATE OF EVENT: _____

TIME OF EVENT: _____

INTENSITY OF DISTRESS: Then _____ %

INTENSITY OF DISTRESS: Now _____ %

NAME: _____

DAILY SCHEDULE OF MINDFULNESS PRACTICE

Your Name: …………… ……………	Date	a.m. (circle)	Duration	Rating % (How difficult was your practice?)	p.m. (circle)	Duration	Rating % (How difficult was your practise?)
Monday		Yes / No			Yes / No		
Tuesday		Yes / No			Yes / No		
Wednesday		Yes / No			Yes / No		
Thursday		Yes / No			Yes / No		
Friday		Yes / No			Yes / No		
Saturday		Yes / No			Yes / No		
Sunday		Yes / No			Yes / No		

If you missed your practice, explain why:_____

_____

DAILY RECORD OF MINDFULNESS PRACTICE

NAME……………..   STARTED TRAINING (date)…………………..

DATE TIME	SITUATION Describe the stressful situation?	TYPE OF SENSATION(s) Rate strength 1–100	TYPE OF THOUGHT	HOW LONG DID IT LAST?	WHAT DID YOU DO?
Monday:					
Tuesday:					
Wednesday:					
Thursday:					
Friday:					
Saturday:					
Sunday:					

Interoceptive Signature

Instructions

Use the frame below to rate your experience of body sensations during or following an event that you believe was distressing. Identify the experience in your body by placing a small dot on each of the lines representing a category of body sensation. Then join the dots with a line and rate the intensity of your experience during the event out of 100 in the lower left corner of the frame. After a short practice (less than 1 minute) of body scanning, place another dot on each line, re-draw another line to join the dots, and re-rate your distress out of 100 in the lower right corner of the frame.

Name:		Date: / /

MASS	Lightest	Neutral		Heaviest
TEMPERATURE	Coldest	Neutral		Hottest
MOTION	Most Still	Neutral		Most Agitated
COHESIVENESS	Loosest	Neutral		Densest

Percent Distress

Before: %   After: %

In the frame below, please write a short summary of the circumstance in which you experienced the distressing experience.

Place:..

Date: .... Time: .... Were you alone?...... If not, with who?............

What happened?...

....

....

....

Interoceptive Signature – Pocket Form

Instructions

Use one of the blank forms below to record how you experience body sensations on each of the four categories (**Mass, Temperature, Motion, Cohesiveness**). When you experience stress, notice your body sensations and identify the experience in your body by placing a dot on each of the four lines representing a category of sensation. Then join each dot with a full line. After a short practice of body scanning (about half a minute), place another dot on each of the four categories to represent how you are experiencing body sensations after practice. Then join those dots with another line (dotted line) to show any change.

Date: **Time:**   Describe the event:

		Neutral	
Mass	Light		Heavy
Temperature	Cold	Neutral	Hot
Motion	Still	Neutral	Movement
Cohesiveness	Loose	Neutral	Dense

Date: **Time:**   Describe the event:

		Neutral	
Mass	Light		Heavy
Temperature	Cold	Neutral	Hot
Motion	Still	Neutral	Movement
Cohesiveness	Loose	Neutral	Dense

Date: **Time:**   Describe the event:

		Neutral	
Mass	Light		Heavy
Temperature	Cold	Neutral	Hot
Motion	Still	Neutral	Movement
Cohesiveness	Loose	Neutral	Dense

Date: **Time:**   Describe the event:

		Neutral	
Mass	Light		Heavy
Temperature	Cold	Neutral	Hot
Motion	Still	Neutral	Movement
Cohesiveness	Loose	Neutral	Dense

Date: **Time:**   Describe the event:

		Neutral	
Mass	Light		Heavy
Temperature	Cold	Neutral	Hot
Motion	Still	Neutral	Movement
Cohesiveness	Loose	Neutral	Dense

Interoception Form(Front/Back)

Name:.. **Age:**.........**Sex:**........ **Date:**.............................

Date when training started:.............. **Scanning methods this week:**.....................................

Please color the parts in the silhouette where you can feel any type of body sensations. Try not to spend too long coloring the parts. It is OK if you go slightly over the silhouette edge.

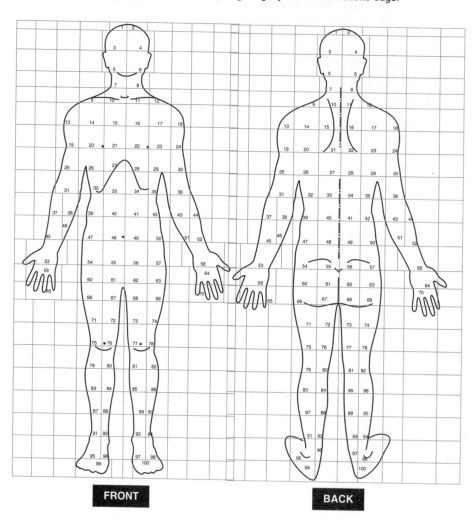

FRONT   BACK

Results

There are 100 numbered boxes (square and rectangular shapes) within or crossing the outline of the silhouette. To calculate the percentage of interoceptive awareness, count the total number of coloured boxes. A numbered box is counted as valid if at least half of its surface, which falls within the silhouette, is colored. **Total interoceptive awareness = (%back + %front / 2) = ...%**

Bi-polar Exposure/Exercise Form

Instructions

Choose a situation that you are avoiding or likely to avoid. For the first 5 minutes, visualize the *worst* case scenarios that could occur if you were not avoiding this situation while *remaining equanimous*. Then rest your mind for a minute by practicing mindfulness of breath. Finally, continue with 5 minutes of visualizing the very *best* case scenarios that would occur in this situation while *remaining equanimous*.

This exercise lasts about 11 minutes. It needs to be practiced in four separate sessions (usually twice daily) for two days, after each 30-minute practice of mindfulness meditation. This method helps desensitize from the consequences of both positive and negative unrealistic expectations. After four sessions of "bi-polar exposure" (experiencing 2 extremes), enter the situation in real live ("*in vivo*") doing your best to *remain equanimous*.

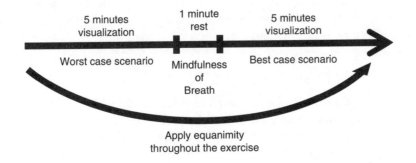

What is MiCBT?

Introduction

There is a growing number of therapy approaches that incorporate mindfulness training. Mindfulness-integrated Cognitive Behavior Therapy or MiCBT is one of these approaches. It offers a practical set of evidence-based techniques derived from mindfulness training together with principles of Cognitive Behavior Therapy (CBT) to address a broad range of psychological disorders and general stress conditions. Below is a brief overview of the foundations of MiCBT as well as the core mechanisms and basic practice components of this valuable therapeutic approach.

What is mindfulness?

Mindfulness involves paying attention to each event experienced in the present moment within our body and mind, with a non-judgmental, non-reactive and accepting attitude. In learning to be mindful, we can begin to counter many of our everyday sufferings such as stress, anxiety and depression because we are learning to experience events in a more impersonal and detached way. Mindfulness has its roots in an Eastern meditation technique called *Vipassana* and shares with it a number of central principles and mechanisms including what are known as *equanimity* and *impermanence*.

Equanimity
Equanimity is best described as a neutral response to something we experience. It is a state of awareness where we neither feel an aversion for unpleasant experiences nor craving for pleasant ones. Other ways of describing *equanimity* are balance, calmness and composure. The development of *equanimity*, or an *equanimous* mind as it is sometimes called, is an important part of mindfulness skills because it gives us the ability to remain less reactive and less judgmental no matter what is experienced, thereby giving us a feeling of ease, self-control and composure as we go about our daily lives.

Impermanence
Mindfulness incorporates the notion of *impermanence*, the changing nature of all things including our own mental and emotional experiences. By experiencing the changing nature of internal experiences, we can learn to see ourselves in a more objective and scientific way. We can detach ourselves from rigid views that can sometimes lead to stress and unhappiness.

How do we practice?
While we can practice being mindful in everyday life by just observing what is happening around and within us, formal training by way of sitting meditation is most

effective for developing mindfulness skills. During mindfulness meditation we sit closed eyes and initially focus the breath to develop concentration and take control of our attention. This alone helps decrease the intrusion of unhelpful thoughts that we may have.

During this training, all sorts of thoughts frequently arise. Instead of being caught up in a thought, we learn to see it for what it is, just a thought, an impermanent mental event, no matter what the content of the thought may be, and go back to our focus of attention. In this way, we learn not to react to thoughts. We gain a direct experience that thoughts cannot truly affect us or define who we are.

Similarly, when we pay attention to our body sensations, we also learn to perceive a body sensation merely as a body sensation, regardless of how pleasant or unpleasant it is. Mindfulness training helps us realise that body sensations, like thoughts and all other experiences, are also impermanent by nature and no matter how pleasant or unpleasant they are, they pass away. As we become more mindful of this reality, it becomes increasingly easy to observe that body sensations are essentially an experience that cannot affect us unless we react to them. Body sensations are significant because they are the only means by which we can feel emotions. Accordingly, training ourselves to not react to them helps us accept and let go of emotions, rather than suffer from them. This is called *emotional regulation*.

What is CBT?

The way we think often affects our emotions and behavior and CBT or Cognitive Behavior Therapy helps people with such conditions as anxiety and depression change the content of unhelpful thoughts and their maladaptive ways of coping, such as avoidance or addictive behavior.

MiCBT: mindfulness-integrating and CBT

MiCBT is a 4-stage therapeutic approach which integrates mindfulness and some of the basic principles of CBT in order to help people improve the way they feel and change unhelpful behaviors. However, MiCBT helps people make changes in a different way to CBT. While CBT attempts to change maladaptive behavior by modifying people's unrealistic thoughts and beliefs, MiCBT tries to help people learn to develop control over the processes that maintain the unrealistic thoughts and beliefs through mindfulness training. MiCBT helps change the process of thinking, not just the content of our thoughts.

Changing reactive habits

Like CBT, MiCBT draws on the principles of *exposure* and *desensitization* to help us change habitual unhelpful reactions or coping strategies. However, unlike other models of cognitive-behavior therapy, MiCBT regards learned reactive habits as being the result of our own way of reacting towards the body sensations that result from our judgmental thoughts. Preventing such reactions, while remaining fully aware and accepting of bodily experiences, leads to rapid change in our habitual feelings and behaviors. We feel emotionally relieved.

Interpersonal mindfulness
MiCBT can not only help people change distressing thoughts, feelings and behaviors, it can also help people change their relationships with others. The skills we learn in MiCBT can help us not to react to others and foster a greater understanding and acceptance of ourselves and others. This usually culminates in more harmonious relationships and helps prevent relapse into habitual moods and behavior. This is explained during Stage 3 of the program.

Mindfulness And The Power Of Empathy
The fourth stage of MiCBT teaches people to use their own resources for empathy towards themselves and others. The three previous stages lead to the realization that we are the first beneficiary of the emotions we produce, whether this is a positive or negative emotion. A deep sense of empowerment, acceptance and change usually takes place at the end of Stage 4, which is the last stage of the MiCBT program.

Contraindications

MiCBT is usually safe. However, it is not advisable to practice mindfulness meditation on your own during extremely distressing states. In particular, it is not recommended to practice mindfulness meditation while experiencing psychotic states (e.g., delusions, hallucinations, paranoia), manic states (e.g., extreme anxiety or anger, uncontrollable agitation or impulse), or suicidal states in which the person may be at risk. If you experience any of these difficulties, and you are already using mindfulness meditation, it is best stop your practice until you contact your therapist and discuss your experience.

Program duration
The MiCBT program generally requires about 8 sessions, but it may vary between 6 and 12 sessions, according to the problem we intend to address. Sessions are best held weekly or fortnightly for optimum progress.

Dealing with Difficulties in Mindfulness Training

Introduction

At the beginning of mindfulness training, there are various difficulties that need to be addressed early on so that progress can be made during your therapy. Potential difficulties as well as some strategies for dealing with them will be explained below.

Adherence to training

Poor adherence to mindfulness training is the greatest cause of failure to make progress in MiCBT. However on the positive side you are likely to gain significant results if you maintain your commitment to the exercises during the program. Below are some common difficulties that people have early on.

Too tired to practice
Conditions such as stress, anxiety and depression can make you feel tired and sometimes people complain that they cannot get up early enough to practice mindfulness exercises as they need to get as much sleep as they can. Sometimes people feel too tired to practice in the evening too. As you may have already learned, mindfulness training will help you to become less reactive and calmer and thereby better equipped to deal with stressful areas in your life. This will consequently have a positive impact on your energy levels reducing tiredness and the need to sleep for the usual number of hours. Try practicing for a week, twice a day, morning and night, and see how energized you can feel!

Too busy to practice
Time pressures affect all of us. We never seem to have enough time to get everything done, let alone sitting for half an hour twice a day observing our body sensations. Think about how you use your time and you will probably find that there are various activities and tasks that you could eliminate from your daily routine – at least for the short term. Sit down and write out a plan for your day and try to use your time wisely, eliminating time wasters and low priority activities. If you are having difficulties with time management, talk to your therapist for some assistance. You have come to therapy because you want to experience change in your life. Begin by changing your daily routine and make time for what is important to you. The effort will pay off and you will empowered by your effort and notice a significant change in the way you feel due to the skills you will develop.

Lost in thoughts

A difficulty that many people experience when starting mindfulness training is that their mind keeps on being distracted by unwanted thoughts. With continued and correct mindfulness practice, intrusive thoughts can gradually decrease and people feel more in control of what their mind is doing. By remaining equanimous to thoughts that arise during practice, that is, by accepting that thoughts have emerged and systematically shifting your attention back to the breath or body sensations instead of reacting to the thoughts, the activation strength of these thoughts in the brain gradually weaken and decrease over time. If, when practicing mindfulness, intrusive thoughts are too overpowering, a *3-second rule* may help. This consists of an agreed limited time for the duration of distraction; in this case, three seconds. After three seconds, you must commit to make an effort to switch your attention back to the breath or body sensations. This is a little bit like bringing the part of the brain that deals with attentional control to the gym every day. It gets easier with practice.

Dealing with pain

During mindfulness practice, some intense sensations can emerge for numerous reasons, including posture, old injury and the like, and they can be distressing at times, particularly when you are required to keep still and focus on body sensations during body-scanning techniques. The best way to face possible pain when practicing mindfulness is to direct your attention to the centre of the intense body sensation. At first, this can enhance your perception of the pain but it will decrease as you apply equanimity to the experience, partly because you will stop interpreting unpleasant sensations as threats and hence reduce stress hormones in your body. Try to resist the urge to do things to avoid or escape sensations of pain. Reacting with avoidance will only make it appear as though the pain is strengthened or unchangeable. It is always good to remember that like thoughts and all other experiences, body sensations are also impermanent by nature and no matter how intense or painful they are, they eventually pass away.

Drowsiness

Even after a good night sleep people can sometimes feel drowsy when practicing mindfulness. Sometimes this is due to relaxing deeply after some stress. Because our nervous system is not used to the eyes being closed whilst being deeply relaxed unless we are asleep, our brain acts as if it is time to sleep. Sometimes we feel drowsy because the room is too warm or too dark, or we practice with a full stomach.

When drowsiness is overpowering, it is important to assess and modify the environment we practice in, such as increasing light intensity, decreasing room temperature, sitting in a less comfortable seat or modifying posture, keeping your neck and back straight with your knees below the level of your buttocks. If you are still feeling drowsy, try to breathe slightly deeper for a minute or so, feeling the touch of the breath within the nostrils. If drowsiness persists, you can wake the brain by letting a small amount of light enter your eyes. Rather than fully opening your eyes, open your eyelids just enough to let you see the floor not further than about 2.5 meters away from your knees. If this is insufficient to counteract drowsiness, try practicing while standing up for a few minutes. If this is still insufficient, go for a short walk and wet your face with cold water before coming back and continuing the practice. Drowsiness too is impermanent!

Poor interoception

If you have just started practicing body-scanning, you are likely to experience initial difficulties feeling body sensations in some body parts, which is an ability called *interoception*. Low interoception is normal and is to be expected. The reason for this is that, although we can easily feel strong sensations in the body, we are not used to feeling more subtle ones because the parts of the brain which lets us feel certain body parts are not very connected. The brain needs to connect more nerve cells in certain areas to allow us to feel body parts that are initially difficult to feel. As mentioned earlier in relation to dealing with thoughts, scanning the body in order to feel sensations is a bit like *bringing our brain to the gym*. It becomes easier with practice. However, some people do not progress readily or may even decrease their ability to feel body sensations because of a decrease in vigilance during practice. To overcome the lack of sustained attention and interoception, ensure that your posture is appropriate, as explained earlier in the section on drowsiness. Some people may prefer to sit on one or two thick cushions on the floor rather than on a chair, as a small degree of discomfort is an advantage in our ability to remain aware of body sensations. Whether sitting in a chair or on the floor, your buttocks must be slightly above the level of your knees and your back and neck must be kept straight, without straining. In addition, trying to keep completely immobile during practice is likely to help in feeling more sensations.

Agitation

Misunderstanding the techniques of mindfulness in the early stage often leads to some agitation and the desire to distract ourselves, misinterpret the experience, become agitated and ultimately stop practicing. Agitation can occur and be stimulated in many ways. For example, we can feel irritable because of external background noise, intrusive thoughts, uncomfortable room temperature, thinking that we are lacking time or feeling rushed. In addition, we often interpret these unpleasant experiences as *feeling bored*, forgetting that *boredom* is just another experience that can equally be accepted. The lack of stimulation of our senses, along with our personal expectation that we "should" be more skilled at this practice, can also create a sense of frustration, which we attribute to boredom. This is mainly because our levels of awareness and equanimity toward thoughts and associated body sensations are still not very well developed. As a result, we react. Remember that we only react to the unpleasant body sensations that we produce when we judge situations negatively. It is reassuring that after a period of good practice our equanimity improves and agitation usually disappears. Issues such as background noise and temperature don't seem as disturbing anymore and intrusive thoughts and physical pain are understood as part of the present moment experience. We can use them as *tools* to develop qualities such as patience, tolerance and acceptance.

Confusion and doubts

Sometimes people undergoing mindfulness training ask themselves 'What am I doing here with closed eyes watching my breath and body sensations?' Such doubt usually arises when we are still not clear about the reasons for mindfulness training. If you find yourself doubting your training, ask your therapist for further clarification and re-read the introductory handouts you have been given so that you fully understand how mindfulness works. Sometimes, it is also difficult to understand that what benefits you can derive from mindfulness training until you actually experience its effects. This means you need to practice it. Trying to philosophize or rationalize what good such daily effort might bring to you is not likely to fulfill your needs and will increase your doubts instead. It might be helpful if you commit yourself initially to practice for the entire week, as an experiment, and see how much benefit you derive from this practice. If you commit to practice every day diligently, you will soon have an understanding of why you are undergoing the training – an understanding based on your own actual experience. Although we can always doubt the wisdom of someone else, like your therapist, doubts are dispelled by the evidence which emerges from our own experience.

Contraindications

MiCBT is usually safe. However, it is not advisable to practice mindfulness meditation on your own during extremely distressing states. In particular, it is not recommended to practice mindfulness meditation while experiencing psychotic states (e.g., delusions, hallucinations, paranoia), manic states (e.g., extreme anxiety or anger, uncontrollable agitation or impulse), or suicidal states in which the person may be at risk. If you experience any of these difficulties, and you are already using mindfulness meditation, it is best stop your practice until you contact your therapist and discuss your experience.

Conclusion

Because your habits of emotional reactivity have been established for a long time, changing your way of reacting in daily life will require you to train every day for some time. Accordingly, it is important to deal with any difficulties you may experience when practicing mindfulness as soon as possible and get into a good practice routine. If you experience any difficulties during your practice that have not been listed above, please discuss these without delay with your therapist. Best of luck with your training!

Index

Mindfulness-integrated CBT: Principles and Practice, First Edition. Bruno A. Cayoun.
© 2011 John Wiley & Sons, Ltd. Published 2011 by John Wiley & Sons, Ltd.